Korean Grammar

Using the framework of Systemic Functional Linguistics (SFL), this pioneering book provides the first comprehensive functional account of Korean grammar, building foundations for an engagement with Korean texts across a range of spoken and written registers and genres. It treats grammar as a meaning-making resource, comprising experiential resources for construing reality, interpersonal resources for enacting social relations, textual resources for composing coherent discourse, and logical resources for linking clauses. It not only deals with clause systems and structures but also focuses on their realisation as groups and phrases (and clause rank particles), and the realisation of these groups and phrases in words (including clitics and relevant suffixation). Its concluding chapter demonstrates how this grammar can be applied – for teaching Korean as a foreign language and for translation and interpreting studies. This book is essential reading for scholars and students of Asian languages and linguistics and functional approaches to grammar description.

MIRA KIM is Associate Professor of Translation and Interpreting Studies at the University of New South Wales, Sydney. Over two decades, she has explored her passion for Translation Studies, drawing on Systemic Functional Linguistics (SFL), and has provided SFL-inspired text analysis tools for translators-to-be. Notable publications include *Systemic Functional Linguistics and Translation Studies* (2021).

J. R. MARTIN is Professor of Linguistics at the University of Sydney. He is best known for his work on discourse analysis, appraisal and genre and has a longstanding concern with language description. In April 2014 Shanghai Jiao Tong University opened its Martin Centre for Appliable Linguistics, appointing Professor Martin as Director.

GI-HYUN SHIN is Senior Lecturer at the University of New South Wales, Sydney, and is a pioneer in the field of Korean language education in Australia. He has developed a series of Korean language textbooks and numerous Korean teaching and learning aids for adult learners.

GYUNG HEE CHOI is Assistant Professor at Pyeongtaek University. She trained as a professional translator and interpreter, and has worked in the T&I field for over two decades. This experience and her studies in SFL have led her to focus her research on analysis of translation texts using SFL.

Korean Grammar

A Systemic Functional Approach

Mira Kim
University of New South Wales, Sydney

J. R. Martin
University of Sydney

Gi-Hyun Shin
University of New South Wales, Sydney

Gyung Hee Choi
Pyeongtaek University, Korea

Shaftesbury Road, Cambridge CB2 8EA, United Kingdom

One Liberty Plaza, 20th Floor, New York, NY 10006, USA

477 Williamstown Road, Port Melbourne, VIC 3207, Australia

314–321, 3rd Floor, Plot 3, Splendor Forum, Jasola District Centre, New Delhi – 110025, India

103 Penang Road, #05–06/07, Visioncrest Commercial, Singapore 238467

Cambridge University Press is part of Cambridge University Press & Assessment, a department of the University of Cambridge.

We share the University's mission to contribute to society through the pursuit of education, learning and research at the highest international levels of excellence.

www.cambridge.org
Information on this title: www.cambridge.org/9781009011617

DOI: 10.1017/9781009019941

© Mira Kim, J. R. Martin, Gi-Hyun Shin and Gyung Hee Choi 2023

This publication is in copyright. Subject to statutory exception and to the provisions of relevant collective licensing agreements, no reproduction of any part may take place without the written permission of Cambridge University Press & Assessment.

First published 2023
First paperback edition 2025

A catalogue record for this publication is available from the British Library

ISBN 978-1-316-51534-1 Hardback
ISBN 978-1-009-01161-7 Paperback

Cambridge University Press & Assessment has no responsibility for the persistence or accuracy of URLs for external or third-party internet websites referred to in this publication and does not guarantee that any content on such websites is, or will remain, accurate or appropriate.

Contents

List of Figures	page ix
List of Tables	xi
Preface	xv
List of Conventions and Abbreviations	xvii
Romanisation	xxi

1	Introduction to a Systemic Functional Grammar of Korean	1
	1.1 Why This Grammar Book?	1
	1.2 Levels of Language	2
	1.3 Grammatical Units	4
	1.4 Kinds of Meaning in the Clause	7
	1.5 Systems of Choices	13
	1.6 The Organisation of This Grammar	15
2	The Grammar of Groups and Phrases in Korean	17
	2.1 Introduction	17
	2.2 Groups and Phrases: An Overview	17
	2.3 Nominal Group	22
	2.3.1 The System of THING TYPE	23
	2.3.2 The System of CLASSIFICATION	25
	2.3.3 The System of ORDINATION	27
	2.3.4 The System of EPITHESIS	28
	2.3.5 The System of DEIXIS	32
	2.3.6 The System of ORIENTATION	35
	2.3.7 The System of QUALIFICATION	41
	2.3.8 The System of QUANTIFICATION	45
	2.3.9 The System of PERSPECTIVISATION	47
	2.3.10 The System of FUNCTION MARKING	49
	2.3.11 Nominal Group Structure	53
	2.4 Verbal Group	57
	2.4.1 The System of EVENT TYPE	58
	2.4.2 The System of VALENCY	59
	2.4.3 The System of DIMENSION TYPE	65
	2.4.4 The System of POLARITY	70
	2.4.5 The System of VERBAL GROUP MODALITY	73
	2.4.6 The System of HIGHLIGHT	79

	2.4.7	The System of DEGREE	81
	2.4.8	The System of VERBAL GROUP PARTICIPANT DEFERENCE	83
	2.4.9	Tense Systems	85
2.5	Adverbial Group		93
2.6	Co-verbal Phrase		99
2.7	Group and Phrase Complexes		103
2.8	Concluding Remarks		108

3 The Grammar of Interpersonal Meaning in Korean: MOOD — 109

- 3.1 Introduction to Interpersonal Clause Structure — 109
- 3.2 Formal Systems: FORMAL MOOD and ADDRESSEE DEFERENCE — 111
  - 3.2.1 The System of FORMAL MOOD — 111
  - 3.2.2 The System of ADDRESSEE DEFERENCE — 115
- 3.3 Informal Systems: INFORMAL MOOD, STANCE and POLITENESS — 120
  - 3.3.1 The System of INFORMAL MOOD — 121
  - 3.3.2 The System of STANCE — 124
  - 3.3.3 The System of POLITENESS — 135
- 3.4 The System of PARTICIPANT DEFERENCE — 139
- 3.5 The System of POLARITY — 143
- 3.6 The System of MODALITY — 148
  - 3.6.1 Modalisation — 150
  - 3.6.2 Modulation — 158
  - 3.6.3 Adverbs Realising Modal Adjuncts — 163
- 3.7 The System of HIGHLIGHT — 165
- 3.8 The System of VOCATION — 168
- 3.9 The System of COMMENT — 173
- 3.10 The System of EXPLETION — 175
- 3.11 Concluding Remarks on MOOD — 177

4 The Grammar of Experiential Meaning in Korean: TRANSITIVITY — 180

- 4.1 Introduction to Experiential Clause Structure — 180
- 4.2 The System of EXPERIENTIAL CLAUSE TYPE — 187
  - 4.2.1 Material Clauses — 188
    - 4.2.1.1 Actor — 189
    - 4.2.1.2 Undergoer — 190
    - 4.2.1.3 Recipient — 191
    - 4.2.1.4 Source — 193
    - 4.2.1.5 Entity-Range and Process-Range — 195
  - 4.2.2 Mental Clauses — 198
    - 4.2.2.1 Senser and Phenomenon — 199
    - 4.2.2.2 Mental-Range — 200
    - 4.2.2.3 Phenomenon Construing Acts, Facts and Ideas — 202
  - 4.2.3 Relational Clauses — 212
    - 4.2.3.1 Carrier and Attribute — 213
    - 4.2.3.2 Token and Value — 216
    - 4.2.3.3 Carrier-Domain — 219
    - 4.2.3.4 Emoter — 221
    - 4.2.3.5 Non-intensive Relational Clauses and the Features [presence] vs [absence] — 223
    - 4.2.3.6 Located and Location — 224
    - 4.2.3.7 Possessor and Possession — 228

	4.2.4	Verbal Clauses		231
		4.2.4.1	Sayer and Verbiage	232
		4.2.4.2	Receiver	235
		4.2.4.3	Verbal-Range	235
4.3	The System of DIATHESIS			235
4.4	The System of CIRCUMSTANTIATION			245
	4.4.1	Location		245
	4.4.2	Extent		252
	4.4.3	Manner		255
	4.4.4	Comparison		256
	4.4.5	Means		257
	4.4.6	Cause		260
	4.4.7	Purpose		263
	4.4.8	Concession		265
	4.4.9	Accompaniment		268
	4.4.10	Role		268
	4.4.11	Product		269
	4.4.12	Angle		270
	4.4.13	Matter		272
4.5	Concluding Remarks on TRANSITIVITY			275

5 **The Grammar of Textual Meaning in Korean: THEME** — 277
  5.1 Introduction to Textual Clause Structure — 277
  5.2 Topical Theme — 281
    5.2.1 The System of ANGLING THEME — 281
    5.2.2 The System of POSITIONING THEME — 289
  5.3 Interpersonal Theme — 292
  5.4 Textual Theme — 294
  5.5 Theme Systems — 296
  5.6 Topical Theme Identification and Thematic Progression — 297
  5.7 Conclusion — 305

6 **The Grammar of Logical Meaning in Korean: CLAUSE COMPLEXING** — 307
  6.1 Introduction to Clause Complexing — 307
  6.2 Verbal Group Complex vs Clause Complex — 310
  6.3 Clause Nexus and Relevant Notation — 313
  6.4 CLAUSE COMPLEXING — 320
    6.4.1 Paratactic vs Hypotactic Relations — 321
    6.4.2 PROJECTION and EXPANSION — 330
    6.4.3 Projection — 331
      6.4.3.1 Paratactic Projection — 331
      6.4.3.2 Hypotactic Projection — 337
    6.4.4 Expansion — 348
      6.4.4.1 Hypotactic Elaboration — 348
      6.4.4.2 Paratactic and Hypotactic Extension — 351
      6.4.4.3 Hypotactic Enhancement — 355
  6.5 Discussion of a Long Clause Complex — 363
  6.6 Conclusion — 370

viii   Contents

7 Two Applications — 371
7.1 Introduction to Using Our Korean Grammar — 371
7.2 Teaching Korean as a Foreign Language — 372
    7.2.1 Traditional Approaches to Teaching Korean as a Foreign Language — 373
    7.2.2 An Alternative 'Reading to Learn' (R2L) Perspective — 377
7.3 Translation and Interpreting Korean — 397
    7.3.1 Interpretation Example — 397
    7.3.2 Translation Examples — 404
        7.3.2.1 Survey Results — 405
        7.3.2.2 Analysis — 407
7.4 Further Applications — 413
Appendix — 414

References — 415
Index — 422

Figures

1.1	Levels of language	page 3
1.2	Rank scale	4
1.3	Two MOOD options	13
1.4	Two MOOD systems	14
1.5	A system network cross-classifying clauses	15
2.1	Rank scale in Korean	19
2.2	The system of basic THING TYPE	24
2.3	The system of CLASSIFICATION	27
2.4	The system of ORDINATION	28
2.5	The system of EPITHESIS	31
2.6	The system of DEIXIS	34
2.7	The system of ORIENTATION	39
2.8	The system of QUALIFICATION	45
2.9	The system of QUANTIFICATION	47
2.10	The system of PERSPECTIVISATION	49
2.11	The system of FUNCTION MARKING	53
2.12	Nominal group systems	53
2.13	The system of EVENT TYPE	59
2.14	The system of VALENCY	65
2.15	The system of DIMENSION TYPE	70
2.16	The system of POLARITY	72
2.17	The system of VERBAL GROUP MODALITY	76
2.18	The system of HIGHLIGHT	80
2.19	The system of DEGREE	82
2.20	The system of VERBAL GROUP PARTICIPANT DEFERENCE	83
2.21	The system of ABSOLUTE TENSE	88
2.22	The system of RELATIVE TENSE	92
2.23	Verbal group systems	92
2.24	Adverbial group systems	98
2.25	Co-verbal phrase systems	101
3.1	The system of FORMALITY	110

3.2	The system of FORMAL MOOD	112
3.3	The system of ADDRESSEE DEFERENCE	116
3.4	More delicate formal systems	120
3.5	The system of INFORMAL MOOD	121
3.6	The system of STANCE	125
3.7	The systems of STANCE and INFORMAL MOOD	134
3.8	The system of POLITENESS	135
3.9	The system of FORMALITY (extended)	139
3.10	The system of PARTICIPANT DEFERENCE	140
3.11	The system of POLARITY	147
3.12	The system of MODALITY	149
3.13	The system of HIGHLIGHT	165
3.14	The system of VOCATION	170
3.15	The system of COMMENT	173
3.16	The system of EXPLETION	176
3.17	The system of MOOD: interpersonal systems in Korean	178
4.1	The system of EXPERIENTIAL CLAUSE TYPE	187
4.2	The system of MATERIAL CLAUSE TYPE	189
4.3	The system of MENTAL CLAUSE TYPE	198
4.4	The system of RELATIONAL CLAUSE TYPE	213
4.5	Non-intensive relational clauses	224
4.6	The system of VERBAL CLAUSE TYPE	231
4.7	The system of DIATHESIS	237
4.8	The system of CIRCUMSTANTIATION in relation to other experiential systems	247
4.9	The system of TRANSITIVITY in Korean	276
5.1	The system of ESTABLISHING THEME	282
5.2	The system of CONTINUING THEME	285
5.3	The system of POSITIONING THEME	292
5.4	The system of INTERPERSONAL THEME	294
5.5	The system of TEXTUAL THEME	296
5.6	The system network of THEME in Korean	297
5.7	Three types of thematic progression	298
6.1	Clause complex systems (primary delicacy)	310
6.2	The system of CLAUSE COMPLEXING in Korean	321
7.1	Complementary perspectives on comparing and contrasting languages	372
7.2	R2L's teaching/learning cycle	377
7.3	Rose's model of R2L curriculum genres	378
7.4	T & I as a process of reinstantiation	412

Tables

1.1	Experiential Function Marking	page 10
1.2	Function/rank matrix for the grammar of Korean	16
2.1	Word classes and their functions in groups and phrases	21
2.2	The system of basic THING TYPE: realisation statements	24
2.3	The system of CLASSIFICATION: realisation statements	27
2.4	The system of ORDINATION: realisation statements	28
2.5	The system of EPITHESIS: realisation statements	31
2.6	Types of determiner	32
2.7	Possessive determiners	33
2.8	Possessive pronoun alternatives	34
2.9	The system of DEIXIS: realisation statements	35
2.10	The system of ORIENTATION: realisation statements	39
2.11	The system of QUALIFICATION: realisation statements	45
2.12	The system of QUANTIFICATION: realisation statements	47
2.13	The system of PERSPECTIVISATION: realisation statements	49
2.14	The system of FUNCTION MARKING	52
2.15	Nominal group functions	57
2.16	The system of EVENT TYPE: realisation statements	59
2.17	The system of VALENCY: realisation statements	65
2.18	Types of Dimension	68
2.19	The system of DIMENSION TYPE: selected realisation statements	70
2.20	The system of POLARITY: realisation statements	73
2.21	The system of VERBAL GROUP MODALITY: realisation statements	76
2.22	The system of HIGHLIGHT: realisation statements	80
2.23	Adverbs realising the Degree function	81
2.24	The system of DEGREE: realisation statements	83
2.25	The system of VERBAL GROUP PARTICIPANT DEFERENCE: realisation statements	83
2.26	The system of ABSOLUTE TENSE: realisation statements	88
2.27	The system of RELATIVE TENSE: realisation statements	92
2.28	Adverbs realising the Property and Grader functions	95

xi

2.29	Adverbs deployed as Modal Adjunct and Comment functions	97
2.30	Adverbs deployed as Conjunctive Adjuncts	98
2.31	Realisation statements for adverbial group systems	99
2.32	Realisation statements for co-verbal phrases	101
2.33	Some examples of co-verbal phrases	102
2.34	Naming conventions for terms across ranks	108
3.1	The system of FORMALITY: realisation statements – simplified	110
3.2	The system of FORMAL MOOD: realisation statements (affixes specified for [dominant] clauses only)	112
3.3	FORMAL MOOD suffixes in [dominant] clauses	114
3.4	The system of ADDRESSEE DEFERENCE: realisation statements	116
3.5	FORMAL MOOD; ADDRESSEE DEFERENCE suffixes	120
3.6	The system of INFORMAL MOOD: realisation statements – only for [pronounce] clauses	121
3.7	The system of STANCE: realisation statements	125
3.8	The system of POLITENESS: realisation statements	135
3.9	The system of PARTICIPANT DEFERENCE: realisation statements	140
3.10	The system of POLARITY: realisation statements	148
3.11	Realisation statements for the system of MODALITY	149
3.12	Constraints on the realisation of MODALITY	150
3.13	Some realisations of MODALISATION	157
3.14	Some realisations of MODULATION	162
3.15	Some adverbs realising the Modal Adjunct function	163
3.16	Realisation statements for the system of HIGHLIGHT	166
3.17	Realisation statements for the system of VOCATION	171
3.18	Realisation statements for the system of COMMENT	173
3.19	Adverbial groups realising the Comment function	174
3.20	Lexicalised phrases and a nominal group realising the Comment function	175
3.21	Realisation statements for the system of EXPLETION	176
4.1	Experiential Function Marking (EFM) clitics	184
4.2	Key Participants in experiential clause types	188
4.3	Entity-Range examples	197
4.4	Process-Range examples	197
4.5	Acts, facts and ideas and embedding strategies	211
4.6	Key Participants in clauses with differing DIATHESIS features	244
4.7	Realisation of Circumstances	273
5.1	Realisation statements for ESTABLISHING THEME	282
5.2	Interpersonal Themes	292
5.3	Conjunctive Adjuncts	294
6.1	Primary and secondary clauses in a clause nexus	313

6.2 Logico-semantic relations between clauses in a clause nexus	316
6.3 Basic types of inter-clausal connectors in Korean	362
7.1 Results of the Survey	405
7.2 Reasons for Preferring Translation 1	405
7.3 Reasons for Preferring Translation 2	405

Preface

Sitting down to draft this preface, the first thing that came to Mira Kim's mind was an old proverb, *Necessity is the mother of invention*. She had never dreamt of writing this book herself in her professional role as a translation scholar. Her wish was simply that someone would do it for her, so that she could apply it to translation studies and teaching translation. When it looked like that person would not appear, she began to ask around to find someone to work with. In 2008 Jim Martin had stepped forward with the idea of holding a weekly typology seminar at the University of Sydney – to work with PhD students who were developing language descriptions. That is how our work together began.

Gi-Hyun Shin, a Korean language specialist from the University of New South Wales (UNSW), joined this seminar. He had been trained as a linguist in a related functional school (Role and Reference Grammar) and became fascinated by Michael Halliday's work when he read the first edition of *An Introduction to Functional Grammar*. Gi had in fact examined Mira's PhD thesis on Korean THEME (2007), which reawoke his interest in Systemic Functional Linguistics (SFL) (it had been hibernating for years).

Gyung Hee Choi and Mira started their postgraduate study in the same year when training to become professional translators and interpreters at Hankuk University of Foreign Studies in Korea. After many years apart, Gyung Hee came to visit Mira in Sydney (2007) to discuss her burning questions about translation and they ended up working together as supervisee and superviser at Macquarie University and later at UNSW for her PhD on Korean clause complexes (2013).

Kyoung-hee Park started her PhD on Korean transitivity at Macquarie University, with Christian Matthiessen as primary supervisor and Mira as secondary supervisor. Once both Christian and Mira left (Christian for the Polytechnic University of Hong Kong and Mira for UNSW), Kyoung-hee completed her PhD under the supervision of Canzhong Wu as primary supervisor and Mira as adjunct supervisor (2013).

As you can see, Mira attracted members of the team in different ways; but they all shared a keen interest in SFL and how it could be applied to Korean. Mira, Jim, Gi-Hyun, Gyung Hee and Kyoung-hee started to meet every week to work specifically on this book in 2014. After completing their PhD projects, Gyung Hee and Kyoung-hee returned to Korea. Mira, Jim and Gi-Hyun continued the work together from that time. Gyung Hee rejoined the team in the latter part of 2019 via Zoom from Korea.

Initially we drew on three PhD theses: Kim (2007) for Chapter 5 on THEME, Park (2013) for Chapter 4 on TRANSITIVITY and Choi (2013) for Chapter 6 on clause complexes. We have however revisited all these descriptions, further developing the analyses. In addition, we began work on four chapters from scratch. Chapter 1 has been written as a user-friendly introduction to the major SFL concepts informing this grammar. Chapter 2 is a comprehensive description of Korean below clause. It took Mira, Gi-Hyun and Jim more than a year to draft this one chapter. We faced a number of difficult questions during that time; but we could not give up on that chapter because there is so much going on below the clause in Korean. Chapter 3 is Gi-Hyun's original contribution, based on a spoken corpus and focusing on interpersonal meaning (Shin 2018). Chapter 7 is an introduction to how this grammar can be applied for Korean language teaching and translation/interpreting.

We are of course indebted to our many colleagues who have provided us with feedback on presentations over the years – in our seminal typology workshop, in local research seminars and at national and international SFL conferences. In particular we would like to thank Bob Hong for his comments on each chapter, Wang Pin for his careful reading of draft chapters as they appeared, David Rose for his advice on Chapter 7 and Susan Hood for her help with proofing. Any mistakes and limitations that remain are our responsibility alone.

We hope that our book is used to answer many questions related to Korean grammar and discourse and that it will inspire functional descriptions of many other languages around the world.

Conventions and Abbreviations

Labels for terms

lower case	name of a feature in a system (feature), e.g., declarative
small capitals	name of a system, e.g., FORMALITY
initial capital	name of a structural function, e.g., Dimension

When a feature is referred to in running text it is enclosed in square brackets, e.g., [declarative].

When two or more simultaneous features are referred to they are connected by ';', e.g., interrogative;dominant in analysis tables or [interrogative;dominant] in running text.

Markers in Analysis Tables and Realisation Statements

‖‖	clause complex boundary
‖	clause boundary
[[ ]]	embedded clause
[ ]	embedded group
<< >>	enclosed clause
< >	enclosed word
*	ungrammatical
"	locution
'	idea
=	elaborating
+	extending
x	enhancing
^	immediate sequence
.	may precede or follow
1 2 3...	paratactic
...γ β α	hypotactic

xvii

xviii   List of Conventions and Abbreviations

Conventions in System Networks

a → [x / y]	**system:** if [a] then [x] or [y]
a, b → [x / y]	**disjunctive entry condition:** if [a] or [b] then [x] or [y]
a, b → [x / y]	**conjunctive entry condition:** if [a] and [b] then [x] or [y]
a → { [x/y], [m/n] }	**simultaneous systems:** if [a] then both [x] or [y] and [m] or [n]
a → [x/y], x → [m/n]	**delicacy:** if [a] then [x] or [y]; if [x] then [m] or [n]
a → { [x^l / y], [m^T / n] }	**conditional marking:** if [x] then also [m]
a → [x^n / y]	**recursive feature:** choose [x] one or more times

List of Conventions and Abbreviations

Conventions for Realisation Statements

The most common types of realisation statement are presented below (variations and extensions are introduced at point of need):

(1) Presence of Functions in the structure: the presence of a Function in a structure is specified by inserting the Function into the structure; the operation of insertion is symbolised by '+'; e.g., +Exchange Mark.

(2) Relative ordering of Functions and ordering relative to unit boundaries: two Functions may be ordered relative to one another in the Function structure, and this relative ordering is symbolised by '^'; e.g., Classifier ^ Thing.

The ordering may also be relative to the left or right boundary of a grammatical unit (represented by #), e.g., # ^ Qualifying and Politeness Marker ^ #.

A distinction can be made between sequencing Functions directly after one another, e.g., Classifying ^ Thing, and sequencing Functions with respect to one another, e.g., Ordering → Thing (meaning that Ordering comes before the Thing but that another function, for example Classifying function, might intervene). Intervening Functions, if specified, are enclosed in parentheses (e.g., Ordering → (Classifying) Thing).

(3) Conflation of one Function with another: one Function is conflated with another Function, i.e., the two Functions specified are realised by the same constituent. Conflation is symbolised by '/'; for example, Attribute/Process means that the Attribute and Process Functions are together realised by the constituent (i.e., verbal group).

(4) Realisation of a Function in terms of features from the rank below: the realisation of a Function in a Function structure is stated by preselecting one or more features from the unit realising it; preselection is symbolised by ':', e.g., Thing:proper noun.

(5) Two or more realisation statements for a single feature (or combination of features) are separated by ';', e.g., +Ordering; Ordering → Thing.

Abbreviations

Acc	accompaniment
adj	adjective
adv	adverb
advg	adverbial group
Ang	angle
aux	auxiliary
b noun	bound noun

b verb	bound verb
C-Domain	Carrier-Domain
Cau	cause
Cir	Circumstance
Class	Classifying
cvp	co-verbal phrase
decl	declarative
def	deferential
dom	dominant
E-Range	Entity-Range
EFM	Experiential Function Marking
EM	Exchange Mark
Ext	extent
IFM	Interpersonal Function Marking
imp	imperative
inter	interrogative
jus	jussive
Loc	location
Man	manner
Mod Adj	Modal Adjunct
M-Range	Mental-Range
ng	nominal group
P0	Participant 0
P1	Participant 1
P2	Participant 2
P3	Participant 3
PDM	Participant Deference Mark
PM	Politeness Marker
PMM	Projected Mood Mark
P-Range	Process-Range
ptcl	particle
RTM	Relative Tense Mark
sfx	suffix
SM	Stance Mark
TFM	Textual Function Marking
TM	Tense Mark
ven	venerate
vg	verbal group
VM	Voice Mark
V-Range	Verbal-Range

Romanisation

We use the Revised Romanisation of Korean (RRK) in presenting the Korean data in this book. The RRK was devised by the Korean government in 2000, and as such it has an official status in the Republic of Korea. We use RRK because it allows the reader an easier access to natural Korean pronunciation than the other existing systems such as the Yale system. Also, RRK is useful for learners of Korean who visit Korea, where all the names of streets and places are romanised using this system.

RRK romanises Korean as it is pronounced (Han and Shin 2006). For instance, 집 'house' will be romanised as *jip* when cited in our explanation of examples; but when it is followed by a word beginning with a vowel in examples, such as 안 *an* 'inside', the 'p' would be romanised as 'b' (so 집 안 'inside the house' would be romanised as *jib an* not *jip an*).

The table relates Hangeul letters to their RRK Roman counterparts.

Consonants 자음			Vowels 모음	
Hangeul letters 한글 자모	Romanisation 로마자		Hangeul letters 한글 자모	Romanisation 로마자
	before a vowel 초성, 종성: 모음 앞에서	before a consonant 종성: 자음 앞에서		
Stops 파열음			Monophthongs 단모음	
ㄱ	*g*	*k*	ㅏ	*a*
ㄲ	*kk*	*k*	ㅐ	*ae*
ㅋ	*k*	*k*	ㅓ	*eo*
ㄷ	*d*	*t*	ㅔ	*e*
ㄸ	*tt*	N/A	ㅗ	*o*
ㅌ	*t*	*t*	ㅜ	*u*

(cont.)

Consonants 자음			Vowels 모음	
Hangeul letters 한글 자모	**Romanisation** 로마자		**Hangeul letters** 한글 자모	**Romanisation** 로마자
	before a vowel 초성, 종성: 모음 앞에서	before a consonant 종성: 자음 앞에서		
ㅂ	*b*	*p*	ㅡ	*eu*
ㅃ	*pp*	N/A	ㅣ	*i*
ㅍ	*p*	*p*	Diphthongs 이중모음	
Affricates 파찰음			ㅑ	*ya*
ㅈ	*j*	*t*	ㅒ	*yae*
ㅉ	*jj*	N/A	ㅕ	*yeo*
ㅊ	*ch*	*t*	ㅖ	*ye*
Fricatives 마찰음			ㅛ	*yo*
ㅅ	*s*	*t*	ㅠ	*yu*
ㅆ	*ss*	*t*	ㅘ	*wa*
ㅎ	*h*	*h*	ㅙ	*wae*
Nasals 비음			ㅚ	*oe*
ㄴ	*n*	*n*	ㅝ	*wo*
ㅁ	*m*	*m*	ㅞ	*we*
ㅇ	N/A	*ng*	ㅟ	*wi*
Liquid 유음			ㅢ	*ui*
ㄹ	*r*	*l*		

1 Introduction to a Systemic Functional Grammar of Korean

1.1 Why This Grammar Book?

This is the first grammar book to describe Korean grammar from a systemic functional linguistic perspective. It grew out of the much-felt need to be able to use grammar to analyse Korean texts for practical purposes such as translation and interpreting, and Korean language teaching and learning.[1] Two of the authors (Kim and Choi) have been professional translators and interpreters, and have also taught translation for over two decades. Both authors found the existing descriptions of Korean limited as a tool for translation due to the focus of these descriptions on form rather than meaning. Shin, another author, has been teaching Korean at Australian universities for over 30 years. He felt there was a need for a description that could explain a wider range of phenomena in the texts, written and spoken, that he was using with his students as models. The bond that united these different concerns was our interest in systemic functional linguistics (SFL), an appliable linguistics (Halliday 2008), which we felt could inform a description of Korean grammar that would better suit our needs – i.e., an appliable grammar that practitioners could use.

This book makes a number of distinctive contributions when compared with other Korean grammar books. First of all, whereas existing grammar books have been largely concerned with relations among elements within a clause (i.e., syntagmatic structure), this book focuses in addition on relations of alternative grammatical elements to each other (i.e., paradigmatic relations) – describing how meaning changes when one choice is made rather than another. In other words, this book is concerned with the way in which Korean grammar is used to make meaning.

Secondly, the grammar description in this book is based on Korean texts that were collected as the foundation for three PhD dissertations (Kim 2007, Choi 2013, Park 2013) and a new spoken corpus used by Shin (2018). The corpora

---

[1] This practical concern underpins our decision not to use Leipzig glossing for examples; instead we provide word glosses for lexical items and unpack the relevant structure of examples so that the meaning of the grammar is clear.

are limited in terms of size. But they have been selected to provide a representative sample of Korean texts across a range of registers and genres including recounts, news stories, narratives, reports, descriptions, explanations, arguments and chat.[2] As such they have allowed us to explore a comprehensive range of Korean grammatical resources across various text types.

Thirdly, this book interprets lexicogrammatical features in a way that is sensitive to both discourse semantics (co-text) and context (register and genre). In other words, it describes Korean grammar in ways that help us see how Korean texts are organised to do what Korean speakers and writers need them to do across a range of communicative tasks. We will outline the ways in which this grammar contributes to this task in Chapter 7, with special reference to the fields of practice we introduced above – namely translation and interpreting, and teaching Korean as a foreign or heritage language.

Alongside these contributions our grammar addresses dimensions of Korean grammar that have not been thoroughly explored before (e.g., the structure of the Korean verbal group) and engages productively with the reasoning SFL deploys to ground paradigmatic relations in syntagmatic ones. This puts us in a stronger position to interpret Korean from a functional perspective.

We have adopted SFL as the informing theory for this grammar of Korean. In doing so we draw specifically on the principles of the linguistic theory that were devised by Halliday and his colleagues in the 1950s and 1960s, as inspired by earlier work by Firth and Hjelmslev in this initial conceptual period (cf. Martin 2016 for a short history of SFL; foundational papers have been republished as Martin and Doran 2015a, b, c, d, e). In the rest of this chapter, we will introduce the theoretical principles of SFL that underpin this grammar book.

1.2   Levels of Language

In SFL, language is regarded as a meaning-making resource modelled at different levels of abstraction or strata: discourse semantics, lexicogrammar and phonology.[3] Phonology is concerned with phonemes, syllable structure, rhythm and intonation; lexicogrammar deals with the organisation of clauses, groups and phrases, words and morphemes; and discourse semantics focuses on patterns of coherence in texts. The relation between levels is termed realisation. Figure 1.1 uses cotangential circles to model the way the levels are related. Technically speaking, discourse semantics is realised through lexicogrammar, which is in turn realised through phonology.

---

[2] The genre categories used in this book are taken from Martin and Rose (2008) and Eggins and Slade (1997).

[3] Or graphology, for written language.

1.2 Levels of Language

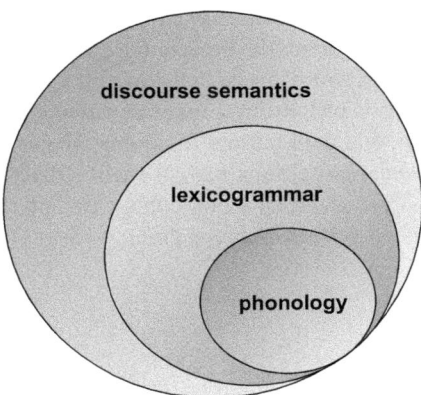

Figure 1.1 Levels of language

In SFL, lexicogrammar is explored from a functional perspective as a meaning-making resource. In Halliday's terms:

One way of thinking of a 'functional' grammar ... is that it is a theory of grammar that is orientated towards the discourse semantics. In other words, if we say we are interpreting the grammar functionally, it means that we are foregrounding its role as a resource for construing meaning (Halliday 1994: 15).

Alongside the three strata represented in Figure 1.1, language is modelled with respect to three simultaneous strands of meaning (Halliday 1994: 35) in SFL. These strands of meaning are referred to as metafunctions and comprise ideational resources for construing our experience of the world, interpersonal resources for enacting our social relations and textual resources for composing ideational and interpersonal meanings as a coherent flow of information in text. The ideational metafunction is split into two sub-components: the experiential (resources for organising configurations of experience) and the logical (resources for chaining configurations of experience in relation to one another).

Seen as an appliable linguistics, one of the most valuable aspects of this tradition is that it looks at grammar as a resource for making different kinds of meaning. In order to see clearly how it does this we need to acknowledge the distinction SFL makes between function and class. This grammar makes use of two types of grammatical labels: names of classes, including terms such as clause, noun, adjective, adverb, verbal group and nominal group; and names of functions, e.g., Actor, Undergoer, Process, Theme and Rheme. Function labels are used to distinguish the role played by a particular unit in a function structure and the class labels are used to categorise the unit playing a role. In SFL class and function are interconnected in a relationship called realisation. For example, in a simple clause such as 아기 원숭이가 나무에서 떨어졌다 *agi wonsungi ga namu eseo tteoreoj-eot-da* 'A baby monkey fell down from a tree', the Process (i.e., what happened) is realised by a verbal group, 떨어졌다 *tteoreoj-eot-da* 'fell down'; the Actor (i.e., the entity participating in the Process) is realised by a nominal group, 아기 원숭이가 *agi wonsungi ga* 'baby monkey'; and the Location (outlining where) is realised by a nominal group, 나무에서 *namu eseo* 'from a tree'. We will write all function labels (Actor, Location, Process etc.) with an initial upper-case letter to distinguish them clearly from class labels (clause, nominal group, verb etc.); the latter are written in lower case.

1.3 Grammatical Units

When we take a closer look at the lexicogrammar level, we can see it has units of different size. These grammatical units are organised in relation to one another along a constituency hierarchy known as rank in SFL. For Korean this means that a clause is interpreted as consisting of one or more groups and phrases; in turn groups and phrases consist of one or more words; and words consist of one or more morphemes. The scale of ranks we use for Korean grammar is outlined in Figure 1.2.

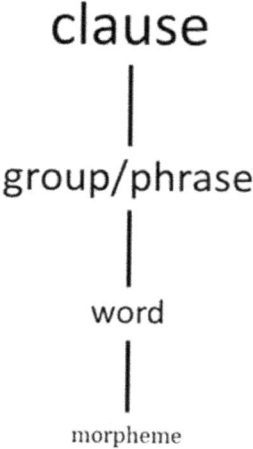

Figure 1.2 Rank scale

We next preview the ranks in Korean grammar, moving down the constituency hierarchy from the clause through groups and phrases to words and morphemes. We will later intersect this perspective on rank with the

1.3 Grammatical Units

perspective on metafunction developed earlier on to provide an overview of the organisation of this grammar as a whole (Table 1.2). Consider (1).

(1)

서울에		비가		오고	있나	보다.
seoul	e	bi	ga	o-go	in-na	bo-da
Seoul	in	rain		come	be ... -ing	seems
Circumstance		Participant		Process		
nominal group		nominal group		verbal group		
'It seems to be raining in Seoul.'						

Example (1) is a clause that consists of two nominal groups and a verbal group. Each of the nominal groups includes two words, 서울 *seoul* 'Seoul' and 에 *e* 'in, at' and 비 *bi* 'rain' and 가 *ga* clitic; and the verbal group has three words, 오고 *o-go* 'come', 있나 *in-na* 'is ... -ing' and 보다 *bo-da* 'seems'. As far as the experiential meaning of the clause is concerned, the Process is realised by the verbal group, the Participant by the second nominal group and a Circumstance by the first nominal group. The clitic 에 *e* in the first nominal group indicates that the nominal group is a Circumstance (specifically a Location); the clitic 가 *ga* in the second nominal group indicates that the nominal group is a Participant (functioning in this clause type as an Actor).[4]

The verbal group in (1) consists of three verbs: 오다 *o-da*[5] (main), 있다 *it-da* (auxiliary) and 보다 *bo-da* (auxiliary). In Korean, a number of verbs can be connected to each other to realise a Process. When they are, the main verb comes at the beginning, indicating the main Event. Auxiliary verbs follow, connected to preceding verbs by a connecting suffix such as 고 *–go* and 나 *–na* in (1) (see Chapter 2 for details). The final verb may come with what we call an Exchange Mark, such as 다 *–da*; this is a suffix indicating MOOD and ADDRESSEE DEFERENCE (see Chapter 3 for details).

The first auxiliary verb in the verbal group in (1), 있나 *in-na*, plays the role of Dimension, indicating the event hasn't finished; and the second auxiliary verb, 보다 *bo-da*, plays the role of Modal, indicating that the proposition is not certain but probable. The hyphens in 오고 *o-go*, 있나 *in-na* and 보다 *bo-da* indicate that each of these verbs consists of two morphemes – a stem followed by a suffix. The stem realises the Head of the verb; the suffix functions as a

---

[4] We will use the term 'clitic' to refer to dependent grammatical word classes at group/phrase rank (e.g., 에 *e*, 가 *ga*) and reserve the term particle for dependent grammatical word classes at clause rank (e.g., 요 *yo*); see Chapter 2 for discussion.

[5] In Korean, when cited as words, verbs and verbalised adjectives are customarily presented in the form of stem plus the suffix 다 *-da*. This is their dictionary entry format, and in this book we follow this tradition when we cite verbs and verbalised adjectives.

Link for 오고 *o-go* and 있나 *in-na* but as an Exchange Mark for 보다 *bo-da* (see Chapter 2 for details).

The function and class analysis just outlined for the verbal group in (1) is consolidated as in (2).

(2)

1	Hangeul	오고 있나 보다				
2	Romanisation	*o-go*		*in-na*		*bo-da*
3	word gloss	come		be ...-ing		seem
4	clause functions	Process				
5	group classes	verbal group				
6	group functions	Event		Dimension		Modal
7	word classes	verb		auxiliary verb		auxiliary verb
8	word functions	Head	Link	Head	Link	Head	Exchange Mark
9	morpheme classes	stem	suffix	stem	suffix	stem	suffix
10	clause gloss	'seem to be coming'				

The first row in (2) provides the Korean script (Hangeul), following Korean spelling and spacing conventions; and the second row presents the example in Roman script; we place each unit we treat as a grammatical word in this grammar in a separate cell (clitics are preceded by '=' following the Leipzig conventions). This means that all affixes are included in these cells, with morpheme boundaries marked by a hyphen ('-'). The third row provides a plausible English gloss for each word.

Note that as far as structure is concerned, our analysis provides information about both the function and class of units. The fourth, sixth and eighth rows provide function labels for the groups/phrases, words and morphemes involved, and the fifth, seventh and ninth rows provide class labels for the units realising each function. In the final row a fairly literal English gloss for the example as a whole is provided; we don't attempt a fully idiomatic translation (which in any case would depend on a specific co-text and context). As far as the English determiners *a*, *the* and *some* are concerned, in the absence of Korean determiners we will assume that the entity in question is known to the interactants and so use *the* unless the reference is clearly non-specific.

In this book we consider choices for meaning and their structural realisation at clause, group/phrase, word and morpheme rank in Korean. We will be concentrating on clause and group/phrase rank systems and structures – but will bring word and morpheme ranks into the picture in order to specify the realisation of clause and group/phrase rank systems.

With respect to the Romanisation in row 2, for this book we use the Revised Romanisation of Korean (RRK), which was devised by the Korean government in 2000. We do so because it allows the reader an easier access to natural Korean pronunciation[6] than the other existing systems such as the Yale system. RRK has an official status in the Republic of Korea. And it is useful for learners of Korean who visit Korea, where all the names of streets and places are romanised using this system.

1.4 Kinds of Meaning in the Clause

Adopting SFL as our informing theory allows us to draw on the experience of SFL grammarians' descriptions of different languages around the world; this gives rise to the expectation that at clause rank our grammar will be organised paradigmatically around three bundles of clause classes (Caffarel et al. 2004, Mwinlaaru and Xuan 2016). This has proved to be the case for Korean. In SFL, each of these bundles is modelled as a system of choices; and these systems of choices (i.e., TRANSITIVITY, MOOD and THEME) comprise choices for making different kinds of meaning (we follow the convention of writing the names of systems of choices in small caps in this grammar). For example, the TRANSITIVITY system consists of choices for experiential meaning (i.e., construing our experience of the world), the MOOD system of choices for interpersonal meaning (i.e., enacting social relations) and the THEME system of choices for textual meaning (i.e., composing discourse). One consequence of this is that we will propose a distinctive function structure for each system of choices. These clause rank function structures allow for one tier of analysis for each layer of structure – i.e., one TRANSITIVITY tier, one MOOD tier and one THEME tier.

In SFL distinctive bundles of clause systems are interpreted with respect to the metafunctional organisation of language – the idea that we tend to mean three things at once. In terms of metafunctions, Korean TRANSITIVITY construes experiential meaning, Korean MOOD enacts interpersonal meaning and Korean THEME composes textual meaning. It is in this respect that SFL allows us to interpret Korean grammar as a resource for making different kinds of meaning.

---

[6] RRK romanises Korean as it is pronounced. For instance, 집 'house' will be romanised as *jip* when cited in our explanation of examples; but when it is followed by a word beginning with a vowel in examples, such as 안 *an* 'inside', the '*p*' would be romanised as '*b*' (so 집 안 'inside the house' would be romanised as *jib an* not *jip an*). Accordingly, in the example tables in this book, we will romanise taking the morphophonemic environment into account (so *jib an* not *jip an*).

We now take a further step into our systemic functional grammar of Korean. In this section we focus on single clauses, such as that in (1) (combinations of clauses, i.e., clause complexes, will be addressed in Chapter 6).

We begin with experiential meaning as our way in. In Korean clauses there is a Process, a central element of structure that construes something going on, or alternatively a relationship of some kind. In (1), the Process 오고있나보다 *o-go in-na bo-da* 'seems to be coming' construes material activity (something going on in the world). In (3), the Process 보았다 *bo-at-da* 'saw' construes mental activity (our perceptions, feelings and thoughts about the world). And in (4), the Process 이다 *i-da* 'be' construes a relationship of identity between two entities.

(3)

아이가 고양이를 보았다.				
ai	*ga*	*goyangi*	*reul*	*bo-at-da*
child		cat		saw
Participant		Participant		Process
nominal group		nominal group		verbal group
'The child saw the cat.'				

(4)

저 분이 우리 영어 선생님이다.						
jeo	*bun*	*i*	*uri*	*yeongeo*	*seonsaengnim*	*i-da*
that	person		our	English	teacher	is
Participant			Participant			Process
nominal group			nominal group			verbal group
'That person is our English teacher.'						

In each of the examples, the grammatical function Process is realised by the class verbal group, as indicated in the analyses. Note that we consider a group that consists of a single word as a group because it has the potential to be expanded via optional group systems (see Chapter 2 for details).

Exploring further we can note that in (3) and (4) the grammatical function Process is accompanied by two additional units involved with the Process – realised by nominal groups and functioning as Participants in the clause. In this chapter, we won't introduce the types of Participant involved with different kinds of clause (to be presented in Chapter 4), but will use general terms – Participant 1 (P1), typically for an entity that undertakes an activity or is described or identified; Participant 2 (P2), typically for an entity subjected to an activity; and Participant 3 (P3), typically for an entity that is less centrally involved (as for example the recipient of goods and services or the receiver of information). We reserve the term Participant 0 (P0) for a participant function that lacks a post-positional clitic

1.4 Kinds of Meaning in the Clause

explicitly signalling its relation to other elements in its clause (i.e., lacks clitics such as the 가 *ga* and 를 *reul* noted in (3) and 이 *i* in (4)).[7]

Clauses involving a Process and one or more Participants can be further extended by adding Circumstances, as we saw in (1). Circumstances deal with a range of meanings, including how long the Process was going on, where it took place, how it was done and/or why it was done. A Circumstance of Location in time and a Circumstance of Location in space are illustrated in (5).

(5)

아이가 아침에 정원에서 고양이를 보았다.							
ai	*ga*	*achim*	*e*	*jeongwon*	*eseo*	*goyangi*	*reul*	*bo-at-da*
child		morning	in	garden	in	cat		saw
P1		Circumstance		Circumstance		P2		Process
ng[8]		ng		ng		ng		vg
'The child saw the cat in the morning in the garden.'								

Korean uses a small set of post-positional clitics (이/가 *i/ga*, 을/를 *eul/leul*, 에게 *ege*, 에 *e*, 에서 *eseo*, 부터 *buteo* etc.)[9] to help sort out who is doing what to whom or what is related to what, how, when and where etc. In this grammar, as shown in Table 1.1, we will treat 이/가 *i/ga* as marking Participant 1, 을/를 *eul/leul* as marking Participant 2, 에게 *ege*, 한테 *hante* and 에 *e* as marking Participant 3 and 에 *e*, 에서 *eseo*, 부터 *buteo* etc. as marking Circumstances. In addition, as noted above, we will recognise a Participant 0 (P0), which has no marker (mainly in relational clauses).[10] Note that 에게 *ege* and 한테 *hante* are employed when P3 is 'animate' and 에 *e* is used for an 'inanimate' P3. Note also that 께서 *kkeseo* and 께 *kke* in Table 1.1 are honorific variants of 이/가 *i/ga* and 에게 *ege* respectively (see Chapter 3 for details).

---

[7] As mentioned in Chapter 2 (Section 2.3.10), a post-positional clitic signalling the relation of the Participant concerned to other elements in the clause can often be elided in colloquial spoken Korean. However, Participant 0 (P0) is not used for a Participant function where the clitic is elided, but rather for a Participant function where deploying a clitic is not possible, e.g., the second Participant in (4).
[8] The abbreviation 'ng' in the examples below stands for nominal group, 'vg' for verbal group.
[9] Clitics given in pairs and separated by a slash (/) are morphophonemically conditioned variants. In our representation, the first one occurs after a consonant, and the second after a vowel. The parenthesised syllables 써 *sseo* and 서 *seo* in 으로/(써) *euro/ro(sseo)* and 으로/로(서) *euro/ro (seo)* can be omitted without affecting the experiential meaning.
[10] Part of the inspiration for this P1, P2, P3 convention comes of course from Perlmutter and Postal's relational grammar (Perlmutter 1983, Perlmutter and Rosen 1984, Postal and Joseph 1990); P1 and P2 can also be related to what in other models are referred to as macro-roles (e.g., van Valin and Lapolla 1997); we were also influenced by Quiroz's use of these terms in her work on Spanish TRANSITIVITY (Quiroz 2013).

Table 1.1 *Experiential Function Marking*

Participant 0	[no marking]
Participant 1	이/가 i/ga; 께서 kkeseo (honorific)
Participant 2	을/를 eul/reul
Participant 3	에게 ege, 한테 hante; 께 kke (honorific); 에 e (inanimate)
Circumstance	에 e, 에서 eseo 'on, at, in'; 에서 eseo, 부터 buteo 'from'; 으로/로(써) euro/ro(sseo) 'with'; 으로/로(서) euro/ro(seo) 'as' etc.

As far as the group or phrase function of the classes of post-positional clitics noted in Table 1.1 are concerned, we will use the function label Experiential Function Marking (EFM for short). Example (6) illustrates the way we will present the experiential structure of clauses unless we need to refer more specifically to Participant and Circumstance roles (e.g., Participant:Senser or Circumstance: Location, as outlined in Chapter 4). Note that in Korean the clitics distinguishing P1, P2, P3 and Circumstances come last in the nominal group realising these functions.[11]

(6)

할머니가 시장에서 손자에게 과자를 사 주셨다.									
halmeoni	*ga*	*sijang*	*eseo*	*sonja*	*ege*	*gwaja*	*reul*	*saju-si-eot-da*	
grandma		market	in	grandson	to	cookies		bought	
P1		Circumstance		P3		P2		Process	
ng		ng		ng		ng		vg	
'Grandma bought cookies for her grandson in the market.'									

The classes of unit realising clause functions (i.e., the nominal, verbal and adverbial groups, co-verbal phrases and embedded clauses realising Process, Participant and Circumstances) will be explored in Chapter 2.

We now move on to two additional perspectives on Korean clauses. The first is interpersonal (the system of MOOD). Alongside construing experience, clauses enact social relations. One important dimension of this is the way they establish a relationship between the speaker and addressee. In Korean this is mainly done at the end of the clause, through suffixes on the final verb in the clause and an optional particle that follows the final verb – all of which position the clause as a dialogic interact. As further explained in Chapter 3, we use the function Negotiator for the part of the structure that does the work of positioning the clause in dialogue (basically its culminative verbal group);

---

[11] Post-positional clitics are also used to distinguish the role of co-verbal phrases and embedded clauses, as outlined in Chapters 2 and 4.

1.4 Kinds of Meaning in the Clause

the other elements of interpersonal structure are Expletive, Vocative, Comment, Modal Adjunct, Inquirer and Politeness Marker.

In (7), the speaker is positioning the addressee to receive information she is proffering (declarative mood).

(7)   (with declarative suffix 다 -*da* and MOOD functions highlighted in bold)

		아이가 과자를 먹었다.				
		ai	*ga*	*gwaja*	*reul*	*meog-eot-**da***
		child		cookies		ate-declarative
TRANSITIVITY		P1		P2		Process
MOOD						**Negotiator**
		ng		ng		vg
		'The child ate the cookies.'				

In (8) she is asking the addressee for information (interrogative mood).

(8)   (with interrogative suffix 니/냐 -*ni/nya* and MOOD functions highlighted in bold)

		아이가 과자를 먹었니?				
		ai	*ga*	*gwaja*	*reul*	*meog-eon-**ni***
		child		cookies		ate-interrogative
TRANSITIVITY		P1		P2		Process
MOOD						**Negotiator**
		ng		ng		vg
		'Did the child eat the cookies?'				

And in (9) she is telling him to do something (imperative mood).

(9)   (with imperative suffix 아라/어라 –*ara/eora* and MOOD functions highlighted in bold)

		과자를 먹어라.			
		gwaja	*reul*	*meog-**eora***	
		cookies		eat-imperative	
TRANSITIVITY		P2		Process	
MOOD				**Negotiator**	
		ng		vg	
		'Eat the cookies!'			

The verbal group realising the Negotiator can be expanded to include additional interpersonal meanings such as MODALITY and POLARITY as we will see in Chapter 3.

Alongside variations in MOOD, Korean also has extensive resources for fine-tuning the relationship between the speaker and addressee in terms of their respective social positions (their tenor relation in SFL terms). These interpersonal resources will be introduced in Chapter 2 and discussed in further detail in Chapter 3.

The final perspective on Korean clause grammar we will introduce here is a textual one. Compare now (10) and (11). In these examples we have added a tier of thematic structure. As will be further explained in Chapter 5, we use the function Theme for the part of the clause that sustains or shifts a clause's orientation to what it is talking about (its field in SFL terms). The rest of the clause, from this textual perspective, is referred to as Rheme.

(10) (with 이/가 *i/ga* marker and THEME functions highlighted in bold)

	아이가 고양이를 보았다.				
	ai	***ga***	*goyangi*	*reul*	*bo-at-da*
	child		cat		saw
TRANSITIVITY	P1		P2		Process
MOOD					Negotiator
THEME	**Theme**		Rheme		
	ng		ng		vg
	'The child saw the cat.'				

(11) (with 은/는 *eun/neun* marker and THEME functions highlighted in bold)

	아이는 고양이를 보았다.				
	ai	***neun***	*goyangi*	*reul*	*bo-at-da*
	child		cat		saw
TRANSITIVITY	P1		P2		Process
MOOD					Negotiator
THEME	**Theme**		Rheme		
	ng		ng		vg
	'The child saw the cat.'				

Note that in (11), the 이/가 *i/ga* marking appearing in (10) has been replaced with 은/는 *eun/neun*. This marking signals that the news value of the Participant function it marks is in some sense predictable – because for example it has been established in preceding clauses as the orientation to the topic being discussed. Participants or Circumstances marked by 은/는 *eun/neun* tend to appear as the first experiential element of clause structure, and so can be taken as a textual resource marking the beginning of a Korean clause.

Our perspective on the interpersonal structure of Korean clauses will be further developed in Chapter 3, where a fuller range of interpersonal systems and structures is considered. Experiential structure is further developed in Chapter 4 including a more detailed description of Participant and Circumstance roles in material, mental and relational clauses. Textual structure is further developed in Chapter 5, including discussion of different kinds of Theme in relation to news value. We will ground these analyses by providing a description of what is going on below clause rank in Chapter 2.

1.5 Systems of Choices

As noted briefly above, one of the distinctive contributions of this grammar of Korean is its focus on paradigmatic relations. In SFL, system networks are used to formalise the choices that are available to construe, enact or compose a particular type of meaning.

By way of exemplification, let's consider clause choices in the system of MOOD, which were briefly introduced above. Examples (7) and (8) illustrated the distinction between declarative and interrogative clauses, signalled by the culminative suffixes 다 *–da* and 니/냐 *–ni/nya* respectively. This opposition is formalised as a system in Figure 1.3. The system's entry condition is [clause] and the two features are alternatives: [declarative] vs [interrogative]. The arrow and square bracket indicate that a clause can be declarative or interrogative, but not neither and not both (i.e., logical 'or').

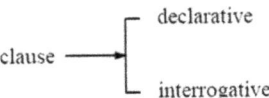

Figure 1.3 Two MOOD options

However, as (9) indicates, there is in fact an alternative mood to declarative and interrogative, namely imperative, which has a distinctive culminative suffix 아라/어라 *-ara/eora*. From a discourse semantic perspective imperative clauses differ from declarative and interrogative ones in that they negotiate an exchange of goods and services rather than an exchange of information. From a lexicogrammatical perspective imperative clauses also differ from declarative and interrogative ones in that they never involve MODALITY or STANCE MARKING (as detailed in Chapter 3). On the basis of this reasoning, we can revise the description in Figure 1.3 as Figure 1.4. We now have two systems, one opposing imperative to indicative clauses (to capture the generalisations just reviewed), and another for [declarative] vs [interrogative].

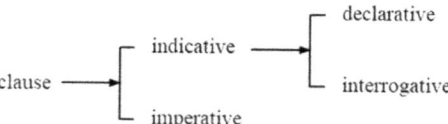

Figure 1.4 Two MOOD systems

In Figure 1.4 the entry condition for the indicative/imperative system is [clause], and the entry condition for the declarative/interrogative system is [indicative]. The two systems together are referred to as a system network. And the names of clauses classes (i.e., imperative, indicative, declarative and interrogative) are referred to as features. A system typically consists of two, sometimes three, and very occasionally four or more features. Korean MOOD systems are further developed in Chapter 3.

Alongside showing the dependency of one system on another, system networks also have to represent parallel systems. The metafunctional organisation of language for example means that the MOOD systems just outlined operate in tandem with TRANSITIVITY systems distinguishing one clause type from another (i.e., material vs mental vs relational clauses).[12] Each experiential clause type can combine with declarative, interrogative or imperative just as each type of mood can combine with material, interrogative or imperative. This relationship is formalised in Figure 1.5 by setting up two systems with the same entry condition ([clause]). The curly bracket (brace) shows that the systems are simultaneous (logical 'and'); technically speaking they cross-classify clauses along two dimensions (TRANSITIVITY and MOOD).

---

[12] Material clauses feature Processes such as 오다 *o-da* 'come', mental clauses Processes such as 보다 *bo-da* 'see' and relational clauses Processes such as 이다 *i-da* 'be'.

1.6 The Organisation of This Grammar

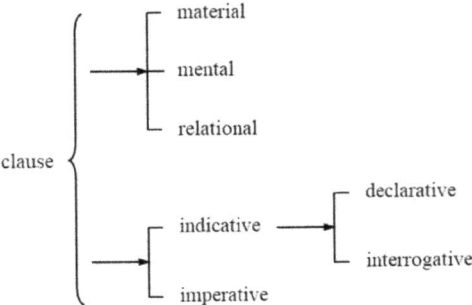

Figure 1.5 A system network cross-classifying clauses

In SFL choices from system network are realised through the function structures introduced earlier in this chapter (for example Participant, Circumstance and Process, or Negotiator), along with conditioned selections from lower ranking systems. This axial relation between system and structure (between paradigmatic and syntagmatic relations) will be further specified in Chapter 2, along with extensions of the system network formalism that we have introduced in simplified terms here.

1.6 The Organisation of This Grammar

Our next step in the development of this grammar in Chapter 2 involves consideration of group and phrase rank systems and structures. This is a necessary step because Korean does so much work at group and word rank distinguishing clauses from one another. The following three chapters focus on clauses and are organised with respect to metafunction – interpersonal meaning (MOOD systems) in Chapter 3, experiential meaning (TRANSITIVITY systems) in Chapter 4 and textual meaning (THEME systems) in Chapter 5. In Chapter 6 we turn to logical meaning and focus on clause complexes.

In Table 1.2 we present a simplified overview of the grammatical systems for clauses, nominal groups and verbal groups we consider in this book, organised by metafunction. The rows name these units, the columns show metafunction, and small caps name systems.

Table 1.2 *Function/rank matrix for the grammar of Korean*

metafunction / rank	ideational		interpersonal	textual
	logical	experiential		
clause	TAXIS, LOGICO-SEMANTIC RELATIONS	TRANSITIVITY, DIATHESIS, CIRCUMSTANTIATION	MOOD, ADDRESSEE DEFERENCE, INFORMAL MOOD, STANCE, POLITENESS, PARTICIPANT DEFERENCE, POLARITY, MODALITY, VOCATION, COMMENT, EXPLETION	THEME
nominal group		THING TYPE, CLASSIFICATION, ORDINATION, EPITHESIS, ORIENTATION, QUALIFICATION, QUANTIFICATION, PERSPECTIVISATION, FUNCTION MARKING	FUNCTION MARKING,	DEIXIS, FUNCTION MARKING
verbal group		EVENT TYPE, VALENCY, DIMENSION TYPE, ABSOLUTE TENSE, RELATIVE TENSE	POLARITY, VERBAL GROUP MODALITY, DEGREE, VERBAL GROUP PARTICIPANT DEFERENCE, HIGHLIGHT	

2 The Grammar of Groups and Phrases in Korean

2.1 Introduction

As noted in Chapter 1, Korean grammar does a lot of work at group/phrase rank and at word rank as far as the realisation of the different strands of meaning (ideational, interpersonal and textual) at clause rank is concerned. Accordingly, before turning to a consideration of systems and structures at clause rank, we focus here on systems and structures at group/phrase and word ranks.

2.2 Groups and Phrases: An Overview

For Korean we recognise three kinds of group – nominal group, verbal group and adverbial group; and we recognise one kind of phrase – which we will call a 'co-verbal phrase' (introduced below). The groups are realised by one or more words; and the phrase is realised by a co-verb preceded by a nominal group. These units align with clause rank experiential functions as follows:[1]

Process	realised by	a verbal group
Participant	realised by	a nominal group
Circumstance	realised by	an adverbial group, nominal group or co-verbal phrase

---

[1] Participants and Circumstances can also be realised by embedded clauses, as reviewed in Chapter 4.

By way of illustration, let's consider the clause in (1):[2]

(1)

저 어린 소년이 조국을 위해 전쟁터에서 ...		
jeo eori-n sonyeon =i	*joguk =eul wihae*	*jeonjaengteo =eseo*
that young boy	for his mother country	in the battlefield
Participant 1	Circumstance:Cause	Circumstance: Location
nominal group	co-verbal phrase	nominal group
'The young boy ... for his mother country in the battlefield.'		

... 매우 용감하게 싸우고 있었다.	
maeu yonggamha-ge	*ssau-go iss-eot-da*
very bravely	was fighting
Circumstance:Manner	Process
adverbial group	verbal group
... was fighting very bravely...	

This clause has four groups and one phrase; it exemplifies one way in which experiential clause functions are realised by units at group/phrase rank. The Participant 저 어린 소년이 *jeo eorin sonyeon i* 'that young boy' is realised by a nominal group; the Circumstance of Cause 조국을 위해 *joguk eul wihae* 'for his mother country' is realised by a co-verbal phrase; the Circumstance of Location 전쟁터에서 *jeonjaengteo eseo* 'in the battlefield' is realised by a nominal group; the Circumstance of Manner 매우 용감하게 *maeu yonggamha-ge* 'very bravely' is realised by an adverbial group; and finally the Process 싸우고 있었다 *ssau-go iss-eot-da* 'was fighting' is realised by a verbal group.

From the perspective of SFL, in all languages a group is made up of words, and for languages like Korean a word is further analysed as made up of morphemes. We need to adjust this picture a little for co-verbal phrases, which consist of a nominal group (realised by one or more words) followed by a 'bound' verb. We call the verb in a co-verbal phrase (e.g., 위해 *wihae* 'for') a bound verb because it has limited conjugation possibilities. Since co-verbal

---

[2] Note that as the example is too long to fit into a single analysis table, we have divided it into two tables. The '...' in Hangeul line indicates that more words are following (in the first table) or preceding (in the second table). The first instance of '...' in the translation line represents the gap that can be 'filled' with the expressions between two sets of '...' in the translation line of the following table. This is inevitable as we are providing fairly literal translations in the face of grammatical differences between Korean and English.

2.2 Groups and Phrases: An Overview

phrases function like groups as far as realising clause rank functions is concerned, we interpret the scale of ranks in Korean grammar in general terms as outlined in Figure 2.1.

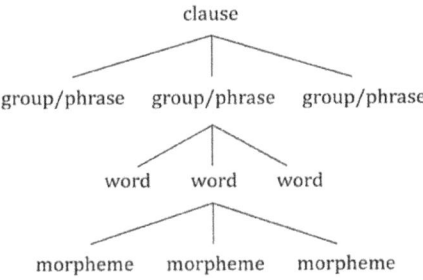

Figure 2.1 Rank scale in Korean

We return now to (1) and take a closer look at the first nominal group and the verbal group. The nominal group 저 어린 소년이 *jeo eorin sonyeon i* 'that young boy' in (1) is a group of four words, 저 *jeo* 'that' (determiner), 어린 *eorin* 'young' (adjective), 소년 *sonyeon* 'boy' (noun) and 이 *i* (clitic). Just as groups and phrases realise grammatical functions at clause rank (e.g., a nominal group realising Participant or Circumstance), each of the words realises a grammatical function at group/phrase rank. As analysed here, (2) includes the nominal group functions Deictic, Epithet, Thing and Function Marking (FM)[3] – each of which will be explained in following sections.

(2)

저 어린 소년이 ...			
jeo	*eori-n*	*sonyeon*	*=i*
that	young	boy	
Participant			
nominal group			
Deictic	Epithet	Thing	Function Marking (FM)
determiner	adjective	noun	clitic
'That young boy ...			

Turning to the verbal group 싸우고 있었다 *ssau-go iss-eot-da* 'was fighting' in (3), we have a group of two verbs, 싸우고 *ssau-go* 'fight' (lexical verb) and

---

[3] Experiential Function Marking, Interpersonal Function Marking and Textual Function Marking functions will be distinguished in Section 2.3.10.

있었다 *iss-eot-da* 'was...ing' (auxiliary verb).[4] Here the lexical verb 싸우고 *ssau-go* 'fight' realises the Event function, and the auxiliary verb 있었다 *iss-eot-da* 'was...ing' realises the Dimension function (a verbal group function introduced in Chapter 1). Example (3) is analysed in these terms.

(3)

... 싸우고 있었다.	
ssau-go	*iss-eot-da*
fight	be doing
Process	
verbal group	
Event	Dimension
lexical verb	auxiliary verb
... was fighting.'	

Words can be divided into classes reflecting their grammatical potential. In this grammar we recognise four primary classes:[5] nominal, verbal, phrasal and adverbial. The four primary classes correlate with the role they play in Korean groups and phrases. In proposing these classes, we privilege their combinatorial potential in a given structure. Table 2.1 lists these classes alongside the functions they play in groups and phrases (and via groups and phrases in clauses). For instance, nouns, adjectives, numerals, determiners, bound nouns and clitics are the classes of word that can occur in a nominal group in Korean. The typical roles they play are listed in column 3 in Table 2.1.

Note that we are treating clitics as a word class, not a suffix. The main criterion we apply in distinguishing a word from a suffix is that of 'independency'. A clitic is not part of the word that it follows; the preceding word is 'complete' whether the clitic is there or not. Suffixes, however, are different; if they are not there, the word in the structure being considered is incomplete.

In addition, while verbal suffixes only enter into a grammatical relation with conjugatable word classes (i.e., with verbs and adjectives), clitics can follow many word classes, conjugatable or not. A clitic like *neun*, for instance, can be

---

[4] Note that when two verbs realise a Process as in (3), the first culminates with a connecting suffix and the second (even if it is not a lexical verb) gets marked for tense and mood. Thus, in (3), 싸우고 *ssau-go* consists of the stem and the connecting suffix, and 있었다 *iss-eot-da* comprises the stem, the suffix for tense (past) and the suffix for mood (declarative).

[5] Further subdivisions are possible. For instance, nouns can further be divided into three types: common nouns, proper nouns and pronouns. And adjectives in a nominal group can further be divided into two types: the conjugatable adjective class, e.g., 어린 *eori-n* 'young' and the non-conjugatable adjective class, e.g., 새 *sae* 'new' as in 새 책 *sae chaek* 'new book'. Conjugatable adjectives can realise the Event in verbal groups while non-conjugatable adjectives cannot.

2.2 Groups and Phrases: An Overview

Table 2.1 *Word classes and their functions in groups and phrases*

		word class	their typical function(s) in groups/phrases	
nominal group		noun	Thing, Classifying, Quantity	
		pronoun	Thing	
		adjective	Epithet, Classifying	
		adverb	Classifying	
		numeral	Classifying, Ordering, Quantity	
		determiner	Deictic	
		bound noun	Quantity, Perspective	
		clitic	Function Marking, Linking	
verbal group		verb	Event	
		verbalised adjective	Event	
		copula auxiliary verb	Event Valence, Dimension, Negating, Modal	
		auxiliary adjective	Dimension, Negating, Modal, Highlight	
		adverb	Negate, Degree	
		bound noun	Dimension, Modal, Highlight	
		clitic[6]	Function Marking	
adverbial group		adverb	Property, Grader, Head	
		clitic[7]	Function Marking	
co-verbal phrase	nominal group	same as nominal group above	same as nominal group above	Incumbent
		bound verb	Role	

a function marker for a nominal group (e.g., 우리 엄마는 *uri eomma* **neun** 'our mum'), a co-verbal phrase (e.g., 우리 엄마를 위해서는 *uri eomma reul wihaeseo* **neun** 'for our mum'), an adverbial group (e.g., 철저하게는 *choljeohage* **neun** 'thoroughly') or an embedded clause (e.g., 중요한 것은 *jungyohan gos* **eun** 'what is important').

---

[6] The functions of this clitic are interpersonal, and will be discussed in Chapter 3 (Section 3.6.1 Modalisation).
[7] As for the clitic in verbal groups, its function is interpersonal or textual. See Chapters 3 (Section 3.9 The System of COMMENT) and 5 (Section 5.3 Interpersonal Theme) for details.

We distinguish clitics from particles according to the rank at which they function. For example, 요 *yo* (the Politeness Marker, which will be discussed in Chapter 3) and 라고 *rago* or 하고 *hago* (Linkers, which will be discussed in Chapter 6) are particles that function as part of clause structure; clitics on the other hand function in groups and phrases. The clitics can be divided into two groups: 의 *ui* and 와/과 *wa/gwa* (which make a connection between units within a nominal group) and 이/가 *i/ga*, 을/를 *eul/reul*, 은/는 *eun/neun*, 도 *do* etc. (which mark the function of groups and phrases in clause structure). These will be discussed toward the end of Section 2.3.

Following the Korean spelling convention that clitics, particles and suffixes are not separated by a space from the word, group/phrase or morpheme they enter into a construction with, no space is provided before a clitic, a particle or a suffix in our Hangeul examples. However, in our Romanised examples and analysis, a space is provided before a clitic and a particle but not a suffix – in order to distinguish their classes (as word vs morpheme). Further, an equals sign '=' is used before a clitic, to show that clitics are dependent words. And we use a hyphen '-' before a suffix, to show they are part of a word. For more discussion of the Korean spelling system and the grammatical status of what we call clitics, particles and suffixes, see Yu et al. (2018: 219).

Below we explore group and phrase functions in detail, beginning with the nominal group.[8]

2.3   Nominal Group

The nominal group in Korean typically involves some combination of nouns (including common nouns, proper nouns, pronouns and bound nouns), adjectives, numerals, determiners and clitics. In addition, the Korean nominal group has the potential to include embedded groups/phrases and embedded clauses in its structure. These units realise a number of group functions: Qualifying, Orient, Deictic, Epithet, Ordering, Classifying, Thing, Quantity, Perspective and Function Marking. We will introduce each of the functions in terms of the systems they realise. We begin our discussion with the nucleus of the nominal group, the Thing, which is always present (it is not possible in Korean to elide the Thing as it is an obligatory nuclear function). We then introduce the functions realised by a word or word complex before the Thing (e.g., Deictic, Epithet, Ordering and Classifying), then the functions realised by an embedded group/phrase or clause before the Thing (i.e., Orient or Qualifying) and finally the functions realised after the Thing (i.e., Quantity, Perspective and Function Marking).

---

[8] For a fuller interpretation of nominal group structure, see Martin and Shin (2021).

2.3 Nominal Group

2.3.1 The System of THING TYPE

The **Thing** is the core element in a nominal group; it construes conscious beings, non-conscious entities, or abstractions. The Thing may or may not be expanded by various pre- or post-modifying elements. Each of (4), (5) and (6) shows a simple nominal group consisting of just a pronoun, proper name and common noun.

(4)
너
neo
you
nominal group
Thing
pronoun
'you'

(5)
수지
suji
Suji
nominal group
Thing
proper noun
'Suji'

(6)
나무
namu
tree
nominal group
Thing
common noun
'tree'

The network in Figure 2.2 presents the basic thing types illustrated in (4), (5) and (6), and the relevant realisation statements for THING TYPE are given in Table 2.2.

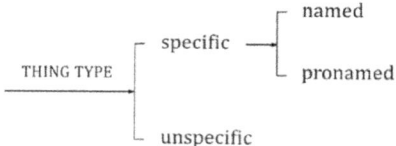

Figure 2.2 The system of basic THING TYPE

Realisation statements specify the relationship between choices in the system (e.g., [named]) and their realisation in structure (e.g., Thing: proper noun).[9] In these statements '+' indicates that a function will be present in the structure (e.g., +Thing); ':' signals the relation between function and the class that realises it (e.g., Thing:proper noun).

Table 2.2 *The system of basic* THING TYPE: *realisation statements*

nominal group	+Thing
named	Thing:proper noun
pronamed	Thing:pronoun
unspecific	Thing:common noun

Example (7) 조국을 *jogug eul* 'mother country' and (8) 전쟁터에서 *jeonjaengteo eseo* 'in the battlefield' are not pre-modified or post-modified; but they include a clitic that indicates what kind of function the nominal group has at clause rank. We'll set aside discussion of Function Marking elements here and return to their culminative role in nominal group structure toward the end of this section.

(7)

조국을	
jogug	=*eul*
mother country	
nominal group	
Thing	Function Marking
noun	clitic
'mother country'	

---

[9] The realisation statements in our descriptive grammar are less explicit than those which might be required for alternative purposes – for example, implementation of a computer program for automatic parsing or for text generation. They have been phrased for the benefit of users in appliable linguistics research.

(8)

전쟁터에서	
jeonjaengteo	=eseo
battlefield	in
nominal group	
Thing	Function Marking
noun	clitic
'in the battle field'	

Korean has a nominal suffix, 들 -deul, operating at word rank, for marking plural. It can be used with common nouns (e.g., 나무들 namu-deul 'trees'), pronouns (e.g., 너희들 neohui-deul 'you plural') and proper nouns (e.g., 수지들 Suji-deul 'Sujis' – i.e., 'people whose names are Suji'). This suffix is not obligatory in nominal groups understood as referring to more than one entity. In colloquial Korean, one often finds additional uses of the suffix, in association with an adverb or verb (see Song 1977 for discussion).

2.3.2 The System of CLASSIFICATION

Classifying functions are pre-modifiers that come immediately before the Thing. They subclassify the Thing and involve relatively persistent distinguishing features. They are not gradable and in Korean they are typically realised by nouns (e.g., 나무 *namu* 'wood' in 나무 의자 *namu uija* '*wooden chair*' and 금 *geum* 'gold' in 금 목걸이 *geum mokgeori* 'gold necklace'). Over time, some structures that were once Classifying ^ Thing constructions have been lexicalised as compound nouns – for example, 책가방 *chaekgabang* is a compound noun that literally means 'book bag'. It refers to schoolbag, a particular kind of bag that students use when they go to school (which may or may not have any books in it). Example (9) presents a nominal group with a Thing modified by a Classifying function.

(9)

전기 자동차	
jeongi	jadongcha
electricity	car
nominal group	
Classifying	Thing
noun	noun
'electric car'	

There can be more than one Classifying function in a Korean nominal group as exemplified in (10) and (11).

(10)

장난감 전기 자동차		
jangnamgam	*jeongi*	*jadongcha*
toy	electricity	car
nominal group		
Classifying	Classifying	Thing
noun	noun	noun
'toy electric car'		

(11)

전기 통신 금융 사기			
jeongi	*tongsin*	*geumnyung*	*sagi*
electricity	communication	finance	fraud
nominal group			
Classifying	Classifying	Classifying	Thing
noun	noun	noun	noun
'voice phishing (Lit. electric communication finance fraud)'			

A single Classifying function is sometimes realised by a word complex, as in 조선 시대 관습 *Joseon sidae gwanseup* 'Chosun era conventions' (12); these can be analysed as involving a dependency structure (e.g., *Joseon* 'Chosun' as β and *sidae* 'era' as α).

(12)

조선 시대 관습		
Joseon	*sidae*	*gwanseup*
Chosin	era	conventions
nominal group		
Classifying		Thing
word complex		noun
β	α	
noun	noun	
'Chosun era conventions'		

The Classifying function is typically realised by nominals, but can also be realised by adjectives, numerals, verbs and adverbs in Korean. Some examples are given in (13).

2.3 Nominal Group

(13) 새신랑   *sae* (adjective) *sillang*   'just married husband'
      수천 마리   *sucheon* (numeral:cardinal) *mari* 'thousand head (e.g., animals)'
      1 차 조사   *il cha* (numeral:ordinal) *josa*   'first (initial) investigation'
      지정된 장소 *jijeongdoen* (verb) *jangso*   'designated area'
      몰래카메라 *mollae* (adverb) *kamera*   'hidden camera'

Figure 2.3 illustrates the system of CLASSIFICATION in Korean, and shows that the Thing may or may not be classified (through the symbol '–') and that multiple classification is possible (through the superscript ^{n}). The '^' operator in the realisation statements (Table 2.3) specifies that one function immediately precedes another (e.g., Classifying ^ Thing).

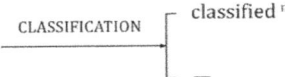

Figure 2.3 The system of CLASSIFICATION

Table 2.3 *The system of CLASSIFICATION: realisation statements*

Classified	+Classifying; Classifying ^ Thing; Classifying:(various)

2.3.3 The System of ORDINATION

A Thing can be also modified by the function Ordering. Ordering functions are realised by ordinal numbers such as 첫번째 *cheotbeonjjae* 'first', 두번째 *dubeonjjae* 'second', or by nouns such as 중간 *junggan* 'middle', 마지막 *majimak* 'end', 오른쪽 *oreunjjok* 'right side' etc. They position the Thing relative to other entities in the co-text or context. Example (9) is expanded as (14) to include an Ordering function.

(14)

첫 번째 전기 자동차		
cheotbeonjjae	*jeongi*	*jadongcha*
first	electricity	car
nominal group		
Ordering	Classifying	Thing
numeral	noun	noun
'first electric car'		

The system of ORDINATION presented in Figure 2.4 shows that a Thing may or may not be modified by an Ordering function and when it is, it can be ordered numerically or positionally.

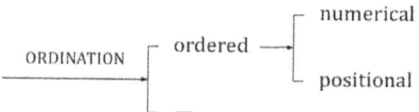

Figure 2.4 The system of ORDINATION

The relevant realisation statements for ORDINATION are given in Table 2.4. Note that '→' indicates that the Ordering function, if present, precedes the Thing and sometimes one or more Classifying functions.

Table 2.4 *The system of ORDINATION: realisation statements*

ordered	+Ordering; Ordering → (Classifying) ^ Thing
numerical	Ordering:ordinal numeral
positional	Ordering:positional noun

2.3.4 The System of EPITHESIS

Another modifier that can come before the Thing is **Epithet**. Epithets realise relatively less persistent qualities of Things – for example, age, size, length, height, loudness, degree, weight, behavioural propensity, rating, emotion, dimension, colour or taste.

This function is realised by adjectives – both conjugatable (e.g., 친절한 *chinjeolhan* 'kind', 조그만 *jogeuman* 'small', 아름다운 *areumdaun* 'beautiful', 뚱뚱한 *ttungttunghan* 'fat', or 푸른 *pureun* 'blue') and non-conjugatable (e.g., 새 *sae* 'new', 헌 *heon* 'old (much used)', 옛 *yet* 'old (time-wise)', 온갖 *ongat* 'all sorts of', 모든 *modeun* 'all', or 여러 *yeoreo* 'various'). The distinction between conjugatable and non-conjugatable adjectives rests on the ability of some adjectives to be 'verbalised' and function as a conflated Attribute/Process in relational attributive clauses; this distinction affects the need for a linker and also influences how these adjectives are positioned in Korean nominal groups.

2.3 Nominal Group

Example (14) is expanded as (15) to include an Epithet function.

(15)

혁신적인 첫 번째 전기 자동차				
hyeoksinjeogi-n		*cheotbeonjjae*	*jeongi*	*jadongcha*
innovative		first	electric	car
noinal group				
Epithet		Ordering	Classifying	Thing
adjective		numeral	noun	noun
Head	Link			
stem	suffix			
'innovative first electric car'				

The qualities realised by Epithets are gradable (e.g., 매우 친절한, *maeu chinjeolhan* 'very kind', 더 아름다운 *deo areumdaun* 'more beautiful', etc.). Example (16) presents a nominal group in which the Thing is modified by a graded Epithet. In such cases the Epithet is realised by a word complex, with an adjective as head (α) and a submodifying adverb as dependent (β).

(16)

매우 혁신적인 첫 번째 전기 자동차				
maeu	*hyeoksinjeogi-n*	*cheotbeonjjae*	*jeongi*	*jadongcha*
very	innovative	first	electric	car
nominal group				
Epithet		Ordering	Classifying	Thing
word complex		numeral	noun	noun
β	α			
adverb	adjective			
	Head	Link		
	stem	suffix		
'very innovative first electric car'				

When a comparison is made, there is the additional option of declaring the standard of comparison – as illustrated in (17). To this effect a Standard function has been added, preceding the Epithet. It is realised by an embedded nominal group culminating with the linking clitic 보다 *boda* (by convention we enclose embedded groups and phrases in single square brackets in our analyses).

(17)

나보다 더 큰 사람				
na	=boda	deo	keu-n	saram
I	than	more	big	person
nominal group				
Standard		Epithet		Thing
[nominal group]		word complex		noun
Thing	Linking	β	α	
noun	clitic	adverb	adjective	
			Head	Link
			stem	suffix
'a taller person than me'				

Like CLASSIFICATION and GRADING, EPITHESIS is a recursive system. However, unlike CLASSIFICATION and GRADING, with EPITHESIS additional descriptors are arranged as a progressive paratactic word complex which "coordinates" the adjectives (and so are annotated 1, 2, 3 etc. in SFL). These paratactic complexes contrast with the regressive hypotactic ones introduced above for CLASSIFICATION and GRADING (notated ...γ β α there).

In this respect Korean reflects nicely the difference between CLASSIFICATION (where each expansion subclassifies the item or items to its right) and EPITHESIS (where each expansion separately characterises the Thing). This explains why the adjectives in a complex realising an Epithet can come in different sequences without affecting the description – since each separately modifies the Thing. Items realising CLASSIFICATION on the other hand have to be strictly sequenced – respecting hyponymic relations in the taxonomy they are construing. An example adding three qualities to an entity is illustrated in (18). The first and second adjectives involve a paratactic linking suffix (i.e., 고 -go).

(18)

빠르고 아름답고 매우 혁신적인 전기 자동차							
ppareu-go		areumdap-go		maeu	hyeoksinjeogi-n	jeongi	jadongcha
fast		beautiful		very	innovative	electricity	car
nominal group							
Epithet						Classifying	Thing
word complex						noun	noun
1		+2		+3			
adjective		adjective		word complex			
Head	Link	Head	Link	β	α		
stem	sfx	head	sfx	adverb	adjective		
					Head	Link	
					stem	sfx	
'fast, beautiful and very innovative electric car'							

2.3 Nominal Group

In Korean there is no typical or obligatory sequence among attitudinal and depictive Epithets. Both 작고 예쁜 아이 *jak-go yeppeu-n ai* 'small and pretty child' and 예쁘고 작은 아이 *yeppeu-go jag-eun ai* 'pretty and small child' are natural.

The system of EPITHESIS shown in Figure 2.5 takes into account that when an Epithet is used, it can be realised by either a conjugatable or non-conjugatable adjective. The network also allows for submodification that intensifies or mitigates the quality being ascribed to the Thing. And for comparative grading the network allows the standard of comparison to be made explicit through inclusion of a Standard function.

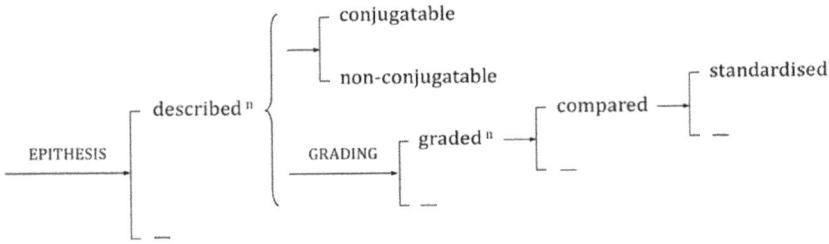

Figure 2.5 The system of EPITHESIS

The relevant realisation statements are specified in Table 2.5. Epithets always precede the Thing. If an Ordering function is also present, conjugatable adjectives precede (e.g., 혁신적인 첫 번째 전기 자동차 *hyeoksinjeogi-n cheot beonjjae jeongi jadongcha* 'innovative first electric car') and non-conjugatable adjectives follow (e.g., 첫 번째 새 전기 자동차 *cheotbeonjjae sae jeongi jadongcha* 'first new electric car').

Table 2.5 *The system of* EPITHESIS: *realisation statements*

described	+Epithet; Epithet ⇀ Thing; Epithet:adjective
conjugatable	Epithet ⇀ (Ordering)
non-conjugatable	(Ordering) ⇀ Epithet
graded	Epithet:word complex:+β; β ^ α; β:adverb
compared	β:comparative adverb
standardised	+Standard; Standard ^ Epithet; Standard:nominal group (with culminative 보다 =*boda*)

2.3.5 The System of DEIXIS

A Thing can be also pre-modified by a **Deictic**. The Deictic function indicates whether the identity of the entity realised in the nominal group is specific (i.e., identity recoverable) or non-specific (i.e., identity not recoverable, or identity recovery irrelevant). In (19) 저 *jeo* 'that' signifies that the speaker is referring to a specific car that is not near the speaker or the addressee but that they can see.

(19)

저 매우 혁신적인 전기 자동차				
jeo	*maeu*	*hyeoksinjeogi-n*	*jeongi*	*jadongcha*
that	very	innovative	electricity	car
nominal group				
Deictic	Epithet		Classifying	Thing
determiner	word complex		noun	noun
	β	α		
	adverb	adjective		
		Head	Link	
		stem	suffix	
'that very innovative first electric car'				

The Deictic function is realised by determiners. Korean determiners are outlined in Table 2.6.

Table 2.6 *Types of determiner*

Types			Examples (Deictic ^ Thing)
specific		possessive	내 재산 **nae** *jaesan* 'my property' 우리 사회 **uri** *sahoe* 'our society' etc.
	demonstrative	determinative	이 여아 **i** *yeoa* 'this (near speaker) girl' 그 선녀 **geu** *seonnyeo* 'that (near addressee) nymph' 저 건물 **jeo** *geonmul* 'that (not near speaker/addressee) building'
		interrogative	어느 집 **eoneu** *jip* 'which house' 무슨 뜻 **museun** *tteut* 'what meaning' etc.
non-specific			한 사람 **han** *saram* 'one person' 아무런 해법 **amureon** *haebeop* 'any solution' 어떤 질문 **eotteon** *jilmun* 'certain question' etc.

2.3 Nominal Group

When used exophorically to identify someone or something in the speech situation, the demonstratives 이 *i* 'this', 그 *geu* 'that', and 저 *jeo* 'that' realise three kinds of interpersonal distance: 이 *i* marks near the speaker, 그 *geu* near the addressee, and 저 *jeo* near neither. Of these it is the demonstrative 그 *geu* that is used for anaphoric reference (to the co-text). In fact, when the identity of a participant is recoverable from the material situational setting (exophoric reference), the Deictic is usually not made explicit (and the most readily recoverable clause Participants[10] do not need to be mentioned at all in Korean). When one asks someone to close the door, one usually says 문 닫아주세요 ***mun dad-a juse yo*** 'close (the) door', or simply 닫아주세요 ***dad-a juse yo*** 'close' rather than 그 문 닫아주세요 ***geu mun dad-a juse yo*** 'close that door'. The Deictic is also not used when the identity of an entity is recoverable with respect to knowledge shared by a particular social group (e.g., homophoric reference to the sun or the moon, the president or the boss, or to the car in a one-car family).

Table 2.6 included examples of possessive determiners (내 *nae* 'my' and 우리 *uri* 'our'). The complete set of Korean possessive determiners is outlined in Table 2.7.

Table 2.7 *Possessive determiners*

		singular (only)	plural (plus others)
1st person (speaker)	by non-deferential speaker	내 *nae*	우리 *uri*
	by deferential speaker	제 *je*	저희 *jeohui*
2nd person (addressee)	by non-deferential speaker	네 *ne*	너희 *neohui*
	by deferential speaker	–	–
3rd person (non-interlocutor)	by non-deferential speaker	–	–
	by deferential speaker	–	–

Note the gaps in Table 2.7. Korean lacks a possessive determiner that could be used by a deferential speaker for 2nd person; it also lacks possessive determiners for 3rd person – comparable to English *his/her/its* and *their*.

As exemplified in Table 2.8, Korean fills in gaps in the paradigm by utilising an embedded nominal group with a non-possessive pronoun followed by the

---

[10] In SFL the term Participant is used to refer to 'agentive', 'affected' and 'benefactive' arguments in the transitivity structure of a clause (Halliday 1985); they are complemented in this structure by Circumstances (of extent, location, manner, matter, role and so on); see Chapter 4 for details.

linking clitic 의 *ui*; we take these syntagms to be realisations of a different function, Orient, which unlike Deictics is realised by an embedded nominal group and culminates with the linking clitic 의 *ui* (see Section 2.3.6).

Table 2.8 *Possessive pronoun alternatives*

		singular (only)	plural (plus others)
2nd person (addressee)	by deferential speaker	선생님의 재산 *seonsaengnim =ui jaesan* 'your (literally, the teacher's) property'	선생님들의 재산 *seonsaengnim-deul =ui jaesan* 'your (literally, the teachers') property'
3rd person (non-interlocutor)	by non-deferential speaker[11]	그 사람의 재산 *geu saram =ui jaesan* 'his/her (literally, the person's) property'	그 사람들의 재산 *geu saram-deul =ui jaesan* 'their (literally, the persons') property'
	by deferential speaker	그분의 재산 *geu bun =ui jaesan* 'his/her (literally the respected person's) property'	그분들의 재산 *geu bun-deul =ui jaesan* 'their (literally, the respected persons') property'

The general options in the DEIXIS system are outlined in Figure 2.6. Reading left to right, the first system allows for the presence of a Deictic or not. If a Deictic is present (i.e., marked), then the Deictic function can be realised by a specific or non-specific determiner. If the Deictic is specific, then there is a choice between demonstrative and possessive (realised by a possessive pronoun). If demonstrative, there is a choice between a determinative or interrogative determiner.

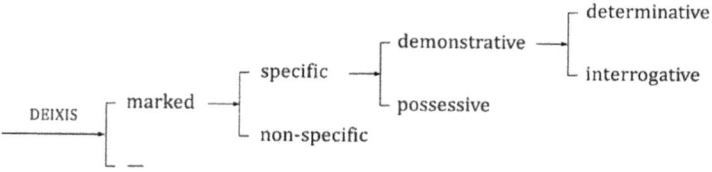

Figure 2.6 The system of DEIXIS

---

[11] We acknowledge here 그(의) *geu (ui)* 'his', 그들(의) *geu-deur (ui)* 'their (masculine)', 그녀(의) *geunyeo (ui)* 'her' and 그녀들(의) *geunyeo-deur (ui)* 'their (feminine)', which can appear without the clitic 의 *ui* but which until recently have been restricted in usage to formal (e.g., literary and legal) registers.

2.3 Nominal Group

The relevant realisation statements are shown in Table 2.9. Deictics always precede the Thing and an Epithet and/or Ordering function if present (the '·' notation acknowledges that the Epithet and Ordering functions can occur in either sequence, as noted above).

Table 2.9 *The system of* DEIXIS: *realisation statements*

marked	+Deictic; Deictic ⇁ (Epithet) · (Ordering) Thing
determinative	Deictic:demonstrative determiner
interrogative	Deictic:interrogative determiner
possessive	Deictic:possessive determiner (cf. Table 2.7)
non-specific	Deictic:non-specific determiner

2.3.6 The System of ORIENTATION

We now move to systems that come before the Thing, but are realised by an embedded group/phrase or clause. One of them is **Orient**. The Orient function is realised by an embedded nominal group (i.e., a nominal group inside another nominal group), which culminates with the clitic 의 *ui* as in (20). By convention we enclose embedded groups and phrases in single square brackets in our analyses.

(20)

혁신적인 프로젝트의 개발			
hyeoksinjeogi-n	*peurojekteu*	=*ui*	*gaebal*
innovative	project		development
nominal group			
Orient			Thing
[nominal group]			noun
Epithet	Thing	Link	
adjective	noun	clitic	
Head	Linking		
stem	suffix		
'development of innovative project'			

In (20), the Orient involves an entity related to the Thing. Another example is 하나님의 은혜 *hananim ui eunhye* 'God's grace'.

The Orient function may also specify the Thing in terms of circumstantial meanings such as space, time or degree as in (21), explain its function as in (22), or exemplify it as in (23).

(21)

고단수의 사기			
godansu	=*ui*		*sagi*
high-level			fraud
nominal group			
Orient			Thing
[nominal group]			noun
Thing	Linking		
noun	clitic		
'highly organised fraud' (literally 'fraud of high-level')			

(22)

평화의 종소리			
pyeonghwa	=*ui*	*jong*	*sori*
peace		bell	sound
nominal group			
Orient		Classifying	Thing
[nominal group]		noun	noun
Thing	Linking		
noun	clitic		
'bell-sound for peace'			

(23)

산소 등의 물질			
sanso	*deung*	=*ui*	*muljil*
oxygen	etc.		substance
nominal group			
Orient			Thing
[nominal group]			noun
Thing		Linking	
word complex		clitic	
α	β		
noun	bound noun		
'substances such as oxygen etc.'			

2.3 Nominal Group

The Orient function can also be used to count the number of entities construed by the Thing – as in (24). This counting resource is in addition to the Quantity function, which is a post-nominal function (see Section 2.3.8).

(24)

35 명의 사상자				
35		*myeong*	=*ui*	*sasangja*
35		person		casualty
nominal group				
Orient				Thing
[nominal group]				noun
Thing		Linking		
word complex		clitic		
α	β			
cardinal numeral	bound noun			
'thirty-five casualties'				

As we saw above in our discussion of DEIXIS, the Orient function also modifies the Thing function by setting up 'possessive' relations. A very common one is ownership, as in (25).

(25)

친절한 수학 선생님의 책				
chinjeolha-n	*suhak*	*seonsaengnim*	=*ui*	*chaek*
kind	math	teacher		book
nominal group				
Orient				Thing
[nominal group]				noun
Epithet	Classifying	Thing	Linking	
adjective	noun	noun	clitic	
Head	Link			
stem	suffix			
'kind math teacher's book'				

In fact, employing a non-possessive pronoun followed by the linking clitic 의 *ui* (i.e., realising possession relations through the Orient function) is also possible as an alternative to the possessive determiners illustrated in Table 2.7.

So, we have a contrast in Korean between a Deictic function realised directly by a possessive determiner as in (26) and an Orient function realised by an embedded nominal group with a non-possessive pronoun as Thing like that in (27). As noted above, possessive Orient functions such as the one in (27) are used to 'fill the gaps' in the paradigm of possessive determiners in Table 2.7 (cf. the examples in Table 2.8).

(26)

내 책	
nae	chaek
my	book
nominal group	
Deictic	Thing
possessive determiner	noun
'my book'	

(27)

나의 책		
na	=ui	chaek
I		book
nominal group		
Orient		Thing
[nominal group]		noun
Thing	Linking	
noun	clitic	
'my book'; literally 'book of me'		

An example like (27) can be expanded as (28) to include both an Orient and a Deictic function – further confirming the distinction between these two functions.

(28)

나의 저 책			
na	=ui	jeo	chaek
I		that	book
nominal group			
Orient		Deictic	Thing
[nominal group]		determiner	noun
Thing	Linking		
noun	clitic		
'that book of mine'			

2.3 Nominal Group

Possessive examples like (28) aside,[12] the Orient will be sequenced after a Deictic, Epithet and/or Ordering function if present – as in (29). Further work on its position will have to take into account the wide range of meanings the ORIENTATION system involves, including the realisation of entities associated with Things involving nominalisation (as in (20)).

(29)

저 아름다운 세 번째 평화의 종소리							
jeo	areumdau-n	sebeonjjae	pyeonghwa	=ui	jong		sori
that	beautiful	third	peace		bell		sound
nominal group							
Deictic	Epithet	Ordering	Orient		Classifying		Thing
determiner	adjective	numeral	[nominal group]		noun		noun
	Head	Link		Thing	Linking		
	stem	sfx		noun	clitic		
'that beautiful third bell-sound for peace'							

The system of ORIENTATION is presented in Figure 2.7.

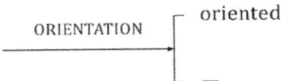

Figure 2.7 The system of ORIENTATION

The feature [oriented] is realised by the insertion of an Orient function. The Orient precedes the Thing and precedes or follows a Deictic, Epithet and/or Ordering functions if present. It is realised by an embedded nominal group, which culminates with a Linking function realised by the clitic 의 *ui* as noted in Table 2.10.

Table 2.10 *The system of ORIENTATION: realisation statements*

oriented	+Orient; Orient • (Deictic) (Epithet) (Ordering) ^ (Classifying) ^ Thing; Orient:nominal group (culminative 의 *ui*)

As indicated in (20) (혁신적인 프로젝트의 개발 *hyeoksinjeogi-n peurojekteu ui gaebal* 'development of innovative project'), the Orient function has a role to play in nominal groups involving a nominalised Thing. Compare (30) and (31).

---

[12] Using the Orient function to realise pronominal possession clearly influences sequencing; alongside (28), note the following Orient ^ Deictic ^ Epithet ^ Thing sequence: 너의 그 작은 어깨 *neo ui geu jag-eun eokkae* 'your (the) small shoulders', which comes from a Korean pop song.

(30)

기사들이 계획안을 준비했다.				
gisa-deur	=*i*	*gyehoegan*	=*eul*	*junbiha-et-da*
engineers		plan		prepared
P1		P2		Process
ng		[ng]		vg
Thing	FM	Thing	FM	
noun	clitic	noun	clitic	
'The engineers developed (lit. prepared) a plan.'				

(31)

기사들의 계획안 준비			
gisa-deur	=*ui*	*gyehoegan*	*junbi*
engineers		plan	preparation
nominal group			
Orient		Classifying	Thing
[nominal group]		noun	noun
Thing	Linking		
noun	clitic		
'The engineers' plan development (lit. preparation)'			

In (30) we have a ranking clause, with a Process and two Participants. In (31) the same meanings are reconfigured as a nominal group – with what happened realised as Thing, the P1 entity as Orient and the P2 entity as a Classifying function. As illustrated in (32) it would also be possible to realise both the P1 and P2 entities as Orient functions, although (31) would be the preferred nominalisation (probably because having more than one Orient function is strongly marked in Korean).

(32)

기사들의 계획안의 준비				
gisa-deur	=*ui*	*gyehoegan*	=*ui*	*junbi*
engineers		plan		preparation
nominal group				
Orient		Orient		Thing
[nominal group]		[nominal group]		noun
Thing	Linking	Thing	Linking	
noun	clitic	noun	clitic	
'The engineers' development (lit. preparation) of a plan'				

2.3.7 The System of QUALIFICATION

A nominal group can be further modified by an embedded clause or co-verbal phrase that defines, specifies or delimits the Thing in question, as exemplified in (33). By convention we enclose embedded clauses in double square brackets in analyses. These embedded clauses are referred to as **Qualifying** functions and come at the beginning of the nominal group – before the Thing and any of its associated pre-modifiers. They differ from Orient functions with embedding, both in terms of the class of unit embedded (embedded clause or co-verbal phrase for Qualifying vs embedded nominal group for Orient), the kind of connector deployed (suffixes for Qualifying vs the linking clitic 의 *ui* for Orient) and position in a nominal group (initial for Qualifying vs typically next to Thing for Orient).

(33)

내가 존경하는 ...			
nae	=*ga*		*jongyeongha-neun*
I			respect
nominal group			
Qualifying			
[[clause]]			
Participant		Process	
nominal group	clitic	verbal group	
Thing	Function Marking	Event	
		verb	
		Head	Link
		stem	sfx
... whom I respect'			

... 이 친절한 수학 선생님			
i	*chinjeolha-n*	*suhak*	*seonsaengnim*
this	kind	math	teacher
nominal group			
Deictic	Epithet	Classify	Thing
determiner	adjective	noun	noun
	Head	Link	
	stem	sfx	
'this kind math teacher ...			

The linking suffixes (known as 관형사형 어미 *gwanhyeongsahyeong eomi* 'adnominal suffixes' in Korean school grammars) that are used to culminate embedded clauses in Qualifying functions include those marking relative tense: (으)ㄴ -*(eu)n* (relative past), 는 -*neun* (relative present) and (으)ㄹ -*(eu)l* (relative future). Note that 은 -*eun* and 을 -*eul* occur after a consonant, and ㄴ -*n* and ㄹ -*l* after a vowel. The 'past', 'present' and 'future' tenses here are all 'relative' tenses in the sense that the reference point is the tense in the main clause (see Kim et al. 2005a: 166 for further details).

Qualifying functions can also be realised by an embedded co-verbal phrase. The co-verbal phrase in Korean involves a bound verb preceded by a nominal group. Its function structure is Incumbent followed immediately by Role. The Role function specifies the function of the co-verbal phrase in a clause or nominal group and the Incumbent function specifies the entity that plays the Role. Alongside realising Qualifying functions in nominal groups they regularly realise various types of Circumstance in clause structure (see Chapter 4).

Co-verbal phrases in nominal groups manage a range of circumstantial meanings specified by their culminative bound verb (i.e., a verb with a very restricted range of suffixation) – including means, cause, purpose, matter, accompaniment and so on. The connecting suffix employed is (으)ㄴ -*(eu)n*. This is the same suffix we saw in our discussion of EPITHESIS above where it is deployed to connect a conjugatable adjective to the following item (typically a noun) in a nominal group (34).

(34)

민주주의에 대한 시험 문제				
minjujuui	=*e*	*daeha-n*	*siheom*	*munje*
democracy		about	examination	question
nominal group				
Qualifying			Classifying	Thing
[co-verbal phrase]			noun	noun
Incumbent		Role		
[nominal group]		bound verb		
Thing	FM			
noun	clitic			
'exam question about democracy'				

Qualifying functions can be realised more than once in a nominal group, as illustrated in (35).

2.3 Nominal Group

(35)

jangnyeon	=e	nao-n	aideur	=i	joaha-neun	aiseukeurim
last year		appeared	children		like	ice cream

nominal group						
Qualifying			Qualifying			Thing
[[clause]]			[[clause]]			noun
Circumstance		Process	Participant		Process	
nominal group		verbal group	nominal group		verbal group	
Thing	FM	Event	Thing	FM	Event	
noun	clitic	verb	noun	clitic	verb	
		Head			Head	
		stem / sfx — Link			stem / sfx — Link	

'ice cream that appeared last year which children love'

There are two reasons why we analyse (35) as involving iterative Qualifying functions (rather than as a single Qualifying function realised by a clause complex). One reason is that a single Qualifying function realised by a clause complex has a different structure – as in (36). Note in this example the paratactic linking suffix 고 -*go* coordinating the two clauses, which contrasts with the relative tense marking suffix 는 -*neun* linking the clause complex as a whole to the Thing it modifies.

(36)

jangnyeon	=e	naw-at-go	ai-deur	=i	joaha-neun	aiseukeurim
last year		appeared and	children		like	ice cream

nominal group							
Qualifying							Thing
[[clause complex]]							noun
1				+2			
[[clause]]				[[clause]]			
Circumstance		Process		Participant		Process	
nominal group		verbal group		nominal group		verbal group	
Thing	FM	Event		Thing	FM	Event	
noun	clitic	verb		noun	clitic	verb	
		Head / stem	TM / sfx	Link / sfx		Head / stem	Link / sfx

'ice cream which appeared last year and children love'

The other reason is that the Qualifying functions in (35) can appear in either order; compare (35) with (37).

(37)

아이들이 좋아하는 작년에 나온 아이스크림

aideur	=i	joaha-neun	jangnyeon	=e	nao-n	aiseukeurim
children		like	last year		appeared	ice cream
nominal group						
Qualifying			Qualifying			Thing
[[clause]]			[[clause]]			noun
Participant		Process	Circumstance		Process	
nominal group		verbal group	nominal group		verbal group	
Thing	FM	Event	Thing	FM	Event	
noun	clitic	verb	noun	clitic	verb	
		Head / Link			Head / Link	
		stem / sfx			stem / sfx	

'ice cream that children love which appeared last year'

A Qualifying function realised by an embedded clause tends to precede one realised by a co-verbal phrase, as illustrated in (38).

(38)

아침에 본 민주주의에 대한 ...

achim	=e	bo-n	minjujuui	=e	daeha-n	
morning		took	democracy		about	
nominal group						
Qualifying			Qualifying			
[[clause]]			[co-verbal phrase]			
Circumstance		Process	Incumbent		Role	
nominal group		verbal group	[nominal group]		bound verb	
Thing	FM	Event	Thing	FM	Head	Link
noun	clitic	verb	noun	clitic	stem	sfx
		Head / Link				
		stem / sfx				

'... about democracy which we took in the morning'

2.3 Nominal Group

... 시험 문제	
siheom	*munje*
examination	question
nominal group	
Classify	Thing
noun	noun
'exam question ...	

The system of QUALIFICATION is presented in Figure 2.8.

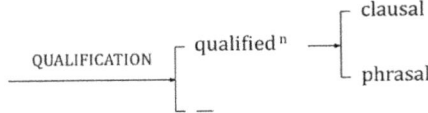

Figure 2.8 The system of QUALIFICATION

In the realisation statements the symbol '#' represents the left or right boundary of a grammatical unit. The superscript 'n' on the feature [qualified] indicates that more than one Qualifying function can be deployed (Table 2.11). The feature [clausal] allows for Qualifying functions realised by embedded clauses in initial position in a nominal group, with an appropriate relative tense culminative suffix. The [phrasal] alternative allows for Qualifying functions realised by a co-verbal phrase culminating with the suffix (으)ㄴ *-(eu)n* (see Table 2.32).

Table 2.11 *The system of QUALIFICATION: realisation statements*

qualified	+Qualifying; # ^ Qualifying ^{n}
clausal	Qualifying:[[clause]]
phrasal	Qualifying:[co-verbal phrase]

2.3.8 The System of QUANTIFICATION

We turn now to systems that are realised after the Thing (i.e., QUANTIFICATION, PERSPECTIVISATION and FUNCTION MARKING).

Turning to post-modification, there are two nominal group functions that come directly after the Thing but before a Function Marking function. One of them is **Quantity**, which is concerned with quantifying the Thing through cardinal numbers such as 하나 *hana* 'one', 둘 *dul* 'two', 셋 *set* 'three', etc. (39). This is an alternative to counting with an Orient function as illustrated in (24).

(39)

선녀 셋이		
seonnyeo	*ses*[13]	=*i*
nymph	three	
nominal group		
Thing	Quantity	FM
noun	cardinal number	clitic
'three nymphs'		

These numbers are optionally followed by the unit of measure with respect to which the Thing is quantified (e.g., 명 *myeong* or 사람 *saram* (for people), 마리 *mari* (for animals), 자루 *jaru* (for pencils), 권 *gwon* (for books), 대 *dae* (for vehicles) etc.);[14] see Sohn (1999: 204–6) for a more detailed discussion of this structure. In many descriptions these units of measure are referred to as "classifiers"; but in SFL descriptions this can be confusing since many descriptions informed by SFL have used the term Classifier in a different way, as a label for a function that subclassifies the Thing (e.g., Halliday 1985 and subsequent editions). Rather than treating this unit as directly realising a nominal group rank function, we'll treat it as a bound noun sub-modifying the numeral in a Quantity function.

This means that when the Quantity function involves a measure noun, it is realised as a word complex, with the head numeral (α) followed by a bound noun (β) – as shown in (40).

---

[13] Note that here we put *ses*, not *set*, since in our glossing we reflect morphophonemic changes across the cell boundaries.
[14] Lee and Chae (2013: 141–2) classify Korean's unit nouns (about 70 of them) into six categories: (i) general – the use of 개 *gae* 'item', (ii) clothing, (iii) food, (iv) housing, (v) reading and writing, and (vi) machines and furniture.

2.3 Nominal Group

(40)

선녀 세[15] 명이			
seonnyeo	se	myeong	=i
nymph	three	people	
nominal group			
Thing	Quantity		Function Marking
noun	word complex		clitic
	α	β	
	cardinal numeral	bound noun	
'three nymphs'			

The system of QUANTIFICATION is presented in Figure 2.9 and specifies that when the Thing in a nominal group is quantified, it can be realised with a unit of measure or without one (Table 2.12).

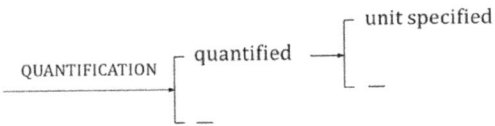

Figure 2.9 The system of QUANTIFICATION

Table 2.12 *The system of QUANTIFICATION: realisation statements*

quantified	+Quantity; Thing ^ Quantity
unit specified	Quantity:word complex (α:cardinal numeral ^ β:bound noun)

2.3.9 The System of PERSPECTIVISATION

Another possible post-modifier is the **Perspective** function; it can be found in nominal groups that realise a Circumstance of Location in space or time in a clause. This function is used to specify the locative meaning of the culminative clitic deployed in these nominal groups. For example, the clitics 에 *e* or 에서 *eseo* can both be glossed as 'in, at, on, etc.'; they are not specific enough to distinguish among different types of location. A Perspective function is needed to make the finer distinctions. The Perspective function is realised by a noun

---

[15] The first four cardinal numerals 하나 *hana* 'one', 둘 *dul* 'two', 셋 *set* 'three' and 넷 *net* 'four' become 한 *han*, 두 *du*, 세 *se* and 네 *ne* respectively when used with a bound noun indicating a measure unit.

designating a specific location – e.g., 안 *an* 'inside', 밖 *bak* 'outside', 앞 *ap* 'front', 뒤 *dwi* 'back', etc.

The general locative meaning in (41), which does not have a Perspective nominal group function, is further specified by a Perspective function in examples (42)–(44).

(41)

방에	
bang	=*e*
room	in
nominal group	
Thing	FM
noun	clitic
'in the room'	

The Perspective function follows the Thing, as exemplified in (42) and (43). If the Thing is specified through a Quantity function, realised by a cardinal numeral or word complex, the Perspective function follows – as in (44).

(42)

방 안에		
bang	*an*	=*e*
room	inside	in
nominal group		
Thing	Perspective	FM
noun	noun	clitic
'inside the room'		

(43)

방 앞에		
bang	*ap*	=*e*
room	front	in
nominal group		
Thing	Perspective	FM
noun	noun	clitic
'in front of the room'		

2.3 Nominal Group

(44)

책 한 권 위에				
chaek	*han*	*kwon*	*wi*	*=e*
book	one	unit	above	at
nominal group				
Thing	Quantity		Perspective	FM
noun	word complex		noun	clitic
	α	β		
	cardinal numeral	bound noun		
'on the top of a book'				

Other nouns that may realise the Perspective function include 아래 *arae* 'under' in 선반 아래에, *seonban arae e* 'under the shelf', 옆 *yeop* in 책상 옆에 *chaeksang yeop e* 'next to the desk' and 뒤 *dwi* in 문 뒤에, *mun dwi e* 'behind the door', or in 30 분 뒤에, 30 *bun dwi e* 'after/in 30 minutes'.

The system of PERSPECTIVISATION and the realisation statements are presented in Figure 2.10 and Table 2.13. The feature [perspectivised] is realised by the presence of a Perspective function realised by a 'locative' noun in penultimate position in a nominal group with function marking (the FM in (41) to (44)).

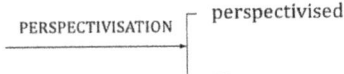

Figure 2.10 The system of PERSPECTIVISATION

Table 2.13 *The system of PERSPECTIVISATION: realisation statements*

perspectivised	+Perspective;Thing (Quantity) ⁀ Perspective; Perspective:locative noun

2.3.10 The System of FUNCTION MARKING

It remains to discuss culminative function in nominal groups. As noted in passing above, nominal groups functioning at clause rank (i.e., unembedded nominal groups) may include culminative **Function Marking**. In colloquial spoken Korean, where interlocutors share understandings and expectations based on shared experience and/or the language in action mode, this function is often elided (see Kim et al. 2005a: 406 and Lee I. and Chae W. 2013: 194–8 for details). Function Marking can be divided into three types: Experiential Function Marking (or EFM), which we introduced briefly in Chapter 1, Interpersonal Function Marking (or IFM) and Textual Function Marking (or TFM). Function Marking is realised by post-positional clitics[16] that help distinguish the role the nominal group plays at clause rank.

The EFM function plays a role in determining how the element it culminates functions in a clause in terms of who does what to whom, and how. These function-marking clitics include 이/가 *i/ga* (for 'agentive' Participants), 을/를 *eul/reul* (for 'affected' Participants), 에게 *ege* (for 'benefactive' Participants) and 에 *e*, 에서 *eseo*, 으로 *euro* etc. (for Circumstances).

The EFM of 'agentive' and 'affected' Participants may be replaced by Interpersonal Function Marking (IFM) to signal aspects of a speaker's stance toward the entity expressed in the nominal group (e.g., modal assessments such as 도 *do* 'also', 'even', 만 *man* 'only' and deference marking). For 'benefactive' Participants the IFM is added after the EFM function.

In addition, the EFM of 'agentive' and 'affected' Participants may be replaced by Textual Function Marking (TFM), realised as 은/는 *eun/neun*. For 'benefactive' Participants the TFM is added after the EFM function. This clitic has been described in a number of existing Korean grammar books as a clitic that has two primary functions – (i) as a topic marker often glossed as 'as for' and (ii) as a contrast marker. These descriptions are compatible with an SFL perspective in that the primary function of this clitic is textual. The TFM is used when a specific element is foregrounded as a Theme. For instance, the EFM, 이 *i* occurring after 선녀 셋 *seonnyeo set* 'three nymphs' in (45) tells us who descended; the TFM, 은 *eun* in (46) flags the orientation to the field by thematising three nymphs (see Chapter 5 for a more detailed discussion); and the IFM, 만 *man* in (47), indicates the speaker's unsatisfied expectation about the number of nymphs descending (cf. Chapter 3, Section 3.6.1, note 21).

---

[16] In Korean school grammars, what we call clitics belong to a class labelled as 조사 *josa*, which literally means 'assisting part of speech'; this term is commonly translated into English as 'particle', 'postposition', and so on. In this study, most of these 'josa' are called clitics because they are operating at group rank and realising Function Marking or Linking functions. We reserve the term 'particle' for those *josa* operating at clause rank, of which the common examples are 요 *yo*, 그려 *geuryeo* and 마는 *maneun*. They all occur clause-finally (except for 요 *yo*, which can occur group/phrase-finally). Note that (i) 요 *yo* is the particle realising the Politeness Marker function in an informal clause (see Chapter 3); (ii) 그려 *geuryeo* is a dialectal, archaic expression employed by aged males to convey their 'certainty' over the proposition realised by the clause; (iii) 마는 *maneun* conveys the sense of 'contrariness', and there is controversy over its grammatical class – i.e., whether it belongs to *josa* or verbal suffix. For more details, see Yu et al. (2018: 312). In this book, we only consider 요 *yo* a particle.

2.3 Nominal Group

(45)

선녀 셋이 내려왔다.			
seonnyeo	*ses*	=*i*	*naeryeow-at-da*
nymph	three		descended
P1			Process
nominal group			verbal group
Thing	Quantity	EFM	Event
noun	numeral	clitic	verb
'Three nymphs descended'			

(46)

선녀 셋은 내려왔다.			
seonnyeo	*ses*	=*eun*	*naeryeow-at-da*
nymph	three		descended
P1			Process
nominal group			verbal group
Thing	Quantity	TFM	Event
noun	numeral	clitic	verb
'Three nymphs descended'			

(47)

선녀 셋만 내려왔다.			
seonnyeo	*sen*	=*man*	*naeryeow-at-da*
nymph	three	only	descended
P1			Process
nominal group			verbal group
Thing	Quantity	IFM	Event
noun	numeral	clitic	verb
'Only three nymphs descended'			

A basic list of clitics that indicate a nominal group's clause rank function is presented in Table 2.14 (cf. Lee H. and Lee J. 2010, who consider over a hundred realisations of our EFM, TFM and IFM functions). The clitics that most 'commonly' indicate a nominal group's clause rank function are presented in Table 2.14. As the number of clitics in Korean is nearly 480 (*Encyclopedia of Korean Culture*, Academy of Korean Studies, 2nd ed., 2017), the list in Table 2.14 cannot be treated as exhaustive.

Table 2.14 *The system of* FUNCTION MARKING

FUNCTION MARKING		Examples
experiential	Participant 1	이/가 =*i*/=*ga* 에서 =*eseo*
	Participant 2	을/를/ㄹ =*eul*/=*reul*/=*l*
	Participant 3	에게 =*ege* 한테 =*hante*
	Circumstances	에 =*e* 'on, at, in, to' 더러 =*deoreo* 'to' 에서 =*eseo* 'in, at, on, from' 에게서 =*egeseo* 'from' 한테서 =*hanteseo* 'from' (으)로 =*(eu)ro* 'with' 에로 =*ero* 'toward' 에게로 =*egero* 'toward' 한테로 =*hantero* 'toward' (으)로써 =*(eu)rosseo* 'with' (으)로서 =*(eu)roseo* 'as' 처럼 =*cheoreom* 'like'
interpersonal		도 =*do* 'also, even' 만 =*man* 'only' 조차 =*jocha* 'even, as well' 께서 =*kkeseo* (hon) 께 =*kke* (hon) 부터 =*buteo* 'from' 까지 =*kkaji* 'even, up to' 마저 =*majeo* 'even, so far as' (이)나마 =*(i)nama* 'in spite of' (이)나 =*(i)na* 'as many (much) as' (이)라도 =*(i)rado* 'even if' (이)야 =*(i)ya* 'surely'
textual		은/는 =*eun*/=*neun* 'as for' (이)란 =*(i)ran* 'speaking of'

General choices for FUNCTION MARKING are presented in Figure 2.11. The system is an optional one, since function-marking clitics are often omitted in casual Korean conversation. The choice of experiential and/or interpersonal and/or textual FUNCTION MARKING is determined, as noted above, by the role played by a nominal group in clause structure and has not been formalised in this network.

2.3 Nominal Group

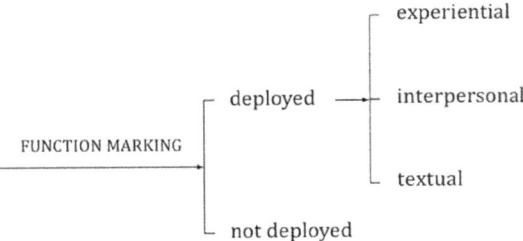

Figure 2.11 The system of FUNCTION MARKING

In this section, we have introduced a number of nominal group functions and included system networks for several systems where more delicate choices affect nominal group structure. A synoptic overview of the nominal group systems discussed above is presented in Figure 2.12.

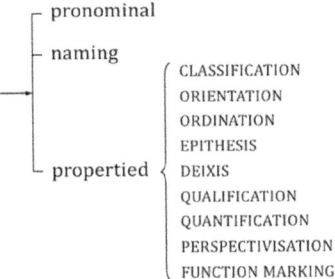

Figure 2.12 Nominal group systems

2.3.11 Nominal Group Structure

We have presented the nominal group systems in three groups: first, systems that are realised by a word or word complex before the Thing (i.e., DEIXIS, EPITHESIS, ORDINATION and CLASSIFICATION); second, systems that are realised by an embedded group, phrase or clause before the Thing (i.e., QUALIFICATION and ORIENTATION); and third, systems that are realised after the Thing (i.e., QUANTIFICATION, PERSPECTIVISATION and FUNCTION MARKING).

Although it is not natural for a Thing to be modified by all the possible functions, browsing Internet examples confirms that it is not uncommon for a Thing to be modified by three to four modifiers. Some examples of these longer nominal groups are presented in (48)–(50).

(48)   Qualifying ^ Epithet ^ Classifying ^ Thing

아이들이 좋아하는 간단한 간식 레시피							
ai-deur	*=i*	*joaha-neun*		*gandanha-n*	*gansik*		*resipi*
children		like		simple	snack		recipe
nominal group							
Qualifying				Epithet	Classifying		Thing
[[clause]]				adjective	noun		noun
P1		Process		Head	Link		
ng		vg		stem	sfx		
Thing	EFM	Event					
noun	clitic	verb					
		Head	Link				
		stem	sfx				
'a recipe for a simple snack which children like'							

(49)   Deictic ^ Epithet ^ Thing ^ Experiential Function Marking

저 붉은 태양처럼				
jeo	*bulg-eun*		*taeyang*	*=cheoreom*
that	red		sun	like
nominal group				
Deictic	Epithet		Thing	EFM
demonstrative	adjective		noun	clitic
	Head	Link		
	stem	sfx		
'like that red sun'				

2.3 Nominal Group

(50)   Epithet ^ Thing ^ Quantity ^ Experiential Function Marking

귀여운 강아지 두 마리를					
gwiyeou-n	gangaji	du		mari	=reul
cute	puppy	two			
nominal group					
Epithet	Thing	Quantity			EFM
adjective	noun	word complex			clitic
		α		β	
		cardinal numeral		bound noun	
'two cute puppies'					

When a nominal group has multiple modifiers, the systems that belong to the second group (QUALIFICATION and ORIENTATION) are realised first, followed by the first group systems (DEIXIS, EPITHESIS, ORDINATION and CLASSIFICATION) – both before the Thing; and the Thing is followed by the third group systems (QUANTIFICATION, PERSPECTIVISATION and FUNCTION MARKING). These sequences are exemplified in (48), (49) and (50).

The ordering among the systems realised in each of the three groups is fixed. In the second group, if both are realised, QUALIFICATION precedes ORIENTATION as in (51). The sequence in the first group is generally DEIXIS, EPITHESIS, ORDINATION and CLASSIFICATION if they all appear– as illustrated in (52), an example slightly modified from (29). The systems in the third group, if they are all realised, follow the order of QUANTIFICATION, PERSPECTIVISATION and FUNCTION MARKING as shown in (53) – this example appeared as (44).

(51)   Qualifying ^ Orient ^ Classifying

내가 좋아하는 할머니의 김치 만두						
nae	=ga	joaha-neun	halmeoni	=ui	gimchi	mandu
I		like	grandma		kimchi	dumpling
nominal group						
Qualifying			Orient		Classifying	Thing
[[clause]]			[ng]		noun	noun
P 1			Process			
ng			vg			
Thing			Thing	Linking		
noun			noun	clitic		
	EFM		Event			
	clitic		verb			
			Head	Link		
			stem	sfx		
'grandma's kimchi dumpling that I like'						

(52)   Deictic ^ Epithet ^ Order ^ Classifying

저 아름다운 세 번째 종소리				
jeo	*areumdau-n*	*sebeonjjae*	*jong*	*sori*
that	beautiful	third	bell	sound
nominal group				
Deictic	Epithet	Ordering	Classifying	Thing
determiner	adjective	numeral	noun	noun
	Head	Link			
	stem	sfx			
'that beautiful third bell-sound'				

(53)   Quantity ^ Perspective ^ Experiential Function Marking

책 한 권 위에				
chaek	*han*	*gwon*	*wi*	*=e*
book	one	unit	above	at
nominal group				
Thing	Quantity		Perspective	EFM
noun	word complex		noun	clitic
	α	β		
	cardinal numeral	bound noun		
'on the top of a book'				

Note that one system, ORIENTATION, has more flexibility. The Orient function is realised before first group systems, such as the DEIXIS and EPITHESIS systems – as in (54).

(54)   Orient before Epithet

할머니의 이 맛있는 김치 만두					
halmeoni	*=ui*	*i*	*massin-neun*	*gimchi*	*mandu*
grandma		this	tasty	kimchi	dumpling
nominal group					
Orient		Deictic	Epithet	Classifying	Thing
[ng]		determiner	adjective	noun	noun
Thing	Linking		Head	Link		
noun	clitic		stem	sfx		
'grandma's this tasty kimchi dumpling'					

2.4 Verbal Group

However, as illustrated in (55), the system of ORIENTATION can be realised after first group systems. This happens particularly when the Orient function includes a short embedded nominal group specifying the Thing through a circumstantial meaning or an explanation of its function.

(55)　Orient after Epithet

저	아름다운	평화의		종소리	
jeo	areumdau-n	pyeonghwa	=ui	jong	sori
that	beautiful	peace		bell	sound
Deictic	Epithet	Orient		Classifying	Thing
determiner	adjective	[nominal group]		noun	noun
		Thing	Linking		
		noun	clitic		
'that beautiful bell-sound for peace'					

The structure of a Korean nominal group with multiple functions would typically unfold as indicated in Table 2.15 (for further consideration, see Martin and Shin 2021).

Table 2.15 *Nominal group functions*

Qualifying ^ Orient ^ Deictic ^ Epithet ^ Ordering ^ Orient ^ Classifying ^ **Thing** ^ Quantity ^ Perspective ^ Function Marking

2.4   Verbal Group

We turn now to the consideration of system and structure in Korean verbal groups. The verbal group in Korean is a group of elements featuring verbs, but also including nouns, adjectives, auxiliary verbs, adverbs and bound nouns; it is positioned as the final experiential element of structure in a Korean clause. It involves a number of ideational and interpersonal systems. Some of them are realised at group rank and some at word rank (and some at both ranks). In this section, we will concentrate on the systems realised at group rank through verbal group structure: DEGREE, EVENT TYPE, VALENCY, DIMENSION TYPE, POLARITY, VERBAL GROUP MODALITY and HIGHLIGHT. Systems realised at word rank will be briefly introduced (and elaborated as needed in later chapters).

We begin our discussion with the Event function, which is the nucleus of the verbal group (comparable to the Thing in the nominal group) and is always present. We then introduce the functions that follow the Event (i.e., Valence, Dimension, Negating, Modal and Highlight). We continue with Negate and Degree, which are realised before the Event. We complete this section by introducing three relevant word rank functions: Participant Deferent Mark (PDM), Tense Mark (TM) and Relative Tense Mark (RTM).

2.4.1 The System of EVENT TYPE

In Korean the verbal group begins with a lexical verb or adjective that realises the obligatory function of **Event**. An action-type Event is realised by a lexical verb (e.g., 가르치다 *gareuchi-da* 'teach', 보다 *bo-da* 'see' and 말하다 *malha-da* 'say') and a state-type Event is realised by a verbalised adjective (e.g., 예쁘다 *yeppeu-da* '(be) pretty', 시끄럽다 *sikkeureop-da* '(be) noisy') or copula (i.e., 이다 *i-da* 'be' and 아니다 *a-ni-da* 'not be').

Example (56) illustrates a verbal Event, while (57) illustrates an adjectival Event. In (56) the Event is realised by the verb 가르치니 *gareuchi-ni*, which consists of a stem, *gareuchi*, and a suffix *-ni*. As touched on briefly in Chapter 1, Korean verbs always include a stem that functions as the head of the group (where it helps signal the process type of a clause) and a suffix that indicates whether or not a clause is the last clause in a clause complex or is followed by another clause. If the clause is the last one in a clause complex, the suffix realises the function Exchange Mark or Stance Mark – which realises the system of MOOD (in case of Exchange Mark) or the system of INFORMAL MOOD (in case of Stance Mark) interacting with the systems of VALENCY, ABSOLUTE TENSE, RELATIVE TENSE, FORMALITY and ADDRESSEE DEFERENCE (see Chapter 3 for details). The suffix 니 *-ni* in (56), for instance, marks dominant (i.e., non-deferential), formal, interrogative mood. In this example the tense is present, since there is no suffix marking it as past; and the valency is neutral (i.e., 'active'), since there is no suffix marking it as shifted (i.e., neither 'passive' nor 'causative').

(56)

가르치니?	
gareuchi-ni	
teach	
Process	
verbal group	
Event (action-type)	
lexical verb	
Head	Exchange Mark
stem	suffix (non-deferential interrogative)
'Are (you) teaching?'	

2.4 Verbal Group

In (57) the Event is realised by the verbalised adjective 예쁘다 *yeppeu-* 'be pretty' and 다 *-da* ('non-deferential, formal, declarative' suffix). The tense is present, since there is no suffix marking it as past.

(57)

예쁘다.	
yeppeu-da	
pretty	
Process	
verbal group	
Event (state-type)	
verbalised adjective	
Head	Exchange Mark
stem	suffix (non-deferential declarative)
'(She) is pretty.'	

The system of EVENT TYPE is presented in Figure 2.13.

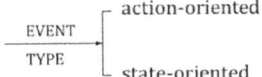

Figure 2.13 The system of EVENT TYPE

The realisation statements in Table 2.16 specify that the Event is realised first in a verbal group (unless it is preceded by a Degree or Negate function; see Sections 2.4.7 and 2.4.4 respectively). For [action-oriented] verbal groups the Event is realised by a verb, and for [state-oriented] ones by a verbalised adjective or copula.

Table 2.16 *The system of* EVENT TYPE: *realisation statements*

verbal group	+Event; # (Degree) (Negate) ⌐ Event
action-oriented	Event:verb
state-oriented	Event:verbalised adjective or copula

2.4.2 The System of VALENCY

The system realised after EVENT TYPE in Korean verbal group structure is the system of VALENCY. It covers what is traditionally termed 'passivisation' and 'causativisation' in other linguistic traditions. This system specifies the verbal group realisations of the system of DIATHESIS at clause rank (discussed in Chapter 4, Section 4.3). Accordingly it is involved in increasing or decreasing the number of Participants in a clause ([augment] vs [diminish] respectively). Increasing the number of Participants involves selecting what is traditionally referred to as 'causative', while decreasing the number of Participants involves selecting what is traditionally referred to as 'passive voice'. Both the augment and diminish options are realised at either group rank (through an auxiliary verb) or word rank (by a suffix).

Group rank augmentation involves the auxiliary verb 하다 *ha-da* preceded by the connecting suffix 게 *-ge*. We refer to the function realised by this augmenting auxiliary as **Valence**. In examples (58) and (59), [neutral] and [augment] options are illustrated: [neutral] (먹다 *meok-da* 'eat') and [augment] (먹게 하다 *meok-ge ha-da* 'make (someone) eat'). Note that in (59) we use abbreviations TM and EM for the Tense Mark and Exchange Mark functions, respectively.

(58)

아이가 빵을 먹었다.						
ai	*=ga*	*ppang*	*=eul*	*meog-eot-da*		
child		bread		ate		
P1		P2		Process		
nominal group		nominal group		verbal group		
Thing	EFM	Thing	EFM	Event		
noun	clitic	noun	clitic	verb		
				Head	Tense Mark	Exchange Mark
				stem	suffix	suffix
'The child ate the bread.'						

(59)

엄마가 아이한테 빵을 먹게 했다.									
eomma	*=ga*	*ai*	*=hante*	*ppang*	*=eul*	*meok-ge*	*ha-et-da*		
mum		child	to	bread		made eat			
P1		P3		P2		Process			
ng		ng		ng		vg			
Thing	EFM	Thing	EFM	Thing	EFM	Event	Valence:augment		
noun	clitic	noun	clitic	noun	clitic	verb	auxiliary verb		
						Head	Link	Head	TM	EM
						stem	sfx	stem	sfx	sfx
'Mum made the child eat the bread.'									

2.4 Verbal Group

The augmenting verbal group realised through the auxiliary verb 하다 *ha-da* used in a clause such as (59) indicates that Participant 1, who made Participant 3 'eat', is an instigator of the process; s/he does not take part directly in the Event 'eating'. This is a much-discussed phenomenon among Korean grammarians (see Yu et al. 2018: 558 and references cited there).

By contrast, word rank augmentation is realised through a suffix 이 *-i* as in (60); the suffix indicates that the Participant 1 is directly involved in the Event 'eating'. We refer to the function of this suffix in verb structure as Voice Mark (abbreviated as VM).

(60)

엄마가 아이한테 빵을 먹였다.									
eomma	*=ga*	*ai*	*=hante*	*ppang*	*=eul*	*meog-i-eot-da*			
mum		child	to	bread		fed (made eat)			
P1		P3		P2		Process			
ng		ng		ng		vg			
Thing	EFM	Thing	EFM	Thing	EFM	Event			
noun	clitic	noun	clitic	noun	clitic	verb			
						Head	VM:augment	TM	EM
						stem	sfx	sfx	sfx
'Mum fed the bread to the child.'									

This [augment] option is realised by the suffixes 이 *-i*, 히 *-hi*, 리 *-ri*, 기 *-gi*, 우 *-u*, 구 *-gu*, 추 *-chu* and 애 *-ae* – attached not just to verbs as in (60), but also to a limited number of verbalised adjectives (as illustrated in (62)). Compare (61), with [neutral] valency, to (62), which realises the feature [augment] (although the instigating participant is left implicit in this imperative clause).

(61)

온도가 낮다.			
ondo	*=ga*	*nat-da*	
temperature		is low	
P1		Process	
nominal group		verbal group	
Thing	EFM	Event	
noun	clitic	verbalised adjective	
		Head	Exchange Mark
		stem	suffix
'The temperature is low.'			

(62)

온도를 낮추어라.			
ondo	=*reul*	*nat-chu-eora*	
temperature		lower	
P2		Process	
nominal group		verbal group	
Thing	EFM	Event	
noun	clitic	verb	
		Head	VM:augment	Exchange Mark
		stem	suffix	suffix
'Lower the temperature!'			

Group rank diminishment involves the auxiliary verb 지다 *ji-da* preceded by the connecting suffix 아 -*a* or 어 -*eo*. In examples (63) and (64), [diminish] and [neutral] options are exemplified – [neutral] (만들다 *mandeul-da* 'make') and [diminish] (만들어지다 *mandeur-eo ji-da* 'be made'). We refer to this option as [diminish] because in (63), for instance, we only have a P1 (다리가 *dari ga* 'bridge'), while in (64), its related clause with the neutral valency, there is both a P1 (군인들이 *gunin-deur i*, 'soldiers') and a P2 (다리를 *dari reul*, 'bridge').

(63)

다리가 만들어졌다.						
dari	=*ga*	*mandeur-eo*	*ji-eot-da*			
bridge		was made				
P1		Process				
nominal group		verbal group				
Thing	EFM	Event		Valence:diminish		
noun	clitic	verb		auxiliary verb		
		Head	Link	Head	TM	EM
		stem	suffix	stem	suffix	suffix
'The bridge was made (built).'						

2.4 Verbal Group

(64)

군인들이 다리를 만들었다.				
gunin-deur	=*i*	*dari*	=*reul*	*mandeur-eot-da*
soldiers		bridge		made
P1		P2		Process
nominal group		nominal group		verbal group
Thing	EFM	Thing	EFM	Event
noun	ptcl	noun	ptcl	verb
				Head / TM / EM
				stem / suffix / suffix
'The soldiers made the bridge.'				

At word rank, the [diminish] option is realised by the suffixes 이 -*i*, 히 -*hi*, 리 -*ri* and 기 -*gi*, as in (65) – attached to verbs or verbalised adjectives realising Events. Note the system of VALENCY is not available for a handful of verbs, including 이다 *i-da* 'be', 있다 *it-da* 'there-be', 하다 *ha-da* 'do' and 주다 *ju-da* 'give' in Korean.

(65)

도둑이 잡혔다.		
dodug	=*i*	*jap-hi-eot-da*
burglar		was caught
P1		Process
nominal group		verbal group
Thing	EFM	Event
noun	clitic	verb
		Head / VM:diminish / TM / EM
		stem / suffix / suffix / suffix
'The burglar was caught.'		

In clauses with the feature [diminish], which realise 'passive' figures, the demoted Actor functions as P3. There are two ways of realising P3 (i.e., the demoted P1) in Korean. One is through a nominal group with the EFM 에게 *ege*; the other is through a co-verbal phrase (see Section 2.6) 에 의해 *e uiha-e* 'by'. The demoted P1 (i.e., P3) in diminished clauses with a Voice Mark can be realised either by a nominal group with the EFM 에게 *ege* or by a co-verbal phrase 에 의해 *e uiha-e* as in (65') and (65"). P3 in diminished clauses with a Valence function is realised only by a co-verbal phrase, as in (64').

(65′)

도둑이 경찰에게 잡혔다.

dodug	=i	gyeongchar	=ege	jap-hi-eot-da			
burglar		police		was caught			
P1		P3		Process			
ng		ng		vg			
Thing	EFM	Thing	EFM	Event			
noun	clitic	noun	clitic	verb			
				Head	VM:diminish	TM	EM
				stem	suffix	suffix	suffix

'The burglar was caught by the police.'

(65″)

도둑이 경찰에 의해 잡혔다.

dodug	=i	gyeongchar	=e	uiha-e		jap-hi-eot-da				
burglar		police		by		was caught				
P1		P3				Process				
ng		co-verbal phrase				vg				
Thing	EFM	Incumbent		Role		Event				
noun	clitic	[ng]		b verb		verb				
		Thing	EFM	Head	Link	Head	VM:diminish		TM	EM
		noun	clitic	stem	sfx	stem	sfx		sfx	sfx

'The burglar was caught by the police.'

(64′)

다리가 군인들에 의해 만들어졌다.

dari	=ga	gunin-deur	=e	uiha-e		mandeur-eo		ji-eot-da			
bridge		soldiers		by		was made					
P1		P3				Process					
ng		co-verbal phrase				vg					
Thing	EFM	Incumbent		Role		Event		Valence:diminish			
noun	clitic	[ng]		b verb		verb		aux verb			
		Thing	EFM	Head	Link	Head	Link	Head	TM	EM	
		noun	clitic	stem	sfx	stem	sfx	stem	sfx	sfx	

'The bridge was made by the soldiers.'

The system of VALENCY is presented in Figure 2.14. Both [augment] and [diminish] are realised by an auxiliary or suffix (Table 2.17).

2.4 Verbal Group

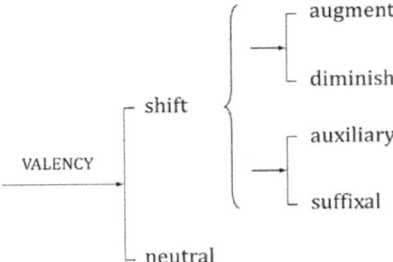

Figure 2.14 The system of VALENCY

Table 2.17 *The system of* VALENCY: *realisation statements*

auxiliary	+Valence; Event ^ Valence
suffixal	(at word rank) +Voice Mark; Head ^ VM
augment	Valence:aux verb (게 하- *-ge ha-*); VM:suffix (이 *-i*, 히 *-hi*, 리 *-ri*, 기 *-gi*, 우 *-u*, 구 *-gu*, 추 *-chu*, 애 *-ae*)
diminish	Valence:aux verb (아/어 지- *-a/eo ji-*); VM:suffix (이 *-i*, 히 *-hi*, 리 *-ri*, 기 *-gi*)

2.4.3 The System of DIMENSION TYPE

The verbal group can also be expanded to include what we are calling a **Dimension** function.

The Dimension function realises a wide range of ideational meanings (e.g., 'aspectual', 'phasing' and 'projective') and is typically realised by an auxiliary verb or auxiliary verbalised adjective, and, less commonly, by a word complex involving a bound noun.

In (66) the Dimension is realised by the auxiliary verb 있다 *it-da*, which signals that the Event is in progress. In this kind of example, a connecting suffix such as 고 *-go* links the Event to the Dimension.

(66)

가르치고 있다.			
gareuchi-go	*it-da*		
teach	is ...ing		
verbal group			
Event		Dimension	
lexical verb		auxiliary verb	
Head	Link	Head	Exchange Mark
Stem	suffix	stem	suffix
'(He) is teaching.'			

Example (67) is an imperative clause and includes a Dimension function that indicates that the service or action demanded by the clause is for the benefit of a third party who may be realised in the clause as P3. The Dimension function is realised by the auxiliary verb 주다 *ju-da*, and and the connecting suffix that connects the Event to the Dimension in this case is 아 *-a* or 어 *-eo*.

(67)

동생한테 읽어 줘라.			
dongsaeng	*=hante*	*ilg-eo*	*ju-eora*
younger sibling	to	read	for
P3		Process	
nominal group		verbal group	
Thing	EFM	Event	Dimension
noun	clitic	lexical verb	auxiliary verb
		Head	Link	Head	Exchange Mark
		stem	suffix	stem	suffix
'Read it to your younger sibling (for their benefit)'			

Most auxiliary verbs functioning as Dimension in structures of this kind have the potential to realise an Event (action or state) in a different grammatical context. For example, 주다 *ju-da* 'give' in (68) realises the Event in a verbal group realising the Process in a material clause.

(68)

동생한테 책을 주었다.				
dongsaeng	*=hante*	*chaeg*	*=eul*	*ju-eot-da*
younger sibling	to	book		gave
P3		P2		Process
nominal group		nominal group		verbal group
Thing	EFM	Thing	EFM	Event
Noun	clitic	noun	clitic	verb
				Head	TM	EM
				stem	suffix	suffix
'(I) gave the book to my younger sibling.'				

Likewise, 있다 *it-da* 'there is or are' in (69) realises the Event in a verbal group realising the Process in a relational clause.

2.4 Verbal Group

(69)

꽃병이 선반 위에 있다.							
kkotbyeong	=i	seonban	wi	=e	it-da		
vase		shelf	top	on	there is		
P1		Circumstance			Process		
nominal group		nominal group			verbal group		
Thing	EFM	Thing	Perspective	EFM	Event		
noun	clitic	noun	bound noun	clitic	verb		
					Head		Exchange Mark
					stem		suffix
'There's a vase on the shelf.'							

But verbs such as 있다 *it-da* 'there is or are' and 주다 *ju-da* 'give' can also be used as an auxiliary verb realising Dimension, as illustrated in (66) and (67). In such cases, the verbs have been 'grammaticalised' to construe the continuity of the Event (66) and to render the benefactor of the Event (67).

In (70) the Dimension is realised by an auxiliary verbalised adjective 싶다 *sip-da* 'want'.[17]

(70)

추천하고 싶다.			
chucheonha-go		sip-da	
recommend		want	
verbal group			
Event		Dimension	
lexical verb		auxiliary adjective	
Head	Link	Head	Exchange Mark
stem	suffix	stem	suffix
'(I) want to recommend (him/it)'			

In (71) the word complex 척하다 *cheok ha-da* realises pretence. The Dimension is realised through a word complex and the connecting suffix is (으)ㄴ *-(eu)n*.

---

[17] The auxiliary verbalised adjective is conjugated like a verbalised adjective. As we shall see in Chapter 3, like other verbalised adjectives, 싶다 *sip-da* 'want' cannot occur with (으)ㄴ *–(eu)n* 'the tense mark in declarative/formal:dominant clause'.

(71)

<table>
<tr><td colspan="5">모른 척 하자.</td></tr>
<tr><td colspan="2">moreu-n</td><td>cheok</td><td colspan="2">ha-ja</td></tr>
<tr><td colspan="2">not know</td><td>pretend</td><td colspan="2">let's</td></tr>
<tr><td colspan="5">verbal group</td></tr>
<tr><td colspan="2">Event</td><td colspan="3">Dimension</td></tr>
<tr><td colspan="2">verb</td><td colspan="3">word complex</td></tr>
<tr><td>Head</td><td>Link</td><td>β</td><td colspan="2">α</td></tr>
<tr><td rowspan="3">stem</td><td rowspan="3">suffix</td><td rowspan="3">bound noun</td><td colspan="2">auxiliary verb</td></tr>
<tr><td>Head</td><td>Exchange Mark</td></tr>
<tr><td>stem</td><td>suffix</td></tr>
<tr><td colspan="5">'Let's pretend not to know (about it).'</td></tr>
</table>

Table 2.18 outlines the range of meanings realised as Dimension.[18]

Table 2.18 *Types of Dimension*

Types	Realisations	Examples
aspectual	고 있다 *-go it-da* 'is doing . . .'	먹고 있었다. *meog-go it-eot-da* '(He) was eating.'
	아/어 있다 *-a/eo it-da* 'has been in the state of . . .'	죽어 있었다. *jug-eo it-eot-da* '(He) was dead (already, when we arrived).'
	아/어 오다 *-a/eo o-da* 'has been the case'	전해 온다. *jeonha-e o-n-da* '(the story) has been passed down (from a long time ago).'
	아/어 가다 *-a/eo ga-da* 'continues to be the case'	이어 간다. *i-eo ga-n-da* '(the tradition) continues'
	기 시작하다 *-gi sijaka-da* 'start to do'	검토하기 시작했다. *geomtoha-gi sijaka-et-da* '(They) started to review.'
	다가 말다 *-da(ga) mal-da* 'stop doing . . .'	설득하다 말았다. *seoldeuka-da mar-at-da* '(They) persuaded (him) but then stopped.'
	곤하다 *-gon ha-da*, 'used to . . .'	말하곤 했다. *malha-gon ha-et-da* '(They) used to say . . .'
	아/어 대다/쌓다 *-a/eo dae-da/ssa-ta* 'do . . . vigorously'	먹어 댔다. *meog-eo dae-t-da* '(They) were gobbling (must be very hungry!)'
	(으)ㄴ 적 있다/없다 *-(eu)n jeog it-da* 'have done . . .'	가본 적이 있다. *gabo-n jeog i it-da* '(I) have been there.'

[18] Here we are drawing on Halliday and Matthiessen (2014: 517–18) and Sohn (1999: 381–8); we regard this outline of Dimension resources as a first step, which needs to be followed up in future research.

2.4 Verbal Group

Table 2.18 *(cont.)*

Types	Realisations	Examples
phasal	아/어 내다 *-a/eo nae-da* 'succeed in; do all the way; to the very end'	해 냈다. *ha-e nae-t-da* '(I)'ve finally done it!'
	아/어 버리다/치우다 *-a/eo beori-da/chiu-da* 'finish (it) off'	먹어 버렸다. *meog-eo beori-eot-da* '(I) ate it up.'
	고 말다 *-go mal-da* 'have done it regrettably'	먹고 말았다. *meog-go mar-at-da* '(I) ate it (regrettably).'
	아/어 놓다/두다 *-a/eo no-ta/du-da* 'did something and put aside (for future use)'	심어 놓았다. *sim-eo no-at-ta* '(I) planted it (for future use).'
	게 되다 *-ge doe-da* 'come to do (it)'	가게 되었다. *ga-ge doe-eot-da* '(I) came to go.'
projective	고 싶다/싶어하다 *-go sip-da/sipeoha-da* 'want to do . . .'	먹고 싶었다. *meog-go sip-eot-da* '(I) want to eat.'
	기로 하다 *-giro ha-da* 'decided to do . . .'	가기로 했다. *ga-giro ha-et-da* '(I)'ve decided to go.'
	고 하다 *-go ha-da* '(it) is said . . .'	어렵다고 한다. *eoryeopda-go ha-n-da* 'It is said that (the task) is difficult.'
others	아/어 주다 *-a/eo ju-da* 'do . . . for the benefit of someone'	읽어 주었다. *ilg-eo ju-eot-da* '(I) read it for the benefit of (them).'
	아/어 드리다 *-a/eo deuri-da* 'do . . . for the benefit of someone respected'	만들어 드렸다. *mandeur-eo deuri-eot-da* '(I) made it for (them, respected).'
	아/어 보다 *-a/eo bo-da* 'try to do, have a go'	입어 보았다. *ip-eo bo-at-da* '(I) tried (it) on (to see if it fits).'
	은/ㄴ/는 척/체/양 하다 *-(eu)n/neun cheok/che/yang ha-da* 'pretend to do'	아픈 척 했다. *apeu-n cheok ha-et-da* '(They) pretended to be sick.'

The system of DIMENSION TYPE is presented in Figure 2.15 and Table 2.19. Note that from this point we will not state the entry condition for systems, which is 'verbal group' for all verbal group systems.

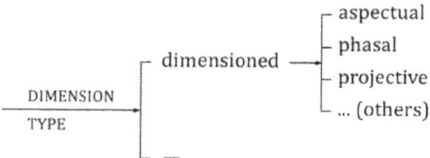

Figure 2.15 The system of DIMENSION TYPE

Table 2.19 *The system of DIMENSION TYPE: selected realisation statements*

dimensioned	+Dimension; Event (Valence) ← Dimension
aspectual	Dimension:aux verb, aux verbalised adjective or word complex (see Table 2.18)
phasal	Dimension:aux verb, aux verbalised adjective or word complex (see Table 2.18)
projective	Dimension:aux verb, aux verbalised adjective or word complex (see Table 2.18)
others	Dimension:aux verb, aux verbalised adjective or word complex (see Table 2.18)

2.4.4 The System of POLARITY

The system of POLARITY in Korean is realised through verbal group structure but in two different ways. In one, the choice of negative polarity involves a **Negate** function, positioned immediately before the Event and realised by a negative adverb 안 *an* 'not'. In the other, it involves a **Negating** function, positioned after Event and realised through an auxiliary verb, 않다 *an-ta* 'not'; in this case the main verb culminates with the connecting suffix 지 *-ji*. Examples (72) and (73) illustrate the alternative realisations of negative polarity.

2.4 Verbal Group

(72)

안 간다.	
an	*ga-n-da*
not	go
Process	
verbal group	
Negate	Event
adverb	verb
	Head	Exchange Mark
	stem	suffix
'(I)'m not going.'	

(73)

가지 않는다.			
ga-ji		*an-neun-da*	
go		don't	
Process			
verbal group			
Event		Negating	
verb		auxiliary verb	
Head	Link	Head	Exchange Mark
stem	suffix	stem	suffix
'(I)'m not going.'			

In (72) an indicative clause involving the proposition '(I)'m going' is negated through an adverb 안 *an* 'not'. By contrast, in (73) the clause is negated by adding an auxiliary verb 않 *an-* 'do not';[19] in this case the main verb culminates with the connecting suffix 지 *-ji*.

Imperative clauses can only be negated by adding the auxiliary verb 말 *mal-*[20] 'don't do ...' after the main verb; the main verb culminates with the

---

[19] The difference between the negative adverb 안 *an* 'not' and the negative auxiliary verb 않 *an-* 'do not' is not immediately clear because of the Romanisation system we use; but the difference is clear in Hangeul. Unlike the adverb, the auxiliary verb ends in ㅎ /h/, which is silent in syllable-final position. Also, unlike the negative adverb 안 *an* 'not', the Romanisation of the negative auxiliary verb 않 *an-* 'do not' has a dash, '-', which indicates that it is a conjugatable category.

[20] Note that the auxiliary verb 말 *mal-* is irregular in the sense that the stem final consonant 'l' frequently drops when suffixed.

72 The Grammar of Groups and Phrases in Korean

connecting suffix 지 *-ji*, as with other negative auxiliary verbs. Thus, while employing an adverb and attaching an auxiliary verb are both possibilities for indicative clauses (declaratives and interrogatives), using a negative adverb is not available as an option for imperatives. Example (74) illustrates a negative imperative clause and Figure 2.16 summarises the system of POLARITY.

(74)

가지 마라.			
ga-ji	*ma-ra*[21]		
go	don't		
Process			
verbal group			
Event	Negating		
verb	auxiliary verb		
Head	Link	Head	Exchange Mark
stem	suffix	stem	suffix
'Don't go.'			

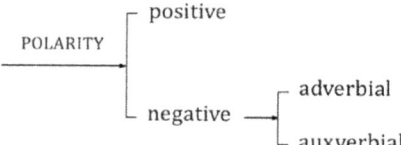

Figure 2.16 The system of POLARITY

The realisation statements in Table 2.20 clarify that the Negate function comes before the Event (preceded by a Degree function if present; see Section 2.4.7). In contrast, the Negating function follows the Event (and a Valence or Dimension function if present).[22]

---

[21] 마라 *ma-ra* has an accepted variant: 말아라 *mar-ara*.
[22] Note that this sequencing is a general tendency, not a strict rule. Some realisations of the Dimension do allow the Negating function to precede or to follow. Realisations of the projective-type Dimension all allow Negating to precede or follow, but those of the other types do so only in limited cases. For instance, for the aspectual type, 고 있다 *-go it-da* 'is ...ing' allows Negating to precede or follow – 술을 마시고 있지 않다 *sur eul masi-go it-ji an-ta* **Dimension** ^ <u>Negating</u> '(They) are not drinking alcohol' vs 술을 마시지 않고 있다 *sur eul masi-ji an-ko it-da* <u>Negating</u> ^ **Dimension** '(They) are there not drinking alcohol'.

2.4 Verbal Group

Table 2.20 *The system of* POLARITY: *realisation statements*

positive	–
negative:adverbial	+Negate; # (Degree) ^ Negate ⁀ Event; only for [indicative]
negative:aux verbial	+Negating; Event (Valence) (Dimension) ⁀ Negating; Negating: aux verb 지 말- -*ji mal*-, if imperative; aux verb/verbalised adjective 지 않- -*ji an*-, if indicative

2.4.5 The System of VERBAL GROUP MODALITY

VERBAL GROUP MODALITY deals with degrees of uncertainty between the positive and negative poles of POLARITY in terms of probability and usuality or obligation and inclination. Systemic functional grammars (e.g., Halliday and Matthiessen (2014)) have grouped modalities of probability and usuality together as modalisation, and modalities of obligation and inclination together as modulation.

In Korean, both modalisation and modulation are realised at group rank, with the former generally involving word complexes and the latter auxiliary verbs and adjectives. Exceptions to this generalisation have to do with usage of the suffix 겠 -*get* 'will' and the word complex (으)ㄹ 거 -*(eu)lgeo*- 'will' or 'am/are/is going to' – each of which realises probability as well as inclination. These realisations will be further discussed in Chapter 3.

The probability **Modal** function is realised at group rank through word complexes such as 수 있다 *su it-da* 'could' or 수 없다 *su eop-da* 'couldn't'. Note that this pair of word complexes involve (i) the bound noun 수 *su* 'possibility' and (ii) the verbs 있다 *it-da* 'there is' or 없다 *eop-da* 'there is not', which both require the preceding verbal to culminate with (으)ㄹ -*(eu)l* (realising the Link function).[23] This Modal function is exemplified in (75).

(75)

죽을 수 있다.				
jug-eul		*su*	*it-da*	
die		could		
Event		Modal		
verb		word complex		
Head	Link	β	α	
stem	suffix	bound noun	auxiliary verb	
			Head	Exchange Mark
			stem	suffix
'(You) could die (e.g., if you do that).'				

---

[23] Note that 을 -*eul* is used after a consonant and ㄹ -*l* after a vowel.

The usuality Modal function is also realised at group rank, through various word complexes. In (76) the word complex involves a bound noun 때 *ttae* 'time', followed by the verb 있다 *it-da* 'there is or are'. As in (75) the Event in (76) culminates with the connecting suffix ㄹ *-l*.

(76)

마실 때 있다.				
masi-l		*ttae*	*it-da*	
drink		would (literally, there are times when ...)		
Event		Modal		
verb		word complex		
Head	Link	β	α	
stem	suffix	bound noun	auxiliary verb	
			Head	Exchange Mark
			stem	suffix
'(I) would drink (when I feel ...).'				

Turning to modulation, the obligation Modal function is realised by an auxiliary verb 하다 *ha-da* 'do' or 되다 *doe-da* 'be done' preceded by the connecting suffix (아 or 어)야 *-(a or eo)ya* (which culminates the Event), as exemplified in (77).

(77)

가야 된다.					
ga-ya		*doe-n-da*			
go		must			
Event		Modal			
verb		auxiliary verb			
Head	Link	Head	Tense Mark[24]	Exchange Mark	
stem	suffix	stem	suffix	Suffix	
'(You) must go.'					

The inclination Modal function is also realised by the auxiliary verb 하다 *ha-da* 'do' as in (78); but its connecting suffix is (으)려고 *-(eu)ryeogo*, not 야 *-ya*.

---

[24] See Section 2.4.9 Tense Systems.

2.4 Verbal Group

(78)

가려고 한다.				
ga-ryeogo		*ha-n-da*		
go		intend/be keen		
Event		Modal		
verb		auxiliary verb		
Head	Link	Head	Tense Mark	Exchange Mark
stem	suffix	stem	suffix	suffix
'(He) is keen to go.'				

As noted, modalisation is realised by a word complex, involving a bound noun (realising β) and the auxiliary verb 있다 *it-da* 'there is/are' (realising α). Negation of the word complex (realising modalisation) involves suppletion at word rank – that is, replacing 있다 *it-da* (realising α) with another auxiliary verb 없다 *eop-da* 'there is/are not' as illustrated in (79).

(79)

죽을 수 없다.			
jug-eul		*su*	*eop-da*
die		could not	
Event		Modal	
verb		word complex	
Head	Link	β	α
stem	suffix	bound noun	negative auxiliary verb
			Head	Exchange Mark
			stem	suffix
'(You) cannot die.'			

By contrast, modulation is realised by an auxiliary verb, negation of which is through the Negate or Negating function, as (80) and (81) show.

(80)

안 가려고 한다					
an	*ga-ryeogo*		*ha-n-da*		
not	go		intend/be keen		
Negate	Event		Modal		
adverb	verb		auxiliary verb		
	Head	Link	Head	Tense Mark	Exchange Mark
	stem	suffix	stem	suffix	suffix
'(He) is not keen to go.'					

(81)

가려고 하지 않는다		
ga-ryeogo	*ha-ji*	*an-neun-da*
go	intend/be keen	not
Event verb	Modal auxiliary verb	Negating auxiliary verb
Head	Link	Head	Link	Head	Tense Mark	Exchange Mark
stem	suffix	stem	suffix	stem	suffix	suffix
'(He) is not keen to go.'		

The system of VERBAL GROUP MODALITY is presented in Figure 2.17 and Table 2.21.

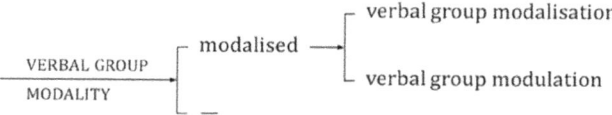

Figure 2.17 The system of VERBAL GROUP MODALITY

Table 2.21 *The system of* VERBAL GROUP MODALITY: *realisation statements*

modalised	+Modal; (Negate) ^ Event (Valence) (Dimension) ← Modal → (Negating); Negate and Negating are mutually exclusive
verbal group modalisation	Modal:word complex (+β:bound noun ^ α:있- *it-* or 없- *eop-*, etc.)
verbal group modulation	Modal:aux verb (아 or 어야 하- *-a* or *eoya ha-* or (으)려(고) 하- *-(eu)ryeo(go) ha-*, etc.)

In closing, we consider differences between the DIMENSION TYPE system and VERBAL GROUP MODALITY system. Although there are similarities (e.g., both are realised at group rank), there are a number of differences. First, if both are present, then a Dimension function is always realised before a Modal, as in (82) and (83). Changing the order of Modal and Dimension results in ungrammaticality.

2.4 Verbal Group

(82)   possibility Modal

가르치고 있을 수 있다						
gareuchi-go	*iss-eul*		*su*	*it-da*		
teach	continuity		could			
verbal group						
Event	Dimension		Modal			
verb	aux verb		word complex			
Head	Link	Head	Link	β	α	
stem	suffix	stem	suffix	bound noun	auxiliary verb	
					Head	Exchange Mark
					stem	suffix
'(He) could be teaching (now).'						

(83)   inclination Modal

읽어 주려고 한다						
ilg-eo		*ju-ryeogo*		*ha-n-da*		
read		for		intend/be keen		
verbal group						
Event		Dimension		Modal		
verb		aux verb		aux verb		
Head	Link	Head	Link	Head	Tense Mark	Exchange Mark
stem	suffix	stem	suffix	stem	suffix	suffix
'(I) am keen to read (it) to (them for their benefit).'						

Second, while VERBAL GROUP MODALITY is an interpersonal system (dependent on the feature indicative as we shall see in Chapter 3), DIMENSION TYPE is ideational (and so independent of MOOD). Dimension functions can thus be used across moods, including imperative, whereas Modals cannot function in imperative clauses. Examples (84)–(86) show that a Dimension function can operate in different moods.

(84)

가르치고 있니?			
gareuchi-go		*in-ni*	
teach		continuity	interrogative
Event		Dimension	
verb		auxiliary verb	
Head	Link	Head	Exchange Mark
stem	suffix	stem	suffix
'Is (he) teaching?'			

(85)

가르치고 있다.			
gareuchi-go		*it-da*	
teach		continuity	declarative
Event		Dimension	
verb		auxiliary verb	
Head	Link	Head	Exchange Mark
stem	suffix	stem	suffix
'(He) is teaching.'			

(86)

가르치고 있어라.			
gareuchi-go		*iss-eora*	
teach		continuity	imperative
Event		Dimension	
verb		auxiliary verb	
Head	Link	Head	Exchange Mark
stem	suffix	stem	suffix
literally, 'Keep teaching!'			

In contrast, Modals are limited to indicative mood, as in (87) and (88). One cannot say in Korean, for instance, *가르쳐야 해라 *gareuchy-ya ha-era* 'must teach', which attempts to use Modal in imperative mood.

2.4 Verbal Group

(87)

가르쳐야 한다				
gareuchi-eoya	ha-n-da			
teach	obligation	present	declarative	
Event	Dimension			
verb	aux verb			
Head	Link	Head	Tense Mark	Exchange Mark
stem	suffix	stem	suffix	suffix
'(I) have to teach.'				

(88)

가르쳐야 하니?				
gareuchi-eoya	ha-ni			
teach	obligation	interrogative		
Event	Dimension			
verb	aux verb			
Head	Link	Head	Exchange Mark	
stem	suffix	stem	suffix	
'Do (you) have to teach?'				

2.4.6 The System of HIGHLIGHT

The system of HIGHLIGHT in Korean provides resources for raising the significance of a proposition. It is only realised in indicative clauses (for both formal and informal moods; see Chapter 3). This system is optional. It is realised at group rank by a word complex involving the bound noun 것 *geot* and the copula 이다 *i-da*, as in 것이다 *geos i-da*, or 거다 *geo-da* in short, which literally means 'It is that ...'.

Speakers use this word complex to dramatise (i.e., highlight) propositions. Example (89) illustrates a proposition without 'dramatisation'; (90) exemplifies the **Highlight** function. As will be noted in Chapter 3, 요 *yo* is a Politeness Marker which functions directly in the structure of a clause.

(89)

꿈을 버렸어요				
kkum	=eul	beory-eoss-eo		yo
dream		discarded		
P2		Process		Politeness Marker
nominal group		verbal group		particle
Thing	EFM	Event		
noun	clitic	verb		
		Head	Tense Mark	Stance Mark
		stem	suffix	suffix
'(He)'s given up on (his) dream.'				

(90)

꿈을 버린 거에요						
kkum	=eul	beori-n	geo-y-e			yo
dream		discarded	it is			
P2		Process				PM
nominal group		verbal group				particle
Thing	EFM	Event	Highlight			
noun	clitic	verb	word complex			
		Head	Link	β	α	
		stem	suffix	bound noun	copula	
					Head	Stance Mark
					stem	suffix
'What happened was, (he)'s given up on (his) dream.'						

In Figure 2.18 and Table 2.22 we propose the following HIGHLIGHT system.

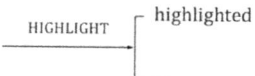

Figure 2.18 The system of HIGHLIGHT

Table 2.22 *The system of HIGHLIGHT: realisation statements*

verbal group	+Highlight; Highlight ^ #
highlighted	Highlight:word complex (α:bound noun (것 *geot* or 거 *geo*) ^ β:copula)

2.4.7 The System of DEGREE

The Event is in general the first function realised within the verbal group structure in Korean. There are two exceptions for this generalisation. One is, as we saw above, the Negate function, realised by the negative adverb 안 *an* 'not' or 못 *mot* 'cannot' and positioned before the Event. The other precedes Negate – the Degree function.

The Degree function is realised only in a relational clause where the Event is realised by a verbalised adjective. There are a handful of adverbs that realise the Degree function in Korean, as illustrated in Table 2.23.

Table 2.23 *Adverbs realising the Degree function*

adverbs of intensification	degreed	upgraded	참	*cham*	'really'
			진짜	*jinjja*	'really'
			매우	*maeu*	'extremely'
			아주	*aju*	'very'
			되게	*doege*	'very'
			너무	*neomu*	'too'
			제법	*jebeop*	'fairly'
			꽤	*kkwae*	'fairly'
		downgraded	약간	*yakgan*	'slightly'
			조금	*jogeum*	'a little'
	compared		더	*deo*	'more'
			덜	*deol*	'less'

Example (91) illustrates a typical example of the Degree function. Note that a verbal group can have more than one Degree function, as shown in (92).

(91)

김치가 조금 맵다.			
gimchi	=*ga*	*jogeum*	*maep-da*
Kimchi		a little	spicy
P1		Process/Attribute	
nominal group		verbal group	
Thing	EFM	Degree	Event
noun	clitic	adverb	verbalised adjective
			Head	Exchange Mark
			stem	suffix
'Kimchi is a little spicy.'			

(92)

수애는 정말 참 친절하다.					
suae	*=neun*	*jeongmal*	*cham*	*chinjeolha-da.*	
Suae		truly	really	is kind	
P1		Process/Attribute			
nominal group		verbal group			
Thing	TFM	Degree	Degree	Event	
noun	clitic	adverb	adverb	verbalised adjective	
				Head	Exchange Mark
				stem	suffix
'Suae is really, truly kind.'					

In (93), the price of a piano is described as higher than that of a guitar. We analyse 기타 보다 *gita boda* 'than guitar' as an additional clause rank function in this clause type. Unlike the adverb 더 *deo* 'more', it can occur before 피아노가 *piano ga* 'piano' (as P1). In addition, the clitic 보다 *boda* 'than' can be followed by a Textual or Interpersonal Function Marking, e.g., 는 *neun* or 도 *do*.

(93)

피아노가 키타보다 더 비싸다.					
piano	*=ga*	*kita*	*=boda*	*deo*	*bissa-ta*
piano		guitar	than	more	is expensive
P1		Standard		Process/Attribute	
nominal group		nominal group		verbalised adjective	
Thing	EFM	Thing	Linking	Degree	Event
noun	clitic	noun	clitic	adverb	verbalised adjective
					Head / Exchange Mark
					stem / suffix
'A piano is more expensive than a guitar.'					

We propose the DEGREE system in Figure 2.19 and the realisation statements in Table 2.24.

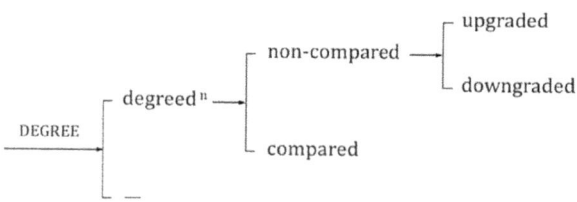

Figure 2.19 The system of DEGREE

2.4 Verbal Group 83

Table 2.24 *The system of* DEGREE: *realisation statements*

degreed	+Degree; # Degree ⇀ (Negate) Event; only for Event realised by verbalised adjective
compared	+Standard (clause rank); Standard:nominal group (with culminative 보다 *boda*)

2.4.8 The System of VERBAL GROUP PARTICIPANT DEFERENCE

The VERBAL GROUP PARTICIPANT DEFERENCE is an optional system that allows Korean speakers to 'exalt' a person who is construed experientially as the main participant (P1) in a clause (e.g., the Actor in an action process, the Sayer in a verbal process, the Senser in a mental process etc., as detailed in Chapter 4).

The system is realised at word rank through suffixation on the last element of the verbal group, which can be a lexical or auxiliary verb or verbalised adjective. The realisation involves the Participant Deference Mark (PDM), which is realised by the non-culminating suffix (으)시 *-(eu) si*.[25] The PDM is positioned before the Tense Mark and the Mood Mark or Stance Mark.

The VERBAL GROUP PARTICIPANT DEFERENCE system we propose is displayed in Figure 2.20 and the realisation statements are in Table 2.25.

Figure 2.20 The system of VERBAL GROUP PARTICIPANT DEFERENCE

Table 2.25 *The system of* VERBAL GROUP PARTICIPANT DEFERENCE: *realisation statements*

honoured	+Participant Deference Mark (PDM); Head ^(VM) ⇀ PDM; PDM:(으)시 *-(eu)si*

In (94) the main participant is not honoured. By contrast, (95) and (96) illustrate Participant Deference resources – P1, the main participant, is explicitly honoured. In the examples, PDM stands for Participant Deference Mark. In (96) deference to P1 is reinforced through the clitic 께서 *kkeseo*, an Interpersonal Function Mark (IFM).

---

[25] After a consonant 으시 *-eusi* is used, otherwise 시 *-si* is used.

(94)   Speaker is deferential to Addressee, but not to P1

동생이 신문을 봅니다.					
dongsaeng	=*i*	*sinmun*	=*eul*	*bo-mnida*	
younger sibling		newspaper		read	
P1				Process	
nominal group				verbal group	
Thing	EFM			Event	
noun	clitic			verb	
				Head	EM
				stem	venerate;declarative suffix
'(My) younger sibling is reading a newspaper.'					

(95)   Speaker is deferential to Addressee and P1

아저씨가 신문을 보십니다.						
ajeossi	=*ga*	*sinmun*	=*eul*	*bo-**si**-mnida*		
uncle		newspaper		read		
P1				Process		
nominal group				verbal group		
Thing	EFM			Event		
noun	clitic			verb		
				Head	PDM	EM
				stem	suffix	venerate; declarative suffix
'Uncle is reading a newspaper.'						

2.4 Verbal Group

(96) Speaker is deferential to Addressee and to P1; deference to P1 reinforced

할아버지께서 신문을 보십니다.							
harabeoji	*=kkeseo*	*sinmun*	*=eul*	*bo-si-mnida*			
grandfather		newspaper		read			
P1				Process			
nominal group				verbal group			
Thing	IFM			Event			
noun	clitic			verb			
				Head	PDM	EM	
				stem	suffix	venerate; declarative suffix	
'Grandfather is reading a newspaper.'							

2.4.9 Tense Systems

The tense systems are realised through word rank resources in Korean. Specifically, the Tense Mark function is realised by a suffix on the stem of the last element of the verbal group of a clause (which can be a lexical verb, a verbalised adjective, a copula or an auxiliary verb).

We include tense in our discussion of verbal group resources because we need to distinguish between [tensed] and [non-tensed] verbal groups (see Figure 2.23). Verbal groups without tense operate in imperative clauses, and in embedded clauses culminating with 기 *-gi*.

Korean has two tense marking systems. One operates in a ranking clause, and the other in an embedded clause. We will call them ABSOLUTE TENSE and RELATIVE TENSE respectively. The ABSOLUTE TENSE system allows for two choices: [now] and [then]. The feature [now] involves 'zero' marking; the tense is 'present' when no tense suffix is employed, as in (97). The exception is when (i) the verbal group is [action-oriented], (ii) the last element of the verbal group is a lexical or auxiliary verb in declarative mood and (iii) the formality choice is non-deferential; in this case the suffix (는)ㄴ–*(neu)n*[26] is employed, as exemplified in (98) and (99).

---

[26] Note that we choose *-neun* after a consonant, and *-n* after a vowel.

(97)

작다.	
jak-da	
small	
Process	
vg	
Event	
verbalised adjective	
Head	Exchange Mark
stem	suffix
'(It's) small.'	

(98)

대학교에 간다.			
daehakkyo	=*e*	*ga-**n**-da*	
university	to	go	
Circumstance:Location		Process	
ng		vg	
Thing	EFM	Event	
noun	clitic	verb	
		Head	**Tense Mark**	Exchange Mark
		stem	suffix	suffix
'(She) is going to the university.'			

(99)

점심을 먹는다.			
jeomsim	=*eul*	*meong-**neun**-da*	
lunch		eat	
P2		Process	
ng		vg	
Thing	EFM	Event	
noun	clitic	verb	
		Head	**Tense Mark**	Exchange Mark
		stem	suffix	suffix
'(He) is eating lunch.'			

2.4 Verbal Group

The feature [then] (i.e., past tense) is realised through the suffix ㅆ -*t*, 았 -*at* or 었 -*eot*, as shown in examples (100)–(102).[27]

(100)

대학교에 갔다.		
daehakkyo	=*e*	*ga-t-da*
university	to	go
Circumstance:Location		Process
ng		vg
Thing	EFM	Event
noun	clitic	verb
		Head	**Tense Mark**	Exchange Mark
		stem	suffix	suffix
'(She) went to the university.'		

(101)

작았다.	
*jag-**at**-da*	
small	
Process	
vg	
Event	
verbalised adjective	
Head	Tense Mark	Exchange Mark
stem	suffix	suffix
'(It) was small.'	

---

[27] Suffixes given in pairs (or triplets) are morphophonemically conditioned variants. In case of the ㅆ -*t*, 았 -*at* or 었 -*eot* triplet, broadly stated, the first one is chosen when the stem ends in either 아 *a* or 어 *eo*; the second one is chosen when the stem ends in a consonant and the vowel of the last syllable of the stem is either 아 *a* or 어 *o*; elsewhere the third one is chosen.

(102)

jeomsim	=*eul*	*meog-eot-da*		
lunch		eat		
P2		Process		
ng		vg		
Thing	EFM	Event		
noun	clitic	verb		
			Head	**Tense Mark**	Exchange Mark
			stem	suffix	suffix
'(He) ate lunch.'				

In Figure 2.21 and Table 2.26 we propose the following ABSOLUTE TENSE system in Korean.

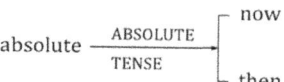

Figure 2.21 The system of ABSOLUTE TENSE

Table 2.26 *The system of* ABSOLUTE TENSE: *realisation statements*

absolute	+Tense Mark; Head ^ (Voice Mark) ^ (PDM) ⸺ Tense Mark
now	(if event type is [action-oriented] and non-deferential) +Tense Mark; Tense Mark: (ㄴ)ㄴ –(*neu*)*n*
then	+Tense Mark; Tense Mark: ㅆ -*t*, 앗 -*at* or 엇 -*eot*

RELATIVE TENSE, which is realised in one type of embedded clause, involves five choices in Modern Korean: [not happened], [happened], [ongoing], [witnessed] and [remote]. All these tenses are relative to the absolute tense expressed in the 'main' clause. For instance, when the tense in the 'main' clause is [now] and that in the embedded clause is [not happened], the Event realised in the embedded clause means 'has not happened'; but when the tense in the 'main' clause is [then], and that in the embedded clause is [not happened], the Event in the embedded clause means 'had not happened (at that point in time in the past)'.

2.4 Verbal Group

Note that an embedded clause involving a relative tense marker typically realises the Qualifying function within the nominal group structure (other types of embedding will be discussed later in this book; see Sections 4.2.2.3 and 4.2.2.4 in Chapter 4.)

The feature [not happened] is realised through the suffix (으)ㄹ –(eu)l; the feature [happened] is realised through the suffix (으)ㄴ –(eu)n; the feature [ongoing] is realised through the suffix 는 –neun; the feature [witnessed] is realised through the suffix 던 –deon; the feature [remote] is realised through the suffixes ㅆ던 -t-deon, 았던 -at-deon or 었던 -eot-deon. Note that the features [remote] or [ongoing:witnessed:remote] are realised through syntagms formed by combining ㅆ -t, 았 -at or 었 -eot (the absolute past tense marker we saw above) with 던 -deon (the suffix realising [witnessed]).[28] In examples (103)–(107), RTM stands for Relative Tense Mark.

(103)   not happened

친구가 읽을 책이 여기 있다						
chingu	=ga	ilg-eul	chaeg	=i	yeogi	it-da
friend		read	book		here	is
P1					Cir:loc	Process
ng					adv	vg
Qualifying			Thing	EFM		Event
[[clause]]			noun	clitic		verb
P1		Process				Head	EM
ng		vg				stem	sfx
Thing	EFM	Event					
noun	clitic	verb					
		Head	RTM				
		stem	sfx				
'The book (which) the friend will read is here.'						

---

[28] Note that 을 -eul and 은 -eun are employed after a consonant, and ㄹ -l and ㄴ -n after a vowel. However, both 는 -neun and 던 -deon are used after a consonant or a vowel. The difference among the ㅆ던 -tdeon, 았던 -atdeon or 었던 -eotdeon triplet, broadly stated, is that the first one is chosen when the stem ends in either ㅏ a or ㅓ eo, the second one is chosen when the stem ends in a consonant and the vowel of the last syllable of the stem is either ㅏ a or ㅗ o, and the third one is chosen elsewhere.

(104) happened

친구가 읽은 책이 여기 있다							
chingu	=ga	*ilg-eun*		*chaeg*	=i	*yeogi*	*it-da*
friend		read		book		here	is
P1						Cir:loc	Process
ng						adv	vg
Qualifying				Thing	EFM		Event
[[clause]]				noun	clitic		verb
P1		Process					Head	EM
ng		vg					stem	sfx
Thing	EFM	Event						
noun	clitic	verb						
		Head	RTM					
		stem	sfx					
'The book (which) the friend read is here.'							

(105) ongoing

친구가 읽는 책이 여기 있다							
chingu	=ga	*ing-neun*		*chaeg*	=i	*yeogi*	*it-da*
friend		read		book		here	is
P1						Cir:loc	Process
ng						adv	vg
Qualifying				Thing	EFM		Event
[[clause]]				noun	clitic		verb
P1		Process					Head	EM
ng		vg					stem	sfx
Thing	EFM	Event						
noun	clitic	verb						
		Head	RTM					
		stem	sfx					
'The book (which) the friend is reading is here.'							

2.4 Verbal Group

(106)   witnessed (or ongoing witnessed)

친구가 읽던 책이 여기 있다							
chingu	*=ga*	*ik-deon*		*chaeg*	*=i*	*yeogi*	*it-da*
friend		read		book		here	is
P1						Cir:loc	Process
ng						adv	vg
Qualifying				Thing	EFM		Event
[[clause]]				noun	clitic		verb
P1		Process					Head	EM
ng		vg					stem	sfx
Thing	EFM	Event						
noun	clitic	verb						
		Head	RTM					
		stem	sfx					

'The book (which) the friend was (I saw) reading is here.'

(107)   remote (or ongoing witnessed remote)

친구가 읽었던 책이 여기 있다							
chingu	*=ga*	*ilg-**eot**-deon*		*chaeg*	*=i*	*yeogi*	*it-da*
friend		had read		book		here	is
P1						Cir:Loc	Process
ng						adv	vg
Qualifying				Thing	EFM		Event
[[clause]]				noun	clitic		verb
P1		Process					Head	EM
ng		vg					stem	sfx
Thing	EFM	Event						
noun	clitic	verb						
		Head	RTM					
		stem	suffixes[29]					

'The book (which) the friend **had been** (I saw) reading is here.'

---

[29] The pair of suffixes 었던 *-eot-deon* taken together realise the [ongoing:witnessed:remote] relative tense here.

In Figure 2.22 and Table 2.27 we propose the following RELATIVE TENSE system in Korean.

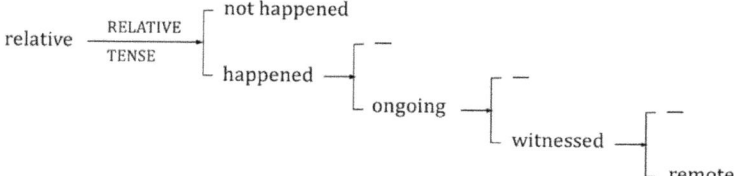

Figure 2.22 The system of RELATIVE TENSE

Table 2.27 *The system of RELATIVE TENSE: realisation statements*

relative	+Relative Tense Mark; Head (VM) (PDM) ⌐ RTM ^ #
not happened	RTM:(으)ㄹ –(eu)l
happened	RTM:(으)ㄴ –(eu)n
ongoing	RTM:는 –neun
witnessed	RTM:던 –deon
remote	RTM:ㅆ던 -t-deon, 았던 -at-deon or 었던-eot-deon

In Figure 2.23 we provide a synoptic overview of verbal group systems.

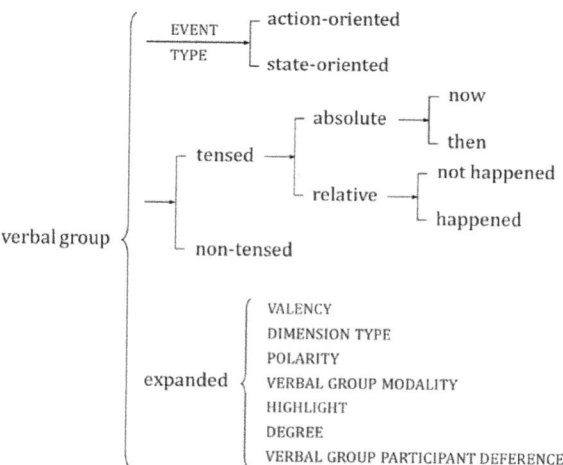

Figure 2.23 Verbal group systems

2.5 Adverbial Group

The adverbial group consists of one or more adverbs, and its role in clause structure can be looked at from three different perspectives. From the perspective of experiential meaning, the adverbial group typically realises a Circumstance.

The basic structure of an adverbial group realising a Circumstance is a **Property** function, which can be optionally preceded by a **Grader**. The Property function is realised by one or more adverbs of 'manner' or by adverbs of 'time' or 'space'. The optional Grader can be realised through one or more adverbs of 'degree'. Examples (108) and (109) illustrate these functions.

(108) Grader ^ Property

꽤 멀리 날아갔다.				
kkwae	*meolli*	*naraga-t-da*		
fairly	far	flew		
Circumstance:Extent		Process		
adverbial group		verbal group		
Grader	Property	Event		
adverb	adverb	verb		
		Head	TM	EM
		stem	suffix	suffix
'(It) flew fairly far.'				

(109) Grader ^ Property

아주 천천히 조심스럽게 먹는다.				
aju	*cheoncheonhi*	*josimseureopge*	*meong-neun-da*	
very	slowly	cautiously	eat	
Circumstance:Manner			Process	
adverbial group			verbal group	
Grader	Property		Event	
adverb	[adverb complex]		verb	
	1	+2	Head	TM	EM
	adverb	adverb	stem	suffix	suffix
'(He) eats very slowly and cautiously.'				

Graded adverbial groups can also involve a Standard function as part of its structure (specifying the comparison being made), as illustrated in (110).

(110)   Standard ^ Grader ^ Property

나보다 더 천천히 먹는다.						
na	*=boda*	*deo*	*cheoncheonhi*	*meong-neun-da*		
I	than	more	slowly	eat		
Circumstance:Manner				Process		
adverbial group				verbal group		
Standard		Grader	Property	Event		
[nominal group]		adverb	adverb	verb		
Thing	Linking			Head	TM	EM
noun	clitic			stem	sfx	sfx
'(He) eats more slowly than me.'						

The Property function can be followed by IFM or TFM Function Marking (111).[30] This optional Function Marking reflects the speaker's stance or adds informational prominence.

(111)

꽤 멀리도 날아갔다!					
kkwae	*meolli*	*=do*[31]	*naraga-t-da*		
fairly	far		flew		
Circumstance:Manner			Process		
adverbial group			verbal group		
Grader	Property	IFM	Event		
adverb	adverb	clitic	verb		
			Head	TM	EM
			stem	suffix	suffix
'(It) flew fairly far to my surprise!'					

Some examples of adverbs of 'manner', of 'time' and 'space', and of 'degree' (which realise the Property and Grader functions) are provided in Table 2.28.

---

[30] TFM or IFM Function Marking can also follow the Standard function (even though it is an element of adverbial group structure), for contrastive force.
[31] The clitic 도 *do* signals counter-expectation of some kind.

2.5 Adverbial Group

Table 2.28 *Adverbs realising the Property and Grader functions*

Property:quality	깨끗이	*kkaekkeusi*	'neatly'
	빨리	*ppalli*	'quickly'
	완전히	*wanjeonhi*	'completely'
	부지런히	*bujireonhi*	'diligently'
	가득히	*gadeuki*	'fully'
	슬며시	*seulmyeosi*	'subtly'
	갑자기	*gapjagi*	'suddenly'
	정확하게	*jeonghwakhage*	'accurately'
	부드럽게	*budeureopge*	'softly'
	예쁘게	*yeppeuge*	'prettily'
Property:distance	아까	*akka*	'a while ago'
	여기	*yeogi*	'here'
	지금	*jigeum*	'now'
	어제	*eoje*	'yesterday'
	멀리	*meolli*	'far'
	가까이	*gakkai*	'near'
	길이 길이	*giri giri*	'forever'
	한참	*hancham*	'for a good while'
	넓게	*neolge*	'widely'
	좁게	*jopge*	'narrowly'
Grader	조금	*jogeum*	'a little bit'
	많이	*mani*	'lots'
	더	*deo*	'more . . .'
	덜	*deol*	'less . . .'
	가장	*gajang*	'most'
	거의	*geoui*	'almost, nearly'
	너무	*neomu*	'too . . .'
	매우	*maeu*	'very'
	몹시	*mopsi*	'very'
	아주	*aju*	'very'

Turning to interpersonal meaning, adverbial groups can function as Modal Adjuncts or Comment; these will be further discussed in Chapter 3. Example (112) includes a Modal Adjunct, and (113) a Comment. Note that Comment may occur with the IFM such as 도 *do* 'even', which conveys a more intense feeling.

(112)

아이가 아직도 자고 있다.						
ai	=*ga*	*ajikdo*	*ja-go*		*it-da*	
child		still	sleep		continue	
Participant		Modal Adjunct	Process			
nominal group		adverbial group	verbal group			
Thing	EFM	Head	Event		Dimension	
noun	clitic	adverb	verb		aux verb	
			Head	Link	Head	Exchange Mark
			stem	suffix	stem	suffix
'The child is still sleeping.'						

(113)

다행스럽게도 아이가 울음을 그쳤다.								
dahaengseureopge	=*do*	*ai*	=*ga*	*ureum*	=*eul*	*geuchy-eot-da*		
fortunately		child		crying		stopped		
Comment		Participant		Participant		Process		
adverbial group		nominal group		nominal group		verbal group		
Head	IFM	Thing	EFM	Thing	EFM	Event		
adverb	clitic	noun	clitic	noun	clitic	verb		
						Head	TM	EM
						stem	suffix	suffix
'Fortunately, the child stopped crying.'								

Some examples of adverbs that are deployed as Modal Adjuncts and Comment are listed in Table 2.29.

2.5 Adverbial Group

Table 2.29 *Adverbs deployed as Modal Adjunct and Comment functions*

Modal Adjunct	가끔	*gakkeum*	'sometimes'
	자주	*jaju*	'frequently'
	항상	*hangsang*	'always'
	아직	*ajik*	'yet'
	아직도	*ajikdo*	'still'
	벌써	*beolsseo*	'already'
	아마	*ama*	'perhaps'
	모처럼	*mocheoreom*	'finally able'
	꼭	*kkok*	'absolutely'
	반드시	*bandeusi*	'without fail'
Comment	놀랍게도	*nolapge do*	'to my surprise'
	슬프게도	*seulpeuge do*	'sadly'
	다행히	*dahaenghi*	'fortunately'
	불행하게도	*buraenghage do*	'unfortunately'
	유감스럽게도	*yugamseureopge do*	'regrettably'

From the perspective of logical meaning, adverbial groups can function as Conjunctive Adjuncts – connecting clause complexes (sentences) to one another.

Example (114) illustrates one such instance.

(114)

그래서 엄마는 책을 읽었다.							
geuraeseo	*eomma*	=*neun*	*chaek*	=*eul*	*ilg-eot-da.*		
as a result	mother		book		read		
Conjunctive Adjunct	Participant		Participant		Process		
adverbial group	nominal group		nominal group		verbal group		
Head	Thing	EFM	Thing	EFM	Event		
adverb	noun	clitic	noun	clitic	verb		
					Head	TM	EM
					stem	suffix	suffix
'As a result, mother read the book.'							

Table 2.30 lists some adverbs that function as the head of an adverbial group of this kind.

Table 2.30 *Adverbs deployed as Conjunctive Adjuncts*

Conjunctive Adjuncts	그리고	*geurigo*	'in addition, and'
	그러나	*geureona*	'in contrast, however'
	하지만	*hajiman*	'however'
	그런데	*geureonde*	'by the way'
	그래서	*geuraeseo*	'as a result'
	따라서	*ttaraseo*	'as a result'
	그러니까	*geureonikka*	'consequently'

In Figure 2.24 and Table 2.31 we propose the following system network for adverbial groups in Korean.

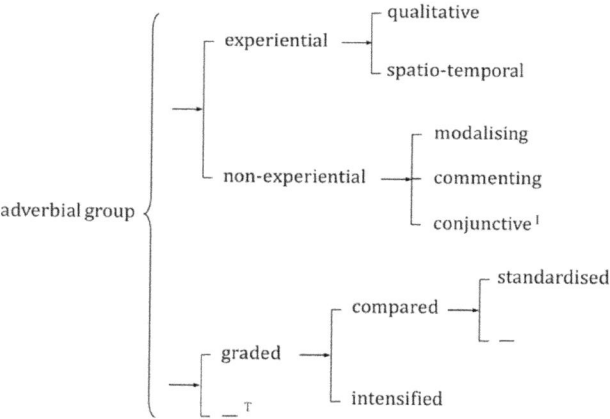

Figure 2.24 Adverbial group systems

Realisation statements for these systems are provided in Table 2.31.

Table 2.31 *Realisation statements for adverbial group systems*

experiential	+Property
qualitative	+Property:depictive adverb
spatio-temporal	+Property:spatio-temporal adverb
graded	+Grader; Grader^Property
compared	Grader:comparative adverb
intensified	Grader:degree adverb
standardised	+Standard; Standard^Grader; Standard:nominal group (with culminative 보다 *boda*)
non-experiential	+Head
modalising	Head:adverb (modal)
commenting	Head:adverb (comment)
conjunctive	Head:adverb (conjunctive)

2.6 Co-verbal Phrase

The co-verbal phrase in Korean involves a bound verb preceded by a nominal group. We have adopted the term co-verbal phrase from the analysis of a similar unit in Chinese by Halliday and McDonald (2004: 311). Teruya (2004: 188) refers to the Japanese counterpart of our co-verbal phrase as a postpositional phrase.

The structure we propose for the Korean co-verbal phrase is Incumbent followed immediately by Role. The Role function specifies the function of the co-verbal phrase in a clause or nominal group and the Incumbent function specifies the entity that plays the Role. The Incumbent is realised by a nominal group (or an embedded clause) and Role by a bound verb. We refer to the realisation of Role as a 'bound verb', by analogy with a 'bound noun', because it has a very restricted range of suffixation. As noted above (Section 2.3.7), co-verbal phrases can realise Qualifying functions (with an appropriate connecting suffix) in nominal groups; and they regularly realise various types of Circumstance in clause structure (see Chapter 4, Section 4.4).

In (115) the co-verbal phrase is embedded in a nominal group Qualifying function; in (116) it realises a Circumstance of purpose.

(115)

문제 해결을 위한 협력이 필요하다.						
munje	*haegyeor*	=*eul*	*wiha-n*	*hyeomnyeog*	=*i*	*piryoha-da*
problem	solution		for	cooperation		is needed
P1						Process
nominal group						verbal group
Qualifying				Thing	EFM	Event
[co-verbal phrase]				noun	clitic	verb
Incumbent			Role			Head	EM
[nominal group]			bound verb			stem	sfx
Classifying	Thing	EFM	Head	Link		
noun	noun	clitic	stem	sfx		
'Cooperation for a solution to the problem is needed.'						

(116)

문제 해결을 위해 협력이 필요하다.						
munje	*haegyeor*	=*eul*	*wiha-e*	*hyeomnyeog*	=*i*	*piryoha-da*
problem	solution		for	cooperation		is needed
Circumstance:Purpose				P1		Process
co-verbal phrase				nominal group		verbal group
Incumbent			Role	Thing	EFM	Event
[nominal group]			bound verb	noun	clitic	verb
Classifying	Thing	EFM	Head	Link		Head	EM
noun	noun	clitic	stem	sfx		stem	sfx
'Cooperation is needed for a solution to the problem.'						

Two points need to be noted here. One relates to the bound verb that realises the Role – 위한 *wiha-n* 'for' in (115) and 위해 *wiha-e* 'for' in (116). These illustrate two of the very restricted conjugation possibilities that the verb 위하다 *wiha-da* 'care' can enter into in a co-verbal phrase. The culminating suffix in the Qualifying function is (으)ㄴ *-(eu)n* and the culminating suffix in Circumstances is 아(서) *-a(seo)* or 어(서) *-eo(seo)*. There are some idiosyncratic exceptions to these possibilities that will not be detailed here.

Second, in both of the examples, the Incumbent is realised by a nominal group marked by 을 *eul* (EFM for P2). This is required by the bound verbs 위한 *wiha-n* 'for' and 위해 *wiha-e* 'for'. The choice of EFM in the realisations of the Incumbent can vary because different bound verbs require different EFMs.

Example (117) shows another example of a co-verbal phrase. Here, the Role is realised by the bound verb 인해 *inha-e* 'because of' and the Incumbent is realised by a nominal group marked by 으로 *euro* (the EFM for Circumstance:Instrument); this EFM is determined by the bound verb 인해 *inha-e* 'caused'.

2.6 Co-verbal Phrase

(117)

지진으로 인해 건물이 무너졌다.								
jijin	*=euro*	*inha-e*		*geonmur*	*=i*	*muneojy-eot-da*		
earthquake		because of		building		collapsed		
Circumstance:Cause				P1		Process		
co-verbal phrase				nominal group		verbal group		
Incumbent		Role		Thing	EFM	Event		
[nominal group]		bound verb		noun	clitic	verb		
Thing	EFM	Head	Link			Head	TM	EM
noun	clitic	stem	sfx			stem	sfx	sfx
'A building got collapsed because of earthquake.'								

In Figure 2.25 we propose a network for co-verbal phrase systems in Korean.

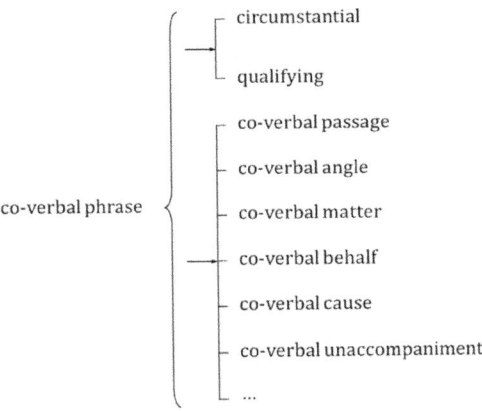

Figure 2.25 Co-verbal phrase systems

A general realisation statement for co-verbal phrases is provided in Table 2.32.

Table 2.32 *Realisation statements for co-verbal phrases*

co-verbal phrase	+Incumbent; + Role; Incumbent ^ Role; Incumbent:[nominal group] or [[clause]] with appropriate EFM
circumstantial	Role:bound verb with 아(서) -*a*(*seo*) or 어(서) -*eo*(*seo*)
qualifying	Role:bound verb with (으)ㄴ -(*eu*)*n*

Table 2.33 lists a limited number of examples of co-verbal phrases. As noted, the realisations of the Role function are bound verbs, and different EFMs are required in the nominal groups which realise the respective Incumbent function.

Table 2.33 *Some examples of co-verbal phrases*

	co-verbal phrases (Hangeul, Romanisation and 'meaning')		Notes
	Circumstance	Qualifying	
co-verbal passage	을 or 를 통해, 통하여 or 통해서 (r)eul tongha-e, tongha-yeo or tongha-eseo 'through . . .'	을 or 를 통한 (r)eul tongha-n 'through . . .'	• the clitic 을 or 를 (r) eul is EFM for P2 • the verb 통하다 tongha-da means 'go through'
co-verbal angle	에 의하면 e euiha-myeon 'according to . . .'	에 의한 e euiha-n 'according to . . .'	• the clitic 에 e is EFM for Cir:Angle • the verb 의하다 euiha-da means 'rely'
co-verbal matter	과 or 와 관련해, 관련하여 or 관련해서 (g)wa gwallyeonha-e, gwallyeonha-yeo or gwallyeonha-eseo 'regarding . . .'	과 or 와 관련한 (g)wa gwallyeonha-n 'regarding . . .'	• the clitic 과 or 와 (g)wa is EFM for Cir: Accompaniment • the verb 관련하다 gwallyeonha-da means 'relate'
	에 대해, 대하여 or 대해서 e daeha-e, daeha-yeo or daeha-eseo 'with respect to . . .'	에 대한 e daeha-n 'with respect to . . .'	• the clitic 에 e is EFM for Cir:Location • the verb 대하다 daeha-da means 'encounter'
co-verbal behalf	을 or 를 위해, 위하여 or 위해서 (r)eul wiha-e, wiha-yeo or wiha-eseo 'for the sake of . . .'	을 or 를 위한 (r)eul wiha-n 'for the sake of . . .'	• the clitic 을 or 를 (r) eul is EFM for P2 • the verb 위하다 wiha-da means 'care, serve'
co-verbal cause	(으)로 인해, 인하여 or 인해서 (eu)ro inha-e, inha-yeo or inha-eseo 'because of . . .'	(으)로 인한 (eu)ro inha-n 'because of . . .'	• the clitic (으)로 (eu)ro is EFM for Cir:Means • the verb 인하다 inha-da means 'be caused'
co-verbal unaccompaniment	이 or 가 없이 i or ga eops-i 'without . . .'	이 or 가 없는 i or ga eom-neun 'without . . .'	• the clitic 이 or 가 ga is EFM for P1 • the verb 없다 eop-da means 'there is/are not, not have'

In school grammars in Korea, what we have been calling a co-verbal phrase is not recognised; it is treated as a kind of 'adverbial phrase' on the grounds that it in some sense 'modifies' the main verb of the clause as adverbs do. Structurally, however, a co-verbal phrase is very different from an adverbial group in our grammar. It is not headed by an adverb and involves a verb with limited conjugation potential and a nominal group.

2.7 Group and Phrase Complexes

We have already provided examples of 'word complexes' in (82) and (90); there two or more elements at word rank are combined to realise a single group/phrase rank function. We now consider nominal group complexes and verbal group complexes (clause complexes are explored in Chapter 6).

In simple terms, a group complex is a combination of groups realising a single function. Nominal group complexes deploy a Linking function realised by the clitic 와 *wa* or 과 *gwa* to make explicit the connection. In (118), Participant 1 is realised by a nominal group complex 오랜 경험의 공연 *oraen gyeongheom ui gongyeon* 'long experienced performance' and 창의적인 미술 *changuijeogin misul* 'creative art'. The structure of the first nominal group is Orient ^ Thing ^ Linking; the structure of the second is Epithet ^ Thing. The two nominal groups are paratactically linked (notated as 1 ^ +2) by the clitic 과 *gwa*.

(118)

오랜 경험의 공연과 창의적인 미술이 ...							
oraen	*gyeongheom*	=*ui*	*gongyeon*	=*gwa*	*changuijeogin*	*misul*	=*i*
long	experience		performance		creative	art	
P1							
nominal group complex							
1				+2			EFM
nominal group				nominal group			clitic
Orient			Thing	Linking	Epithet	Thing	
[nominal group]			noun	clitic	adjective	noun	
Epithet	Thing	Linking					
adjective	noun	clitic					
'Long experienced performance ('accomplished performance') and creative art ...							

... 만났습니다.		
manna-t-seumnida		
met		
Process		
verbal group		
Event		
verb		
Head	Tense Mark	Exchange Mark
stem	suffix	suffix
... met.'		

When more than two nominal groups are combined, the Linking function tends to be realised between the first two groups (not between the last two as in English). So in a nominal group complex such as 공연 예술과 디지털 미디어, 상호 매체성 *gongyeon yesul gwa digiteol midieo, sangho maecheseong* 'performing arts, digital media and intermediality', the connecting clitic 과 *gwa* tends to appear between the first two nominal groups.

In Korean, it is often not clear how to treat a 'complex' involving multiple verbs – as a clause complex, as a verbal group complex or as a verb complex. We outline our approach below.

As further discussed in Chapter 6, a clause complex may resemble a verbal group complex when the Participants in the second clause are elided – as in (119). Note that in (120) the elided P1 and P2 in the second clause play different roles to the roles played by the P1 and P2 in the first clause. In the first clause, the P1 is Senser and the P2 is Phenomenon while in the second clause the elided P1 is Actor and the elided P2 is Undergoer. There are two distinct transitivity configurations involved; accordingly we would treat this example as a clause complex (notated as 1 +2 below; see Chapter 6).

(119)   clause complex: two Processes

마니아들은 연극의 장점을 알고 ...							
mania-deur	=*eun*	*yeongeog*	=*ui*	*jangjeom*	=*eul*	*al-***go**	
enthusiasts		play		merits		know and	
1							
clause							
P1:Senser		P2:Phenomenon				**Process: mental**	
nominal group		nominal group				verbal group	
Thing	EFM	Orient		Thing	EFM	Event	
noun	clitic	[ng]		noun	clitic	verb	
		Thing	Linking			Head	Link
		noun	clitic			stem	sfx
'Enthusiasts know the merits of plays (in general) and ...'							

2.7 Group and Phrase Complexes

... 찾는다.		
chan-neun-da		
seek		
+2		
clause		
Process:material		
verbal group		
Event		
verb		
Head	Lk	EM
stem	sfx	sfx
... seek out (plays).'		

In (120) on the other hand the elided P1 function and the P2 function play the same role in relation to each verb. In this case there is just one transitivity configuration and so it is simpler to recognise a verbal group complex realising a single Process.

(120)

원하는 좌석을 선택하여 예약한다.								
wonha-neun	*jwaseog*	*=eul*	*seontaekha-yeo*		*yeyaka-n-da*			
want	seat		select		reserve			
P2			Process					
nominal group			verbal group complex					
Qualifying	Thing	EFM	β		α			
[[clause]]	noun	clitic	verbal group		verbal group			
Process			Event		Event			
verbal group			verb		verb			
Event			Head	Link	Head	TM	EM	
verb			stem	suffix	stem	suffix	suffix	
Head	Link							
stem	suffix							
'(You) reserve, by selecting, the seat (you) want.'								

We prefer to analyse (120) as involving a Process realised by a verbal group complex (rather than a verb complex) because each verbal group has the possibility of being expanded – potentially in different ways. An expanded example is presented in (121). Here, the Negating function in the first verbal group does not apply to the second verbal group; and the Modal function in the second verbal group does not apply to the first verbal group.

(121)

원하는 좌석을 선택하지 않고 ...				
wonha-neun	*jwaseog*	*=eul*	*seontaeka-ji*	*an-ko*
want	seat		select	don't
P2			Process ...	
nominal group			verbal group complex ...	
Qualifying	Thing	EFM	β	
[[clause]]	noun	clitic	verbal group	
Process			Event	Negating
verbal group			verb	aux verb
Event			Head / Link	Head / Link
verb			stem / suffix	stem / suffix
Head / Link				
stem / suffix				
... without selecting, the seat (you) want?'				

... 예약할 수 있나?		
yeyaka-l	*su*	*in-na*
reserve		can
...		
...		
α		
verbal group		
Event	Modal	
verb	word complex	
Head / Link	β	α
stem / suffix	bound noun	aux verb
		Head / EM
		stem / suffix
'Can (you) reserve ...		

2.7 Group and Phrase Complexes

There are no grammatical strategies available in Korean for constructing adverbial group complexes or co-verbal phrase complexes. Instead, we find juxtaposed adverbial groups or co-verbal phrases realising separate elements of clause or nominal group structure – as illustrated in (122) and (123).

(122)

아주 천천히 정말 조심스럽게 먹는다.						
aju	*cheoncheonhi*	*jeongmal*	*josimseureopge*	*meong-neun-da*		
very	slowly	really	cautiously	eat		
Cir:Manner		Cir:Manner		Process		
adverbial group		adverbial group		verbal group		
Grader	Property	Grader	Property	Event		
adverb	adverb	adverb	adverb	verb		
				Head	TM	EM
				stem	suffix	suffix
'(He) is eating very slowly and really cautiously.'						

(123)

학생에 의한 학생을 위한 ...							
haksaeng	=e	*uiha-n*		*haksaeng*	=eul	*wiha-n*	
student		by		student		for	
P0 ...							
nominal group ...							
Qualifying				Qualifying			
[co-verbal phrase]				[co-verbal phrase]			
Incumbent		Role		Incumbent		Role	
[nominal group]		bound verb		[nominal group]		bound verb	
Thing	EFM	Head	Link	Thing	EFM	Head	Link
noun	clitic	stem	suffix	noun	clitic	stem	suffix
... by the students for the students'							

... 서점입니다.	
seojeom	*i-pnida*
bookshop	is
... P0	Process
... nominal group	verbal group
Thing	Event
noun	copula
	Head	Exchange Mark
	stem	suffix
'(It) is a bookshop ...'	

2.8 Concluding Remarks

In the following chapters the description of Korean groups and phrases developed in this chapter will be used to specify the structural realisation of clause systems. Since choices in clause systems have implications for clause, group/phrase and/or word structure, we have adopted two conventions to help make the rank we are discussing clear. One is to use the term particle at clause rank, the term clitic at group/phrase rank and the term suffix at word rank – whenever we are referring to grammatical items that don't require further structural analysis at a rank below. In addition, for our terminology, we have reserved the English *-er* suffix for names of functions at clause rank, the suffix *-ing* for names of functions at group/phrase rank and avoided suffixes completely for names of functions at work rank. These conventions are outlined in Table 2.34.

Table 2.34 *Naming conventions for terms across ranks*

rank	item	term suffix
clause	particle	-er
group/phrase	=clitic	-ing
word	-suffix	-0

3 The Grammar of Interpersonal Meaning in Korean: MOOD

3.1 Introduction to Interpersonal Clause Structure

As introduced in Chapter 1, a clause realises multiple strands of meaning. It construes experience, enacts social relations, composes information flow, and potentially enters into logical relations with other clauses. Our focus in this chapter is on the clause enacting social relations, and our goal is to discuss the interpersonal grammar of a Korean clause. The other strands of meaning and their respective grammars (i.e., experiential, textual and logical) of a Korean clause will be considered in the following three chapters.

To describe interpersonal systems and structures, we first recognise the crucial grammatical distinction Korean makes between formal and informal resources. The two are identified in Korean as 격식체 *gyeoksikche* 'formal style' and 비격식체 *bigyeoksikche* 'informal style' respectively. Note that we are not using these labels to characterise a text in terms of its register; the formal and informal categories as used here are features of the clause. Formal resources emphasise status relations in the negotiation of dialogic exchanges; informal resources on the other hand are more concerned with establishing common ground for affiliation.

As outlined in Figure 3.1 and discussed in detail in Section 3.2, the two key formal systems are FORMAL MOOD and ADDRESSEE DEFERENCE;[1] and the three key informal systems are INFORMAL MOOD, STANCE and POLITENESS. Mood marking, in other words, deploys different strategies in clauses with the feature [formal] and those with the feature [informal] in Korean. Exchange marking (a set of resources for portmanteau realisations of FORMAL MOOD and ADDRESSEE DEFERENCE) characterises [formal] clauses; and stance marking (a rich set of resources for establishing the common ground on which speaker and addressee can align around a proposition or proposal) is only available in [informal] clauses. In addition, the speaker's status relationship with the addressee is finely tuned in formal clauses by delicate ADDRESSEE DEFERENCE

---

[1] The system of ADDRESSEE DEFERENCE is not available for projected clauses (see Chapter 6).

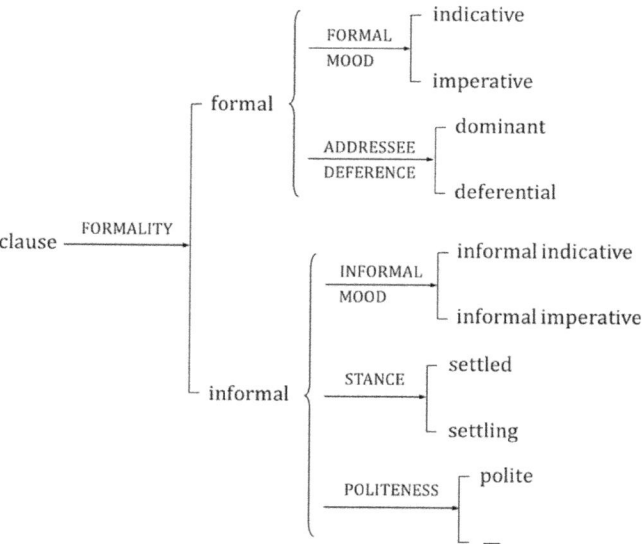

Figure 3.1 The system of FORMALITY

systems, whereas in informal clauses social distance simply involves a binary choice of polite or not.

As in Chapter 2, we continue to specify realisation statements in tables following the system networks. The relevant realisation statements for formality are given in Table 3.1. In the realisation statements '+' indicates that a function will be present in the structure (e.g., +Exchange Mark); ':' signals the relation between function and the class that realises it (e.g., Exchange Mark:suffix).

Table 3.1 *The system of* FORMALITY: *realisation statements – simplified*

clause	+Exchange Mark ^ # (for formal clause); +Stance Mark ^ # (for informal clause)
formal	Exchange Mark:culminating suffix
informal	Stance Mark:culminating suffix

In specifying how a Korean clause is structured, we will propose a dedicated **interpersonal** tier of structure. A key function in this tier is the function Negotiator. As introduced in Chapter 1, the Negotiator does the work of specifying the mood of a clause in dialogue, and is by and large realised through the culminative verbal group of the clause. Other functions that occur

3.2 FORMAL MOOD and ADDRESSEE DEFERENCE

on this tier are **Vocative**, **Expletive**, **Comment** and **Inquirer**;[2] they occur before the Negotiator. The **Politeness Marker** (realised through the particle 요 *yo*) occurs after the Negotiator.[3] Example (1) illustrates a number of these interpersonal clause functions.

(1)

언니, 엄마 언제 나가셨어요?				
eonni	*eomma*	*eonje*	*naga-sy-eoss-eo*	*yo*
big sister	mum	when	went out	
clause				
Vocative		Inquirer	Negotiator	Politeness Marker
ng		advg	vg	particle
'Big sister, when did mum go out?'				

In what follows, we begin with description of the formal systems (FORMAL MOOD and ADDRESSEE DEFERENCE), and then move on to the informal systems (INFORMAL MOOD, STANCE and POLITENESS). We subsequently consider further interpersonal systems that are not dependent on the formal vs informal distinction: PARTICIPANT DEFERENCE, POLARITY, MODALITY, HIGHLIGHT, COMMENT, VOCATION and EXPLETION. All these systems are operative at clause rank in the sense that they position the whole of the clause as a discourse move; but as detailed below their structural realisations are dispersed across clause, group/phrase and word ranks in Korean (Shin 2018). In order to give a complete picture of the interpersonal grammar of Korean and the interaction among its systems, we recapitulate below some of the information on verbal group systems and structures introduced in Chapter 2.

3.2 Formal Systems: FORMAL MOOD and ADDRESSEE DEFERENCE

As noted above, the two key formal systems are FORMAL MOOD and ADDRESSEE DEFERENCE. Both are realised at word rank through suffixation.

3.2.1 The System of FORMAL MOOD

As outlined in Figure 3.2, and the subsequent realisation statements in Table 3.2, Korean makes basic distinctions among indicative and imperative clauses. Indicative clauses are either declarative or interrogative while imperative clauses have a further distinction between imperatives excluding the

---

[2] We take the term Inquirer from Wang (2020), to avoid using the Anglocentric term Wh.
[3] As we will note below, the Politeness Marker 요 *yo* may appear more than once in a clause.

112 The Grammar of Interpersonal Meaning: MOOD

speaker (2nd person jussives) and imperatives including the speaker (1st plus 2nd person cohortatives).

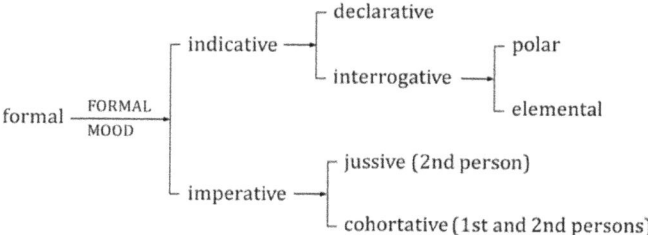

Figure 3.2 The system of FORMAL MOOD

Table 3.2 *The system of FORMAL MOOD: realisation statements (affixes specified for [dominant] clauses only)*

formal	+Exchange Mark ^ #
declarative	Exchange Mark:culminating suffix: 다 -*da*
interrogative	Exchange Mark:culminating suffix: 냐 -*nya*, 니 -*ni*
elemental	+Inquirer:adverbial group or nominal group
jussive	Exchange Mark:culminating suffix: 아라 -*ara* or 어라 -*eora*
cohortative	Exchange Mark:culminating suffix: 자 -*ja*

In making these distinctions we need to take into account the fact that in Korean the verb morphology distinguishing moods interacts with the morphology realising ADDRESSEE DEFERENCE. To begin we will focus on just the set of culminative verbal suffixes that we characterise as [dominant][4] in Figures 3.1 and 3.3.

Consider (2)–(5). They exemplify [declarative], [interrogative], [imperative: jussive] and [imperative:cohortative] clauses, respectively.

---

[4] Korean grammarians generally speak of 'speech levels', such as 'deferential', 'polite', 'semi-formal', 'familiar', 'intimate' and 'plain', to group and characterise what they call 'sentence-enders' (our culminative verbal suffixes). In our grammar culminative verbal suffixes realise choices formalised as 'features', which cover comparable ground. Thus, the feature [venerate] deals with what speakers do when they employ the traditional 'deferential' speech level, and the feature [dominant] addresses what they do when deploying the traditional 'plain' one. See Shin (2018: 21) and references cited there for further explanation.

3.2 FORMAL MOOD and ADDRESSEE DEFERENCE

(2)

아침을 먹었다.		
achim	=*eul*	*meog-eot-**da***
breakfast		eat-past-**declarative;dominant**
		Negotiator
		verbal group
		Event
		verb
		Head / Tense Mark / Exchange Mark
		stem / suffix / declarative suffix
'(I) had breakfast.'		

(3)

아침을 먹었니?		
achim	=*eul*	*meog-eon-**ni***
breakfast		eat-past-**interrogative;dominant**
		Negotiator
		verbal group
		Event
		verb
		Head / Tense Mark / Exchange Mark
		stem / suffix / interrogative suffix
'Did (you) have breakfast?'		

(4)

아침을 먹어라.		
achim	=*eul*	*meog-**eora***
breakfast		eat-**jussive;dominant**
		Negotiator
		verbal group
		Event
		verb
		Head / Exchange Mark
		stem / jussive suffix
'Have breakfast.'		

(5)

아침을 먹자.		
achim	=*eul*	*meog-ja*
breakfast		eat-**cohortative;dominant**
		Negotiator
		verbal group
		Event
		verb
		Head / Exchange Mark
		stem / cohortative suffix
'Let's have breakfast.'		

As illustrated, FORMAL MOOD in Korean is realised at word rank through verb suffixes; the suffixes in clauses with [dominant] addressee deference are presented in Table 3.3.

Table 3.3 FORMAL MOOD suffixes in [dominant] clauses

MOOD		suffix	
indicative	declarative	다	-*da*
	interrogative	냐, 니	-*nya*, -*ni*
imperative	jussive	아라/어라	-*ara*/-*eora*
	cohortative	자	-*ja*

Note that the suffixes 냐 -*nya* and 니 -*ni* both mark the interrogative mood in dominant clauses; but semantically 니 -*ni* conveys what can be described as softer or more intimate feelings than 냐 -*nya*.[5] Note also that the choice between the two imperative:jussive suffixes 아라 -*ara* and 어라 -*eora* is morphophonemically conditioned – when the vowel of the last syllable of the verb stem is either 아 *a* or 오 *o*, 아라 -*ara* is used; otherwise 어라 -*eora* will be chosen.[6]

---

[5] See Standard Korean Language Dictionary, National Institute of Korean Language (https://stdict.korean.go.kr/main/main.do).

[6] Note that there is another jussive suffix, 여라 -*yeora*, which is chosen when the verb stem is 하 *ha*- 'do' or ends in 하 -*ha*- 'do'. However, 여라 -*yeora* is an archaic suffix. In current usage, 하 *ha*- in jussive mood conjugates as 해라 -*haera* – with a fusion of sounds across the boundaries between the stem and the jussive suffix. As this happens only when the verb stem is *ha*- 'do' or ends in 하 -*ha*-, we do not include 여라 -*yeora* in Table 3.3.

3.2 FORMAL MOOD and ADDRESSEE DEFERENCE

The declarative and interrogative options can be grouped together as [indicative] for various reasons. From a paradigmatic perspective, indicative clauses make choices for MODALITY and HIGHLIGHT available, whereas imperative ones do not (see Sections 3.6 and 3.8). And as we shall see in Section 3.5 indicative clauses have different realisations for negative polarity than imperative clauses do. From a discourse semantic perspective we can think of indicative clauses as negotiating propositions (exchanges of information) and imperative clauses as negotiating proposals (exchanges of goods-&-services).

Interrogative clauses can be further categorised as [polar] or [elemental]. Compare (3) with (6). In (6) the suffix 냐 *-nya* marks the clause as an interrogative, and this means that the highlighted Inquirer, 언제 *eonje* 'when', would be interpreted as indicating the missing experiential meaning the addressee is expected to provide.

(6)

아침을 언제 먹었냐?				
achim	=*eul*	*eonje*	*meog-eon*[7]-*nya*	
breakfast		when	eat-past-**interrogative;dominant**	
		Inquirer	Negotiator	
		adverbial group	verbal group	
			Event	
			verb	
			Head	Tense Mark	Exchange Mark
			stem	suffix	interrogative suffix
'When did (you) have breakfast?'				

3.2.2 The System of ADDRESSEE DEFERENCE

We now turn our attention to ADDRESSEE DEFERENCE. The system of ADDRESSEE DEFERENCE and its realisation statements are outlined in Figure 3.3 and Table 3.4 respectively.

Consider (7)–(10), which are deferential alternatives for the dominant declarative, interrogative and imperative clauses in (2) to (5). The verbs culminating these clauses display a different paradigm of suffixes than they did above (as summarised in Table 3.1 for (2)–(5)).

---

[7] Note that the base form of the past tense mark in Korean is 았/었 *-at/-eot* and the final /t/ is realised as [ss] when a vowel follows, and as [n] before a nasal sound.

116   The Grammar of Interpersonal Meaning: MOOD

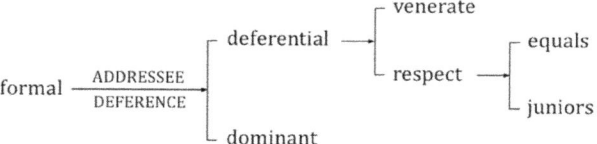

Figure 3.3 The system of ADDRESSEE DEFERENCE

Table 3.4 *The system of* ADDRESSEE DEFERENCE: *realisation statements*

formal	+Exchange Mark ^ #
dominant	Exchange Mark: culminating suffix: 다 -*da* (for declarative); 냐 -*nya*, 니 -*ni* (for interrogative); 아라/어라 -*ara*/-*eora* (for jussive); 자 -*ja* (for cohortative)
venerate	Exchange Mark: culminating suffix: (see Table 3.5 for details)
equals	Exchange Mark: culminating suffix: (see Table 3.5 for details)
juniors	Exchange Mark: culminating suffix: (see Table 3.5 for details)

At this point we need to take into account that the culminating suffixes we have been discussing have two roles. As noted above, they distinguish FORMAL MOOD options (i.e., declarative vs interrogative vs jussive vs cohortative); and they also realise ADDRESSEE DEFERENCE. Examples (2)–(5) illustrated [dominant] options; examples (7)–(10) enact [deferential] options.[8] As mentioned in Chapter 1, we label the verb function encoding this portmanteau realisation as an Exchange Mark.

(7)

아침을 먹었습니다.				
achim	=*eul*	*meog-eot-**seumnida***		
breakfast		eat-past-**declarative;deferential**		
		Negotiator		
		verbal group		
		Event		
		verb		
		Head	Tense Mark	Exchange Mark
		stem	suffix	suffix
'(I) had breakfast.'				

---

[8] In examples we use ';' to indicate simultaneous systemic features and ':' to indicate subclassification.

3.2 FORMAL MOOD and ADDRESSEE DEFERENCE

(8)

아침을 먹었습니까?		
achim	=*eul*	*meog-eot-**seumnikka***
breakfast		eat-past-**interrogative;deferential**
		Negotiator
		verbal group
		Event
		verb

			Head	Tense Mark	Exchange Mark
			stem	suffix	suffix

'Did (you) have breakfast?'

(9)

아침을 드십시오.		
achim	=*eul*	*deusi-**psio***
breakfast		eat (exalted)-**jussive;deferential**
		Negotiator
		verbal group
		Event
		verb

			Head	Exchange Mark
			stem	suffix

'Please have breakfast.'

Note that in (9), a deferential speaker would choose 드시 *deusi-* 'eat (exalted)' over 먹 *meog-* 'eat (plain)' to show more respect to the addressee.

(10)

아침을 먹읍시다.		
achim	=*eul*	*meog-**eupsida***
breakfast		eat-**cohortative;deferential**
		Negotiator
		verbal group
		Event
		verb

			Head	Exchange Mark
			stem	suffix

'Let's have breakfast.'

If we now reconsider (2)–(5) in relation to (7)–(10) we can see that there are alternative ways of realising declarative mood; in (11)–(13) further distinctions in ADDRESSEE DEFERENCE are registered. These distinctions encode different levels of respect. We distinguish [venerate], signalling great respect, from [respect]; and [respect] is further divided into respect for [equals] and respect for [juniors].

(11) venerate

아침을 먹었습니다.		
achim	=*eul*	*meog-eot-**seumnida***
breakfast		eat-past-**declarative;deferential:venerate**
		Negotiator
		verbal group
		Event
		verb

		Head	Tense Mark	Exchange Mark
		stem	suffix	suffix

'(I) had breakfast.'

(12) respect:equals

아침을 먹었소.		
achim	=*eul*	*meog-eot-**so***
breakfast		eat-past-**declarative;deferential:respect:equal**
		Negotiator
		verbal group
		Event
		verb

		Head	Tense Mark	Exchange Mark
		stem	suffix	suffix

'(I) had breakfast.'

3.2 FORMAL MOOD and ADDRESSEE DEFERENCE

(13) respect:juniors

아침을 먹었다네.		
achim	=*eul*	*meog-eot-**dane***
breakfast		eat-past-**declarative;deferential:respect:juniors**
		Negotiator
		verbal group
		Event
		verb
		Head	Tense Mark	Exchange Mark
		stem	suffix	suffix
'(I) had breakfast.'		

In (12) and (13) the deferential speaker who chooses the [equals] and the [juniors] levels of respect would tend to be an elderly man. Younger people and female speakers do not normally choose these levels, which are in effect dying out; see for example Kwon (2012: 318) and Lee I. and Chae W. (1999: 354–9) for discussion. The typical target of the [equals] level respect would be someone who is similar in age and position to the speaker, and the typical target of the [juniors] level respect would be someone who is an adult and is younger than, and junior to, the speaker.

Deference level distinctions are also available for interrogative and imperative clauses. The relevant morphological distinctions are presented in Table 3.5.[9]

In summary, the FORMAL MOOD and the ADDRESSEE DEFERENCE options are available only in clauses with the feature [formal] in Korean, as formalised in Figure 3.4. Once the feature [formal] is chosen, the culminating suffix that is appropriate in terms of FORMAL MOOD and ADDRESSEE DEFERENCE must be deployed. Note that in the system network, one portmanteau realisation statement is given as an example (so as not to make the network unnecessarily complicated). There, the notation '+Exchange Mark' after the 'down-right arrow' indicates the

---

[9] Suffixes given in pairs and separated by a slash (/) in Table 3.5 are morphophonemically conditioned variants. Except for the pair 아라/어라 -*ara*/*eora* in non-deferential imperative (jussives), the first member of each pair occurs after a consonant and the second after a vowel. In case of the 아라/어라 -*ara*/*eora* pair, the first one is chosen when the vowel of the last syllable of the stem is either 아 *a* or 오 *o*; elsewhere the second is selected.
Note also that the resources for deferential [venerate] and [respect:equals] imperative (cohortatives) appear to be collapsing as well as shifting in modern Korean usage. For example, while avoided in deferential [venerate] imperatives (cohortatives), the pair 으십시다/십시다 -*eusipsida*/*sipsida* is regularly used to register [respect:equals] level deference.

120   The Grammar of Interpersonal Meaning: MOOD

Table 3.5 FORMAL MOOD; ADDRESSEE DEFERENCE suffixes

	declarative	interrogative	imperative (jussive)	imperative (cohortative)
deferential: venerate	습니다/ㅂ니다 -seumnida/ mnida	습니까/ㅂ니까 -seumnikka/ mnikka	으십시오/십시오 -eusipsio/ sipsio	으십시다/십시다 읍시다/ㅂ시다 -eusipsida/ sipsida -eupsida/psida
deferential: respect: equals	으오/오, 소 -euo/o, -so	으오/오, 소 -euo/o, -so	으시오/시오, 으소/소 -eusio/sio, -euso/so	
deferential: respect: juniors	으네/네, 다네 -eune/ne, -dane	나 -na	게 -ge	세 -se
dominant	다 -da	니, 냐 -ni, -nya	아라/어라 -ara/eora	자 -ja

word rank function through which features are realised. This is another (more traditional) way of providing realisation statements in SFL. The combination of [declarative] and [venerate] is realised through what we term an Exchange Mark function, which is realised in turn through a suffix indicating declarative mood and venerate addressee deference. A list of the relevant suffixes was presented in Table 3.5.

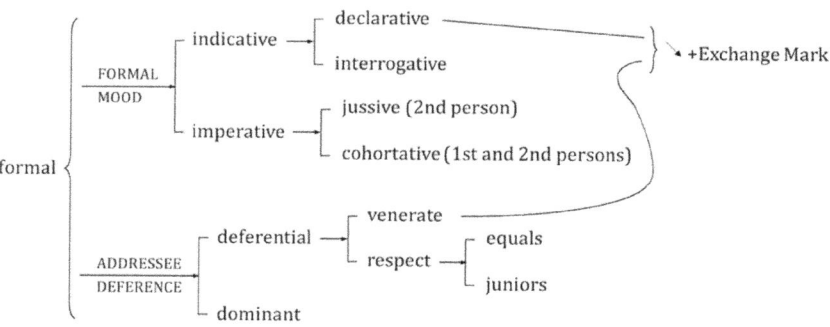

Figure 3.4 More delicate formal systems

3.3   Informal Systems: INFORMAL MOOD, STANCE and POLITENESS

Informal clauses in Korean involve different resources to formal ones. For one thing, moods are not distinguished by suffixes, as was the case with [formal] clauses. For another, the speaker's status relationship with the addressee is not finely tuned; and whether to mark social distance or not is a choice speakers can make. What informal clauses do offer is a rich set of resources for establishing the grounds on which speaker and addressee can align around a

3.3 INFORMAL MOOD, STANCE and POLITENESS

proposition or a proposal. The three key informal systems are INFORMAL MOOD, STANCE and POLITENESS.

3.3.1 The System of INFORMAL MOOD

In informal clauses, moods are distinguished not by suffixes but by intonation, adjacent moves in dialogue, co-text, constraints such as unavailability of TENSE MARKING and MODALITY in imperative clauses, and/or punctuation marks in written language. We will refer to the mood system for informal clauses as INFORMAL MOOD (Figure 3.5); its realisation statements are given in Table 3.6. In the statements, the doubled plus symbols, '++', indicate inter-stratal realisations (i.e., between grammar and phonology for spoken language, or grammar and graphology in case of written sentences).

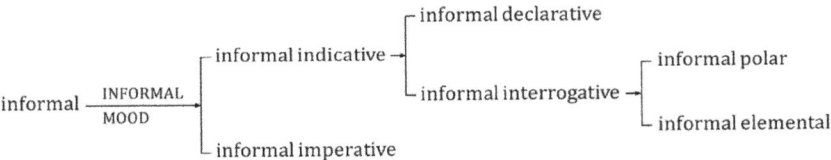

Figure 3.5 The system of INFORMAL MOOD

Table 3.6 *The system of INFORMAL MOOD*: realisation statements – only for [pronounce] clauses

informal	+Stance Mark ^ #
informal declarative	Stance Mark: culminating suffix: 아/어 -*a/eo*; ++Intonation(falling); '.'
informal polar	Stance Mark: culminating suffix: 아/어 -*a/eo*; ++Intonation(rising); '?'
informal elemental	Stance Mark: culminating suffix: 아/어 -*a/eo*; +Inquirer; ++Intonation(falling); '?'
informal imperative	Stance Mark: culminating suffix: 아/어 -*a/eo*; ++Intonation(rising/falling); '.'

Consider (14)–(16), which demonstrate that in informal speech the verbal morphology does not play a part in distinguishing one mood from another. As can be seen, the same suffix 아/어 -*a/eo*, highlighted in bold, is used in a statement, in a question and in a command – with INFORMAL MOOD choices distinguished by means of phonological, discourse semantic and contextual factors. The suffix 어 -*eo* is a Stance Mark in these clauses. Based on the punctuation mark employed, '.', and falling intonation, we recognise (14) as a declarative clause – informal declarative. Likewise, we recognise (15) as an informal interrogative clause, based on the punctuation mark there, '?', and rising intonation. Example (16) is an informal imperative clause based on the punctuation mark employed, '.', and rising/falling intonation. In the data we studied there does not seem to be clear evidence of two informal imperatives subtypes, comparable to formal [jussive] and [cohortative].[10]

(14)   with falling intonation

아침 먹어.	
achim	*meog-eo*
breakfast	eat-**informal declarative**
	Negotiator
	verbal group
	Event
	verb
	Head / Stance Mark
	stem / suffix
'(I) am having breakfast.'	

(15)   with rising intonation

아침 먹어?	
achim	*meog-eo*
breakfast	eat-**informal interrogative**
	Negotiator
	verbal group
	Event
	verb
	Head / Stance Mark
	stem / suffix
'Are (you) having breakfast?'	

---

[10] If the distinction needs to be made, speakers may include the first person plural pronoun 우리 *uri* 'we' to make the clause [cohortative]. Thus, we have the contrast 우리 아침 먹어 **uri** *achim meog-eo* 'Let's eat breakfast (literally, we … eat breakfast)' vs 아침 먹어 *achim meog-eo* 'Eat breakfast'. Alternatively they can simply deploy a formal clause: 아침 먹자 *achim meok-ja* 'Let's eat breakfast'.

3.3 INFORMAL MOOD, STANCE and POLITENESS

(16)   with rising/falling intonation

아침 먹어.		
achim	*meog-eo*	
breakfast	eat-**informal imperative**	
	Negotiator	
	verbal group	
	Event	
	verb	
	Head	Stance Mark
	stem	suffix
'Have breakfast.'		

The choice between [polar] and [elemental] questions is available in [informal] clauses, as (17) and (18) illustrate.

(17)

아침 먹었어?			
achim	*meog-eoss-eo*		
breakfast	eat-past-**informal interrogative**		
	Negotiator		
	verbal group		
	Event		
	verb		
	Head	Tense Mark	Stance Mark
	stem	suffix	suffix
'Did (you) have breakfast?'			

(18)

아침 언제 먹었어?		
achim	***eonje***	*meog-eoss-**eo***
breakfast	**when**	eat-past-**informal interrogative**
	Inquirer	Negotiator
	adverbial group	verbal group
		Event
		verb
		Head / Tense Mark / Stance Mark
		stem / suffix / suffix
'When did (you) have breakfast?'		

3.3.2 The System of STANCE

Like the system of INFORMAL MOOD, the STANCE system is a defining characteristic of the [informal] clause; it is realised through the Stance Mark function at word rank. The Stance Mark is realised in the very last element of the verbal group structure; it is realised through various culminative verbal suffixes. The Stance Mark function is to an informal clause what the Exchange Mark is to a formal clause.

The options in the system of STANCE represent grammatical resources Korean speakers draw on to enhance the negotiation of propositions and proposals in dialogic interaction. In particular, they are resources for solidarity-oriented language use, establishing grounds for agreeing about a proposition and thus contracting the negotiability of a proposition (i.e., reducing the space for alternative opinions). In Martin and White's terms (2005: 102–17), what is at stake here are heteroglossic engagement resources for contracting the play of voices around an exchange of meaning by enhancing the grounds for accepting the proposition.

Figure 3.6 presents the STANCE system and Table 3.7 the suffixes that realise the options in the system we propose.

The features [settled] and [settling] capture the sense that the clause realises a move in which a proposition or a proposal may be presented as 'case closed' as opposed to 'case open'.

We consider [settled] propositions first. The feature [settled] indicates 'I now see and accept', and is realised through the culminating suffixes 구나 *-guna* and 군 *-gun*. Note that 군 *-gun* is a shortened form of 구나 *-guna* (cf. Heo (1995: 629)); and only 군 *-gun* can be used with the particle 요 *yo* by a deferential speaker in informal speech (see Section 3.3.3).

3.3 INFORMAL MOOD, STANCE and POLITENESS

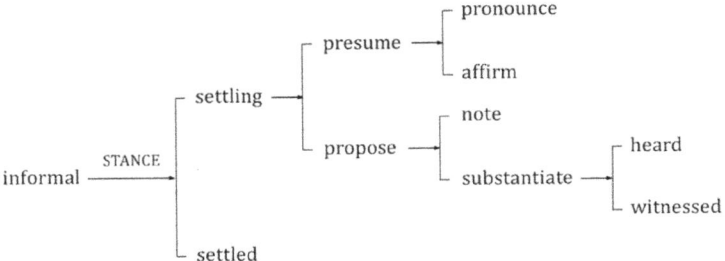

Figure 3.6 The system of STANCE

Table 3.7 *The system of STANCE*: realisation statements

informal	+Stance Mark ^ #
pronounce	Stance Mark: culminating suffix: 아/어 -a/eo[11]
affirm	Stance Mark: culminating suffix: 지 -ji
note	Stance Mark: culminating suffix: 네 -ne
heard	Stance Mark: culminating suffix: 대/내/래/재 -dae/nyae/rae/jae
witnessed	Stance Mark: culminating suffix: 더라구 -deoragu, 던가 -deonga
settled	Stance Mark: culminating suffix: 군 -gun, 구나 -guna, (으)ㄹ게 -(eu)lge

The suffixes 군 -gun and 구나 -guna indicate that the proposition is something that the speaker comes to believe at the moment of speaking. The factors contributing to his/her realisation do not have to be present in the speech situation; they may have arisen in another context but have only just precipitated a moment of awareness (cf. Lee K. 1993, Sohn 1999, Strauss 2005). Critically, these suffixes confirm that there is no room for alternative propositions.

For example, (19) and (20) include different Stance Mark suffixes – [settling] and [settled] respectively. The idea in (19) can be challenged with an opposing idea, e.g., 틀려 *tteuli-eo* 'wrong', because it is presented with a

---

[11] Many grammar books in Korea customarily identify the suffix, 여 -yeo, as additional 'intimate sentence-ender' – a [pronounce] suffix in our grammar. Similar to what was mentioned in footnote 6, this is an archaic suffix and chosen when the verb stem is 하 *ha-* 'do' or ends in 하 -*ha-* 'do'. In contemporary Korean, the verb 하 *ha-* in pronounce stance conjugates 해 *hae*, with fusion of sounds at the boundaries between the stem and the pronounce suffix. Once again, as this happens only when the verb stem is 하 *ha-* or ends in 하 -*ha-*, we do not include the suffix 여 -*yeo* in Table 3.7.

settling suffix 어 *-eo* in (19). The same idea in (20) would be unlikely to be challenged as the 구나 *-guna* suffix indicates that the 'case is closed.'

(19)

맞어	
maj-a	
right	
Negotiator	
verbal group	
Event	
verbalised adjective	
Head	Stance Mark
stem	pronounce suffix
'(It is) right.'	

(20)

맞구나	
mat-guna	
right	
Negotiator	
verbal group	
Event	
verbalised adjective	
Head	Stance Mark
stem	settled suffix
'(It is) right.'	

Now, consider (21). The suffix (으)ㄹ게 *-(eu)lge* indicates two things. First, what is given is a proposal (i.e., concerned with exchanging goods-&-services), not a proposition (i.e., concerned with exchanging information); and second, the proposal is something that the speaker has decided to undertake, instigated by the addressee (and perhaps others too), and is now marked as [settled]. The proposal is presented as 'case closed' in the sense that the speaker now agrees to actualise it, implying that there is no room for alternatives.

3.3 INFORMAL MOOD, STANCE and POLITENESS

(21)

나 그만둘게.		
na	geumandu-**lge**	
I	quit	
	Negotiator	
	verbal group	
	Event	
	verb	
	Head	Stance Mark
	stem	settled suffix
'OK, I'll quit.'		

The usage of the suffix (으)ㄹ게 -(eu)lge is restricted grammatically; this is related to the fact that what is being negotiated is a proposal, not a proposition. In comparison with 구나/군 -guna/-gun, (으)ㄹ게 -(eu)lge has a person constraint – namely that the person who actualises the goods-&-services transaction is always first person (the speaker). It also has a tense constraint – namely that it cannot be used with a Tense Mark. If (으)ㄹ게 -(eu)lge was used in moves conveying information (in propositions), these constraints would not be present.

As Stance Marks with the feature [settled], (으)ㄹ게 -(eu)lge and 군 -gun share important properties. They both can be used with the Politeness Marker 요 yo by a deferential speaker (see Section 3.3.3); and neither can be used in a question nor in a command, and hence they realise only [informal declarative].

Turning to [settling] clauses, where grounds for agreement remain open, there are two possibilities – [presume] and [propose]. We deal first with the feature [propose], which is available only for propositions, and which covers realisations widely discussed in the literature concerned with evidentiality (Aikenvald 2004, Aikenvald and Dixon 2003, Chafe and Nichols 1986). In Korean, there are three sub-categories that need to be recognised: [note], [witnessed] and [heard].

The feature [note] is realised by the culminating suffix 네 -ne, which indicates that the proposition is based on what the speaker has grasped through observation and/or inference in the speech situation. Consider (22). Here, the speaker and the hearer, both young female professionals, are talking about their male colleague's recent engagement. He met his fiancée in China; they had been there for a few months for some job training. Upon hearing that they were both sent to China by the company, the speaker utters (22). We gloss the meaning of -ne in examples of this kind as 'I note'.

(22)

와, 좋네!	
wa	jon-**ne**
wow	good
	Negotiator
	verbal group
	Event
	verbalised adjective
	Head / Stance Mark
	stem / note suffix
'Wow, that's good!'	

The clause ending with -*ne* must be an [informal declarative] clause; one cannot formulate a question using the suffix 네 -*ne*. This stance is less contracted than that realised by 구나/군 -*guna/gun* (realising [settled] clauses); it leaves some room for speakers to further negotiate the proposition.

Whereas realisations of the feature [note] ground the proposition in observations and inferences based on the current speech situation, the feature [substantiate] allows for evidence drawn from previous situations. In Korean the grounds can be [witnessed] or [heard].

The basic means to realise the feature [witnessed] is the non-culminating suffix 더 -*deo*, which some Korean grammarians have regarded as a Tense Mark, marking the 'retrospective' tense (see Heo 1995: 1181 for instance). The non-culminating suffix is mainly found in frozen constructions; but one construction 더라구 -*deoragu* is used as a culminating suffix and only used in [informal declarative] clauses. The meaning of this suffix is something like 'I witnessed'. Through this suffix the speaker indicates that the information s/he gives is based on what s/he saw (in the past) with his/her own eyes. Consider (23), spoken as the speaker talks about a gathering he attended recently, and where he saw many people in attendance.

(23)

사람이 많이 왔더라구.					
saram	=*i*	*mani*	*w-at-**deoragu***		
person		many(adv)	came		
			Negotiator		
			verbal group		
			Event		
			verb		
			Head	Tense Mark	Stance Mark
			stem	suffix	witnessed suffix
'I saw many people came.'					

3.3 INFORMAL MOOD, STANCE and POLITENESS

Another means to realise the [witnessed] is the culminative suffix 던가 -*deonga*, as illustrated in (24). This suffix is used in [informal interrogative] clauses.

(24)

사람이 많이 왔던가?					
saram	=*i*	*mani*	*w-at-**deonga***		
person		many(adv)	came		
			Negotiator		
			verbal group		
			Event		
			verb		
			Head	Tense Mark	Stance Mark
			stem	suffix	witnessed suffix
'Did many people come, did you see?'					

The feature [heard] is realised through the suffixes such as 대/내/래/재 - *dae/nyae/rae/jae* (glossed as 'heard them saying'/'asking'/'telling'/ 'suggesting'). Consider (25), where the proposition is substantiated as [heard] evidence.

(25)

사람이 많이 왔대.					
saram	=*i*	*mani*	*w-at-**dae***		
person		many(adv)	came		
			Negotiator		
			verbal group		
			Event		
			verb		
			Head	Tense Mark	Stance Mark
			stem	suffix	heard suffix
'I heard many people came.'					

As with [witnessed] clauses, a question can be asked in relation to [heard] evidence as shown in (26).

(26)

사람이 많이 왔대?					
saram	=*i*	*mani*	w-at-**dae**		
person		many(adv)	came		
			Negotiator		
			verbal group		
			Event		
			verb		
			Head	Tense Mark	Stance Mark
			stem	suffix	heard suffix
'Many people came, did you hear?'					

Clauses culminating with these [heard] Stance Marks can be usefully contrasted with semantically comparable projecting clause complexes (Chapter 6) such as (27).

(27)

수애가 사람이 많이 왔다고 ...							
Suae	=*ga*	*saram*	=*i*	*mani*	w-at-da-go		
Suae		person		many(adv)	came		
		<<			Negotiator >>		
					verbal group		
					Event		
					verb		
					Head	Tense Mark	Projected Mood Mark	Link
					stem	suffix	suffix	suffix
'Suae ... that many people came.'							

3.3 INFORMAL MOOD, STANCE and POLITENESS

... 했어.		
ha-ess-eo		
said		
Negotiator		
verbal group		
Event		
verb		
Head	Tense Mark	Stance Mark
stem	suffix	pronounce suffix
... said ...		

In (27) the proposition, 사람이 많이 왔다고 *saram i mani w-at-da-go* 'many people came', represents the linguistic content projected by someone called Suae. But in (26) the proposition, 사람이 많이 왔대 *saram i mani w-at-dae* 'many people came', is presented as [heard] evidence – thereby contracting its negotiability in dialogic interaction (i.e., the addressee has a reduced space for alternative opinions, and thus is now pushed closer to agreement).

The alternative to negotiating a proposition on the basis of evidence, either derived from the current speech context (i.e., [note]) or substantiated as previously seen or heard, is [presume].

Notice that while the feature [propose], which opens choices for evidentiality, is not available for proposals, the feature [presume] is. The feature [presume] is selected to indicate that the speaker has grounds for telling the audience to accept the proposal, which involves assumptions about whether the listener is likely to accept or reject.

Where agreement is expected (the feature [affirm]), speakers deploy the culminating suffix 지 *-ji*. In (28), for example, two university students, one female and one male, are conversing with each other. The speaker is explaining an incident that she and her friend called 수애 *Suae*, experienced recently. The speaker thinks that the hearer knows Suae, since they (i.e., Suae, the hearer and the speaker) had lunch together a short time previously. At this particular point in time, noticing that the hearer looks somewhat puzzled, the speaker utters (28) with a rising-falling intonation. She presents, through the suffix 지 *-ji*, the proposition as a kind of 'presumed agreement'; she thinks the hearer will agree with what she says.

(28)

수애 알지?	
Suae	al-ji
Suae	know
	Negotiator
	verbal group
	Event
	verb
	Head — Stance Mark
	stem — affirm suffix
'You know Suae, right?'	

In (29), the speaker affirms his knowledge of the person, Suae; this is an example for an affirmed agreement. The speaker utters (29) with a falling intonation.

(29)

수애 알지.	
Suae	al-ji
Suae	know
	Negotiator
	verbal group
	Event
	verb
	Head — Stance Mark
	stem — affirm suffix
'I do know Suae.'	

When agreement is not expected, the feature [pronounce] is chosen and realised through the suffix 아/어 -a/eo. This suffix is the most common culminating suffix on verbs or verbalised adjectives in informal speech in Korean. Lee K. (1993: 12–15) suggests that the suffix 아/어 -a/eo is used in statements when 'the speaker assumes that the addressee is not accepting what the speaker says and the speaker finds it necessary to emphasise what he says', and in questions when 'the speaker heard something that he cannot accept readily, so he wants to confirm what he has heard'. So, for statements, the suffix can be glossed as 'I need to emphasise ...', and for questions as 'I need to confirm ...'. The feature [pronounce] is intended to

3.3 INFORMAL MOOD, STANCE and POLITENESS

capture the subtle 'emphasis' conveyed by the suffix 아/어 -*a/eo*.[12] Examples (30) and (31) enact this type of STANCE.

(30)

좋아.	
jo-a	
good	
Negotiator	
verbal group	
Event	
verb	
Head	Stance Mark
stem	pronounce suffix
'It's good for sure.'	

(31)

수애 알아?		
suae	*ar-a*	
personal name	know	
	Negotiator	
	verbal group	
	Event	
	verb	
	Head	Stance Mark
	stem	pronounce suffix
'Do you in fact know Suae?'		

Lee (1993: 12–15) further suggests that in commands the suffix 아/어 -*a/eo* is used when 'the addressee is ignoring or does not pay attention to what the speaker says and the speaker needs to emphasise his/her commands'. Consider (32). Selecting the feature [pronounce] in a proposal means that the addressee

---

[12] Lee Keedong (Lee 1993: 13) makes a further observation that Koreans tend to position a declarative clause (with a 다 -*da* suffix) before a pronounce clause (with a 아/어 -*a/eo* suffix) in order to juxtapose the two clauses for emphasis. For instance, 버스 온다 버스 와 *beoseu o-r-da beoseu w-a* 'bus is coming [formal declarative] bus is coming [informal declarative;pronounce]' is much more natural than the reverse sequence. The speaker first informs the hearer that the bus is coming with a [formal declarative] clause and then replays it for emphasis using an [informal declarative;pronounce] clause.

now has a reduced space for alternatives (e.g., refusal) in the sense that the speaker has addressed expected disagreement.

(32)

빨리 먹어!		
ppali	*meog-**eo***	
quickly	eat	
	Negotiator	
	verbal group	
	Event	
	verb	
	Head	Stance Mark
	stem	pronounce suffix
'Do eat quickly!'		

Before considering the system of POLITENESS, we summarise how the systems of INFORMAL MOOD and STANCE interact. In the system network shown in Figure 3.7, the superscript ᴵ (representing 'if') on the feature [note] and [settled] links it to the superscript ᵀ (representing 'then') on the feature [informal declarative]; this if/then convention (cf. Martin et al. 2013) ensures that a note clause and

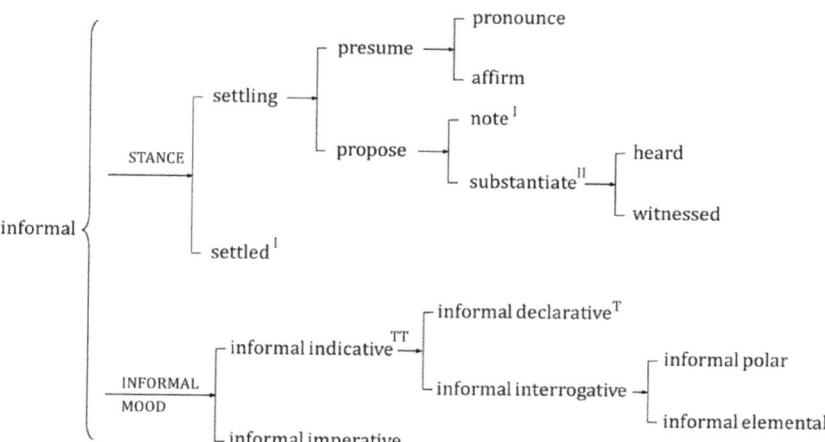

Figure 3.7 The systems of STANCE and INFORMAL MOOD

3.3 INFORMAL MOOD, STANCE and POLITENESS

also a settled clause are always declarative clauses. The superscript ^{II} on the feature [substantiate] links it to the superscript ^{TT} on [informal indicative]; this is to ensure that a substantiating clause cannot be imperative in Korean.

3.3.3 The System of POLITENESS

As mentioned above, the speaker's status relationship with the addressee is not finely tuned in informal clauses. Where necessary, social distance is simply marked through the particle 요 *yo*, which is a 'word' operating as part of clause structure.[13] We identify this as the POLITENESS system.

The informal mood POLITENESS system differs in three respects from the formal mood ADDRESSEE DEFERENCE one. It is realised by a particle at clause rank rather than by a suffix at word rank; it is optional rather than obligatory; and it can be realised more than once in a clause, reflecting the feature [prosodic *yo*]. Figure 3.8 outlines the system of POLITENESS we propose, followed by realisation statements in Table 3.8.

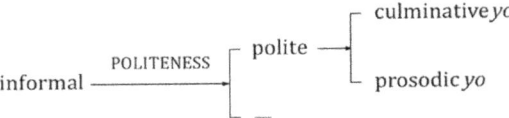

Figure 3.8 The system of POLITENESS

Table 3.8 *The system of POLITENESS*: realisation statements

informal	+Politeness Marker
culminative *yo*	Stance Mark ^ Politeness Marker ^ #
prosodic *yo*	+Politeness Marker^n, following non-culminative elements of clause structure preceding the Negotiator

An informal polite clause is illustrated in (33). In contrast with (30), we can see that the feature [polite] has been selected in (33). Without 요 *yo* the clause

---

[13] As mentioned in footnote 2, 요 *yo* is a particle operating at clause rank; it occurs with [informal] culminating suffixes and can be removed (together with the meaning [polite]) without affecting the suffixes themselves. For instance, looking at the pairs, 아/어요 -*aleo yo* and 아/어 -*aleo*, 네요 -*ne yo* and 네 -*ne*, and 지요 -*ji yo* and 지 -*ji*, etc., we can see that 요 *yo* can be easily removed. In addition, as shown in (39), 요 *yo* can occur at boundaries of nominal groups and co-verbal phrases, indicating that it is operating outside of verbal group structure and at a higher rank. Accordingly we treat 요 *yo* is part of the clause structure.

is not specified as far as politeness is concerned (but it is not necessarily heard as impolite or rude). It is in this sense that POLITENESS is optional.

(33)

좋아요.	
jo-a	*yo*
good	
Negotiator	Politeness Marker
verbal group	particle
Event	
verb	
Head	Stance Mark	
stem	pronounce suffix	
'It's good for sure.'	

Examples (34)–(37) show that the particle 요 *yo* can also be used with other Stance Marks, the presence of which is a hallmark of an informal clause. The non-polite counterparts of the examples are (22), (23), (25) and (28). Whether or not the particle 요 *yo* can be deployed is a critical recognition factor for an [informal] clause.

(34)

와, 좋네요!		
wa	*jon-**ne***	*yo*
wow	good	
	Negotiator	Politeness Marker
	verbal group	particle
	Event	
	verbalised adjective	
	Head	Stance Mark	
	stem	note suffix	
'Wow, that's good!'		

3.3 INFORMAL MOOD, STANCE and POLITENESS

(35)

사람이 많이 왔더라구요.				
saram	*=i*	*mani*	*w-at-**deoragu***	*yo*
person		many	came	Politeness Marker
			Negotiator	particle
			verbal group	
			Event	
			verb	
			Head	Tense Mark	Stance Mark	
			stem	suffix	witnessed suffix	
'I saw many people came.'				

(36)

사람이 많이 왔대요.				
saram	*=i*	*mani*	*w-at-**dae***	*yo*
person		many	came	Politeness Marker
			Negotiator	particle
			verbal group	
			Event	
			verb	
			Head	Tense Mark	Stance Mark	
			stem	suffix	heard suffix	
'I heard many people came.'				

(37)

수애 알지요?		
Suae	*al-**ji***	*yo*
personal name	know	Politeness Marker
	Negotiator	particle
	verbal group	
	Event	
	verb	
	Head	Stance Mark	
	stem	affirm suffix	
'You know Suae, right?'		

In our 'free translations' of (34)–(37) we have not attempted to capture the politeness meanings involved out of a concern that the wide variety of English resources that could be involved might be misleading as far as the Korean POLITENESS system is concerned.

Example (38) illustrates the typical culminative *yo* pattern, while (39) features prosodic 요 *yo*. Note that in the examples PM stands for Politeness Marker, TM for Tense Mark, and SM for Stance Mark; from this point in this chapter, we use abbreviations in the examples wherever space limitations make it necessary. The prosodic 요 *yo* pattern (with more than one occurrence of 요 *yo*) is highly colloquial, and most readily observable in interactions between young speakers and familiar respected adults. In general there is a noticeable pause (a silent beat in the rhythm) after occurrences of 요 *yo* following groups and phrases preceding the Negotiator.

(38)   [culminative *yo*]

어제 호텔에서 아침을 먹었어요.							
eoje	*hotel*	*=eseo*	*achim*	*=eul*	*meog-eoss-eo*		*yo*
yesterday	hotel	at	breakfast		ate		
					Negotiator		PM
					verbal group		ptcl
					Event		
					verb		
					Head	TM	SM	
					stem	sfx	pronounce sfx	
'(We) had breakfast at the hotel yesterday.'							

(39)   [prosodic *yo*]

어제요 ... 호텔에서요 ... 아침을 먹었어요.								
eoje	*yo*	*hotel*	*=eseo*	*yo*	*achim*	*=eul*	*meog-eoss-eo*	*yo*
yesterday		hotel	at		breakfast		ate	
	PM			PM			Negotiator	PM
	ptcl			ptcl			verbal group	ptcl
							Event	
							verb	
							Head	TM	SM	
							stem	sfx	pronounce sfx	
'(We) had breakfast... at the hotel... yesterday.'								

3.4 PARTICIPANT DEFERENCE   139

Figure 3.9 summarises the system of FORMALITY in Korean as discussed so far. The network shows that FORMAL MOOD and ADDRESSEE DEFERENCE are options for [formal] clauses. By contrast, INFORMAL MOOD, STANCE and the optional POLITENESS are available for [informal] clauses.

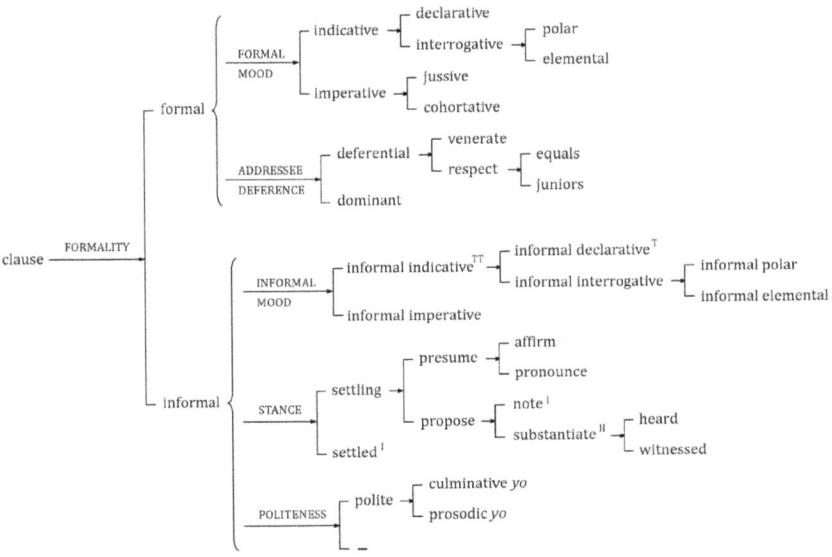

Figure 3.9 The system of FORMALITY (extended)

3.4   The System of PARTICIPANT DEFERENCE

We now consider PARTICIPANT DEFERENCE. As introduced among verbal group systems in Chapter 2, this is an optional system that allows Korean speakers to 'exalt' a person who is construed experientially as the main Participant (P1) in a clause (e.g., the Actor in an action clause, the Senser in a mental clause, the Sayer in a verbal clause, etc. – as detailed in Chapter 4). The system is realised in verbal groups at word rank through suffixation; and it can be reinforced in P1 nominal groups through the choice of an exalting clitic (which is why we extend the system introduced in Chapter 2 here).

PARTICIPANT DEFERENCE is grammaticalised through a Participant Deference Mark (PDM) realised by the non-culminating suffix (으)시 ‒(eu)si[14] and positioned before Tense Mark and Mood or Stance Mark in verb

---

[14] After a consonant 으시 -eusi is used, otherwise 시 -si is used.

structure (including verbal groups with verbalised adjectives). It can be optionally concomitantly realised through the choice of an exalting clitic 께서 *kkeseo* – an IFM that is used in place of the EFM 이/가 *i/ga* in the nominal group realising the honoured Participant.

The system of PARTICIPANT DEFERENCE we propose is displayed in Figure 3.10; realisations are specified in Table 3.9.

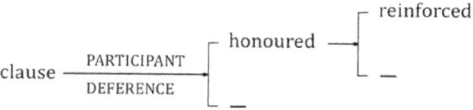

Figure 3.10 The system of PARTICIPANT DEFERENCE

Table 3.9 *The system of PARTICIPANT DEFERENCE*: realisation statements

honoured	+Participant Deference Mark (PDM); Head ⌐ PDM; PDM:(으)시 *-(eu)si*
reinforced	P1:nominal group:IFM: 께서 *kkeseo*

In (40) the main Participant is not honoured. By contrast, (41) and (42) illustrate Participant Deference resources – as P1, the main Participant, is explicitly honoured. In (42), deference to P1 is reinforced through the clitic 께서 *kkeseo*, which realises Interpersonal Function Marking (IFM).

(40)   Speaker is deferential to addressee, but not to P1

동생이 신문을 봅니다.					
dongsaeng	*=i*	*sinmun*	*=eul*	*bo-mnida*	
younger sibling		newspaper		read	
P1				Negotiator	
nominal group				verbal group	
Thing	EFM			Event	
noun	clitic			verb	
				Head	EM
				stem	venerate;declarative suffix
'(My) younger sibling is reading the newspaper.'					

3.4 PARTICIPANT DEFERENCE

(41)   Speaker is deferential to addressee and P1

아저씨가 신문을 보십니다.					
ajeossi	*=ga*	*sinmun*	*=eul*	*bo-si-mnida*	
uncle		newspaper		read	
P1				Negotiator	
nominal group				verbal group	
Thing	EFM			Event	
noun	clitic			verb	
				Head	PDM	EM
				stem	suffix	venerate; declarative suffix
'Uncle is reading the newspaper.'					

(42)   Speaker is deferential to addressee and to P1; deference to P1 reinforced

할아버지께서 신문을 보십니다.					
harabeoji	*=kkeseo*	*sinmun*	*=eul*	*bo-si-mnida*	
grandfather		newspaper		read	
P1				Negotiator	
nominal group				verbal group	
Thing	IFM			Event	
noun	clitic			verb	
				Head	PDM	EM
				stem	suffix	venerate; declarative suffix
'Grandfather is reading the newspaper.'					

As noted above (see Table 3.5), the culminative suffix of a [venerate; jussive] clause is 으십시오/십시오 *-eusipsio/sipsio*. Note that when an honoured P1 is identical with the addressee we cannot add the suffix 시 *-si* (the realisation of PDM); 시 *-si* is in effect part of the culminative suffix (realising Exchange Mark). Figure 3.17 at the end of this chapter shows how the system can be wired to block clauses with the combined features [venerate;jussive].

Nonetheless, PARTICIPANT DEFERENCE is relevant in other imperative clauses – informal imperatives such as (43a) and (43b) as well as formal imperatives such as (43c) and (43d). For example, all the clauses in (43) are leave-taking expressions, and convey varying nuances of deference/politeness due to differing interactions between PARTICIPANT DEFERENCE and FORMALITY.

(43)
a.

그래, 가요.		
geurae	*ga*	*yo*
well then	go-SM:pronounce	Politeness Marker
'Well then, (you) go safely.'		

b.

그래, 가셔.	
geurae	*ga-sy-eo*
well then	go-PDM-SM:pronounce
'Well then, (you) go safely.'	

c.

잘 가시게.	
jal	*ga-si-ge*
well	go-PDM-EM:formal imperative;respect:juniors
'(You) go safely.'	

d.

잘 가게.	
jal	*ga-ge*
well	go-EM:formal imperative;respect:juniors
'(You) go safely.'	

Before closing this section, note that Korean speakers can also express deference to a respected person who is not a P1 – in particular a respected person whom one meets (realised as a P2) or a respected person to whom one gives something (realised as a P3). This type of deference is realised lexically, not grammatically, through the choice of an appropriate verb. For instance, where the P2 is a respected person, the verb 뵙 *boep-* 'to meet (a respected person)' is used instead of 보 *bo-* 'to meet'. Where the P3 (e.g., a Recipient) is a respected person, the verb 드리 *deuri-* 'to give (to a respected person)' is used instead of 주 *ju-* 'to give'. PARTICIPANT DEFERENCE in Korean has been widely discussed in the literature, and often termed 'subject honorification'. The reader is referred to Sohn (1999: 414–17) and the references cited therein.

Note also that the PARTICIPANT DEFERENCE system and the lexical resources for honouring other Participants play a role in tracking the identity of respected persons in discourse. Korean speakers regularly elide honoured Participants, whose identity is implicated by grammatical or lexical realisations of deference in deferential verbal groups.

3.5 The System of POLARITY

Polarity comprises resources for assessing the validity of a proposition (it is vs it isn't) or the actualisation of a proposal (do vs don't!) (Matthiessen et al. 2010: 161). POLARITY in Korean is realised through verbal group structure. As with many languages, it is only negative polarity that involves marking; positive polarity involves 'zero-marking' – by default a proposition or proposal carries positive 'value'. POLARITY is sensitive to MOOD in Korean. As shown below, the marking strategy for negative polarity in an imperative clause differs from that in an indicative clause.

With indicative clauses, POLARITY in Korean is realised in two different ways. In one, negative polarity involves a Negate function – positioned immediately before the Event in verbal groups and realised by a negative adverb 안 *an* 'not' or 못 *mot* 'cannot'. In the other, it involves a Negating function – positioned after Event and realised through an auxiliary verb, 않다 *an-ta* 'not' or 못하다 *mota-da* 'cannot'; in this case the main verb culminates with the linking suffix 지 *-ji*. Examples (44)–(47) illustrate the alternative realisations of negative polarity in indicative clauses.

In (44) and (45), an indicative clause involving the proposition 'the bus goes' is negated through an adverb 안 *an* 'not' positioned before the verb that it modifies. By contrast, in (46) and (47) the clause is negated by adding an auxiliary verb 않 *an-* 'do not'; in these cases the main verb culminates with the linking suffix 지 *-ji*.[15]

(44)

버스가 안 갑니다.			
beoseu	*=ga*	*an*	*ga-mnida*
bus		not	go
		Negotiator	
		verbal group	
		Negate	Event
		adverb	verb
			Head	Exchange Mark
			stem	deferential;declarative suffix
'The bus is not operating.'[16]			

---

[15] The difference between the negative adverb 안 *an* 'not' and the negative auxiliary verb 않 *an-* 'do not' is not immediately clear because of the Romanisation system we use; but the difference is clear in Hangeul. Unlike the adverb, the auxiliary verb ends in ㅎ /h/, which is silent in syllable-final position. Also, unlike the negative adverb 안 *an* 'not', the Romanisation of the negative auxiliary verb 않 *an-* 'do not' has a hyphen, '-', which indicates that it is a conjugatable category.

[16] When P1 is a human and 안 *an* 'not' (adverb) is used, an ambiguity arises; depending on co-text and context, 안 *an* 'not' can signal either 'simple' negation or negative inclination. So clauses like (44) may mean either 'doesn't' or 'won't' with a human P1.

(45)

버스가 안 갑니까?			
beoseu	=ga	**an**	ga-mnikka
bus		**not**	go
		Negotiator	
		verbal group	
		Negate	Event
		adverb	verb
			Head	Exchange Mark
			stem	deferential;interrogative suffix
'Isn't the bus operating?'			

(46)

버스가 가지 않습니다.			
beoseu	=ga	ga-*ji*	**an**-seumnida
bus		go	**do not**
		Negotiator	
		verbal group	
		Event	Negating
		verb	auxiliary verb
		Head	Link	Head	Exchange Mark
		stem	suffix	stem	deferential;declarative suffix
'The bus isn't operating.'			

(47)

버스가 가지 않습니까?			
beoseu	=ga	ga-*ji*	**an**-seumnikka
bus		go	**do not**
		Negotiator	
		verbal group	
		Event	Negating
		verb	auxiliary verb
		Head	Link	Head	Exchange Mark
		stem	suffix	stem	deferential;interrogative suffix
'Isn't the bus operating?'			

3.5 The System of POLARITY

Korean has a negative adverb and a negative auxiliary verb used specifically for realising 'incapability of doing something' – 못 *mot* 'cannot' (adverb) and 못하 *mota-* 'cannot' (auxiliary verb), respectively. Examples (48) and (49) illustrate how 'cannot go' can be expressed in two different ways – with (48) involving the Negate function and (49) the Negating function (in which case the main verb culminates with the linking suffix 지 *-ji*).

(48)

버스가 못 갑니다.			
beoseu	*=ga*	*mot*	*ga-mnida*
bus		**cannot**	go
		Negotiator	
		verbal group	
		Negate	Event
		adverb	verb
			Head	EM
			stem	def;decl suffix
'The bus can't run.'			

(49)

버스가 가지 못합니다.					
beoseu	*=ga*	*ga-ji*		*mota-mnida*	
bus		go		**cannot do**	
		Negotiator			
		verbal group			
		Event		Negating	
		verb		auxiliary verb	
		Head	Link	Head	EM
		stem	suffix	stem	def;decl suffix
'The bus can't run.'					

Since the adverb 못 *mot* and the auxiliary verb 못하다 *mota-da* refer to the 'incapability of doing something', they cannot be used with verbalised adjectives in Korean (as this clause type does not construe activity).

Unlike indicative clauses, imperative clauses can only be negated by adding the auxiliary verb 말 *mal-*[17] 'don't do ...' to the main verb (the main verb

---

[17] Note that the auxiliary verb 말 *mal-* is irregular in the sense that the stem final consonant 'l' frequently drops when suffixed.

culminates with the linking suffix 지 -*ji*, as with other negative auxiliary verbs). Thus while employing an adverb and attaching an auxiliary verb are both possibilities for declarative and interrogative clauses – as in (44) and (45) as well as (46) and (47) – using a negative adverb is not available as an option for imperatives. Example (50) illustrates a negative imperative [venerate] clause, and (51) is its [dominant] variant.

(50)

가지 마십시오.	
ga-ji	*ma-sipsio*
go	**don't**
Negotiator	
verbal group	
Event	Negating
verb	auxiliary verb
Head	Link	Head	EM
stem	suffix	stem	def;jus suffix
'Don't go.'	

(51)

가지 마라.	
ga-ji	*ma-ra*
go	**don't**
Negotiator	
verbal group	
Event	Negating
verb	auxiliary verb
Head	Link	Head	EM
stem	suffix	stem	dom;jus suffix
'Don't go.'	

In closing, note that negation can also be realised through lexical verbs in Korean, as illustrated in (52) and (53). These lexical verbs incorporate negative meaning – e.g., 없 *eop-* 'there be not' as opposed to 있 *it-* 'there be' as in (52). Further examples include 아니 *ani-* 'be not' as opposed to 이 *i-* 'be' as in (53), and 모르 *moreu-* 'not know' as opposed to 알 *al-* 'know'.

3.5 The System of POLARITY

(52)

스키장에 사람이 없습니다.				
skijang	=*e*	*saram*	=*i*	***eop*-*seumnida***
ski resort	at	person		**there is not**
				Negotiator
				verbal group
				Event
				negative verb
				Head	EM
				stem	ven;decl suffix
'There's no one at the ski resort.'				

(53)

여기는 스키장이 아닙니다.				
yeogi	=*neun*	*skijang*	=*i*	***ani*-*mnida***
here		ski resort		**is not**
				Negotiator
				verbal group
				Event
				negative copula
				Head	EM
				stem	ven;decl suffix
'This (place) is not a ski resort.'				

The POLARITY system we propose is presented in Figure 3.11; its realisation statements are given in Table 3.10.

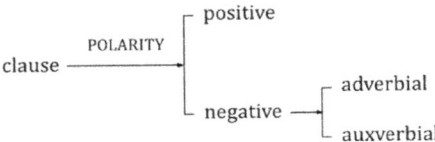

Figure 3.11 The system of POLARITY

Table 3.10 *The system of* POLARITY: *realisation statements*

positive	–
negative:adverbial	+Negate; Negate ⌢ Event; only for [indicative]
negative:auxverbial	+Negating; Event ⌢ Negating; Negating:aux verb 지 말- *-ji mal-* if [imperative]; Negating:aux verb 지 않- *-ji an-* if [indicative]

3.6 The System of MODALITY

In SFL, MODALITY refers to the area of meaning that lies between 'is' and 'isn't', or between 'do' and 'don't' (following Halliday and Matthiessen 2014: 691). For information exchanges, that is, with propositions, MODALITY involves degrees of probability (e.g., 그럴 수 있다 *geureo-l su it-da* 'maybe is') or usuality (e.g., 그럴 때 있다 *geureo-l ttae it-da* 'sometimes is'),[18] which we term modalisation. For goods-&-services exchanges, that is, with proposals, it involves degrees of obligation (e.g., 해야 한다 *ha-eya ha-n-da* 'required to do') or inclination (e.g., 하려 한다 *ha-ryeo ha-n-da* 'inclined to do'),[19] which we term modulation.

Choices for POLARITY and MODALITY are motivated by discourse considerations. From a dialogic perspective, [negative] means to act to challenge, fend off or restrict the scope of alternative positions, and thus it is dialogically contractive (Martin and White 2005: 102-104; 118-120). By contrast, MODALITY can be seen as making space for alternative propositions or proposals as dialogue unfolds – a discourse function Martin and White (2005: 102–17) characterise as dialogic expansion.

MODALITY is an optional system, and once selected, it is realised across ranks in Korean. As discussed in Chapter 2, MODALITY is predominantly realised at group rank through Modal, a verbal group function. This Modal function is realised by word complexes (generally for modalisation, i.e., probability and usuality) or auxiliary verbs (only for modulation, i.e., obligation and inclination).

However, MODALITY is also realised at clause and word rank in Korean. We term the clause rank function Modal Adjunct, and the word rank function Modal Mark. Modal Adjuncts are realised by adverbial groups, and their main

---

[18] See Table 3.13; some realisations of modalisation are provided there with varying degrees of probability and usuality.
[19] See Table 3.14; some realisations of modulation are presented there with differing degrees of obligation and inclination.

3.6 The System of MODALITY

function is to 'intensify' the modality expressed in other parts in the clause. An exception to this is [usuality], where the Modal Adjunct can be the sole means to express the modality (see below). Modal Marks are realised by non-culminating suffixes (only for [probability] and [inclination] as discussed below). The system of MODALITY is presented in Figure 3.12; its realisation statements are presented in Table 3.11.

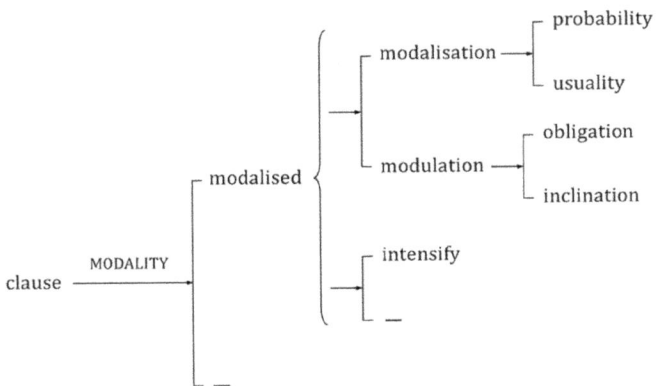

Figure 3.12 The system of MODALITY

Table 3.11 *Realisation statements for the system of* MODALITY

modalised	+Modal; Event ⌐ Modal (in verbal group structure) +Modal Mark if suffixal; Head ⌐ Modal Mark (in verb structure)
modalisation	Modal:word complex; Modal Mark:non-culminative suffix
modulation	Modal:aux verb; Modal Mark:non-culminative suffix (when P1 is the speaker in [declarative] or P1 is the hearer in [interrogative])
intensify	+Modal Adjunct; Modal Adjunct ⌐ Negotiator; Modal Adjunct realised by an adverb expressing a lower degree of usuality occurs in [negative] clauses

Note that not all feature combinations are possible. In addition, Modals realised by word complexes can be reinforced by an 'enclosed' IFM clitic – e.g., ㅌ do 'even' (see below). We outline these 'adjustments' in Table 3.12, instead of making our system network above complex; and we discuss possibilities and limitations in detail in the following sections.

In Table 3.12 '–' blocks impossible realisations (for instance, Modal in [probability] clauses cannot be realised by an auxiliary verb). Note also that the final column indicates how the modality functions are realised in clauses with differing features. For instance, in [probability] clauses, modalisation can be realised by a Modal function at group rank or a Modal Mark at word rank (in either case modalisation can be optionally realised by a Modal Adjunct at clause rank). In Table 3.12, the <...> notation indicates an enclosed clitic (in a word complex realising a Modal function).

Table 3.12 *Constraints on the realisation of* MODALITY

	clause rank	group rank		word rank	
	Modal Adjunct	Modal		Modal Mark	possible structures
probability	adverb	–	word complex	suffix	(Mod Adj) ⌒ Modal; or (Mod Adj) ⌒ Modal Mark; or (Mod Adj) ⌒ Mo... <IFM>...dal
usuality	adverb	–	word complex	–	Mod Adj ⌒ (Modal) or Modal or Mo... <IFM>...dal
obligation	adverb	auxiliary verb	–	–	(Mod Adj) ⌒ Modal
inclination	–	auxiliary verb	–	suffix	(Mod Adj) ⌒ Modal; or (Mod Adj) ⌒ Modal Mark

3.6.1   Modalisation

We now consider modalisation in more detail. Example (54) illustrates a clause with the [probability] feature. Here, modalisation is realised at group rank by a word complex (highlighted in bold) consisting of the bound noun 수 *su* and the auxiliary verb 있 *it-*.[20] The word complex is linked to the (verbalised) adjective 많 *man-* 'there be many', by the linking suffix 을 *-eul*. This particular word complex adds a subjective meaning of possibility to the proposition.

---

[20] Note that the bound noun deployed here is not realising the Installing function and thereby signalling embedding; see Chapter 4, Section 4.2.2.3 for details.

3.6 The System of MODALITY

(54)   probability (group rank Modal)

사람이 많을 수 있어요.							
saram	*=i*	*man-eul*		*su*	*iss-eo*		*yo*
people		there be many		possibility	exist		
		Negotiator					PM
		verbal group					particle
		Event		Modal			
		verbalised adjective		**word complex**			
		Head	Link	β	α		
		stem	suffix	bound noun	auxiliary verb		
					Head	SM	
					stem	suffix	
'There is a possibility that there are many people.'							

The word complex in (54) can be intensified with the IFM clitic 도 *do* 'just, even' to signal a more remote possibility, as shown in (55).[21] In this case, the IFM is 'enclosed' Modal – that is, the Modal function is discontinuously realised by the enclosed clitic. Following SFL conventions, we indicate the enclosure with angled brackets '<...>'.

(55)   probability (group rank Modal; intensified by IFM)

사람이 많을 수도 있어요.								
saram	*=i*	*man-eul*		*su*	*=do*	*iss-eo*		*yo*
people		there be many		possibility	just	exist		
		Negotiator						PM
		verbal group						particle
		Event		Mo...	<IFM>	...dal		
		verbalised adjective		word...	**clitic**	...complex		
		Head	Link	β		α		
		stem	suffix	bound noun		auxiliary verb		
						Head	SM	
						stem	suffix	
'It is just possible that there are many people.'								

---

[21] We saw in Section 2.3.10 in Chapter 2 the clitic 만 *man* 'only' indicating the speaker's unsatisfied expectation (about the number of nymphs descending). The clitic 도 *do* 'even' in (55) indicates the 'opposite'; it tells us that there may be more going on than the speaker expects. Similar clitic functions can also be found in adverbial groups; see Section 3.9.

For [modalisation:probability] the realisation is at word rank through the non-culminative suffix 겠 -get[22] 'will/would'. Consider (56). This statement was made by the speaker who was going to a place in Seoul with friends and heard that a street protest had been organised nearby. The speaker modalises the proposition through the suffix 겠 -get[23] (making the proposition in (56) a possibility). As mentioned above, we refer to the function of the 겠 -get suffix as Modal Mark.

(56)   probability (word rank Modal Mark)

사람이 많겠다.				
saram	=i	man-**ket**-da		
people		there would be many		
		Negotiator		
		verbal group		
		Event		
		verbalised adjective		
		Head	Modal Mark	EM
		stem	**suffix**	suffix
'There would be many people.'				

A possibility can be reinforced (made even more remote) by using both a word complex (수 있 su it-) and a modalising suffix (겠 -get), as in (57). In this case the modality is realised at both group and word ranks.

(57)   probability (word rank Modal Mark; group rank Modal, intensified by IFM)

사람이 많을 수도 있겠다.								
saram	=i	man	-eul	su	=do	it-get-da		
people		there be many		possibility	just	might exist		
		Negotiator						
		verbal group						
		Event		Mo...	<IFM>	...dal		
		verb		word...	clitic	...complex		
		Head	Link	β		α		
		stem	suffix	bound noun		auxiliary verb		
						Head	Modal Mark	EM
						stem	**suffix**	suffix
'It might just be possible that there are many people.'								

---

[22] There are a couple of other suffixes such as 으리 -euri and 으니 -euni, but we disregard them as they are archaic and very rarely used.

[23] Notice that -get is realised as -ket in (56); this is an exhibition of sandhi in Korean. The stem of the verbalised adjective there is /manh/ and the final /h/ combines with the ensuing /g/ in /get/ and become /k/, thus -ket.

3.6 The System of MODALITY

A possibility can also be intensified through a Modal Adjunct, as in (58).

(58) probability (clause rank Modal Adjunct; word rank Modal Mark; group rank Modal, intensified by IFM)

아마 사람이 ...		
ama	*saram*	=*i*
perhaps	people	
Modal Adjunct		
adverbial group		
Head		
adverb		
'Perhaps ... people.'		

... 많을 수도 있겠어요.							
man-eul	**su**	=*do*	*it-get-eo*				*yo*
there be many	possibility	just	might exist				
Negotiator							PM
verbal group							particle
Event	**Mo...**	<IFM>	...**dal**				
verb	word...	clitic	...complex				
Head	Link	β	α				
stem	suffix	bound noun	auxiliary verb				
			Head	**Modal Mark**	SM		
			stem	suffix	suffix		
... it might just be possible that there are many ...							

Example (58) demonstrates that it is possible in Korean for the Modal Adjunct, Modal and Modal Mark functions to be deployed at the same time in a clause. Note, as shown in Table 3.12 for [probability] clauses, the Modal Adjunct, an intensifying function, can only appear if the clause is modalised by a Modal function and/or a Modal Mark function. Compare (58) with (59)–(61), and notice in particular the ungrammaticality of (61), where the Modal Adjunct has neither a Modal nor Modal Mark function to intensify.

(59)

아마 사람이 많을 수도 있어요.							
ama	saram	=i	man-eul	su	=do	iss-eo	yo
perhaps	people		there be many	possibility	just	there be	
Modal Adjunct		Negotiator					PM
		verbal group					
		Event			**Modal**		
'Perhaps it might just be possible that there are many (people).'							

(60)

아마 사람이 많겠어요.				
ama	saram	=i	man-kess-eo	yo
perhaps	people		there would be many	
Modal Adjunct			Negotiator	PM
			verbal group	
			Event	
			verb	
			Head | **Modal Mark** | SM	
'Perhaps there would be many (people).'				

(61) *

아마 사람이 많아요.				
ama	saram	=i	man-a	yo
perhaps	people		there are many	
Modal Adjunct			Negotiator	PM
			verbal group	
			Event	
(Literally) 'Perhaps there are many people.'				

Korean has another resource for realising possibility – (으)ㄹ 것이 *-(eu)lgeosi-*, or its shortened form (으)ㄹ 거 *-(eu)lgeo-*. Structurally, the expression looks like a word complex, consisting of a bound noun 것 *geos* (or 거 *geo* in the shortened form) and the copula 이 *i-* (not in the shortened form), which is linked to the main verb by the connecting suffix (으)ㄹ *-(eu)l*. However, unlike word complexes, such as the one in (55), this resource does not allow for a clitic such as 도 *do* or for the non-culminating suffix 겠 *-get* 'will/would', as in (57). We thus treat it as a suffix – another realisation of modality at word rank (not at group rank), agnate with 겠 *-get*. Compare (62) with (56).

3.6 The System of MODALITY

(62) probability (word rank Modal Mark)

사람이 많을 것이다.				
saram	=*i*	*man-**eulgeosi**-da*		
people		there **would** be many		
		Negotiator		
		verbal group		
		Event		
		verb		
		Head	Modal Mark	EM
		stem	suffix	dom;decl suffix
'There would be many people.'				

This raises the question of the difference between 겠 -*get* and (으)ㄹ 것이 -*(eu)l geos i-*. Korean grammarians vary in their analyses, but here we follow Kim et al. (2005b: 773) who argue that the difference is that of orientation (i.e., a subjective vs an objective orientation). Their position is that 겠 -*get* is relatively subjective, whereas (으)ㄹ 것이 -*(eu)l geos i-* gives the opinion an objective nuance.

Turning to [usuality], as shown in (63), we see the usuality modality is realised at group rank by a word complex (highlighted in bold) consisting of the bound noun 때 *ttae* and the auxiliary verb 있 *it-*.[24] The word complex is linked to the verb 먹 *meog-* 'eat' by the linking suffix 을 -*eul*. This particular word complex adds a subjective meaning of usuality to the proposition.

(63) usuality (group rank Modal)

저녁을 식당에서 먹을 때 있다.							
jeonyeog	=*eul*	*sikdang*	=*eseo*	*meog-eul*	***ttae***	*it-da*	
supper		restaurant		eat	time	there are	
				Negotiator			
				verbal group			
				Event		Modal	
				verb		word complex	
				Head	Link	β	α
				stem	suffix	bound noun	aux verb
							Head	EM
							stem	suffix
'(I) sometimes eat supper at a restaurant.'							

---

[24] The bound noun deployed here is not realising the Installing function; see footnote 19.

As was the case with [probability] in (55), (57) and (58), the word complex realising [usuality] can be reinforced by the IFM clitic 도 *do* 'just, even' and intensified by a Modal Adjunct. These realisations are illustrated in (64).

(64)　usuality (group rank Modal; intensified by IFM; intensified by clause rank Modal Adjunct)

가끔 저녁을 식당에서 . . .				
gakkeum	*jeonyeog*	*=eul*	*sikdang*	*=eseo*
sometimes	supper		restaurant	
Modal Adjunct				
adverbial group				
Head				
adverb				
'(I) sometimes . . . supper at a restaurant.'				

. . . 먹을 때도 있다.					
meog-eul	*ttae*	**=do**	*it-da*		
eat	time	even	exist		
Negotiator					
verbal group					
Event	**Mo…**	<IFM>	**…dal**		
verb	word…	**clitic**	…complex		
Head	Link	β	α		
stem	suffix	bound noun	aux verb		
			Head	EM	
			stem	suffix	
. . . even eat . . .					

There are differences as well. Here, we provide two. One is that unlike [probability], [usuality] is not realised through a verbal suffix. That is, only the Modal and Modal Adjunct functions realise [usuality]. The other is that a Modal Adjunct can be used to realise usuality on its own, without a corresponding Modal function.[25] Compare (65) with ungrammatical (61).

---

[25] We are aware of the problem in our system network in Figure 3.12. A Modal Adjunct is represented as an intensifier but here we have nothing to intensify. We leave this problem for future studies.

3.6 The System of MODALITY

(65) usuality (clause rank Modal Adjunct)

가끔 저녁을 식당에서 먹는다.								
gakkeum	*jeonyeog*	*=eul*	*sikdang*	*=eseo*	*meong-neun-da*			
sometimes	supper		restaurant		eat			
Modal Adjunct					Negotiator			
adverbial group					verbal group			
Head					Event			
adverb					verb			
					Head	TM	EM	
					stem	suffix	suffix	
'(I) sometimes eat supper at restaurant.'								

Table 3.13 presents some realisations of modalisation in Korean. This has been inspired by the topological presentation of modality in English in Halliday and Matthiessen (2014: 691). We are assuming a cline, with finely graded modalisations. Thus, realisations near 그렇다 *geureo-ta* 'is' are more probable/usual than those near 안 그렇다 *an geureo-ta* 'isn't'.

Table 3.13 *Some realisations of* MODALISATION

positive polarity			그렇다	*geureo-ta*
probability	**certainly**	↑	틀림 없다	*teullim eop-da*
			그럴 것이다	*geureol geos-i-da*
			그렇겠다	*geureo-ket-da*
	probably		그럴 수도 있겠다	*geureo-l su do it-get-da*
			그런 모양이다	*geureo-n moyang-i-da*
	possibly	↓	그런 듯싶다	*geureo-n deut-sip-da*
usuality	**always**	↑	그런 법이다	*geureo-n beob-i-da*
			그러기 마련이다	*geureo-gi maryeon-i-da*
			그러기 일쑤다	*geureo-gi ilssu-da*
	usually		그러기 십상이다	*geureo-gi sipsang-i-da*
			그런 편이다	*geureo-n pyeon-i-da*
			그런 셈이다	*geureo-n sem-i-da*
	sometimes	↓	그럴 때 있다	*geureo-l ttae it-da*
negative polarity			안 그렇다	*an geureo-ta*

3.6.2 Modulation

In proposals, modulation opens the possibility of opinions potentially contesting a speaker's desire. Compare (66) – which is an imperative clause, with (67) – a declarative clause in which modulation (more precisely obligation) is realised by an auxiliary verb 하 *ha-* (which means 'must') in conjunction with the linking suffix 어야 *-eoya* (which culminates the main verb 읽 *ik-* 'read').[26] As mentioned above, a Modal function realised through an auxiliary verb is only found in a modulated clause.

(66)

책을 읽어라.		
chaeg	*=eul*	*ilg-eora*
book		read
		Negotiator
		verbal group
		Event
		verb
		Head	EM
		stem	dom;imp suffix
'Read books.'		

(67) obligation (group rank Modal)

책을 읽어야 한다.				
chaeg	*=eul*	*ilg-eoya*	**ha-n-da**	
book		read	**must**	
		Negotiator		
		verbal group		
		Event	Modal	
		verb	**auxiliary verb**	
		Head	Link	Head	TM	EM
		stem	suffix	stem	suffix	dom;decl suffix
'You must read books.'				

---

[26] Notice that 읽 *ik-* 'read' is in fact /ilk/ where /l/ is normally silent unless it is followed by a vowel. This is why the /l/ appears in (58), and /k/ becomes *g* because it is now in an intervocalic environment. Thus, we get 읽어라 *ilg-eora*.

3.6 The System of MODALITY

Obligation can be realised by a Modal Adjunct together with a Modal function in a single clause. This is illustrated in (68).

(68)   obligation (group rank Modal; intensified by clause rank Modal Adjunct)

책을 꼭 읽어야 한다.				
chaeg	=eul	kkok	ilg-eoya	ha-n-da
book		for sure	read	must
		Modal Adjunct	Negotiator	
		adverbial group	verbal group	
		Head	Event	**Modal**
		adverb	verb	auxiliary verb
			Head	Link	Head	TM	EM
			stem	suffix	stem	suffix	dom;decl suffix
'You must for sure read books.'				

A Modal Adjunct cannot realise obligation on its own. Example (69) is not a counterexample to this point. It is not a modulated clause; the Modal Adjunct here would be interpreted as realising usuality.

(69)   usuality (clause rank Modal Adjunct)

책을 꼭 읽는다.			
chaeg	=eul	kkok	ing-neun-da
book		without fail	read
		Modal Adjunct	Negotiator
		adverbial group	verbal group
		Head	Event
		adverb	verb
			Head	TM	EM
			stem	suffix	dom;decl suffix
'(I) never fail to read books.'			

Example (70) realises a modality of permission. As in (67), the modulation is realised by an auxiliary verb – specifically 되 *doe-* (which we gloss as 'may') – together with the linking suffix 어도/아도 *-eodo/ado* (which culminates the main verb 읽 *ik-* 'read'); the clause is declarative.

160 The Grammar of Interpersonal Meaning: MOOD

(70)   obligation (group rank Modal)

책을 읽어도 된다.					
chaeg	=*eul*	*ilg-eodo*	***doe-n-da***		
book		read	**may**		
			Negotiator		
			verbal group		
			Event	**Modal**	
			verb	**auxiliary verb**	
			Head	Head	Tense Mark	EM
			stem	stem	suffix	dom;decl suffix
'You may read books.'					

Inclination is typically realised through an auxiliary verb 하 *ha-* in conjunction with the linking suffix (으)려고 –(*eu*)*ryeogo* (which culminates the main verb).[27] It can be reinforced through an accompanying Modal Adjunct. Example (71) illustrates this pattern.

(71)   inclination (group rank Modal; intensified by clause rank Modal Adjunct)

책을 꼭 읽으려고 한다.				
chaeg	=*eul*	*kkok*	*ilg-euryeogo*	*ha-n-da*
book		for sure	read	am inclined
		Modal Adjunct	Negotiator	
		adverbial group	verbal group	
		Head	Event	**Modal**
		adverb	verb	**aux verb**
			Head	Link	Head	TM	EM
			stem	suffix	stem	suffix	suffix
'I am highly inclined to read books.'				

In addition, inclination can be realised by a Modal Mark (which is not possible with obligation). The non-culminating suffix 겠 -*get* 'will/would' and

---

[27] Notice that when the main verb stem ends in a consonant 으려고 –*euryeogo* is employed, otherwise, 려고 –*ryeogo* will be used.

3.6 The System of MODALITY

the grammaticalised word cluster (으)ㄹ 것이 -*(eu)lgeosi-* (or (으)ㄹ 거 -*(eu)lgeo-*) 'will/would' we saw above can realise modulation (inclination), as well as modalisation (probability). As illustrated in (72), when an [inclination] clause is in declarative mood, Participant 1 is first person; and as shown in (73), when an [inclination] clause is in interrogative mood Participant 1 is second person.

(72) inclination (word rank Modal Mark)

내일 다시 오겠습니다.				
naeil	*dasi*	*o-**get**-seumnida*		
tomorrow	again	**would** come		
		Negotiator		
		verbal group		
		Event		
		verb		
		Head	Modal Mark	EM
		stem	suffix	ven;decl suffix
'(I) would come again tomorrow.'				

(73) inclination (word rank Modal Mark)

지금 가실겁니까?				
jigeum	*ga-si-**lgeo**-mnikka*			
now	**would** go			
	Negotiator			
	verbal group			
	Event			
	verb			
	Head	PDM	Modal Mark	EM
	stem	suffix	suffix	ven;inter suffix
'Would (you) go now?'				

Finally, we note that in Korean modulation can also be realised by 'frozen' expressions, as in (74) (not covered in Figure 3.12 and Table 3.11). We say 'frozen' because the complex structure 지 않으면 안 된다 -*ji an-eumyeon an doe-n-da* '(literally) it's not alright if you don't do ...' is deployed in its entirety to realise an obligation comparable to that in (67).

(74)

책을		읽지		않으면	안	된다.			
chaeg	*=eul*	*ik-ji*		*an-eumyeon*	*an*	*doe-n-da*			
book		read		do not-if	not	is alright			
		Negotiator							
		verbal group							
		Event		Modal					
		verb		word complex					
		Head	Link	β		α			
		stem	suffix	aux verb (negative)		word complex			
				Head	Link	β	α		
				stem	suffix	adverb (negative)	verb		
							Head	TM	EM
							stem	suffix	suffix
'It's not okay if you don't read books.'									

Some realisations of modulation in Korean are presented in Table 3.14. As with realisations of modalisation above, there are two clines assumed (here obligation and inclination) and the realisations near the top of each cline (that is, near 하다 *ha-da* 'do') involve a stronger obligation/inclination than those near the bottom of each cline (that is, near 안 하다 *an ha-da* 'don't').

Table 3.14 *Some realisations of* MODULATION

positive polarity			하다	*ha-da*
obligation	required ↑		해야 하다	*ha-eya ha-da*
			해야 되다	*ha-eya doe-da*
	supposed		안 하면 안 되다	*an ha-myeon an doe-da*
			해도 되다	*ha-edo doe-da*
	allowed ↓		할 수 있다	*ha-l su it-da*
inclination	determined ↑		하겠다	*ha-get-da*
			할 것이다	*ha-lgeos-i-da*
	keen		하려 하다	*ha-ryeo ha-da*
			할까 싶다	*ha-lkka sip-da*
			하는게 좋겠다	*ha-neun-ge jo-ket-da*
	willing ↓		할까 보다	*ha-lkka bo-da*
negative polarity			안 하다	*an ha-da*

3.6.3 Adverbs Realising Modal Adjuncts

Table 3.15 lists some of the adverbs involved in the realisation of Modal Adjuncts.

Table 3.15 *Some adverbs realising the Modal Adjunct function*

not expandable			expandable		
아마	ama	'rather likely'	확실히	hwaksilhi	'certainly'
설마	seolma	'no way'	꼭	kkok	'surely'
다만	daman	'only'	좀	jom	'just'
비록	birok	'even though'	보통	botong	'usually'
만약	manyak	'if'	가끔	gakkeum	'sometimes'
언제나	eonjena	'always'	때때로	ttaettaero	'from time to time'
항상	hangsang	'always'			
자주	jaju	'frequently'			
좀처럼	jomcheoreom	'rarely'			
거의	geoui	'hardly'			
결코	gyeolko	'never'			

Note that those in the 'expandable' column can be modified by 'degree' adverbs such as 정말 *jeongmal* 'really'; 아주 *aju* 'very'; 그냥 *geunyang* 'simply', etc., as shown in (75).

(75)

아주 정말 가끔 전화해도 돼.					
aju	jeongmal	gakkeum	jeonhwaha-edo		doe
very	truly	sometimes	call		is alright
Modal Adjunct			Negotiator		
adverbial group			verbal group		
Head			Event		Modal
adverb complex			verb		auxiliary verb
γ	β	α	Head	Link	Head	SM
adverb	adverb	adverb	stem	suffix	stem	pronounce suffix
'It's okay to call me really very seldom.'					

Modal Adjuncts are optional elements, except for usuality clauses where a Modal Adjunct can be the sole means to realise the modality. Their meaning (i.e., intensity) and realisation as clause rank functions distinguishes them from other types of modality in Korean. As we have seen [modalisation:probability] and [modulation:obligation] can be realised through suffixation at word rank; [modulation] is also realised through auxiliary verbs; and [modalisation] is also realised through word complexes.

Modal Adjuncts occur typically just before the Negotiator; but they can occur clause-initially or even clause-finally (in which case they are taken as an afterthought). As examples (76) and (77) illustrate, a Modal Adjunct is realised outside the Negotiator function in Korean.

(76)

집에 꼭 가야 한다.							
jib	=e	**kkok**		*ga-ya*		*ha-n-da*	
house		**for sure**		go		must	
		Modal Adjunct		Negotiator			
		adverbial group		verbal group			
		Head		Event		Modal	
		adverb		verb		auxiliary verb	
				Head	Link	Head	TM	EM
				stem	suffix	stem	suffix	suffix
'You must definitely go home.'							

(77)

꼭 집에 가야 한다.							
kkok		*jib*	=e	*ga-ya*		*ha-n-da*	
for sure		house		go		must	
Modal Adjunct				Negotiator			
adverbial group				verbal group			
Head				Event		Modal	
adverb				verb		auxiliary verb	
				Head	Link	Head	TM	EM
				stem	suffix	stem	suffix	suffix
'Definitely, you must go home.'							

Among the adverbs in Table 3.15, 'frequency' adverbs such as 언제나 *eomjena* 'always', 자주 *jaju* 'frequently', 보통 *botong* 'usually', 가끔 *gakkeum*

3.7 The System of HIGHLIGHT

'sometimes', 좀처럼 *jomcheoreom* 'rarely', 거의 *geoui* 'hardly', 결코 *gyeolko* 'never', and so on, can realise a Modal Adjunct in usuality clauses. One final note on these adverbs is that those expressing a lower degree of usuality (e.g., *jomcheoreom* 'rarely', *geoui* 'hardly' and *gyeolko* 'never') are found in [negative] clauses in Korean. Example (66) illustrated this point; (78) would be ungrammatical if it was a [positive] clause.

(78)

좀처럼 집에서 저녁을 먹지 않는다.									
jomcheoreom	*jib*	=*eseo*	*jeonyeog*	=*eul*	*meog-ji*		*an-neun-da*		
rarely	house		supper		eat		do not		
Modal Adjunct					Negotiator				
adverbial group					verbal group				
Head					Event		**Negating**		
adverb					verb		aux verb		
					Head	Link	Head	TM	EM
					stem	suffix	stem	suffix	suffix
'(I) rarely eat supper at home.'									

3.7 The System of HIGHLIGHT

As introduced briefly in Chapter 2, the HIGHLIGHT system is realised at group rank by a word complex 것이- *geos i-* 'the thing is that ...' (or 거- *geo-* in short), where 것 *geos* (and also 거 *geo*) is a bound noun and 이 *i* is the copula. We take a closer look at the HIGHLIGHT system here.

The system of HIGHLIGHT provides resources for highlighting or dramatising the significance of a proposition in dialogic interactions. It is only realised in indicative clauses (both formal and informal), and highlighting is only possible with past or ongoing events. As such, the word complex is linked to the main verb, which culminates with one of the connecting suffixes – 는 -*neun* for [ongoing], (으)ㄴ -*(eu)n* for [past] or 았던/었던 -*at-deon/eot-deon* for [remote]. Note also that the Highlight function is always positioned clause-finally.

We propose the following HIGHLIGHT system and realisation statements (Figure 3.13 and Table 3.16).

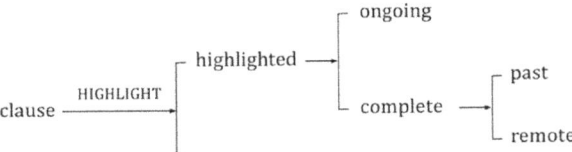

Figure 3.13 The system of HIGHLIGHT

Table 3.16 *Realisation statements for the system of* HIGHLIGHT

highlighted	+Highlight; Event ⌢ Highlight ^ #; Highlight:word complex (β:bound noun (것 or 거 *geot* or *geo*) ^ α:copula)
ongoing	Link ^ Highlight; Link:는 *-neun*
past	Link ^ Highlight; Link:(으)ㄴ *-(eu)n*
remote	Link ^ Highlight; Link:았던/었던 *-at-deon/eot-deon*

Example (79) illustrates a proposition without the Highlight function, and (80) exemplifies a [highlighted:ongoing] clause.

(79)   [not highlighted:ongoing]

거짓말을 해요.			
geojinmar	=*eul*	*hae*	*yo*
lie		do	
		Negotiator	PM
		verbal group	particle
		Event	
		verb	
		Head	SM
		stem	suffix
'(He) is telling a lie.'			

(80)   [highlighted:ongoing]

거짓말을 하는 거예요.					
geojinmar	=*eul*	*ha-**neun***	*geo*	*y-e*	*yo*
lie		tell-**ongoing**	the thing is that ...		
		Negotiator			PM
		verbal group			particle
		Event	Highlight		
		verb	word complex		
		Head	Link	β	α
		stem	suffix	bound noun	copula
					Head	SM
					stem	sfx
'The thing is that (he) is telling a lie.'					

3.7 The System of HIGHLIGHT

Example (81) illustrates a proposition without the Highlight function (but this time in past tense); and (82) and (83) exemplify [highlighted:past:simple] and [highlighted:past:remote] clauses respectively.

(81) [not highlighted:past]

우리가 가까스로 이겼습니다.					
uri	=*ga*	*gakkaseuro*	*igy-eot-seumnida*		
we		narrowly	win-past-declarative		
			Negotiator		
			verbal group		
			Event		
			verb		
			Head	TM	EM
			stem	suffix	ven;decl suffix
'We narrowly won.'					

(82) [highlighted:past:happened]

우리가 가까스로 이긴 것입니다.						
uri	=*ga*	*gakkaseuro*	*igi-n*		*geos*	*i-mnida*
we		narrowly	win-**past: happened**		the thing is that ...	
			Negotiator			
			verbal group			
			Event		Highlight	
			verb		word complex	
			Head	Link	β	α
			stem	suffix	bound noun	copula
						Head	EM
						stem	ven;decl suffix
'The thing is that we've narrowly won.'						

(83) [highlighted:past:remote]

<table>
<tr><td colspan="8">우리가 가까스로 이겼던 것입니다.</td></tr>
<tr><td>uri</td><td>=ga</td><td>gakkaseuro</td><td colspan="2">igy-eotdeon</td><td>geos</td><td colspan="2">i-mnida</td></tr>
<tr><td>we</td><td></td><td>narrowly</td><td colspan="2">win-past:
remote</td><td colspan="3">the thing is that . . .</td></tr>
<tr><td colspan="3" rowspan="8"></td><td colspan="5">Negotiator</td></tr>
<tr><td colspan="5">verbal group</td></tr>
<tr><td colspan="2">Event</td><td colspan="3">Highlight</td></tr>
<tr><td colspan="2">verb</td><td colspan="3">word complex</td></tr>
<tr><td>Head</td><td>Link</td><td>β</td><td colspan="2">α</td></tr>
<tr><td rowspan="3">stem</td><td rowspan="3">suffix</td><td rowspan="3">bound
noun</td><td colspan="2">copula</td></tr>
<tr><td>Head</td><td>EM</td></tr>
<tr><td>stem</td><td>ven;decl
suffix</td></tr>
<tr><td colspan="8">‘The thing is that we narrowly won.’</td></tr>
</table>

3.8 The System of VOCATION

The system of VOCATION makes the addressee of a move in a conversational exchange explicit. Choices for VOCATION thus interact with choices for ADDRESSEE DEFERENCE or POLITENESS to enact social relations of various kinds in Korean clauses. Typically, title terms, kinship terms and personal names are employed for this purpose.

Vocatives typically occur clause-initially, but can also occur clause-finally. In (84) the speaker addresses a teacher; in (85), the speaker and addressee are among a group of university students chatting informally during a class break. Clause-initial Vocatives tend to be used as attention-getters, while clause-final Vocatives are mainly deployed to manage social relations.

3.8 The System of VOCATION

(84)

선생님, 어떻게 생각하십니까?					
seonsaeng-nim	eotteoke	saenggakha-si-mnikka			
teacher	how	think			
Vocative	Inquirer	Negotiator			
nominal group	adverbial group	verbal group			
Thing		Event			
noun		verb			
Head	Honour	Head	PDF	EM	
root	suffix	stem	suffix	venerate;interrogative suffix	
'Teacher, what do (you) think?'					

(85)

줘봐, 선진아.					
jw-eo	bw-a		**Seonjin**	=a	
give	see		**Seonjin**		
Negotiator			Vocative		
verbal group			nominal group		
Event	Dimension		Thing	Title	
verb	auxiliary verb		proper noun	clitic	
Head	Link	Head	SM		
stem	suffix	stem	pronounce suffix		
'Let me have a look, Seonjin.'					

Vocatives are realised by a nominal group. Examples (84) and (85) illustrate two of the common vocative resources in Korean: (i) a noun (with or without a suffix), and (ii) a noun with a clitic or bound noun.

Among vocative resources, a kinship or title term with or without the nominal suffix *-nim*[28] belongs to the first group. Examples such as 사장님 *sajang-nim* 'Mr Boss', 교수님 *gyosu-nim* 'Professor', and so on, are those employed with the suffix *-nim*. Examples such as 아버지 *abeoji* 'Dad', 어머니 *eomeoni* 'Mum', 형 *hyeong* 'Big Brother' (used by a male speaker to an older

---

[28] Following the Standard Korean Language Dictionary published by the National Institute of Korean Language, we take 님 *-nim* to be a suffix on the ground that it is part of each of the words used as vocative terms.

male speaker), 오빠 *oppa* 'Big Brother' (used by a female speaker to an older male speaker) and so on, are those used without the suffix *-nim*. We take the function at word rank realised by the suffix *-nim* to be Honour, as illustrated in (84).

A combination of a personal name and either the clitic, 아/야 *a/ya*,[29] or a bound noun, such as 씨 *ssi* 'Mr, Mrs, Ms, Miss', 군 *gun* 'a title term for a young adult male' and 양 *yang* 'a title term for a young adult female', belongs to the second group.[30] Examples include 수애야 *Suae ya* 'Suae', 수애 양 *Suae yang* 'Miss Suae', 수애 씨 *Suae ssi* 'Miss/Ms Suae', and so on. We take the nominal group function realised by the clitic or the bound nouns to be Title,[31] as illustrated in (85).

We now briefly consider how the VOCATION system works in Korean. As proposed in Figure 3.14 and Table 3.17, VOCATION is an optional system and, when chosen, involves three types of address – upward, downward and equal (i.e., 'neither upward nor downward') and two types of target – distant and close. In other words, there are seven options in Korean vocation: no vocative, [upward;distant], [downward;distant], [equal;distant], [upward;close], [downward;close] and [equal;close].

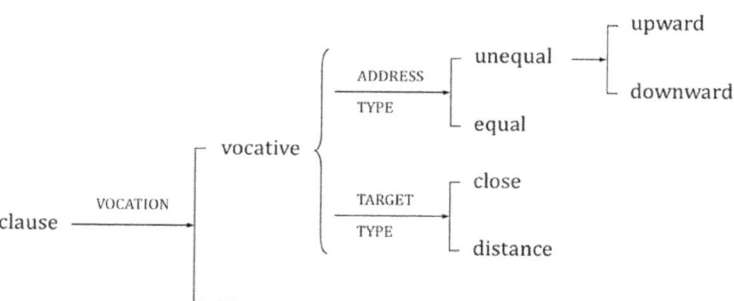

Figure 3.14 The system of VOCATION

---

[29] Note that 아 *a* occurs after a consonant and 야 *ya* after a vowel.
[30] In contrast with 님 *-nim*, 씨 *ssi* 'Mr, Mrs, Ms, Miss', 군 *gun* 'a title term for a young adult male' and 양 *yang* 'a title term for a young adult female' are considered bound nouns; they don't present as distinct dictionary entry words. However, the division 'nominal suffix' vs 'bound noun/clitic' is blurred by the novel use of 님 *nim* in internet chat and SMS messages. There, 님 *nim* is used with common names, forming a paradigm with 씨 *ssi*, 군 *gun* and 양 *yang*.
[31] The Title function is an additional element of nominal group structure that was not introduced in Chapter 2; there we concentrated on nominal groups realising Participants and Circumstances.

3.8 The System of VOCATION

Table 3.17 *Realisation statements for the system of VOCATION*

vocative	+Vocative; # ^ Vocative or Vocative ^ #
upward;distant	Vocative:title terms, professions, positions, kinship terms designating 'upward' kin relations, etc., usually with the 님 -*nim* honorific noun suffix
downward;distant	Vocative:title terms, professions, positions, personal names, etc., usually without the 님 -*nim* honorific noun suffix but can be used with an appropriate bound noun
equal;distant	Vocative:personal names, usually with the 씨 *ssi* bound noun
upward;close	Vocative:kinship terms designating 'upward' kin relations, etc., usually without the 님 -*nim* honorific noun suffix
downward;close	Vocative:personal names with the 아/야 *a/ya* clitic
equal;close	Vocative:title terms, professions, positions, etc., without the 님 -*nim* honorific noun suffix, or personal names with the 씨 *ssi* bound noun

Upward vocation highlights the addressee's social role relation or his/her kinship relation with the speaker. Thus, title terms, expressions for various professions, positions etc., as well as kinship terms designating 'upward' kin relations, are the main means to realise upward vocation. By contrast, downward vocation utilises a personal name as its typical realisation. A possible generalisation here is that in Korea, focusing on the addressee's position in society or the kinship network marks deferential behaviour; identifying an individual as an individual through their name on the other hand is considered non-deferential.

We make two further points here, which follow from the generalisation above. One is that kinship terms designating 'downward' kin relations are not used as vocatives in Korean. For instance, 동생 *dongsaeng* 'younger sibling' is not used as a vocative; but 형 *hyeong* 'older brother' (to a male speaker), 누나 *nuna* 'older sister' (to a female speaker), 오빠 *oppa* 'older brother' (to a male speaker), and 언니 *eonni* 'older sister' (to a female speaker) are all so used. A typical vocative for one's younger sibling is his/her name.

The other point is that in a typical workplace vocatives for senior colleagues refer to their position. As realisations of the [upward;distant] vocative, these titles, professional and position terms always carry 님 -*nim*, which is a deferential nominal suffix. Some examples are: 사장님 *sajang-nim* 'head of company', 부장님 *bujang-nim* 'head of department', 과장님 *gwajang-nim* 'head of section', etc. A typical vocative for one's junior colleague is his/her name. However, unlike the family situation, the personal name is accompanied by a title term bound noun 씨 *ssi* (which cannot be used for upward addresses) to acknowledge that the addressee is an adult.

Consider (86) and (87), which illustrate downward address. Here a personal name is used with the clitic 아/야 *a/ya*, indicating that the name is used as a vocative. Downward vocatives are found in formal [dominant] clauses as in (86), as well as in informal clauses as in (87); in (87) the politeness marker 요 *yo* would not be used.

(86)

수애야, 들어와라.			
Suae	=ya	*deureow-ara*	
Suae		come in	
Vocative		Negotiator	
nominal group		verbal group	
Thing	Title	Event	
proper noun	clitic	Verb	
		Head	EM
		stem	dominant;jussive suffix
'Suae, come in.'			

(87)

수애야, 들어와.			
Suae	=ya	*deureow-a*	
Suae		come in	
Vocative		Negotiator	
nominal group		verbal group	
Thing	Title	Event	
proper noun	clitic	verb	
		Head	SM
		stem	pronounce suffix
'Suae, come in.'			

With equal address, if the speaker and addressee are close to one another, then the realisation of VOCATION is the same as for downward address. A typical example for such a situation would be where the speaker and the addressee spent their childhood together and are interacting in a private domain at the time of speech. This contrasts with parallel address between

3.9 The System of COMMENT

interlocutors who are not close to one another – something that can be observed in public places such as hospitals, banks, government shopfronts etc. In these situations, the personal name is marked by a honorific title term 씨 *ssi*, which is a bound noun, as exemplified in (88). The speaker will be understood as non-committal with respect to his or her relation to the addressee.

(88)

김수애 씨, 들어오십시오.					
Kimsuae	***ssi***	*deureoo-si-psio*			
Kim Suae	**Ms**	come in			
Vocative		Negotiator			
nominal group		verbal group			
Thing	Title	Event			
proper noun	bound noun	Verb			
		Head	PDF	EM	
		stem	suffix	venerate;jussive suffix	
'Ms Kim Suae, please come in.'					

3.9 The System of COMMENT

The system of COMMENT in Korean provides resources for encoding interlocutors' attitude to what is being negotiated (the proposition or the proposal) and as such it operates at clause rank. We propose the system of COMMENT in Figure 3.15 and its realisation statement in Table 3.18.

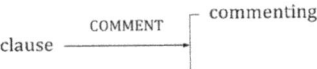

Figure 3.15 The system of COMMENT

Table 3.18 *Realisation statements for the system of COMMENT*

commenting	+Comment; # ^ Comment; Comment:adverbial group, nominal group or lexicalised phrase

The Comment function is typically positioned clause-initially and is in general realised by an adverbial group (Chapter 2, Section 2.5), a nominal group, or a lexicalised phrase.

In (89) the Comment is realised by an adverbial group 다행스럽게도 *dahaengseureopge do*. Here, the Head adverb 다행스럽게 *dahaengseureopge* 'fortunately' is accompanied by Interpersonal Function Marking 도 *do* 'even', which intensifies the attitude. Since the clause is declarative, it encodes the speaker's attitude to the proposition.

(89)

다행스럽게도 친구는 집에 있었습니다.						
dahaengseureopge	=*do*	*chingu*	=*neun*	*jib*	=*e*	*iss-eoss-eumnida*
fortunately		friend		home	at	was
Comment					Negotiator	
adverbial group					verbal group	
Head	IFM				Event	
adverb	clitic				verb	
					Head	TM	EM
					stem	suffix	suffix
'Fortunately, the friend was at home.'						

Some further examples realising a Comment function in declarative clauses, encoding the speaker's attitude to the proposition, are provided in Table 3.19. Notice that like 다행스럽게도 *dahaengseureopge do* 'fortunately', each of the adverbial groups is accompanied by the IFM 도 *do* 'even', which upscales the attitude.

Table 3.19 *Adverbial groups realising the Comment function*

놀랍게도	*nolapge do*	'to my surprise'
슬프게도	*seulpeuge do*	'sadly'
불행하게도	*buraenghage do*	'unfortunately'
어리석게도	*eoriseoke do*	'stupidly'
재미있게도	*jaemi itge do*	'interestingly'

In (90) the Comment is realised by a lexicalised phrase 말이야 바른 말이지 *mar i ya bareu-n mar i-ji* 'truthfully'. This was 'originally' a non-finite clause but now functions as a lexicalised phrase in Korean; so we will not offer a structural analysis here. Since the clause is imperative, the Comment encodes the speaker's attitude to the proposal.

3.10 The System of EXPLETION

(90)

말이야 바른 말이지, 이제 그만하세요.			
mar i ya bareu-n mar i-ji	*ije*	*geumanha-se*	*yo*
in truth	now	stop	
Comment	Modal Adjunct	Negotiator	PM
[[non-finite clause]]	adverbial group	verbal group	particle
	Head	Event	
	adverb	verb	
		Head	TM	EM
		stem	suffix	suffix
'In truth, stop it now! (that's enough!)'			

Table 3.20 lists some more examples of lexicalised phrases and nominal groups that realise the Comment function in indicative clauses. In a declarative clause they express the speaker's angle on a proposition; but in an interrogative clause they seek the addressee's opinion.

Table 3.20 *Lexicalised phrases and a nominal group realising the Comment function*

솔직히 말해서	*soljiki malha-eseo*	'frankly speaking'	phrases
뭐니뭐니해도	*mwo-ni mwo-ni ha-e do*	'no matter what they say'	
우리끼리 얘긴데	*uri kkiri yaegi-nde*	'speaking between you and me'	
아시다시피	*a-si-dasipi*	'as you know'	
예상대로	*yesang daero*	'as expected'	ng

Note that unlike the other four expressions, 예상대로 *yesang daero* 'as expected' is a nominal group – 예상 *yesang* means 'expectation', and 대로 *daero* is an IFM that can be glossed as 'as'.

3.10 The System of EXPLETION

Korean also provides for outbursts of attitude, realised by exclamatory phrases, taboo lexis and euphemisms. We label the function of these expressions Expletive. The system of EXPLETION we propose is provided in Figure 3.16, and its realisation statement in Table 3.21.

Figure 3.16 The system of EXPLETION

Table 3.21 *Realisation statements for the system of EXPLETION*

expleting	+Expletive; # ^ Expletive; Expletive:interjection or nominal group

Realisations of Expletives include interjections, such as 아이구 *aigu*, typically registering surprise (functionally equivalent to 'oops', 'gee', etc. in English) and 이런/저런 *ireon/jeoreon*, registering a mild negative surprise (functionally equivalent to 'crap', 'shit', etc.).

Expletives are also realised by nominal groups in frozen expressions. For some of these, only the Epithet is realised – e.g., 빌어먹을 *bireomeogeul*, literally 'begging' (functionally equivalent 'what the fuck') and 씨팔 *ssipal*, 'fucking'. For others only the Thing is realised – e.g., 병신 *byeongsin*, 'cripple' (functionally equivalent to 'dickhead'), 염병 *yeombyeong*, literally 'typhoid fever' (functionally equivalent to 'damn it').

Expletives operate at clause rank, and are typically realised clause-initially as shown in (91)–(93). The Expletive in (91) is realised by an interjection; and those in (92) and (93) are realised by a nominal group, but consisting of just an Epithet (92) and just a Thing (93).

(91)

이런, 벌써 갔네!		
ireon	*beolsseo*	*ga-n-ne*
what the	already	went
Expletive		Negotiator
interjection		verbal group
		Event
		verb
		Head	TM	SM
		stem	suffix	note suffix
'Bugger, (they)'ve gone already!'		

(92)

빌어먹을, 벌써 갔네!					
bireomeogeul	*beolsseo*	*ga-n-ne*			
begger	already	went			
Expletive		Negotiator			
nominal group		verbal group			
Epithet		Event			
adjective		verb			
		Head	TM	SM	
		stem	suffix	note suffix	
'Shit, (they)'ve gone already!'					

(93)

염병, 벌써 갔네.					
yeombyeong	*beolsseo*	*ga-n-ne*			
typhoid fever	already	went			
Expletive		Negotiator			
nominal group		verbal group			
Thing		Event			
noun		verb			
		Head	TM	SM	
		stem	suffix	note suffix	
'Fucking hell, (they)'ve gone already!'					

3.11   Concluding Remarks on MOOD

In this chapter we have considered the interpersonal grammar of the Korean clause. We began with the system of FORMALITY, describing the formal systems MOOD and ADDRESSEE DEFERENCE; we then moved on to the informal systems INFORMAL MOOD, STANCE and POLITENESS. We continued with other interpersonal systems, which operate alongside the formal vs informal distinction. These are PARTICIPANT DEFERENCE, POLARITY, MODALITY, VOCATION, HIGHLIGHT, COMMENT and EXPLETION.

All these systems take clause as their entry condition, since they position the whole of the clause as a discourse move. As we have noted, however, their structural realisations are dispersed across clause, group/phrase and word ranks in Korean.

We conclude this chapter by providing an overview of interpersonal systems in Korean (Figure 3.17). Note that in addition to the superscript pairs ^{I} and ^{T} and ^{II} and ^{TT}, which we explained in relation to Figure 3.7, there is superscript ^{III} on the features [imperative] and [informal imperative] linking to superscript ^{TTT} on

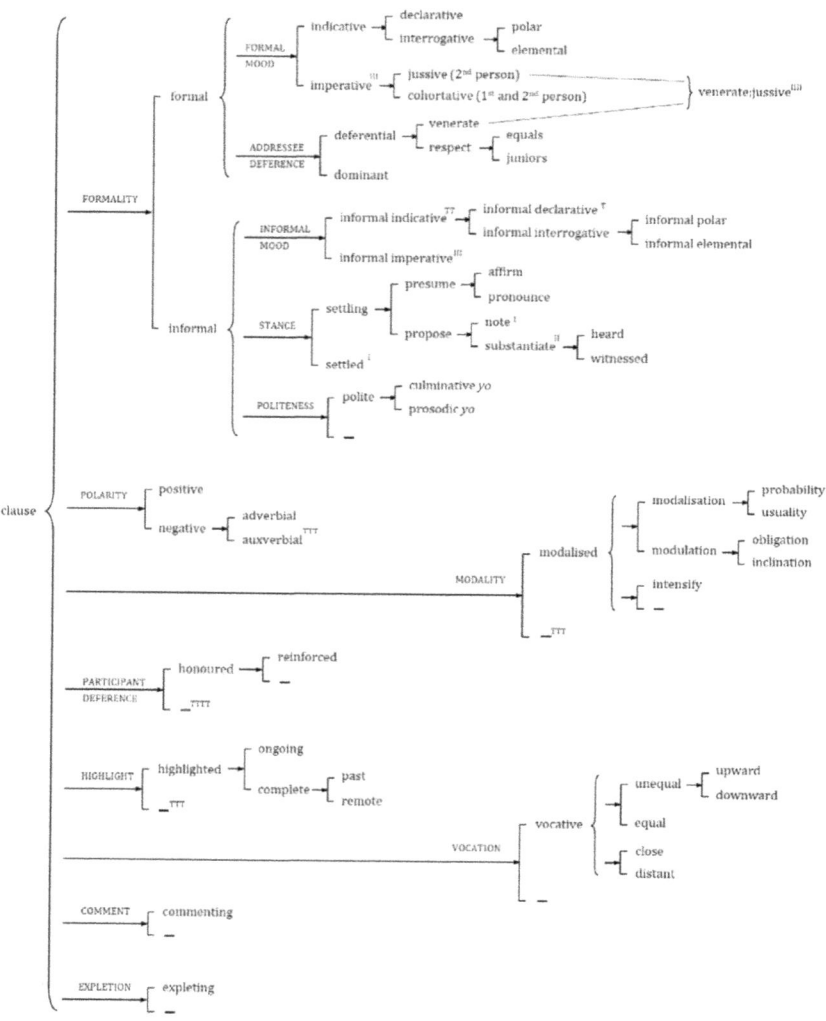

Figure 3.17 The system of MOOD: interpersonal systems in Korean

3.11 Concluding Remarks on MOOD

the feature [aux verbial] and [–] under [modality] and [highlighted]. This additional if/then pair ensures that imperative clauses, whether formal or informal, are neither negated through the negative adverb, 안 *an*, nor are they modalised or highlighted in Korean.

In addition, we have included a superscript pair ^{IIII} and ^{TTTT} between the combined features [venerate;jussive] and [–] in the PARTICIPANT DEFERENCE system. This conditional marking indicates that PARTICIPANT DEFERENCE is not possible (more precisely, redundant) in [venerate;jussive] clauses.

4 The Grammar of Experiential Meaning in Korean: TRANSITIVITY

In Chapter 3 we explored the interpersonal grammar of Korean, as a resource for negotiating meaning in discourse. We now move on to the experiential grammar of Korean and focus on clause resources for construing experience.

4.1 Introduction to Experiential Clause Structure

As mentioned in Chapter 1, experiential meaning is concerned with 'what is going on', 'who does what to whom' and 'when, where, why or how'. The primary grammatical resource managing experiential meanings at the rank of clause is the system of TRANSITIVITY. Through this system experiential meanings map our experience of the world inside us and around us. Following Halliday and Matthiessen (1999: 3; 2014: 213), we treat experience as the reality we construe by means of language.

To understand this experiential clause perspective a little further, consider example (1), which deals with a range of 'goings-on'.

(1) 장마 전선이 북상하면서
<u>jangma</u> <u>jeonseon</u> <u>i</u> | ***buksangha-myeonseo*** ||
rain   front   EFM   northward move-as
'As a rain front is moving northward'

오늘 새벽부터 부산에
oneul saebyeok buteo | *Busan e* |
today dawn   from   Busan in
'from early this morning in Busan,'

많은 비가 내리고 있습니다.
maneun   bi   ga | ***naeri-go   it-seumnida*** |||
lot   rain EFM   fall   is
'a lot of rain has been falling.'

4.1 Introduction to Experiential Clause Structure

경남 함안에서도 철도가 유실돼
<u>Gyeongnam Haman</u>   eseo do | <u>cheoldo</u> ga | **yusildwae** ||
(a Province) (a County) in   IFM   railroad P1 was lost
'In Haman, Gyengnam as well, because railroads were washed away'

열차 운행이 중단됐습니다.
<u>yeolcha unhaeng</u> <u>i</u> | **jungdandwae-t-sumnida** |||
train   operation EFM was halted
'the trains were stopped.'

취재 기자를 연결합니다.
<u>chwijae   gija</u>   reul | **yeongyeolha-mnida** |||
field report reporter EFM connect
'We are connecting to the reporter.'

This text is a short introduction to a TV news story concerning several accidents caused by the day's weather. It was written to be spoken for a TV audience. The text gives an overview of 'what happened – when, where and why' and sets up a reporter to present a fuller picture.

The range of 'goings-on' is realised in the experiential grammar of Korean through five clauses, each of which consists of two or three components – Participant(s) (underlined), Circumstance(s) and a Process (**bold**) in the text above. The Process, realised by a verbal group, is the core element of each clause; the Participants associated with the Process are realised by nominal groups. The second clause of the text is analysed in (2). This clause includes two Circumstances alongside a Participant and a Process – reporting on the day's weather in Busan. This is a typical way of talking about weather in Korean, where a natural phenomenon (here 'rain') is construed as a P1, as if it is 'undertaking' the action of the clause.

(2)

오늘 새벽부터 부산에 ...				
oneul	saebyeok	=buteo	Busan	=e
today	dawn	from	Busan	in
Circumstance:Location:time			Circumstance:Location:space	
nominal group			nominal group	
Class	Thing	EFM	Thing	EFM
noun	noun	clitic	noun	clitic
'From early this morning in Busan ...				

... 많은 비가 내리고 있습니다.						
maneun	*bi*	*=ga*	*naeri-go*		*it-seumnida*	
a lot of	rain		fall		be doing	
Participant 1			Process			
nominal group			verbal group			
Numerative	Thing	EFM	Event		Dimension	
adjective	noun	clitic	verb		auxiliary verb	
			Head	Link	Head	Exchange Mark
			stem	suffix	stem	suffix
'... it has been raining a lot.'						

As shown in (2), the Process is realised by the verbal group 내리고 있습니다 *naeri-go it-seumnida* 'is falling down'; it consists of an Event realised by a lexical verb 내리 *naeri-* 'to fall' with a linking suffix 고 *-go* and a Dimension realised by an auxiliary verb 있 *it-* 'be doing' with a suffix 습니다 *-seumnida* (the suffix realises the verb function Exchange Mark). In (2) the Event function construes basic information about what is going on.

The Participant function and the two Circumstance functions in (2) are realised by nominal groups. In each case the nuclear Thing function is followed by an Experiential Function Marking function (EFM) indicating the role played by the nominal group in the clause (as Participant or Circumstance).[1] Participant 1 (P1) nominal groups are prototypically positioned in relation to the Process by the EFM clitic 이/가 *i/ga*, Participant 2 (P2) nominal groups by the EFM clitic 을/를 *eul/reul* and Participant 3 (P3) nominal groups by the EFM clitic 에게 *ege* or 에 *e* (*ege* is used for a 'conscious' P3 and 에 *e* for an 'unconscious' one).

Examples (3) and (4) have more than one Participant function – two in (3) and three in (4). These examples show the typical sequence of Participants in clause structure – 'P1 ^ P2' and 'P1 ^ P3 ^ P2' respectively. These sequences however can be rearranged without affecting the experiential meaning of the clause. A Circumstance can be realised by an adverbial group as in (3), 깊이 *gipi* 'deeply', as well as a nominal group 카페에서 *kape eseo* 'in the café' as in (4) (where it includes the circumstantial EFM clitic 에서 *eseo* 'in').

---

[1] In colloquial spoken Korean, the EFM function is often elided when marking participant roles (but not circumstantial ones). This happens when interlocutors have common understandings and expectations based on shared experience and/or language in action mode.

4.1 Introduction to Experiential Clause Structure

From example (3) up to the end of this chapter, we use abbreviations, particularly in the (example) tables. For clause rank function labels, we use, in addition to P1, P2 and P3 introduced above, Cir and PM for Circumstance and Politeness Marker respectively. For group rank function labels, we use, in addition to the EFM introduced above, TFM and IFM for Textual Function Marking and Interpersonal Function Marking respectively. For word rank function labels, we use TM, EM and SM for Tense Mark, Exchange Mark and Stance Mark respectively. For class labels, we use ng, vg, advg and ptcl for nominal group, verbal group, adverbial group and particle respectively. At word rank, we use sfx for suffix. Further abbreviations will be introduced below when they are first mentioned.

(3)

여자가 남편을 깊이 사랑한다.							
yeoja	=*ga*	*nampyeon*	=*eul*	*gipi*	*sarangha-n-da.*		
woman		husband		deeply	love		
P1		P2		Cir: Manner	Process		
ng		ng		advg	vg		
Thing	EFM	Thing	EFM	Head	Event		
noun	clitic	noun	clitic	adverb	verb		
					Head	TM	EM
					stem	sfx	sfx
'The woman deeply loves her husband.'							

(4)

카페에서 남자가 여자에게 본심을 털어놓았다.									
kape	=*eseo*	*namja*	=*ga*	*yeoja*	=*ege*	*bonsim*	=*eul*	*teoreono-at-da.*	
café	in	man		woman	to	real mind		reveal	
Cir:Location		P1		P3		P2		Process	
ng		ng		ng		ng		vg	
Thing	EFM	Thing	EFM	Thing	EFM	Thing	EFM	Event	
noun	clitic	noun	clitic	noun	clitic	noun	clitic	verb	
								Head	TM	EM
								stem	sfx	sfx
'In the café the man revealed his real feelings to the woman.'									

Table 4.1 presents a list of clitics realising EFMs in Korean (expanded here from Table 1.1 in Chapter 1).

Table 4.1 *Experiential Function Marking (EFM) clitics*

experiential functions	examples of marking
Participant 0	no mark
Participant 1	이/가 *i/ga*
Participant 2	을/를 *eul/reul*
Participant 3	에게 *ege* 'to' 한테 *hante* 'to' 에 *e* 'by'
Circumstance	에 *e* 'on, at, in, to' 에서 *eseo* 'in, at, on, from' 에게서 *egeseo* 'from' 한테서 *hanteso* 'from' (으)로 *(eu)ro* 'with' 에게로 *egero* 'toward' 한테로 *hantero* 'toward' 에로 *ero* 'toward' (으)로써 *(eu)rosseo* 'with, by' (으)로서 *(eu)roseo* 'as' 보다 *boda* 'than'

Note that the prototypical marker for P1 (*i/ga*) or P2 (*eul/reul*) is not used when an Interpersonal Function Marking (IFM) or Textual Function Marking (TFM) clitic is deployed. However, the other EFMs, including the P3 markers 에게 *ege* and 에 *e*, can be followed by an IFM or TFM.

In (5), the EFM 을 *eul* marks the second nominal group as P2; and the clause initial nominal group marked by the TFM 는 *neun* is thus understood as P1. By contrast, in (6) the EFM 이 *i* marks the second nominal group as P1, and so the clause initial nominal group marked by the TFM 는 *neun* is understood as P2.

4.1 Introduction to Experiential Clause Structure

(5)

여자는 남편을 깊이 사랑한다.					
yeoja	*=neun*	*nampyeon*	*=eul*	*gipi*	*sarangha-n-da.*
woman		husband		deeply	love
P1		**P2**		Cir:Manner	Process
ng		ng		advg	vg
Thing	TFM	Thing	EFM	Head	Event
noun	clitic	noun	clitic	adverb	verb
					Head / TM / EM
					stem / sfx / sfx
'The woman deeply loves her husband.'					

(6)

여자는 남편이 깊이 사랑한다.					
yeoja	*=neun*	*nampyeon*	*=i*	*gipi*	*sarangha-n-da.*
woman		husband		deeply	love
P2		**P1**		Cir:Manner	Process
ng		ng		advg	vg
Thing	TFM	Thing	EFM	Head	Event
noun	clitic	noun	clitic	adverb	verb
					Head / TM / EM
					stem / sfx / sfx
'The woman, her husband deeply loves.'					

Examples (7) and (8) show that EFMs other than 이/가 *i/ga* (P1 marker) and 을/를 *eul/reul* (P2 marker) can be followed by a TFM (in (7)) or an IFM (in (8)).

(7)

카페에서는 남자가 여자에게 ...							
kape	*=eseo*	*=neun*	*namja*	*=ga*	*yeoja*	*=ege*	
café	in		man		woman	to	
Cir:Location			P1		P3		
ng			ng		ng		
Thing	EFM	**TFM**	Thing	EFM	Thing	EFM	
noun	clitic	clitic	noun	clitic	noun	clitic	
'In the café, the man ... to the woman.'							

... 본심을 털어놓았다.		
bonsim	*=eul*	*teoreono-at-da.*
real mind		reveal
P2		Process
ng		vg
Thing	EFM	Event
noun	clitic	verb
		Head / TM / EM
		stem / sfx / sfx
... revealed his real feelings ...		

(8)

남자는 그 여자에게만 ...						
namja	*=neun*	*geu*	*yeoja*	*=ege*	*=man*	
man		that	woman	to	only	
P1		P3				
ng		ng				
Thing	TFM	Deictic	Thing	EFM	IFM	
noun	clitic	determiner	noun	clitic	clitic	
'The man ... only to the woman.'						

4.2 The System of EXPERIENTIAL CLAUSE TYPE

... 본심을 털어놓았다.					
bonsim	=eul	teoreono-at-da.			
real mind		reveal			
P2		Process			
ng		vg			
Thing	EFM	Event			
noun	clitic	verb			
		Head	TM	EM	
		stem	sfx	sfx	
... revealed his real feelings ...					

4.2 The System of EXPERIENTIAL CLAUSE TYPE

As shown in (1)–(4), experience can be construed as a configuration of Process, Participant and (optional) Circumstance functions. We can also observe that clauses (2), (3) and (4) are clearly dealing with different kinds of experience – with 'happening' in (2), with 'emoting' in (3) and with 'communicating' in (4). We will organise clauses construing different kinds of experience into four types. These are outlined in Figure 4.1 as the system of EXPERIENTIAL CLAUSE TYPE: [material], [mental], [relational] and [verbal]. The different clause types involve different kinds of Participant; the obligatory Participant/s for each class are shown following the realisation arrows in Figure 4.1 (e.g., Actor for material clauses, Sayer for verbal clauses and so on).

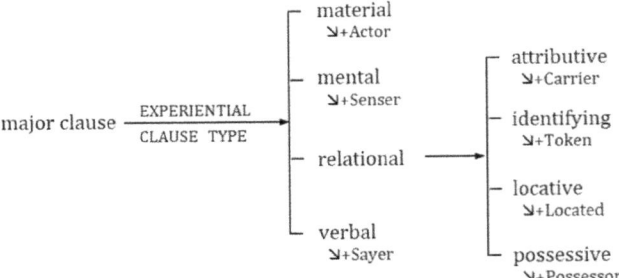

Figure 4.1 The system of EXPERIENTIAL CLAUSE TYPE

These four experiential clause types can be differentiated according to several criteria, including their key Participant roles, their ability to project another clause and their basic meanings. We will deal with these distinguishing characteristics step-by-step in sub-sections below.

A full list of Participants discussed in this chapter is presented in Table 4.2, along with information about whether they have to involve conscious entities or not. These are the Participant functions for each clause type that can be marked formally as P0, P1, P2 or P3 (as specified in Table 1.1, Chapter 1). We will describe them in detail for each clause type in the following sub-sections.

Table 4.2 *Key Participants in experiential clause types*

experiential clause types	key Participants			
	conscious		not conscious	no limitation
	speaker	anyone		
material		Source	Entity-Range Process-Range	Actor Undergoer Recipient
mental		Senser	Mental-Range	Phenomenon
relational	Emoter			Carrier;Attribute Token;Value Carrier-Domain Located;Location Possessor;Possession
verbal		Sayer Receiver	Verbiage Verbal-Range	

4.2.1   Material Clauses

Material clauses construe our experience of the world 'outside' – e.g., actions, activities and events. They involve the meanings of 'creating' or 'transforming' (see Halliday and Matthiessen 2014: 228–36). Figure 4.2 shows the system of MATERIAL CLAUSE TYPE in Korean which we propose.

Material clauses can be classified into non-impacted and impacted depending on whether or not there is an Undergoer that is affected by the unfolding of the Process; they can also be classified depending on whether or not there is a P3 Participant extending the clause. Various Participant functions are discussed below.

4.2 The System of EXPERIENTIAL CLAUSE TYPE

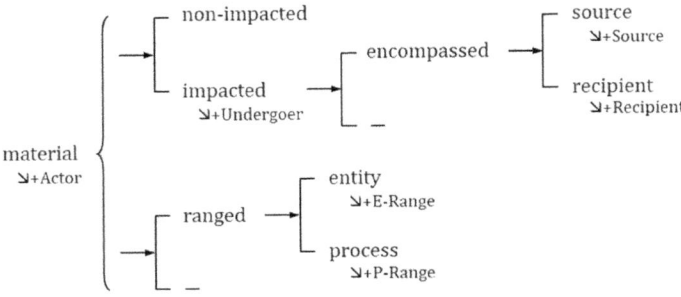

Figure 4.2 The system of MATERIAL CLAUSE TYPE

4.2.1.1 Actor Material clauses include a Participant which is inherently involved in the unfolding of an occurrence of some kind through time – leading to some change from the initial phase of its unfolding. In grammars informed by SFL this inherent Participant in material clauses is typically referred to as Actor, and we adopt this label for our description.

The Actor is prototypically marked by 이/가 *i/ga* (P1) and may be the only Participant in material clauses.

Material clauses construe not only 'doings' as in (9) and (10) but also 'happenings' as in (11). With happenings, there is no intentionality involved as far as the role played by the Actor is concerned.

(9)

하늘에서 선녀가 내려왔다.						
haneul	*=eseo*	*seonnyeo*	*=ga*	*naeryeow-at-da*		
sky	from	nymph		descended		
Cir:Location		**P1:Actor**		Process:material		
ng		ng		vg		
Thing	EFM	Thing	EFM	Event		
noun	clitic	noun	clitic	verb		
				Head	TM	EM
				stem	sfx	sfx
'From heaven, the nymph descended.'						

(10)

선녀가 큰소리로 울었다.				
seonnyeo	=***ga***	*keunsori*	=*ro*	*ur-eot-da*
nymph		loud voice	with	cried
P1:Actor		Cir:Means		Process:material
ng		ng		vg
Thing	EFM	Thing	EFM	Event
noun	clitic	noun	clitic	verb
				Head / TM / EM
				stem / sfx / sfx
'The nymph cried with a loud voice.'				

(11)

기근과 질병으로 인구가 줄어들었다.						
gigeun	=*gwa*	*jilbyeong*	=*euro*	*ingu*	=*ga*	*jureodeur-eot-da*
famine	and	disease	by	population		decreased
Cir:Cause				P1:Actor		Process:material
ng				ng		vg
Thing	EFM	Thing	EFM	Thing	EFM	Event
[ng complex]²				clitic	noun	clitic / verb
1		2				
[ng]		[ng]				Head / TM / EM
Thing	Linking	Thing				stem / sfx / sfx
noun	clitic	noun				
'Because of famine and disease, the population decreased.'						

4.2.1.2 Undergoer Alongside the Actor, material clauses in Korean may involve an Undergoer – a Participant directly affected by something going on.

The Undergoer is prototypically marked by 을/를 *eul/reul* (P2) as shown in (12) and (13).

---

² Following SFL conventions, we use square brackets, [...], to represent an embedded group or group complex.

4.2 The System of EXPERIENTIAL CLAUSE TYPE

(12)

진수가 안경을 발로 짓밟았다.						
Jinsu	*=ga*	*angyeong*	*=eul*	*bal*	*=lo*	*jitbalb-at-da*
Jinsu		glass		foot	with	trampled
P1:Actor		**P2:Undergoer**		Cir:Means		Process:material
ng		ng		ng		vg
Thing	EFM	Thing	EFM	Thing	EFM	Event
noun	clitic	noun	clitic	noun	clitic	verb
						Head	TM	EM
						stem	sfx	sfx
'Jinsu trampled the glasses with his foot.'						

(13)

수상한 물체가 비행기를 쫓고 있다.							
susangha-n	*mulche*	*=ga*	*bihaenggi*	*=reul*	*jjot-go*		*it-da*
suspicious	object		airplane		chase		is...ing
P1:Actor			P2:Undergoer		Process:material		
ng			ng		vg		
Epithet	Thing	EFM	Thing	EFM	Event		Dimension
adjective	noun	clitic	noun	clitic	verb		aux verb
Head	Link				Head	Link	Head	EM
stem	sfx				stem	sfx	stem	sfx
'A suspicious object is chasing the airplane.'							

4.2.1.3 Recipient Material clauses may include another Participant, the Recipient. This Participant is indirectly affected by what is going on, ending up in 'possession' of the entity realised by the Undergoer.

Material clauses with a Recipient can be thought of as 'giving clauses', since the Process is typically realised through the verb 주다 *ju-da* 'give'. The Recipient is marked by 에게 *ege* or 한테 *hante* 'to' when it has the semantic feature of 'consciousness' as in (14), or by 에 *e* 'to' when it lacks this feature as in (15).

(14)

나무꾼이 선녀에게 날개옷을 주었다.									
namukkun	=i	seonnyeo	=ege	nalgae	os	=eul	ju-eot-da		
woodcutter		nymph	**to**	wing	dress		gave		
P1:Actor		**P3:Recipient**		P2:Undergoer			Process:material		
ng		ng		ng			vg		
Thing	EFM	Thing	EFM	Class		Thing	Event		
noun	clitic	noun	clitic	noun		noun	verb		
							Head	TM	EM
							stem	sfx	sfx
'The woodcutter gave the nymph the winged dress.'									

(15)

태풍이 벼농사에 ...					
taepung	=i	byeo	nongsa	=e	
typhoon		rice	farming	**to**	
P1:Actor		**P3:Recipient**			
ng		ng			
Thing	EFM	Class	Thing	EFM	
noun	clitic	noun	noun	clitic	
'The typhoon ... on the rice farming.'					

... 큰 피해를 주었다.					
keun	pihae	=reul	ju-eot-da		
great	damage		gave		
P2:Undergoer			Process:material		
ng			vg		
Epithet	Thing	EFM	Event		
adjective	noun	clitic	verb		
			Head	TM	EM
			stem	sfx	sfx
... inflicted great damage ...					

4.2 The System of EXPERIENTIAL CLAUSE TYPE

4.2.1.4 Source Another Participant we recognise is termed Source. A Process with a Source is typically realised through the verb 받다 *bat-da* 'receive'. Whereas material clauses with a Recipient can be thought of as 'giving clauses' (e.g., (14)), those with a Source can be thought of as 'receiving clauses' as in (16). The Source must be a conscious being in Korean, unlike the Recipient (cf. (15)); but what is notable here is that Recipients and Sources are both aligned as P3s, marked by the same clitics 에게 *ege* or 한테 *hante* 'to/from'.

(16)

선녀가 나무꾼에게 날개 옷을 받았다.									
seonnyeo	=ga	namukkun	=ege	nalgae	os	=eul	bad-at-da		
nymph		woodcutter	from	wing	dress		received		
P1:Actor		P3:Source		P2:Undergoer			Process:material		
ng		ng		ng			vg		
Thing	EFM	Thing	EFM	Class	Thing	EFM	Event		
noun	clitic	noun	clitic	noun	noun	clitic	verb		
							Head	TM	EM
							stem	sfx	sfx
'The nymph received the winged dress from the woodcutter.'									

As (17) shows, non-conscious Sources are unnatural (as indicated by the '??' prefacing the Hangeul in (17)). A more natural expression would construe the 'unconscious' entity as a Circumstance:Means, as shown in (18).

(17)

?? 그 건물이 태풍에게 . . .					
geu	geonmur	=i	taepung	=ege	
the	building		typhoon	'from'	
P1:Actor			P3:Source (?)		
ng			ng		
Deictic	Thing	EFM	Thing	EFM	
determiner	noun	clitic	noun	clitic	
'The building . . . from the typhoon.'					

... 큰 피해를 입었다.					
keu-n	*pihae*	*=reul*	*ib-eot-da*		
great	damage		recieved		
P2:Undergoer			Process:material		
ng			vg		
Epithet	Thing	EFM	Event		
adjective	noun	clitic	verb		
Head	Link		Head	TM	EM
stem	sfx		stem	sfx	sfx
... suffered great damage ...					

(18)

그 건물이 태풍으로 ...				
geu	*geonmur*	*=i*	*taepung*	*=euro*
the	building		typhoon	'by'
P1:Actor			Cir:Means	
ng			ng	
Deictic	Thing	EFM	Thing	EFM
determiner	noun	clitic	noun	clitic
'The building ... from the typhoon.'				

... 큰 피해를 입었다.					
keu-n	*pihae*	*=reul*	*ib-eot-da*		
great	damage		recieved		
P2:Undergoer			Process:material		
ng			vg		
Epithet	Thing	EFM	Event		
adjective	noun	clitic	verb		
Head	Link		Head	TM	EM
stem	sfx		stem	sfx	sfx
... suffered great damage ...					

4.2 The System of EXPERIENTIAL CLAUSE TYPE

The Participant receiving goods in material clauses can also be realised as Circumstance, more precisely, Circumstance:Location. In this case the clitics deployed will be 에게서 *egeseo* or 한테서 *hanteseo* 'from' – as shown in (19).

(19)

선녀가 나무꾼에게서 날개옷을 받았다.									
seonnyeo	=ga	namukkun	=egeseo	nalgae	os	=eul	bad-at-da		
nymph		woodcutter	**from**	wing	dress		received		
P1:Actor		Cir:Location		P2:Undergoer			Process:material		
ng		ng		ng			vg		
Thing	EFM	Thing	EFM	Class	Thing	EFM	Event		
noun	clitic	noun	clitic	noun	noun	clitic	verb		
							Head	TM	EM
							stem	sfx	sfx
'The nymph received the winged dress from the woodcutter.'									

While school grammars in Korea may take (19) to be more 'correct' than (16), our point here is that the 'directional' meaning of the clitics 에게 *ege* or 한테 *hante* (as 'to' or 'from') depends on the relation of the entity they mark to the Process.

In (20) 친구들 *chingu-deul* 'peers' is the Source of the exclusion that 아이 *ai* 'child' experienced in this clause. The role played by 친구들 *chingu-deul* 'peers' could be alternatively realised as a Circumstance:Location:source through the clitic 에게서 *egeseo* or 한테서 *hanteseo* 'from', instead of 에게 *ege* 'from' (the Process-Range function will be introduced in the next section).

(20)

아이가 친구들에게 따돌림을 당했다.									
ai	=ga	chingu-deur	=ege	ttadollim	=eul	dangha-et-da			
child		friends	**from**	bullying		suffered			
P1:Actor		P3:Source		P2:P-Range		Process:material			
ng		ng		ng		vg			
Thing	EFM	Thing	EFM	Thing	EFM	Event			
noun	clitic	noun	clitic	noun	clitic	verb			
						Head	TM	EM	
						stem	sfx	sfx	
'The child suffered from bullying from her friends.'									

4.2.1.5 Entity-Range and Process-Range Some material clauses include a P2 Participant, marked by 을/를 *eul/reul*, which we refer to as Range (rather than Undergoer). A Range differs from an Undergoer in that it is not affected by the unfolding of the Process; and in general clauses with the Range function have no 'passive' (see the discussion of DIATHESIS in Section 4.3).

The Range Participants represent either an entity (often in some sense the 'domain' of the Process) or an occurrence (often specifying a Process that has been realised by a more general verb). The former is called Entity-Range (or E-Range), as in (21); and the latter is called Process-Range (or P-Range), as in (22).

(21)

그 부부는 세상을 두루두루 돌아다녔다.								
geu	*bubu*	*=neun*	*sesang*	*=eul*	*duruduru*	*doradany-eot-da*		
that	couple		world		far and wide	travelled around		
P1:Actor			P2:E-Range		Cir:Manner	Process:material		
ng			ng		advg	vg		
Deictic	Thing	TFM	Thing	EFM	Head	Event		
determiner	noun	clitic	noun	clitic	adverb	verb		
						Head	TM	EM
						stem	sfx	sfx
'The couple travelled all around the world.'								

(22)

나는 친구와 연주를 ...					
na	*=neun*	*chingu*	*=wa*	*yeonju*	*=reul*
I		friend	with	play	
P1:Actor		Cir:Accompaniment		P2:P-Range	
ng		ng		ng	
Thing	TFM	Thing	EFM	Thing	EFM
pronoun	clitic	noun	clitic	noun	clitic
'I ... a performance with a friend.'					

... 하고 있었다.				
ha-go	*iss-eot-da*			
do	be (past) doing			
Process:material				
vg				
Event	Dimension			
verb	aux verb			
Head	Link	Head	TM	EM
stem	sfx	stem	sfx	sfx
... was doing ...				

4.2 The System of EXPERIENTIAL CLAUSE TYPE

The Entity-Range Participants construe meanings involving space (as points of departure or destination), time (as points of starting, ending or passing through), purpose (of an action) or means (of an action); see Table 4.3 for examples.

Table 4.3 *Entity-Range examples*

types	examples
space	학교를 졸업하다 *hakgyo reul joreopha-da* 'graduate from school'; 섬을 떠나다 *seom eul tteona-da* 'leave the island'; 하늘을 날다 *haneul eul nal-da* 'fly the sky'
time	한 학기를 시작하다/마치다 *han hakgi reul sijakha-da/machi-da* 'begin/finish one semester'; 첫날밤을 보내다 *cheonnalbam eul bonae-da* 'spend the wedding (lit. first) night'
purpose	봉사활동을 다녀오다 *bongsahwaldong eul danyeoo-da* 'return from voluntary work'; 마중을 나오다 *majung eul nao-da* 'come to greet'
means	차를 타다 *cha reul ta-da* 'get in (lit. ride) the car'; 매를 맞다 *mae reul mat-da* 'get spanked'

The Process-Range Participants are realised through two types of noun: (i) nouns whose semantics specify some Process – these are predominantly used with the verb 하다 *ha-da* 'do' (and also with the verbs such as 받다 *bat-da* 'receive' and 당하다 *dangha-da* 'encounter (bad things)'); and (ii) nouns with a meaning that is already lexicalised in the verb realising the Process. Some examples are given in Table 4.4.

Table 4.4 *Process-Range examples*

types	examples
(i) specifying the Process	간호를 하다 *ganho reul ha-da* 'nurse, take care of'; 생활을 하다 *saenghwar eul ha-da* 'do life, i.e., lead a life'; 패스를 하다 *paeseu reul ha-da* 'do a pass, i.e., pass'; 공격을 받다 *gonggyeog eul bat-da* 'receive an attack, i.e., be attacked'; 사기를 당하다 *sagi reul dangha-da* 'encounter a swindle, i.e., be swindled'; 따돌림을 당하다 *ttadollim eul dangha-da* 'suffer from bullying'
(ii) cognate with the Process	잠을 자다 *jam eul ja-da* 'sleep a sleep'; 꿈을 꾸다 *kkum eul kku-da* 'dream a dream'; 춤을 추다 *chum eul chu-da* 'dance a dance'

The nouns realising P-Range in type (i) (typically Sino-Korean, that is, Korean words of Chinese origin) can be combined with general verbs (e.g., 하 *ha-*) to construe a single Event in a verbal group; such verbal groups can be used to realise a Process in a material clause. For example, instead of an E-Range Process structure involving 일 *il* 'work', 을 *eul* (P2 marker) and

198   The Grammar of Experiential Meaning: TRANSITIVITY

하 *ha-* 'do', we can have a Process whose Event 'combines' the two meanings – 일하 *ilha-* 'work'. As an additional example compare clause (22) with (23).

(23)

나는 친구와 연주하고 있었다.					
na	*=neun*	*chingu*	*=wa*	*yeonjuha-go*	*iss-eot-da*
I		friend	with	perform	be (past) doing
P1:Actor		Cir:Accompaniment		**Process:material**	
ng		ng		vg	
Thing	TFM	Thing	EFM	Event	Dimension
pronoun	clitic	noun	clitic	verb	aux verb
				Head	Link	Head	TM	EM
				stem	sfx	stem	sfx	sfx
'I was performing with a friend.'					

4.2.2 Mental Clauses

Mental clauses construe experience of the world inside us – as we think, desire, perceive and feel. Depending on their grammatical potential (i.e., their potential to include certain types of phenomena or not), mental clauses can be classified into four types: cognitive, desiderative, perceptive and emotive. Figure 4.3 shows the general system of MENTAL CLAUSE TYPE in Korean that we propose.

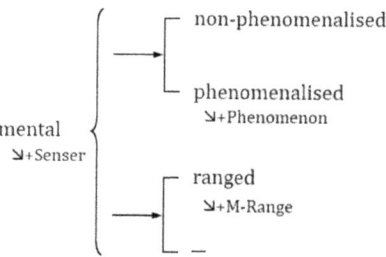

Figure 4.3 The system of MENTAL CLAUSE TYPE

Mental clauses involve two key Participant functions, Senser and Phenomenon; they may also involve a type of Range function (which we call Mental Range or M-Range in short), as discussed below.

4.2.2.1 Senser and Phenomenon

The Senser Participant is prototypically marked by 이/가 *i/ga* (P1), and is imbued with 'consciousness'. The Senser is typically accompanied by another Participant, the Phenomenon, marked by 을/를 *eul/reul* (P2). The Phenomenon construes something that is consciously processed by the Senser. The Senser and Phenomenon functions are illustrated in (24) and (25).

(24)

농부가 아들의 성공을 기뻐했다.								
nongbu	*=ga*	*adeur*	*=ui*	*seonggong*	*=eul*	*gippeoha-et-da*		
farmer		son		success		enjoyed		
P1:Senser		**P2:Phenomenon**				Process:mental		
ng		ng				vg		
Thing	EFM	Orient: possessive		Thing	EFM	Event		
noun	clitic	[ng]		noun	clitic	verb		
		Thing	Linking			Head	TM	EM
		noun	clitic			stem	sfx	sfx
'The farmer enjoyed his son's success.'								

(25)

온 가족이 영화를 봤다.								
on	*gajog*	*=i*	*yeonghwa*	*=reul*	*bw-at-da*			
whole	family		movie		watched			
P1:Senser			**P2:Phenomenon**		Process:mental			
ng			ng		vg			
Epithet	Thing	EFM	Thing	EFM	Event			
adjective	noun	clitic	noun	clitic	verb			
					Head	TM	EM	
					stem	sfx	sfx	
'The whole family watched the movie.'								

The Senser Participant typically involves human beings, but occasionally institutions, as illustrated in (26), or animals such as pets – which are in effect thereby endowed with human consciousness.

(26)

그 회사는 올해 ...				
geu	hoesa	=**neun**	olhae	
that	company		this year	
P1:Senser			Cir:Location	
ng			ng	
Deictic	Thing	TFM	Thing	
determiner	noun	clitic	noun	
'The company ... this year.'				

... 매출 증가를 기대하고 있다.						
maechul	jeunga	=reul	gidaeha-go		it-da	
sale	increase		expect		be doing	
P2:Phenomenon			Process:mental				
ng			vg				
Class	Thing	EFM	Event		Dimension	
noun	noun	clitic	verb		aux verb	
			Head	Link	Head	EM
			stem	sfx	stem	sfx
... is expecting a sales increase ...						

4.2.2.2 Mental-Range

Mental clauses may also involve a type of Range Participant, realised by a nominal group marked by 을/를 *eul/reul* (as P2). This particular function, which we will call Mental-Range, is similar to the Process-Range in material clauses (illustrated in (22)) in the sense that it specifies a Process that is realised through the general verb 하다 *ha-da* 'do' – as shown in (27). The difference is that Mental-Range Participants specify the general verb in terms of 'thinking', 'feeling' or 'hoping'. The nouns involved (typically Sino-Korean) can alternatively be combined with the general verb 하다 *ha-da* 'do' to construe a single Event in a verbal group, which can be used to realise a Process in mental clauses – as shown in (28). Note in passing that in this grammar a projected clause is treated as outside the transitivity structure of the projecting clause and thus we postpone its discussion to Chapter 6.

4.2 The System of EXPERIENTIAL CLAUSE TYPE

(27)

나는 우리가 잘 했다고 . . .

na	=neun	uri	=ga	jal	ha-et-da-go
I		we		well	did
P1:Senser		<<projected clause>>[3]			
ng					
Thing	TFM				
noun	clitic				

'I . . . we did well.'

. . . 생각을 한다.					
saenggag	=eul	ha-n-da			
thought		do			
P2:M-Range		Process:mental			
ng		vg			
Thing	EFM	Event			
noun	clitic	verb			
		Head	TM	EM	
		stem	sfx	Sfx	

. . . think . . .

(28)

나는 우리가 잘 했다고 생각한다.

na	=neun	uri	=ga	jal	ha-et-da-go	saenggakha-n-da
I		we		well	did	think
P1:Senser		<<projected clause>>				Process:mental
ng						vg
Thing	TFM					Event
noun	clitic					verb
						Head	TM	EM
						stem	sfx	sfx

'I think we did well.'

---

[3] Following SFL conventions, we use << >> to represent enclosed clauses.

4.2.2.3 Phenomenon Construing Acts, Facts and Ideas

The Phenomenon in mental clauses may involve not only a thing (as in (25) and (26)), but also an act (a macro-thing) or a fact or an idea (meta-things). In general terms, an act is an unfolding event (사건 *sageon* 'act'), a fact is a presupposed linguistic construal of an event or state of affairs (사실 *sasil* 'fact'), and an idea is the content of a thought (생각 *saenggak* 'idea'). In Korean, all these can be realised by an embedded clause (i.e., a clause that has been 'rank-shifted' to function as a constituent of another clause).

In (29) and (30), the mental clauses involve embedded clauses. In (29) the embedded clause construes an ongoing event that is witnessed (사건 *sageon* 'an act'); in (30) the embedded clause construes an event that is presupposed (사실 *sasil* 'a fact').

From an SFL perspective, the Phenomenon is not 'directly' realised by the embedded clause. Two 'layers' need to be recognised connecting the two, since strictly speaking the Phenomenon is realised through a nominal group consisting of a Thing and EFM structure – with the Thing realised by the embedded clause.

(29)

나는 [[사람이 떨어지는 것을]] 보았다.									
na	=*neun*	[[*saram*	=*i*	*tteoreoji-neun*	*geos*	=*eul*]]	*bo-at-da*		
I		person		falling			saw		
P1:Senser		P2:Phenomenon (act)					Process:mental		
ng		ng					vg		
Thing	TFM	Thing				EFM	Event		
pronoun	clitic	[[clause]]				clitic	verb		
							Head	TM	EM
							stem	sfx	sfx
'I saw a person falling.'									

(30)

우리는 [[국민이 주시하고 있음을]] ...						
uri	=*neun*	[[*gungmin*	=*i*	*jusiha-go*	*iss-eum*	=*eul*]]
we		people		watch	be doing	
P1:Senser		P2:Phenomenon (fact)				
ng		ng				
Thing	TFM	Thing				EFM
pronoun	clitic	[[clause]]				clitic
'We ... that people are watching (us).'						

4.2 The System of EXPERIENTIAL CLAUSE TYPE

... 알아야 한다.	
ar-aya	*ha-n-da*
know	must
Process:mental	
vg	
Event	Modal
verb	aux verb
Head	Link	Head	TM	EM
stem	sfx	stem	sfx	sfx
... must know ...	

In (31) and (32), where the Processes are emotive and desiderative respectively, the Phenomenon Participants are also realised by an embedded clause. In (31) the embedded clause construes an ongoing event that is disliked (an act); in (32) the embedded clause construes an event that is desired but not presupposed (생각 *saenggak* 'an idea').

(31)

그 사람은 [[남한테 지기를]] 싫어한다.							
geu	*saram*	*=eun*	[[*nam*	*=hante*	*ji-gi*	*=reul*]]	*sireoha-n-da*
that	person		others	to	losing		dislike
P1:Senser			P2:Phenomenon(act)				Process
ng			ng				vg
Deictic	Thing	TFM	Thing			EFM	Event
determiner	noun	clitic	[[clause]]			clitic	verb
							Head	TM	EM
							stem	sfx	sfx
'That person hates losing to others.'							

(32)

나는 [[주가가 올라가기를]] 바라고 있다.							
na	*=neun*	[[*juga*	*=ga*	*olaga-gi*	*=reul*]]	*bara-go*	*it-da*
I		stock price		rising		hope	Be doing
P1:Senser		P2:Phenomenon(idea)				Process	
ng		ng				vg	
Thing	TFM	Thing			EFM	Event	Dimension
pronoun	clitic	[[clause]]			clitic	verb	aux verb
						Head	Link	Head	EM
						stem	sfx	stem	sfx
'I am hoping that stock prices rise.'							

The embedded clauses in (29)–(32) are different in type from those we considered in Section 2.3.7 in Chapter 2. There, the embedded clause involved a Relative Tense Mark (RTM) and realised the Qualifier function within nominal group structure – as illustrated in (33); this clause appeared as example (104) in Chapter 2.

(33)

친구가 읽은 책이 여기 있다.							
chingu	=*ga*	*ilg-eun*		*chaeg*	=*i*	*yeogi*	*it-da*
friend		read		book		here	was
P1						Cir: Location	Process
ng						advg	vg
Qualifier				Thing	EFM	Head	Event
[[clause]]				noun	clitic	adverb	verb
P1		Process				Head	EM
ng		vg				stem	sfx
Thing	EFM	Event					
noun	clitic	verb					
		Head	**RTM**				
		stem	**sfx**				
'The book (which) a friend read is here.'							

In contrast, the embedded clauses in (29)–(32) realise clause rank **Participant functions**, as signalled by the accompanying EFM 을/를 *eul/reul* (P2).

There are essentially two strategies available for embedding clauses to realise a Participant function. One is through what we call the **Installing** function, which is realised by a bound noun at group rank; and the other is through what we label as the **Install** function, which is realised by a suffix at word rank.

The **Installing** function is typically realised by a bound noun, such as 것 *geot*, 줄 *jul* or 지 *ji*. The verb preceding the bound noun culminates with one of the suffixes (으)ㄴ *-(eu)n* ([happened]), 는 *neun* ([ongoing]), (으)ㄹ *-(eu)l* ([not happened]), 던 *-deon* ([witnessed]) and 았/었던 *-at/eot-deon* ([remote]); these are also deployed to culminate embedded clauses realising Qualifiers (see Section 2.3.7 in Chapter 2). Example (34) provides a more detailed analysis of (29).

4.2 The System of EXPERIENTIAL CLAUSE TYPE

(34)

나는 [[사람이 떨어지는 것을]] 보았다.							
na	=neun	[[saram	=i	tteoreoji-**neun**	geos	=eul]]	bo-at-da
I		person		falling			saw
P1:Senser		P2:Phenomenon(act)					Process
ng		ng					vg
		Thing				EFM	
		[[clause]]				clitic	
		P1:Actor		Process			
		ng		vg			
		Thing	EFM	Event	Installing		
		noun	clitic	verb	bound noun		
				Head	Link		
				stem	sfx		
'I saw a person falling.'							

The **Install** function on the other hand is realised by the suffix (으)ㅁ -*(eu)m* or 기 -*gi*, which marks a clause as functioning as a constituent – as a P2: Phenomenon followed by the EFM 을/를 *eul/reul* in our examples. This function is illustrated in (35) and (36), which provide a more detailed analysis of (30) and (31).

(35)

우리는 [[국민이 주시하고 있음을]] 알아야 한다.								
uri	=neun	[[gungmin	=i	jusiha-go	iss-**eum**	=eul]]	ar-aya	ha-n-da
we		all		watch	be doing		know	must
P1:Senser		P2:Phenomenon(fact)					Process	
ng		ng					vg	
		Thing				EFM		
		[[clause]]				clitic		
		P1:Senser		Process				
		ng		vg				
		Thing	EFM	Event	Dimension			
		noun	clitic	verb	aux verb			
				Head	Link	Head	Install	
				stem	sfx	stem	sfx	
'We must know that people are watching (us).'								

(36)

그 사람은 [[남한테 지기를]] 싫어한다.							
geu	*saram*	*=eun*	[[*nam*	*=hante*	*ji-gi*	*=reul*]]	*sireoha-n-da*
the	person		others	to	losing		dislike
P1:Senser			P2:Phenomenon(act)				Process
ng			ng				vg
			Thing			EFM	
			[[clause]]			clitic	
			P3		Process		
			ng		vg		
			Thing	EFM	Event		
			noun	clitic	verb		
					Head	Install	
					stem	sfx	
'He dislikes losing to others.'							

Now we have introduced the Installing and Install functions, we can continue with observations concerning types of mental clause (i.e., perceptive, emotive, desiderative and cognitive clauses) and the availability of embedding strategies with respect to acts, facts and ideas.

First, as we saw in (34) and (36), acts can be embedded in perceptive and emotive clauses, via the Installing or Install functions. When embedding is realised through the Installing function ((34)), the connecting suffix to the bound noun 것 *geot* is typically 는 *-neun* ([ongoing]).

Second, facts are embedded in perceptive and cognitive clauses via an Installing function. Facts are different from acts in two respects. One is that the linking suffix is (으)ㄴ *-(eu)n* ([happened]), not 는 *-neun* ([ongoing]). This is illustrated in (37), which contrasts with (34) where the embedded act had the linker 는 *-neun*. The other is that, particularly in cognitive clauses, the bound noun 줄 *jul*, can also be used (as an alternative to 것 *geot*) – as shown in (38). The bound nouns in both (37) and (38) can be replaced by 사실 *sasil* 'fact' in Korean.

4.2 The System of EXPERIENTIAL CLAUSE TYPE

(37)

[[아파트에서 사람이 떨어진 것을]] ...							
[[*apateu*	=*eseo*	*saram*	=*i*	*tteoreoji-n*	*geos*	*eul*]]	
apartment	from	person		fell			
P2:Phenomenon(fact)							
ng							
Thing							EFM
[[clause]]							clitic
Cir:Location		P1:Actor		Process			
ng		ng		vg			
Thing	EFM	Thing	EFM	Event		Installing	
noun	clitic	noun	clitic	verb		bound noun	
				Head	Link		
				stem	sfx		
... that a person fell from the apartment.'							

... 알고 있다.	
al-go	*it-da*
know	be doing
Process	
vg	
Event	Dimension
verb	aux verb
Head	Link	Head	EM
stem	sfx	stem	sfx
'I know ...	

(38)

[[그 사람이 죽은 줄을]] ...					
[[*geu*	*saram*	=*i*	*jug-eun*	*jur*	*eul*]]
the	person		died		
P2:Phenomenon(fact)					
ng					
Thing					EFM
[[clause]]					clitic
P1:Actor			Process		
ng			vg		
Deictic	Thing	EFM	Event	**Installing**	
determiner	noun	clitic	verb	**bound noun**	
			Head	Link	
			stem	sfx	
... that the person had passed away.'					

... 아무도 몰랐다.			
amudo	*moll-at-da*		
nobody	didn't know		
P0	Process		
ng	vg		
Thing	Event		
pronoun	verb		
	Head	TM	EM
	stem	sfx	sfx
'Nobody knew ...			

    Third, ideas are embedded in desiderative clauses via an Install function at word rank – particularly through the suffix 기 -*gi* as in (39). Embedding through an Installing function at clause rank is also possible. But when an embedded idea in a desiderative clause is realised through the Installing function, the linking suffix tends to be (으)ㄹ -*(eu)l*, as shown in (40), and a wider choice of bound nouns (e.g., 지 *ji*, 줄 *jul* and 것 *geot*) is available. Note that ideas are *not* projected by desiderative clauses in Korean; see Chapter 6.

4.2 The System of EXPERIENTIAL CLAUSE TYPE

(39)

빨리 낫기를 기원합니다.					
ppalli	*nat-**gi***		=*reul*	*giwonha-mnida*	
quickly	recovering			wish	
P2:Phenomenon(idea)				Process:mental	
ng				vg	
Thing			EFM	Event	
[[clause]]			clitic	verb	
Cir:Manner	Process			Head	EM:ven;decl
advg	vg			stem	sfx
Head	Event				
adverb	verb				
	Head	**Install**			
	stem	**sfx**			
'I wish you a speedy recovery.'					

(40)

곧 함께 일할 것을 기대합니다.						
got	*hamkke*	*ilha-l*		*geos*	=*eul*	*gidaeha-mnida*
soon	together	work				look forward
P2:Phenomenon						Process:mental
ng						vg
Thing					EFM	Event
[[clause]]					clitic	verb
Cir:Location	Cir:Manner	Process				Head	EM:ven;decl
advg	advg	vg				stem	sfx
Head	Head	Event	**Installing**				
adverb	adverb	verb	**bound noun**				
		Head	Link				
		stem	sfx				
'I look forward to working together soon.'						

Fourth, as illustrated in (41) and (42), ideas can be embedded in perceptive and cognitive clauses through Install or Installing functions. Ideas can be projected as well; see in particular examples (33) and (34) in Chapter 6.

Note that the bound noun 지 *ji* in (42) cannot be replaced by 사실 *sasil* 'fact' (since we are dealing with ideas, not presupposed facts).

(41)

나는 무언가 이상함을 느꼈다.							
na	=neun	mueonga	isangha-m	=eul	neukky-eot-da.		
I		something	being strange		felt		
P1:Senser		P2:Phenomenon(idea)			Process		
ng		ng			vg		
Thing	TFM	Thing		EFM	Event		
pronoun	clitic	[[clause]]		clitic	verb		
		P0	Process		Head	TM	EM
		ng	vg		stem	sfx	sfx
		Thing	Event				
		pronoun	verb				
			Head	Install			
			stem	sfx			
'I felt something being strange.'[4]							

(42)

그는 누가 공격하는 지를 …						
geu	=neun	nuga	gonggyeokha-neun	ji	=reul	
he		who	attack			
P1:Senser		P2:Phenomenon(idea)				
ng		ng				
Thing	TFM	Thing				EFM
pronoun	clitic	[[clause]]				clitic
		P1	Process			
		ng	vg			
		Thing	EFM	Event	Installing	
		pronoun	clitic	verb	bound noun	
				Head	Link	
				stem	sfx	
'He … who is attacking.'						

---

[4] We use a non-finite clause here in the ungrammatical English translation to draw attention to the embedded clause structure.

4.2 The System of EXPERIENTIAL CLAUSE TYPE

... 모르고 있다.	
moreu-go	*it-da*
not know	be ...-ing
Process	
vg	
Event	Dimension
verb	aux verb
Head	Link	Head	EM
stem	sfx	stem	sfx
... does not know ...	

Table 4.5 sums up the possibilities in Korean as far as construing acts, facts and ideas is concerned (note that 'prjt'd' stands for 'projected' in the table)

Table 4.5 *Acts, facts and ideas and embedding strategies*

	act		fact		idea	
	embedded	prjt'd	embedded	prjt'd	embedded	prjt'd
perceptive 보다 *bo-da* 'see'; 듣다 *deut-da* 'hear', etc.	**Installing (ongoing)** 는 것을 *-neun geos eul*	–	**Installing (happened)** (으)ㄴ 것을 *-(eu)n geos eul*	–	**Installing (ongoing/not happened)** 는/(으)ㄹ 것을 *-neun/(eu)l geos eul*	–
	Install ((eu)m) (으)ㅁ을 *-(eu)m eul*				**Install ((eu)m)** (으)ㅁ을 *-(eu)m eul*	
emotive 좋아하다 *joaha-da* 'like'; 싫어하다 *sireoha-da* 'dislike', etc.	**Installing (ongoing)** 는 것을 *-neun geos eul*	–	**Installing (happened)** (으)ㄴ 것을 *-(eu)n geos eul*	–	–	–
	Install (gi) 기를 *-gi reul*					
desiderative 원하다 *wonha-da* 'want'; 바라다 *bara-da* 'wish', etc.	–	–	–	–	**Installing (not happened)** (으)ㄹ 것을 *-(eu)l geos eul*	–
					Install (gi) 기를 *-gi reul*	

Table 4.5 *(cont.)*

	act		fact		idea	
	embedded	prjt'd	embedded	prjt'd	embedded	prjt'd
cognitive 알다 *al-da* 'know'; 모르다 *moreu-da* 'not know'	–	–	**Installing (happened)** (으)ㄴ 것을 *-(eu)n geos eul* (으)ㄴ 줄을 *-(eu)n jul eul*	–	**Installing (ongoing/not happened)** 는/(으)ㄹ 지를 *-neun/(eu)l ji reul* 는/(으)ㄹ 줄을 *-neun/(eu)l jul eul* 는/(으)ㄹ 것을 *-neun/(eu)l geos eul*	Yes
			Install ((eu)m) (으)ㅁ을 *-(eu)m eul*		**Install ((eu)m)** (으)ㅁ을 *-(eu)m eul*	

4.2.3 Relational Clauses

There are four types of relational clauses in Korean: 'attributive', 'identifying', 'locative' and 'possessive'. We will refer to the attributive and identifying types as 'intensive' – they construe a relation between two nominal groups that refer to the same entity.

In attributive clauses, the relation between the two Participants involves a characterisation of phenomena at different levels of generality (e.g., describing or classifying); in identifying clauses, the relation concerns an identity between phenomena construed at different levels of abstraction (e.g., symbolising, defining or exemplifying).

We treat 'locative' and 'possessive' relational clauses as non-intensive, as they construe relationships between two different entities. As explained below in detail, non-intensive relational clauses construe 'being located' or 'having' relations as well as general indications as to the quantity of the Located and the Possession (as 'lots' or 'some').

Figure 4.4 shows the system of RELATIONAL CLAUSE TYPE in Korean we propose.

4.2 The System of EXPERIENTIAL CLAUSE TYPE

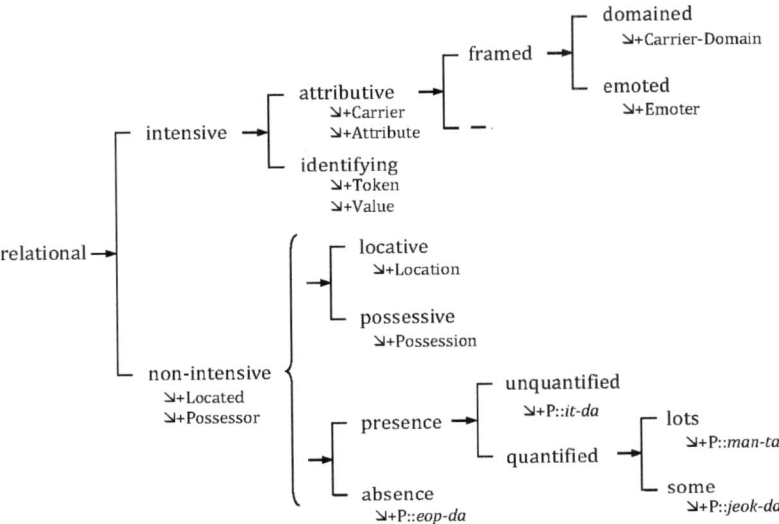

Figure 4.4 The system of RELATIONAL CLAUSE TYPE

Below we discuss Participant roles in intensive relational types first, and then move on to those in non-intensive types.

4.2.3.1 Carrier and Attribute The Carrier and Attribute are the two inherent Participants in attributive clauses; the Carrier construes an entity characterised by the Attribute.

The Carrier is realised by a nominal group, marked prototypically by 이/가 *i/ga* (as P1); but for textual reasons, the Carrier is generally marked by 은/는 *eun/neun*, TFM, rather than by 이/가 *i/ga* EFM:P1.

The Attribute can be realised by a nominal group or by a verbal group (via conflation with the Process). When the Attribute is realised by a nominal group, it is either marked by 이/가 *i/ga* (as a P1 Participant), as in (43), or not marked by a clitic (as a P0 Participant), as in (44). The P0:Attribute is deployed when the Process is realised through the copula 이다 *i-da* 'be' or 같다 *gat-da* 'be like'.

(43)

수애는 꽹장한 미인이다.						
Suae	*=neun*	*goengjangha-n*		*miin*	*i-da*	
Suae		stunning		beauty	is	
P1:Carrier		**P0:Attribute**			Process	
ng		ng			vg	
Thing	TFM	Epithet		Thing	Event	
noun	clitic	adjective		noun	copula	
		Head	Link		Head	EM
		stem	sfx		stem	sfx
'Suae is a stunning beauty.'						

The P1:Attribute on the other hand is deployed when the Process is realised through verbs such as 되다 *doe-da* 'become', as in (44); in this case there is in effect an 'additional' P1 in the clause because the Carrier is realised as P1 as well.

(44)

수애가 벌써 어른이 되었다.							
Suae	*=ga*	*beolsseo*		*eoreun*	*=i*	*doe-eot-da*	
Suae		already		adult		became	
P1:Carrier		Modal Adjunct		**P1:Attribute**		Process	
ng		advg		ng		vg	
Thing	EFM:P1	Head		Thing	EFM:P1	Event	
noun	clitic	adverb		noun	clitic	verb	
						Head	TM	EM
						stem	sfx	sfx
'Suae has already become an adult.'							

The P1:Attribute is also deployed when the Process is realised by the negative copula 아니다 *ani-da* 'be not', as in (45). This contrasts with instances where the Process is realised by the (positive) copula 이다 *i-da* 'be'; in these cases, as we saw in (43), the Attribute is realised as a P0 Participant.

4.2 The System of EXPERIENTIAL CLAUSE TYPE

(45)

수애는 이제 아이가 아니다.					
Suae	*=neun*	*ije*	*ai*	*=ga*	*ani-da*
Suae		now	child		is not
P1:Carrier		Modal Adjunct	**P1:Attribute**		Process
ng		advg	ng		vg
Thing	TFM	Head	Thing	EFM	Event
noun	clitic	adverb	noun	clitic	verb
					Head / EM
					stem / sfx
'Suae is not a child anymore.'					

In Korean, the Attribute can also be realised through a verbal group, whose Event is realised by a verbalised adjective; the Attribute is thus conflated with the Process function, as in (46). As introduced in Chapter 2, a Degree function can also be realised in a relational clause where the Event is realised by a verbalised adjective (see Section 2.4.7 in Chapter 2 for details).

(46)

오늘은 교통 체증이 아주 심하다.						
oneul	*=eun*	*gyotong*	*chejeung*	*=i*	*aju*	*simha-da*
today		traffic	jam		very	is heavy
Cir:Location		P1:Carrier			**Attribute/Process**	
ng		ng			vg	
Thing	TFM	Class	Thing	EFM	**Degree**	Event
noun	clitic	noun	noun	clitic	adverb	verbalised adjective
						Head / EM
						stem / sfx
'Today the traffic is very heavy.'						

Verbalised adjectives can be descriptive, e.g., 심하다 *simha-da* 'be severe', 깊다 *gip-da* 'be deep', 둥글다 *dunggeul-da* 'be round' and 크다 *keu-da* 'be big'; or they can be attitudinal, e.g., 행복하다 *haengbokha-da* 'be happy', 자랑스럽다 *jarangseureop-da* 'be proud', 아름답다 *areumdap-da* 'be beautiful' and 정직하다 *jeongjikha-da* 'be honest'.

The Attribute realised by a nominal group has the function of 'classifying' the Carrier (e.g., (43)–(45)), whereas the Attribute realised through a verbal group (headed by a verbalised adjective) has the function of 'describing' the Carrier (e.g., (46)).

4.2.3.2 Token and Value

Token and Value are the two inherent Participants in identifying clauses. In this clause type the Token is the more 'concrete' manifestation and the Value is the more 'abstract' designation of the Token (cf. Thompson 2014: 104, Halliday and Matthiessen 2014: 279).

As illustrated in (47), Token and Value are usually realised through nominal groups, with a Token ^ Value sequence; and the Process is realised through the copula 이다 *i-da* 'be'. The Participant appearing first in an identifying clause is prototypically marked by *eun/neun* (TFM); the following Participant is not marked by a clitic (and so is a P0 Participant).

(47)

경복궁은 조선시대 제일의 법궁이다.							
Gyeongbokgung	=eun	Joseonsidae	jeil	=ui	beobgung	i-da	
Gyeongbokgung		Joseon era	first		palace	is	
P1:Token		**P0:Value**				Process	
ng		ng				vg	
Thing	TFM	Class	Orient		Thing	Event	
noun	clitic	noun	[ng]		noun	copula	
			Thing	Linking		Head	EM
			noun	clitic		stem	sfx
'Gyeongbokgung is the principal palace of the Joseon Dynasty.'							

The first element in an identifying clause can also be marked by 이/가 *i/ga* (as P1). This is necessary for embedded clauses,[5] where a TFM clitic is not

---

[5] If we compare (47) with the example below, we see that the P1 in an embedded clause is marked by the EFM 이/가 *i/ga*.

경복궁이 제일의 법궁임을 압니까?								
Gyeongbokgung	=i	jeil	=ui	beobgung	i-m		=eul	am-nikka
Gyeongbokgung		first		palace	is			know
P2:Phenomenon								Process
ng								vg
Thing							EFM	Event
[[clause]]							clitic	verb
P1:Token		P0:Value			Process		Head	EM
ng		ng			vg		stem	sfx
Thing	EFM	Orient		Thing	Event			
noun	clitic	[ng]		noun	copula			
		Thing	Linking		Head	Install		
		noun	clitic		stem	sfx		
'Are you aware that Gyeongbokgung is the principal palace?'								

4.2 The System of EXPERIENTIAL CLAUSE TYPE

possible; and it is an alternative to the TFM in various 'marked' situations, such as in a 'challenge' move (Martin and Rose 2007: 242–4) – where, for example, someone denies what has been said before.

Identifying clauses also involve the negative copula 아니다 *ani-da* 'be not'. As illustrated in (48), when the Process is realised by the negative copula, the second Participant is also realised as P1.

(48)

경복궁은 조선시대 제일의 법궁이 아니다.								
Gyeongbokgung	*=eun*	*Joseonsidae*	*jeil*	*=ui*	*beobgung*	*=i*	*ani-da*	
Gyeongbokgung		Joseon era	first		palace		is not	
P1:Token		**P1:Value**					Process	
ng		ng					vg	
Thing	TFM	Class	Orient		Thing	EFM	Event	
noun	clitic	noun	[ng]		noun	clitic	copula	
			Thing	Linking			Head	EM
			noun	clitic			stem	sfx
'Gyeongbokgung is not the principal palace of the Joseon Dynasty.'								

The Token and Value in this type of relational clauses can be resequenced without changing the experiential meaning of the clause. For example, in (47) the first Participant is the Token (P1) and the second the Value (P0). In (49) however the first Participant is the Value (P1) and the second the Token (P0). The difference in meaning is in fact a textual one, having to do with information flow (cf. Chapter 5). As was the case for the Token ^ Value sequence, the first element in a Value ^ Token sequence is prototypically marked by 은/는 *eun/neun* (TFM); it can also be marked by 이/가 *i/ga* (as P1), under the condition noted above for (48) – that is, a negative copula.

(49)

조선시대 제일의 법궁은 경복궁이다.							
Joseonsidae	*jeil*	*=ui*	*beobgung*	*=eun*	*Gyeongbokgung*	*i-da*	
Joseon period	first		palace		Gyeongbokgung	is	
P1:Value					**P0:Token**	Process	
ng					ng	vg	
Class	Orient		Thing	TFM	Thing	Event	
noun	[ng]		noun	clitic	noun	copula	
	Thing	Linking				Head	EM
	noun	clitic				stem	sfx
'The principal palace of the Joseon Dynasty is Gyeongbokgung.'							

Identifying clauses can involve a more specific 'identifying' verb, such as 의미하다 *uimiha-da* 'mean', 상징하다 *sangjingha-da* 'symbolise', 나타내다 *natanae-da* 'represent' or 가리키다 *gariki-da* 'indicate'. As (50) and (51) illustrate, in clauses with this kind of verb, the Token is prototypically realised through P1 (marked by 이/가 *i/ga*) and the Value is prototypically realised through P2 (marked by 을/를 *eul/reul*).

(50)

삼촌은 아버지의 남자형제를 가리킨다.									
samchon	=*eun*	*abeoji*	=*ui*	*namja*	*hyeongje*	=*reul*	*gariki-n-da*		
uncle		father	's	male	sibling		indicate		
P1:Token		**P2:Value**					Process		
ng		ng					vg		
Thing	TFM	Orient		Class	Thing	EFM	Event		
noun	clitic	[ng]		noun	noun	clitic	verb		
		Thing	Linking				Head	TM	EM
		noun	clitic				stem	sfx	sfx
'Uncle means father's male sibling.'									

(51)

비둘기는 평화를 상징한다.						
bidulgi	=*neun*	*pyeonghwa*	=*reul*	*sangjingha-n-da*		
dove		peace		symbolise		
P1:Token		**P2:Value**		Process		
ng		ng		vg		
Thing	TFM	Thing	EFM	Event		
noun	clitic	noun	clitic	verb		
				Head	TM	EM
				stem	sfx	sfx
'The dove symbolises peace.'						

In this clause type, the specific 'identifying' verb can be replaced by the copula 이다 *i-da*. The Value is then realised as P0; it cannot be realised as a P2 (the Token is still realised as P1.) Thus, depending on meaning of the 'identifying' verb, the Value is realised differently. Compare (50) with (52), and also (51) with (53).

4.2 The System of EXPERIENTIAL CLAUSE TYPE

(52)

삼촌은 아버지의 남자 형제이다.							
samchon	=eun	abeoji	=ui	namja	hyeongje	i-da	
uncle		father	's	male	sibling	is	
P1:Token		**P0:Value**				Process	
ng		ng				vg	
Thing	TFM	Orient		Class	Thing	Event	
noun	clitic	[ng]		noun	noun	copula	
		Thing	Linking			Head	EM
		noun	clitic			stem	sfx
'Uncle is father's male sibling.'							

(53)

비둘기는 평화의 상징이다.						
bidulgi	=neun	pyeonghwa	=ui	sangjing	i-da	
dove		peace		symbol	is	
P1:Token		**P0:Value**			Process	
ng		ng			vg	
Thing	TFM	Orient		Thing	Event	
noun	clitic	[ng]		noun	copula	
		Thing	Linking		Head	EM
		noun	clitic		stem	sfx
'The dove is the symbol of peace.'						

4.2.3.3 Carrier-Domain Attributive relational clauses, but not identifying ones, may have additional Participant roles other than the 'Carrier' and 'Attribute' functions described above. One such role is the Carrier-Domain (or C-Domain).

What the Carrier-Domain does is to set up a frame of reference for the following Carrier on the basis of a specific semantic relationship between them – e.g., 'dimensional' (the cell and its shape), as in (54), or 'kinship' (Mr Kim and his brother), as in (55). Both Carrier-Domain and Carrier are P1 Participants in Korean, although for textual reasons the Carrier-Domain tends to be realised through a nominal group with the clitic 은/는 *eun/neun*, TFM.

(54)

백혈구는 모양이 불규칙하다.					
baekhyeolgu	*=neun*	*moyang*	*=i*	*bulgyuchikha-da*	
white blood cell		shape		is irregular	
P1:Carrier-Domain		**P1:Carrier**		Attribute/Process	
ng		ng		vg	
Thing	TFM	Thing	EFM	Event	
noun	clitic	noun	clitic	verbalised adjective	
				Head	EM
				stem	sfx
'Speaking of white blood cells, their shape is irregular.'					

(55)

그 사람은 동생이 의사이다.							
geu	*saram*	*=eun*	*dongsaeng*	*=i*	*uisa*	*i-da*	
that	person		younger brother		doctor	is	
P1:Carrier-Domain			**P1:Carrier**		P0:Attribute	Process	
ng			ng		ng	vg	
Deictic	Thing	TFM	Thing	EFM	Thing	Event	
determiner	noun	clitic	noun	clitic	noun	copula	
						Head	EM
						stem	sfx
'Speaking of that person, his younger brother is a doctor.'							

A similar type of relational clause has been reported for Chinese and Japanese. Halliday and McDonald (2004: 321) treat the first nominal group in this type of clause in Chinese as an 'absolute Theme' (thereby suggesting that it does not have a function in the experiential structure of the clause). According to Teruya (2004: 217), however, the first nominal group in a comparable type of relational clause in Japanese functions is an ordinary Theme; and he also analyses it from an experiential perspective as a Participant, which he calls 'Carrier-Domain'.

In interpreting Korean, we prefer Teruya's analysis in order to capture the experiential relation between the Carrier-Domain and the Carrier. Between the Carrier-Domain and the Carrier there must be a semantic relationship of some kind (e.g., dimensionality or kinship as mentioned above). A useful way to test

4.2 The System of EXPERIENTIAL CLAUSE TYPE

whether such a meaning relationship obtains is to see if the meanings realised by the Carrier-Domain and the Carrier can be alternatively realised in a single nominal group, involving the clitic 의 *ui* 'of'. Compare for example, 백혈구의 모양 *baekhyeolgu ui moyang* 'the shape of white blood cells' in (56) in relation to (54), and 그 사람의 동생 *geu saram ui dongsaeng* 'The person's younger brother' in (57) in relation to (55). The clear relationships encoded in the nominal group structure support our analysis of 백혈구 *baekhyeolgu* 'white blood cells' and 그 사람 *geu saram* 'the person' as Carrier-Domain.

(56)

백혈구의 모양은 불규칙하다.						
baekhyeolgu	=*ui*	*moyang*	=*eun*	*bulgyuchikha-da*		
white blood cell		shape		is irregular		
P1:Carrier				Attribute/Process		
ng				vg		
Orient		Thing	TFM	Event		
[ng]		noun	clitic	verbalised adjective		
Thing	Linking			Head	EM	
noun	clitic			stem	sfx	
'The shape of white blood cells is irregular.'						

(57)

그 사람의 동생은 의사이다.							
geu	*saram*	=*ui*	*dongsaeng*	=*eun*	*uisa*	*i-da*	
that	person		younger brother		doctor	is	
P1:Carrier					P0:Attribute	Process	
ng					ng	vg	
Orient			Thing	TFM	Thing	Event	
[ng]			noun	clitic	noun	copula	
Deictic	Thing	Linking				Head	EM
determiner	noun	clitic				stem	sfx
'That person's younger brother is a doctor.'							

Identifying relational clauses do not have an additional function that is comparable to the Carrier-Domain.

4.2.3.4 Emoter Another Participant role that may appear in attributive relational clauses is the Emoter. As shown in (58) and (59), the Emoter occurs where the Process is realised through a verbalised attitudinal adjective, such as 좋다 *jo-ta* 'likable', 싫다 *sil-ta* 'not likable', 무섭다 *museop-da* 'scary', 자랑스럽다 *jarangseureop-da* 'proud', 반갑다 *bangap-da* 'glad', etc.

The Emoter is the source of the evaluation attributed to the Carrier; the Carrier in turn triggers an emotional reaction in the Emoter. It is prototypically marked by 은/는 *eun/neun* (TFM) and can also be marked by 이/가 *i/ga* (as P1), under the conditions noted above.

(58)

나는 그 사람이 싫다.						
na	=neun	geu	saram	=i	sil-ta	
I		the	person		is not likable	
P1:Emoter		P1:Carrier			Attribute/Process	
ng		ng			vg	
Thing	TFM	Deictic	Thing	EFM	Event	
pronoun	clitic	determiner	noun	clitic	verbalised adjective	
					Head	EM
					stem	sfx
'To me, that person is unlikable.'						

(59)

나는 큰 개가 무섭다.						
na	=neun	keun	gae	=ga	museop-da	
I		big	dog		is scary	
P1:Emoter		P1:Carrier			Attribute/Process	
ng		ng			vg	
Thing	TFM	Epithet	Thing	EFM	Event	
pronoun	clitic	adjective	noun	clitic	verbalised adjective	
					Head	EM
					stem	sfx
'To me, big dogs are scary.'						

In Korean, the Emoter is usually limited to the speaker or writer. Other people's emotional reactions are typically realised through mental clauses (see Section 4.2.2). Compare (60) with (58).

4.2 The System of EXPERIENTIAL CLAUSE TYPE

(60)

수애는 그 사람을 싫어한다.					
Suae	***neun***	*=geu*	*saram*	*=eul*	*sireoha-n-da*
Suae		the	person		dislike
P1:Senser		**P2:Phenomenon**			Process:mental
ng		ng			vg
Thing	TFM	Deictic	Thing	EFM	Event
pronoun	clitic	determiner	noun	clitic	verb
					Head | TM | EM
					stem | sfx | sfx
'Suae dislikes the person.'					

4.2.3.5 Non-intensive Relational Clauses and the Features [presence] vs [absence] Our description of relational clauses so far has focused on the intensive type. Following Halliday (1967: 40), the term 'intensive' indicates that the Participants have 'the same referent as another element in the clause: for example, *she was a good teacher*'. We now turn to the other type of relational clause, that is, non-intensive, where the Participants do not have 'the same referent'.

Two sub-types of non-intensive relational clause are available in Korean. We label them as 'locative' and 'possessive'. We label their Participant roles as 'Located' and 'Location' and 'Possessor' and 'Possession', respectively.

As illustrated in Figure 4.5, which is part of Figure 4.4, there is an important dimension common to locative and possessive clauses. This dimension has to do with existential meanings in Korean – (i) 'there is (quantity irrelevant)', (ii) 'there are many', (iii) 'there are some' and (iv) 'there aren't any'. The first three are 'positive'; we say they share the feature [presence]. And the fourth is 'negative'; we say it has the feature [absence].

Moving along in delicacy from [presence], we have the features [unquantified], [lots] and [some]. Since these features and [absence] are common to [locative] and [possessive] clauses, the system predicts that eight non-intensive relational clause types are available – [locative;unquantified], [locative;lots], [locative;some], [locative;absence], [possessive;unquantified], [possessive;lots], [possessive;some] and [possessive;absence].

Note that the four 'existential' meanings are realised through lexical items in Korean – there is no grammatical evidence in Korean for the recognition of 'existentials' as an independent clause type as in English. The representative[6]

---

[6] We say 'representative' here because for each existential meaning, multiple lexical items are available. For instance, for [lots], 수없다 *sueop-da* 'innumerous', 숱하다 *sutha-da* 'plentiful', 허다하다 *heodaha-da* 'be many', 무진장하다 *mujinjangha-da* 'countless', 무수하다 *musuha-da* 'innumerous', etc. are possible.

224   The Grammar of Experiential Meaning: TRANSITIVITY

lexical items (all verbalised adjectives) for the four existential meanings in Korean are 있다 *it-da* 'there is', 적다 *jeok-da* 'there are some', 많다 *man-ta* 'there are lots', and 없다 *eop-da* 'there is not'.

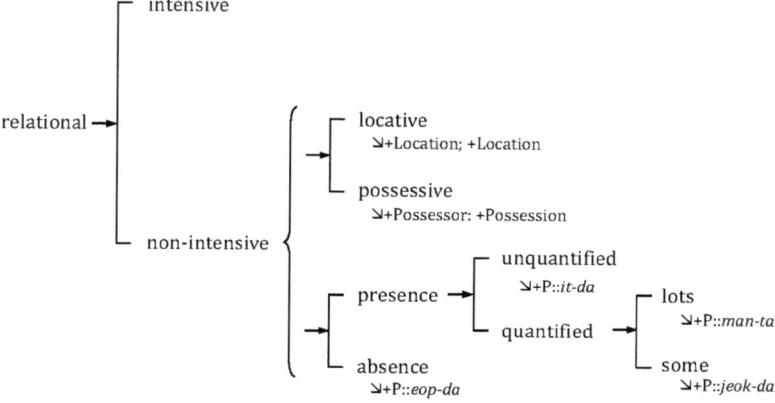

Figure 4.5 Non-intensive relational clauses

In what follows, we explore locative and possessive relational clauses in more detail.

4.2.3.6 Located and Location In Korean, the locative type of relational clause involves two Participants, P1 and P3, which we label as the 'Located' and the 'Location' respectively. The P1 realises the entity that is located, and the P3 the location in space or time where the entity is located. As mentioned above, the Process can construe four types of meaning: 'there-is', 'there-isn't', 'there-are-lots' and 'there-are-some'.

Whereas the copula (positive and negative) and verbalised adjectives are employed to realise the Process in the intensive types of relational clauses, in non-intensive relational clauses verbalised adjectives (e.g., 있다 *it-da* 'be present', 없다 *eop-da* 'be absent', 많다 *man-ta* 'be lots', 적다 *jeok-da* 'be some') are the main means to realise the Process.

The P3 in the locative type of relational clauses has in general the semantic feature of 'unconsciousness' and is marked by the clitic 에 *e* 'at, in, with, to, etc.'; when it has the feature 'consciousness', it is marked by the clitic 에게/한테 *ege/hante* 'at, in, with, to, etc.' (cf. Recipient and Source in Section 4.2.1.3 and 4.2.1.4). In (61) the P3 EFM positions the Located in space.

4.2 The System of EXPERIENTIAL CLAUSE TYPE

(61)   [locative;unquantified]

책이 책상 위에 있다.							
chaeg	*=i*	*chaeksang*	*wi*	*=e*	*it-da*		
book		desk	above	at	is present		
P1:Located		**P3:Location**			Process		
ng		ng			vg		
Thing	EFM	Thing	Perspective	EFM	Event		
noun	clitic	Noun	bound noun	clitic	verbalised adjective		
						Head	EM
						stem	sfx
'The book is on the desk.'							

In (62) the P3 EFM positions the Located in time.

(62)   [locative;unquantified]

회의는 오후에 있다.						
hoeui	*=neun*	*ohu*	*=e*	*it-da*		
meeting		afternoon	at	is present		
P1:Located		**P3:Location**		Process		
ng		ng		vg		
Thing	TFM	Thing	EFM	Event		
noun	clitic	noun	clitic	verbalised adjective		
					Head	EM
					stem	sfx
'The meeting is in the afternoon.'						

In (63) and (64), the P3 EFMs position the Located in space and time respectively, but the Processes are quantified – as 'lots' and 'some' respectively.

(63)   [locative;quantified:lots]

이 나무에 벌레가 많다.					
i	*namu*	*=e*	*beolle*	*=ga*	*man-ta*
this	tree	at	insect		are lots
P3:Location			**P1:Located**		Process
ng			ng		vg
Deictic	Thing	EFM	Thing	EFM	Event
determiner	noun	clitic	noun	clitic	verbalised adjective
					Head / EM
					stem / sfx
'In this tree insects abound.'					

(64)   [locative;quantified:some]

오후에는 방문객이 적다.					
ohu	*=e*	*=neun*	*bangmungaek*	*=i*	*jeok-da*
afternoon	in		visitor		are some
P3:Location			**P1:Located**		Process
ng			ng		vg
Thing	EFM	TFM	Thing	EFM	Event
noun	clitic	clitic	Noun	clitic	verbalised adjective
					Head / EM
					stem / sfx
'In the afternoon visitors are few.'					

In (65), the Process registers the feature [absence]. Note that the Location has the semantic feature 'consciousness', and hence the clitic 한테 *hante* is employed.

4.2 The System of EXPERIENTIAL CLAUSE TYPE

(65)   [locative;absence]

책은 나한테 없다.						
chaeg	*=eun*	*na*	*=hante*	*eop-da*		
book		I	with	is absent		
P1:Located		**P3:Location**		Process		
ng		ng		vg		
Thing	TFM	Thing	EFM	Event		
noun	clitic	pronoun	clitic	verbalised adjective		
				Head		EM
				stem		sfx
'The book is not with me.'						

While Location in non-locative clause types is an optional Circumstance, in the locative type of relational clause it is treated as a Participant – it is an inherent part of the structure. The Location in a locative relational clause is always marked by the clitic 에 *e* (in case of 'unconscious' location) or 에게/한테 *ege/hante* (for 'conscious' location). Location functions in other clause types can be marked by different EFMs depending on their semantic contribution to the clause. For instance, (66) and (67) illustrate two different types of location; we treat them as circumstantial elements.

(66)

이 벌레는 작은 나무에서 산다.								
i	*beolle*	*=neun*	*jag-eun*		*namu*	*=eseo*	*sa-n-da*	
this	worm		small		tree	in	live	
P1			Cir:Location				Process:material	
ng			ng				vg	
Deictic	Thing	TFM	Epithet		Thing	EFM	Event	
determiner	noun	clitic	adjective		noun	clitic	verb	
			Head	Link			Head	TM	EM
			stem	sfx			stem	sfx	sfx
'This worm lives in a small tree.'								

(67)

벌들이 꽃으로 모여든다.				
beol-deur	*=i*	*kkoch*	*=euro*	*moyeodeu-n-da*
bees		flower	**to**	gather
P1		**Cir:Location**		Process:material
ng		ng		vg
Thing	EFM	Thing	EFM	Event
noun	clitic	noun	clitic	verb
Head	Plural			Head	TM	EM
stem	sfx			stem	sfx	sfx
'Bees are gathering around the flowers.'				

As (68) illustrates, the Location can be elided, like other Participants, for textual reasons.

(68)   [locative;absence]

이런, 책이 없네.			
ireon	*chaeg*	*=i*	*eom-ne*
bugger	the book		is absent
Expletive interjection	P1:Located		Process
	ng		vg
	Thing	EFM	Event
	noun	clitic	verbalised adjective
			Head	SM
			stem	sfx
'Bugger, (I note) the book isn't (here).'			

Korean locative relational clauses are often translated into English as an existential clause – for example when an entity is being introduced in a story. However, our position is that (as reflected in our analysis of (61)–(65) and (68)) there is no grammatical evidence in Korean that warrants recognising existential as a distinctive clause type.

4.2.3.7 Possessor and Possession In the possessive type of relational clauses, one Participant supplements another Participant through a 'having' or'not

4.2 The System of EXPERIENTIAL CLAUSE TYPE

having' relation. We will call the two Participants 'Possessor' and 'Possession' respectively.

As mentioned above, the possessive relation is expressed through the verbalised adjective, 있다 *it-da* 'be present' and its negative counterpart 없다 *eop-da* 'be absent'. In addition, two verbalised adjectives, 많다 *man-ta* 'be lots' and 적다 *jeok-da* 'be some', can also be employed to express the 'having' relation, as well as a general quantification of the Possession (i.e., 'lots' or just 'some').

In Korean both the Possessor and the Possession Participants are realised as P1, although for textual reasons, the Possessor is prototypically marked by 은/는 *eun/neun*, TFM, rather than by 이/가 *i/ga*, EFM – as illustrated in (69)–(72).

(69) [possessive;unquantified]

나는 오후에 회의가 있다.						
na	=*neun*	*ohu*	=*e*	*hoeui*	=*ga*	*it-da*
I		afternoon		meeting		is 'present'
P1:Possessor		Cir: Location		**P1:Possession**		Process
ng		ng		ng		vg
Thing	TFM	Thing		Thing	EFM	Event
noun	clitic	noun		noun	clitic	verbalised adjective
						Head	EM
						stem	sfx
'I have a meeting this afternoon.'						

(70) [possessive;quantified:lots]

이 나무는 벌레가 많다.					
i	*namu*	=*neun*	*beolle*	=*ga*	*man-ta*
this	tree		worm		are lots
P1:Possessor			**P1:Possession**		Process
ng			ng		vg
Deictic	Thing	TFM	Thing	EFM	Event
determiner	noun	clitic	noun	clitic	verbalised adjective
					Head	EM
					stem	sfx
'This tree has many worms.'					

(71)   [possessive;quantified:some]

그 사람은 친구가 적다.					
geu	*saram*	*=eun*	*chingu*	*=ga*	*jeok-da*
that	person		friend		are some
P1:Possessor			**P1:Possession**		Process
ng			ng		vg
Deictic	Thing	TFM	Thing	EFM	Event
determiner	noun	clitic	noun	clitic	verbalised adjective
					Head	EM
					stem	sfx
'That person has a few friends.'					

(72)   [possessive;absence]

그 아이는 친구가 없다.					
geu	*ai*	*=neun*	*chingu*	*=ga*	*eop-da*
that	kid		friend		is absent
P1:Possessor			**P1:Possession**		Process
ng			ng		vg
Deictic	Thing	TFM	Thing	EFM	Event
determiner	noun	clitic	noun	clitic	verbalised adjective
					Head	EM
					stem	sfx
'That kid has no friends.'					

Meanings such as 'possession', 'containment' or 'ownership' can also be realised through a different type of clause, that is, material clauses, in Korean. Example (73) in effect construes having money as an activity.

4.2 The System of EXPERIENTIAL CLAUSE TYPE

(73)

수애는 돈을 많이 가지고 있다.								
Suae	*=neun*	*don*	*=eul*	*mani*	*gaji-go*		*it-da*	
Suae		money		a lot	possess		be doing	
P1:Actor		**P2:Undergoer**		Cir:Manner	Process:material			
ng		ng		advg	vg			
Thing	TFM	Thing	EFM	Head	Event		Dimension	
noun	clitic	noun	clitic	adverb	verb		aux verb	
					Head	Link	Head	EM
					stem	sfx	stem	sfx
'Suae possesses lots of money.'								

In (73), the 'possessor' is realised as P1 and the 'possession' as P2. This sort of function configuration, P1 ^ P2, is typical in a material clause, and is clearly different from that for the possessive type of relational clauses, which is essentially P1 ^ P1. Note also that in this example a verbal group function, Dimension, is included; dimensional verbal groups of this kind are never found in relational clauses.

4.2.4 Verbal Clauses

Verbal clauses construe figures of 'saying' and often project direct and indirect speech (further explored in Chapter 6).

Verbal clauses include a Process realised through verbs that can be roughly classified into three types: (i) stating: e.g., 말하다 *malha-da* 'say', 설명하다 *seolmyeongha-da* 'explain', 충고하다 *chunggoha-da* 'advice' or 대답하다 *daedapha-da* 'answer'; (ii) questioning: e.g., 질문하다 *jilmunha-da* or 문의하다 *munuiha-da* 'question'; and (iii) requesting: e.g., 당부하다 *dangbuha-da* or 요청하다 *yocheongha-da* 'request'.

Figure 4.6 shows the system of VERBAL CLAUSE TYPE in Korean we propose. Verbal clauses include various Participant functions as outlined below.

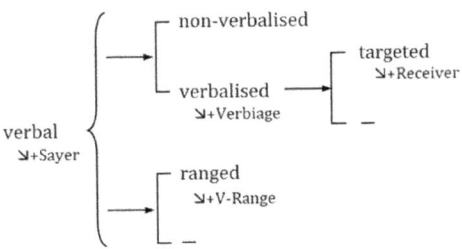

Figure 4.6 The system of VERBAL CLAUSE TYPE

4.2.4.1 Sayer and Verbiage The Sayer is the inherent Participant in verbal clauses, prototypically marked by 이/가 *i/ga* (as P1). This Participant is imbued with consciousness, and represents a person (or an institution) who says (something).

What a Sayer states, asks for or requests can be realised through a second Participant called Verbiage. The Verbiage is typically realised by a nominal group, prototypically marked by 을/를 *eul/reul* (as P2). In (74) an agency (Sayer) asks for thorough preparation (Verbiage).

(74)

기상청은 철저한 대비를 당부했다.					
gisangcheong	*=eun*	*cheoljeoha-n*	*daebi*	*=reul*	*dangbuha-et-da*
weather bureau		thorough	preparation		asked for
P1:Sayer		**P2:Verbiage**			Process
ng		ng			vg
Thing	TFM	Epithet	Thing	EFM	Event
noun	clitic	adjective	noun	clitic	verb
		Head	Link		Head	TM	EM
		stem	sfx		stem	sfx	sfx
'The weather bureau asked for a thorough preparation.'					

The Verbiage can also be realised by an embedded clause, through either the Install (as in (75)) or Installing functions (as in (76)). These embedded clauses do not select for MOOD or ADDRESSEE DEFERENCE; they construe 'locutions', followed by an EFM clitic (e.g., 을/를 *eul/reul* marking the Verbiage as P2).

(75)

대통령은 . . .	
daetongnyeong	*=eun*
president	
P1:Sayer	
ng	
Thing	TFM
noun	clitic
'The president . . .	

4.2 The System of EXPERIENTIAL CLAUSE TYPE

... 군이 중립을 지켜야 함을 ...						
[[gun	=i	jungnib	=eul	jiky-eoya	ha-m	=eul]]
military		neutrality		keep	must	
P2:Verbiage							
ng							
Thing							EFM
						clitic
[[clause]]						
P1:Actor		P2:Undergoer		Process:material		
ng		ng		vg		
Thing	EFM	Thing	EFM	Event		Modal	
noun	clitic	noun	clitic	verb		aux verb	
				Head	Link	Head	Install
				stem	sfx	stem	sfx
... that the military should remain neutral.'								

... 세 번이나 말했다.						
se	beon		=ina	malha-et-da			
three	times			said			
Cir:Extent:frequency				Process			
ng				vg			
Quantity			IFM	Event			
word complex			clitic	verb			
α		β		Head	TM	EM
cardinal number		bound noun		stem	sfx	sfx
... said three times ...								

(76)

사장은 ...	
sajang	=eun
boss	
P1:Sayer	
ng	
Thing	TFM
noun	clitic
'The boss ...	

... 우리가 무엇을 하는 지를 ...						
uri	=ga	mueos	=eul	ha-neun	ji	=reul
we		what		do		
P2:Verbiage						
ng						
Thing						EFM
[[clause]]						clitic
P1		P2		Process		
ng		ng		vg		
Thing	EFM	Thing	EFM	Event	**Installing**	
pronoun	clitic	pronoun	clitic	verb	**bound noun**	
				Head	Link	
				stem	sfx	
... what we are doing.'						

... 물었다.		
mur-eot-da		
asked		
Process		
vg		
Event		
verb		
Head	TM	EM
stem	sfx	sfx
... asked...		

Verbal clauses have a potential to project another clause. The projected clauses construe 'locutions', and unlike the embedded locutions exemplified in (75) and (76), projected locutions do select for MOOD. In addition, when quoting what was said ('direct speech'), ADDRESSEE DEFERENCE is also selected. However, when a verbal clause reports what was said ('indirect speech'), ADDRESSEE DEFERENCE is not possible (see Chapter 6 for further discussion).

4.2 The System of EXPERIENTIAL CLAUSE TYPE

4.2.4.2 *Receiver* Verbal clauses can include another Participant, the Receiver, which construes the Participant to whom the locution is directed; it co-occurs with both Sayer and Verbiage in (77). The possibility of a Receiver is a useful criterion for distinguishing verbal from mental clauses.

(77)

남자가 판사에게 무죄를 호소했다.								
namja	*=ga*	*pansa*	*=ege*	*mujoe*	*=reul*	*hosoha-et-ta*		
man		judge	to	innocence		appealed		
P1:Sayer		**P3:Receiver**		P2:Verbiage		Process		
ng		ng		ng		vg		
Thing	EFM	Thing	EFM	Thing	EFM	Event		
noun	clitic	noun	clitic	noun	clitic	verb		
						Head	TM	EM
						stem	sfx	sfx
'The man appealed to the judge for his innocence.'								

Receiver Participants are imbued with 'consciousness' and typically marked by 에게 *ege* 'to' (P3) as in (77). It is possible to use the EFM 에 *e* 'to' when the Receiver involves organisations (governments, institutions, agencies, etc.) – as in (78).

(78)

선조는 명에 원조를 요청하였다.								
Seonjo	*=neun*	*Myeong*	*=e*	*wonjo*	*=reul*	*yocheongha-yeot-da*		
Seonjo		Myeong	to	reinforcement		asked		
P1:Sayer		**P3:Receiver**		P2:Verbiage		Process		
ng		ng		ng		vg		
Thing	TFM	Thing	EFM	Thing	EFM	Event		
noun	clitic	noun	clitic	noun	clitic	verb		
						Head	TM	EM
						stem	sfx	sfx
'(King) Seonjo asked the Ming Dynasty for reinforcements.'								

4.2.4.3 *Verbal-Range* Verbal clauses may also involve a Verbal-Range (or V-Range) Participant, which is realised by a nominal group marked by 을/를 *eul/reul* (as P2) – as in (79). This Participant function specifies the meaning of a Process that has been realised by a general verb such as 하다 *ha-da* 'do'.

(79)

사람들이 복도에서 잡담을 하고 있다.								
saram-deur	=i	bokdo	=eseo	japdam	=***eul***	ha-go		it-da
people		corridor	in	chat		do		be doing
P1:Sayer		Cir:Location		P2:V-Range		Process		
ng		ng		ng		vg		
Thing	EFM	Thing	EFM	Thing	EFM	Event		Dimension
noun	clitic	noun	clitic	noun	clitic	verb		aux verb
						Head	Link	Head	EM
						stem	sfx	stem	sfx
'People are having a chat in the corridor.'								

These V-Range Process structures contrast with clauses such as (80) in which the Process itself specifies the kind of verbalising taking place.

(80)

사람들이 복도에서 잡담하고 있다.					
saram-deur	=i	bokdo	=eseo	***japdamha***-go	it-da
people		corridor	in	chat	be doing
P1:Sayer		Cir:Location		Process	
ng		ng		vg	
Thing	EFM	Thing	EFM	Event	Dimension
noun	clitic	noun	clitic	verb	aux verb
				Head	Link	Head	EM
				stem	sfx	stem	sfx
'People are chatting in the corridor.'					

The way V-Range Participants operate is similar to what we have observed above for E-Range, P-Range and M-Range Participants – see (21), (22) and (27) for relevant examples. Typically, these Range Participants involve Sino-Korean lexis specifying the general verb 하다 *ha-da* 'do'.

4.3   The System of DIATHESIS

We now move on to another experiential system in Korean, which we will call DIATHESIS. This system applies only to material and verbal clauses.

The system of DIATHESIS describes the alternative ways in which Participants' relations to the Process are coded. These alternatives have been commonly discussed in relation to the term 'voice' (i.e., 'active' versus the

4.3 The System of DIATHESIS

'passive' voice) and also in terms of the contrast between 'causative' and 'non-causative' clauses. In syntagmatically based grammars, e.g., Song (1988: 175–9), these alternatives have been described in terms of 'transformations' (involving 'passivisation of active sentences', 'causativisation of non-causative sentences' and so on). However, in a paradigmatically organised grammar like SFL, these alternatives are agnate expressions (Gleason 1965, Martin and Matthiessen 1991); each of the alternatives is related to the other as paradigmatic options – that is, each of them realises specific distinctive features.

In Figure 4.7 we propose the following system of DIATHESIS in Korean.

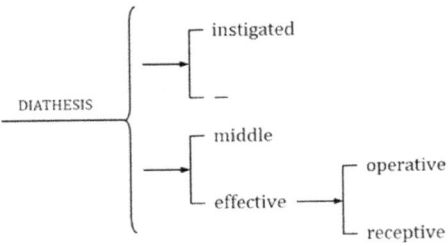

Figure 4.7 The system of DIATHESIS

In (81), we have a material clause that involves a Process and two participants (P1 and P2). The relationship between the Participants and the Process is such that the P1 encodes the Actor and the P2 the Undergoer; this coding realises the feature [effective].

(81)   effective operative

아이가 고양이를 쫓고 있다.							
ai	*=ga*	*goyangi*	*=reul*	*jjot-go*		*it-da*	
child		cat		chase		be . . .ing	
P1:Actor		P2:Undergoer		Process:material			
ng		ng		vg			
Thing	EFM	Thing	EFM	Event		Dimension	
noun	clitic	noun	clitic	verb		aux verb	
				Head	Link	Head	EM
				stem	sfx	stem	sfx
'The child is chasing the cat.'							

This particular material clause has a related clause, illustrated in (82), with an alternative arrangement of Participants. In the alternative, the Undergoer is realised as P1 and the Actor as P3. In a sense, the Actor is 'demoted' to the role of a P3, and the Undergoer on the other hand is 'promoted' to the role of a P1.

(82) effective receptive with a Voice Mark (VM) suffix

고양이가 아이에게 쫓기고 있다.								
goyangi	=*ga*	*ai*	=*ege*	*jjot*-**gi**-*go*			*it*-*da*	
cat		child		chased			be doing	
P1:Undergoer		P3:Actor		Process:material				
ng		ng		vg				
Thing	EFM	Thing	EFM	Event			Dimension	
noun	clitic	noun	clitic	verb			aux verb	
				Head	**VM**	Link	Head	EM
				stem	sfx	sfx	stem	sfx
'The cat is being chased by the child.'								

Notice that in (82) the Process is realised by a verbal group that includes a Voice Mark (VM) function; as we saw in Chapter 2 this VM function operates at word rank and realises the feature [diminish] through a suffix (such as 이 -*i*, 히 -*hi*, 리 -*li* and 기 -*gi*).

We will characterise an 'active' clause such as (81) as realising the feature [operative] – as the clause depicts a situation where someone (the child) does something to someone or something else (the cat). And we characterise a 'passive' clause such as (82) as realising the feature [receptive] – as it depicts a situation where something is done to someone or something (the cat) by someone else (the child). They both are classified as effective clauses because they each include an Actor and Undergoer in the same experiential relationship with one another.

The opposition between [operative] and [receptive] (and other features in DIATHESIS) creates different possibilities for information flow (we discuss the uptake of this potential from the perspective of textual meaning in Chapter 5, examples (5) and (5')).

In contrast with (81)–(82), a material clause like (83) is not an effective clause, since it involves only one inherent Participant. We will characterise clauses like (83) as realising the feature [middle].

4.3 The System of DIATHESIS

(83) middle

고양이가 달려간다.		
goyangi	=*ga*	*dallyeoga-n-da*
cat		run
P1:Actor		Process:material
ng		vg
Thing	EFM	Event
noun	clitic	verb
		Head	TM	EM
		stem	sfx	sfx
'The cat is running.'		

We now turn to a discussion of instigated clauses. The material clause in (81) can be related to a clause such as (84). In this example, an additional Participant, an Instigator, is brought into the picture and realised as P1. The Actor can be thought of as 'demoted' to a P3 role, while the Undergoer remains as a P2 role. The Process in these instigated clauses is realised by a verbal group with a Valence function (as introduced in Chapter 2, Section 2.4.2).

(84) instigated effective operative with a verbal group Valence function

어른이 아이한테 고양이를 쫓게 했다.										
eoreun	=*i*	*ai*	=*hante*	*goyangi*	=*reul*	*jjot-ge*		*ha-et-da*		
adult		child		cat		chase		made		
P1:Instigator		P3:Actor		P2:Undergoer		Process:material				
ng		ng		ng		vg				
Thing	EFM	Thing	EFM	Thing	EFM	Event		**Valence**		
noun	clitic	noun	clitic	noun	clitic	Verb		aux verb		
						Head	Link	Head	TM	EM
						stem	sfx	stem	sfx	sfx
'The adult made the child chase the cat.'										

We will refer to clauses like (84) as instigated clauses, more precisely, instigated effective operative clauses; and we refer to those such as (81)–(83), by contrast, as non-instigated clauses.

Middle clauses like (83) can also be instigated, as exemplified in (85).

(85)   instigated middle with a verbal group Valence function

아이가 고양이를 달려가게 했다.							
ai	*=ga*	*goyangi*	*=reul*	*dallyeoga-ge*		***ha*-et-da**	
child		cat		run		made	
P1:Instigator		P2:Actor		Process:material			
ng		ng		vg			
Thing	EFM	Thing	EFM	Event		**Valence**	
noun	clitic	noun	clitic	verb		aux verb	
				Head	Link	Head	TM	EM
				stem	sfx	stem	sfx	sfx
'The child made the cat run.'							

As introduced in Chapter 2, the group rank system that is related to DIATHESIS at the clause rank is VALENCY. The VALENCY system has three options: neutral, augment and diminish. Accordingly in (84) and (85), the Process includes a verbal group with a Valence function; this function can realise the verbal group feature [augment] or [diminish] through a handful of auxiliary verbs, which we noted in Chapter 2 (Section 2.4.2). In (84) and (85), the auxiliary verb 하다 *ha-da* 'get, make' has been deployed to realise the feature [augment]. Auxiliary verbs such as 지다 *ji-da* 'become' realise the feature [diminish], as in (86).

Notice that there are two strategies in Korean for realising the 'demoted' actor as P3. One is through the clitic 에게/한테 *ege/hante* 'to', as in (82); the other involves a co-verbal phrase[7] with the bound verb 의해 *uihae* 'by', as in (86).

---

[7] We abbreviate co-verbal phrase as 'cvp' in example tables.

4.3 The System of DIATHESIS

(86)   effective receptive with a verbal group Valence function

군인들에 의해 다리가 만들어졌다.									
gunin-deur	=e	uihae	dari	=ga	mandeur-eo		ji-eot-da		
soldiers		by	bridge		was made				
P3:Actor			P1:Undergoer		Process				
cvp			ng		vg				
Incumbent		Role	Thing	EFM	Event		**Valence**		
[ng]		bound verb	noun	clitic	verb		aux verb		
Thing	EFM				Head	Link	Head	TM	EM
noun	clitic				stem	sfx	stem	sfx	sfx
Head	Plural								
root	sfx								
'The bridge was made by soldiers.'									

Note also that not all clauses with the feature [operative] have an agnate [receptive] alternative realised through the word rank Voice Mark (VM) function (involving a [diminish] suffix, such as 이 -i, 히 -hi, 리 -li and 기 -gi). Many verbs in Korean, including 하다 ha-da 'do', 때리다 ttaeri-da 'hit', 만들다 mandeul-da 'make', 사다 sa-da 'buy', 주다 ju-da 'give' and 받다 bat-da 'receive', cannot realise the verbal group [diminish] feature through the suffix.

In contrast, the verbal group Valence function, realised through an auxiliary verb such as 지다 ji-da 'become', is much less restricted; almost all verbal groups can realise the feature [diminish] through an auxiliary verb.

A [receptive] clause with the word rank VM function prototypically realises a P3:Actor through the clitic 에게/한테 ege/hante. However it is not the case that every [receptive] clause with the VM function includes a P3:Actor. In examples such as (87) and (88), a P3:Actor cannot in fact be realised (see Yeon 2011: 128 for details and further references).

(87)   no P3 Actor possible

문이 잘 안 열린다.							
mun	=i	jal	an	yeol-**li**-n-da			
door		well	not	is opened			
P1:Undergoer		Process:material					
ng		vg					
Thing	EFM	Modal Adjunct		Event			
noun	clitic	advg		verb			
		β	α	Head	**VM**	TM	EM
		adverb	adverb	stem	sfx	sfx	sfx
'The door doesn't open well.'							

(88)　　　no P3 Actor possible

요즘 일이 꼬인다.						
yojeum	*il*	=*i*	*kko-**i**-n-da*			
these days	affairs		are twisted			
Cir:Location	P1:Undergoer		Process:material			
advg	ng		vg			
Head	Thing	EFM	Event			
adverb	noun	clitic	verb			
			Head	VM	TM	EM
			stem	sfx	sfx	sfx
'Things are messing up these days.'						

A [receptive] clause with the group rank Valence function on the other hand invariably realises a P3:Actor through the co-verbal phrase 에 의해 *e uihae* (not through the clitic 에게 *ege*) – although the P3:Actor is often elided. Lee K. (1993: 277) describes the P3:Actor realised through the co-verbal phrase 에 의해 *e uihae* as an 'indirect agent actant'; the implication here is that the P3:Actor is someone who is responsible for the event taking place (but who didn't necessarily perform the action depicted).

In (87), as we noted above, the Process includes a word rank VM function; it realises the feature [diminish] through a suffix, such as 이 -*i*, 히 -*hi*, 리 -*li* and 기 -*gi*. The VM function can also realise the feature [augment] through suffixes such as 이 -*i*, 히 -*hi*, 리 -*li*, 기 -*gi*, 우 -*u*, 구 -*gu* and 추 -*chu*. Compare (89) with (90). As with [diminish], not all the verbs can realise [augment] through a suffix.

(89)　　　instigated middle with augmenting Voice Mark (VM) suffix

나뭇꾼이 선녀를 울리고 있다.								
namutkkun	=*i*	*seonnyeo*	=*reul*	*ul-**li**-go*			*it-da*	
woodcutter		nymph		make cry			be doing	
P1:Instigator		P2:Actor		Process:material				
ng		ng		vg				
Thing	EFM	Thing	EFM	Event			Dimension	
noun	clitic	noun	clitic	verb			aux verb	
				Head	VM	Link	Head	EM
				stem	sfx	sfx	stem	sfx
'The woodcutter is making the nymph cry.'								

4.3 The System of DIATHESIS

(90)   non-instigated middle

선녀가 울고 있다.					
seonnyeo	**=ga**	*ul-go*		*it-da*	
nymph		cry		be doing	
P1:Actor		Process:material			
ng		vg			
Thing	**EFM**	Event		Dimension	
noun	clitic	verb		aux verb	
		Head	Link	Head	EM
		stem	sfx	stem	sfx
'The nymph is crying.'					

The generalisation is thus that the feature [instigated] involves the presence of an Instigator Participant function, its coding as P1, and realisation of the feature [augment] by either a Valence function (at group rank) or Voice Mark (at word rank).

In Korean, it is unusual to find instigated effective receptive clauses, such as (91). They are in general highly marked. In addition, there is a restriction on ordering among Participant functions in this clause type – the P2 Undergoer must occur before the P3 Actor. This restriction does not apply to instigated effective operative clauses, such as (84).

(91)   instigated effective receptive with a verbal group Valence function

어른이 고양이를 아이한테 쫓기게 했다.											
eoreun	=*i*	*goyangi*	=*reul*	*ai*	*hante*	*jjot-gi-ge*			*ha-et-da*		
adult		cat		child		chased			made		
P1:Instigator		P2:Undergoer		P3:Actor		Process:material					
ng		ng		ng		vg					
Thing	EFM	Thing	EFM	Thing	EFM	Event			Valence		
noun	clitic	noun	clitic	noun	clitic	verb			aux verb		
						Head	VM	Link	Head	TM	EM
						stem	sfx	sfx	stem	sfx	sfx
'The adult let the cat be chased by the child.'											

To sum up, we present the ways different Participant roles are realised in clauses with different features, and their distributions – as outlined in Table 4.6. Note that the system of DIATHESIS is not available for relational clauses in Korean.

Table 4.6 *Key Participants in clauses with differing DIATHESIS features*

				clause features and participant roles	group or word features and realisations		example Processes
material clause	non-instigated	middle		P1: Actor P1: Undergoer	neutral		울다 *ul-da* 'cry', 줄어들다 *jureodeul-da* 'decrease'
		effective	operative	P1: Actor ^ P2: Undergoer; P2: Undergoer ^ P1: Actor	neutral		쫓다 *jjot-da* 'chase'
			receptive	P1: Undergoer ^ P3: Actor; P3: Actor ^ P1: Undergoer	diminish	VM or Valence	만들어지다 *mandeur-eo ji-da* 'be made' 쫓기다 *jjot-gi-da* 'be chased'
	instigated	middle		P1: Instigator ^ P2: Actor/Undergoer; P2: Actor/Undergoer ^ P1: Instigator	augment	VM or Valence	먹게 하다 *meog-ge ha-da* 'make eat' 먹이다 *meog-i-da* 'feed'
		effective	operative	P1: Instigator ^ P2: Actor ^ P2: Undergoer; P1: Instigator ^ P2: Undergoer ^ P3: Actor; P3: Actor ^ P1: Instigator ^ P2: Undergoer; P3: Actor ^ P2: Undergoer ^ P1: Instigator; P2: Undergoer ^ P1: Instigator ^ P3: Actor; P2: Undergoer ^ P3: Actor ^ P1: Instigator	augment	VM or Valence	먹게 하다 *meog-ge ha-da* 'make eat' 먹이다 *meog-i-da* 'feed'
			receptive	P1: Instigator ^ P2: Undergoer ^ P3: Actor; P2: Undergoer ^ P3: Actor ^ P1: Instigator (Note: the ordering 'P2: Undergoer ^ P3: Actor' cannot be changed.)	augment + diminish	VM or Valence (for diminish) Valence (for augment)	잡히게 하다 *jap-hi-ge ha-da* 'make be caught' 만들어지게 하다 *mandeur-eo ji-ge ha-da* 'make be made'
mental clause	non-instigated	middle		P1: Senser	neutral		생각하다 *saengakha-da* 'think'
		effective	operative	P1: Senser ^ P2: Phenomenon; P2: Phenomenon ^ P1: Senser	neutral		듣다 *deut-da* 'hear'
			receptive	P1: Phenomenon (+P3: Actor through *e uihae*) Possible only with verbs with 하다 *ha-da* 'to do'	diminish	VM (*doe-da* 'to become')	들리다 *deul-li-da* 'be heard'

clause type	instigation	middle/effective	operative/receptive	Participants	augment/diminish	Valence	Example
	instigated	middle		P1: Instigator ^ P2: Senser; P2: Senser ^ P1: Instigator	augment	Valence	생각하게 하다 *saengakha-ge ha-da* 'make think'
		effective	operative	P1: Instigator ^ P3: Senser ^ P2: Phenomenon; P1: Instigator ^ P2: Phenomenon ^ P3: Senser; P3: Senser ^ P1: Instigator ^ P2: Phenomenon; P3: Senser ^ P2: Phenomenon ^ P1: Instigator; P2: Phenomenon ^ P1: Instigator ^ P3: Senser; P2: Phenomenon ^ P3: Senser ^ P1: Instigator	augment	Valence	듣게 하다 *deut-ge ha-da* 'make hear'
			receptive	P1: Instigator ^ P2: Phenomenon ^ P3: Senser; P2: Phenomenon ^ P3: Senser ^ P1: Instigator (Note: the ordering 'P2: Phenomenon ^ P3: Senser' cannot be changed.)	augment + diminish	VM (for diminish) Valence (for augment)	들리게 하다 *deul-li-ge ha-da* 'make be heard'
relational clause							
	—			—	—		
verbal clause							
	non-instigated	middle		P1: Sayer			잡담하다 *japdamha-da* 'chat'
		effective	operative	P1: Sayer ^ P3: Receiver ^ P2: Verbiage; P2: Verbiage ^ P3: Receiver ^ P1: Sayer			설명하다 *seolmyeongha-da* 'explain'
			receptive	P1: Verbiage ^ P2: Receiver (+P3: Sayer through *e uihae*) Possible only with verbs with 하다 *ha-da* 'to do'	diminish	VM (*doe-da* 'to become')	설명되다 *seolmyeong-doe-da* 'explain'
	instigated	middle		P1: Instigator ^ P3: Sayer; P3: Sayer ^ P1: Instigator	augment	Valence	잡담하게 하다 *japdamha-ge ha-da* 'make chat'
		effective	operative	P1: Instigator ^ P3: Sayer ^ P2: Verbiage ^ P3: Receiver;	augment	Valence	설명하게 하다 *seolmyeongha-ge ha-da* 'make explain'
			receptive	P1: Instigator ^ P2: Verbiage ^ P3: Receiver (^ P3: Sayer through *e uihae*)	augment + diminish	VM (for diminish) Valence (for augment)	설명되게 하다 *seolmyeong-doe-ge ha-da* 'make be explained'

4.4 The System of CIRCUMSTANTIATION

As seen in the previous sections, the experiential centre of a clause is construed by a configuration of Participant/s and Process, realising the system of EXPERIENTIAL CLAUSE TYPE. This experiential centre can be expanded by circumstantial elements with various meanings such as time, place, manner and cause. These meanings are construed by different types of Circumstance, realising the system of CIRCUMSTANTIATION.

In general, the status of a Circumstance is less central to the experiential configuration of Participant/s and Process; and circumstantial elements optionally occur in all clause types.

There are a number of different types of Circumstance construing various circumstantial meanings. They tend to be queried in distinctive ways through elemental interrogatives, which we specify below. They are realised by a nominal group, adverbial group, co-verbal phrase or embedded clause in Korean.

We propose the following system of CIRCUMSTANTIATION in Korean (see Figure 4.8). The system we have proposed here overgeneralises the realisation of Circumstances across clause types. Some Circumstances are more strongly associated with some clause types than others; and some (e.g., Matter) are associated with particular clause types (namely verbal and mental). Making explicit these associations and restrictions depends on corpus-based research and is beyond the scope of this grammar.

4.4.1 Location

Circumstances of Location position a clause temporarily or spatially – which we label more specifically as Location:time and Location:space, respectively.

Circumstances of Location:time can be queried through the interrogative expression 언제 *eonje* 'when'. This function is usually realised by a nominal group with a clitic 에 *e* 'in/on/at', as in (92) or without any marking, e.g., 어제 *eoje* 'yesterday' in (93).

4.4 The System of CIRCUMSTANTIATION

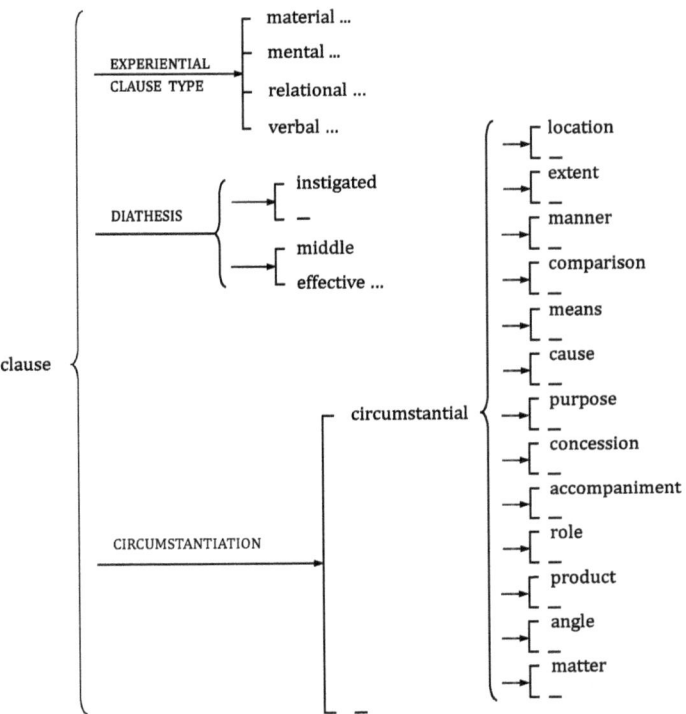

Figure 4.8 The system of CIRCUMSTANTIATION in relation to other experiential systems[8]

(92)

2011 년에 이 작품이 ...						
2011	*nyeon*	*=e*	*i*	*jakpum*	*=i*	
2011	year	in	this	work		
Location:time[9]			P1:Undergoer			
ng			ng			
Quantity		**EFM**	Deictic	Thing	**EFM**	
word complex		clitic	determiner	noun	clitic	
α	β					
numeral	bound noun					
'In 2011 this work ...						

---

[8] DIATHESIS does not freely combine with EXPERIENTIAL PROCESS TYPE, a point we have not formalised in this network; for restrictions see Table 4.6.

[9] To simplify the annotation we will label Circumstances according to sub-type only (i.e., Location:time, not Circumstance:Location:time) in this section.

... 만들어졌다.	
madeur-eo	*jy-eot-da*
made	was
Process:relational	
vg	
Event	Valence:diminish
verb	aux verb
Head	Link	Head	TM	EM
stem	sfx	stem	sfx	sfx
'... was made.'	

(93)

나는 어제 그 사람을 보았다.						
na	*=neun*	*eoje*	*geu*	*saram*	*=eul*	*bo-at-da*
I		yesterday	that	person		saw
P1:Senser		Location: time	P2:Phenomenon			Process:mental
ng		ng	ng			vg
Thing	TFM	Thing	Deictic	Thing	EFM	Event
noun	clitic	noun	determiner	noun	clitic	verb
						Head	TM	EM
						stem	sfx	sfx
'I (saw) that person yesterday.'						

Alternatively Location can be realised by an embedded clause, involving an Installing function realised through a bound noun, with the clitic 에 *e* (which can be elided) as in (94).

4.4 The System of CIRCUMSTANTIATION

(94)

뉴스를 본 뒤에 ...				
nyuseu	*=reul*	*bo-n*	***dwi***	*=e*
news		watched	after	
Location:time				
ng				
Thing				**EFM**
[[clause]]				clitic
P2		Process	**Installing**	
ng		vg	bound noun	
Thing	EFM	Event		
noun	clitic	verb		
		Head	Link	
		stem	sfx	
'After (I) watched the news ...				

... 친구한테 전화를 했다.				
chingu	*=hante*	*jeonhwa*	*=reul*	*ha-et-da*
friend	to	telephone		did
P3		P2		Process
ng		ng		vg
Thing	EFM	Thing	EFM	Event
noun	clitic	noun	clitic	verb
				Head	TM	EM
				stem	sfx	sfx
... (I) called (my) friend.'				

Location:space construes a range of spatial meanings that can be queried with the interrogative expression 어디 *eodi* 'where'. This function is realised by a nominal group with a clitic such as 에서 *eseo* 'in/on/at', 에 *e* 'in/on/at' or (으) 로 *(eu)ro* 'to, toward'. Note that location marked by 에서 *eseo* 'in/on/at' is in general where some action is performed, whereas location marked by 에 *e* 'in/on/at' is where something is, as in (95) and (96).

(95)

나무꾼은 작은 시골 마을에서 ...					
namukkun	=*eun*	*jag-eun*	*sigol*	*maeur*	=*eseo*
wood-cutter		small	country	village	in
P1:Actor		Location:space			
ng		ng			
Thing	TFM	Epithet		Class	Thing	**EFM**
noun	clitic	adjective		noun	noun	clitic
		Head	Link			
		stem	sfx			
'The wood-cutter ... in a small country village.'					

... 나무를 팔고 있었다.				
namu	=*reul*	*pal-go*	*iss-eot-da*	
tree log		sell	be (past) doing	
P2:Undergoer		Process:material		
ng		vg		
Thing	EFM	Event	Dimension	
noun	clitic	verb	aux verb	
		Head	Link	Head	TM	EM
		stem	sfx	stem	sfx	sfx
... was selling tree logs ...				

(96)

나무꾼은 나무를 화로 앞에 ...						
namukkun	=*eun*	*namu*	=*reul*	*hwaro*	*ap*	=*e*
wood-cutter		tree log		stove	front	
P1:Actor		P2:Undergoer		Location:space		
ng		ng		ng		
Thing	TFM	Thing	EFM	Thing	Perspective	**EFM**
noun	clitic	noun	clitic	noun	noun	clitic
'The wood-cutter ... tree logs in front of the stove.'						

4.4 The System of CIRCUMSTANTIATION

... 놓았다.		
no-at-da		
placed		
Process:material		
vg		
Event		
verb		
Head	TM	EM
stem	sfx	sfx
... placed ...		

Note also that 에 *e* 'in/on/at' marks an 'arrival point' (97), whereas (으)로 *(eu) ro* 'to, toward' marks direction (98).

(97)

수애는 학교에 도착했다.						
Suae	*=neun*	*hakgyo*	*=e*	*dochakae-t-da*		
Suae		school		arrived		
P1:Actor		Location:space		Process:material		
ng		ng		vg		
Thing	TFM	Thing	**EFM**	Event		
noun	clitic	noun	clitic	verb		
				Head	TM	EM
				stem	sfx	sfx
'Suae arrived at the school.'						

(98)

수애는 학교로 향했다.						
Suae	*=neun*	*hakgyo*	*=ro*	*hyangha-et-da*		
Suae		school		headed		
P1:Actor		Location:space		Process:material		
ng		ng		vg		
Thing	TFM	Thing	**EFM**	Event		
noun	clitic	noun	clitic	verb		
				Head	TM	EM
				stem	sfx	sfx
'Suae headed for the school.'						

4.4.2 Extent

Circumstances of Extent construe the temporal, spatial and frequential extent of the clause. We label them as Extent:time, Extent:space and Extent:frequency, respectively.

Circumstances of Extent:time deal with temporal duration. They can be queried through the interrogative expression 얼마(나) *eolma(na)* 'how long, to what extent'. They are realised by a nominal group with a clitic such as 동안 *dongan* 'for', as in (99).

(99)

그는 1 시간 동안 . . .				
geu	*=neun*	*han*	*sigan*	***=dongan***
he		one	hour	for
P1:Actor		Extent time		
ng		ng		
Thing	TFM	Quantity		EFM
pronoun	clitic	word complex		clitic
		α	β	
		cardinal number	bound noun	
'He . . . for an hour.'				

. . . 통화를 했다.		
tonghwa	*=reul*	*ha-et-da*
call		did
P2:V-Range		Process:material
ng		vg
Thing	EFM	Event
noun	clitic	verb
		Head / TM / EM
		stem / sfx / sfx
. . . had a phone call . . .		

Circumstances of Extent:time are also used to mark the beginning of an event or its end, or both. Inception is realised by a nominal group marked with the clitic 부터 *buteo* 'from' and culmination is realised by a nominal group with the clitic 까지 *kkaji* 'to', as in (100).

4.4 The System of CIRCUMSTANTIATION

(100)

수애는 . . .	
Suae	*=neun*
Suae	
P1:Actor	
ng	
Thing	TFM
proper noun	clitic
'Suae . . .	

. . . 2 시부터 5 시까지 . . .						
du	*si*	*=buteo*	*daseot*	*si*	*=kkaji*	
two	time	from	five	time	to	
Extent:time						
ng complex						
1			2			
ng			ng			
Quantity		EFM	Quantity		EFM	
word complex		clitic	word complex		clitic	
α	β		α	β		
number	bound noun		number	bound noun		
. . . from 2 o'clock to 5 o'clock.'						

. . . 운동을 했다.					
undong	*=eul*	*ha-et-da*			
exercise		did			
P2:P-Range		Process:material			
ng		vg			
Thing	EFM	Event			
noun	clitic	verb			
		Head	TM	EM	
		stem	sfx	sfx	
. . . exercised . . .					

Circumstances of Extent:space deal with spatial distance; they can be queried through the interrogative expression 얼마(나) *eolma(na)* 'how far, to what extent'. They are realised by a nominal group with the P2 marker 을/를 *eul/reul*, as in (101).

(101)

그는 매일 아침 ...			
geu	*=neun*	*maeil*	*achim*
he		everyday	morning
P1:Actor		Extent:time	
ng		ng	
Thing	TFM	Class	Thing
pronoun	clitic	noun	noun
'He ... every morning.'			

... 5 킬로를 뛴다.					
5	*killo*	*=reul*	*ttwi-n-da*		
5	km		run		
Extent:space			Process:material		
ng			vg		
Quantity		EFM	Event		
word complex		clitic	verb		
α	β		Head	TM	EM
number	bound noun		stem	sfx	sfx
... runs 5 km ...					

Circumstances of Extent:space are also used to indicate the beginning of an event or its end, or both. Origin is realised by a nominal group marked with clitic 에서(부터) *eseo* optionally followed by 부터 *buteo* 'from'; culmination is realised by a nominal group with the clitic 까지 *kkaji* 'to', as in (102).

4.4 The System of CIRCUMSTANTIATION

(102)

그는 집에서 학교까지 걸어다닌다.						
geu	=neun	jip	=eseo	hakgyo	=kkaji	geoleodani-n-da
he		home	from	school	to	walk
P1:Actor		Extent:space				Process:material
ng		ng complex				vg
Thing	TFM	1		2		Event
pronoun	clitic	ng		ng		verb
		Thing	EFM	Thing	EFM	Head	TM	EM
		noun	clitic	noun	clitic	stem	sfx	sfx
'He walks from home to school.'						

A Circumstance of Extent:frequency is used to show the frequency of an event as illustrated in (103). Circumstances of Extent:frequency can be probed through the interrogative expression 몇 *myeot* 'how many' combined with various unit bound nouns, e.g., 번 *beon* 'time', 시간 *sigan* 'hour' and 년 *nyeon* 'year'.

(103)

식사는 하루에 세 번을 한다.						
siksa	=neun	haru	=e	se	beon	=eul	ha-n-da
meal		a day	in	three	times		do
P2:P-Range		Extent:frequency					Process:material
ng		ng complex					vg
Thing	TFM	β		α			Event
noun	clitic	ng		ng			verb
		Thing	EFM	Quantity		EFM	Head	TM	EM
		noun	clitic	word complex		clitic	stem	sfx	sfx
				α	β				
				cardinal number	bound noun				
'Speaking of the meals, we have three times a day.'							

4.4.3 Manner

Circumstances of Manner construe the way in which the Process is actualised; they can be queried by the interrogative expression 어떻게 *eotteoke* 'how' or 'in what way'. They are typically realised by an adverbial group. In (104) the way in which the P1 lived is described in three ways.[10]

---

[10] A Circumstance of Manner can also be used to qualify a Process with respect to the effect of an activity; so the dog ends up more docile in 개는 아주 온순하게 길들여졌다 *gae neun aju onsunhage gildeur-y-eo jy-eot-da* 'the dog has been tamed to be very docile' (literally 'the dog has been

(104)

세 사람은 ...		
se	saram	=eun
three	person	
P1:Actor		
ng		
Quantity		TFM
word complex		clitic
α	β	
cardinal number	bound noun	
'The three ...		

...오순도순 행복하게 열심히 살았다.					
osundosun	haengbokage	yeolsimhi	sar-at-da		
harmoniously	happily	vigorously	lived		
Manner	Manner	Manner	Process:material		
advg	advg	advg	vg		
Head	Head	Head	Event		
adverb	adverb	adverb	verb		
			Head	TM	EM
			stem	sfx	sfx
... lived harmoniously, happily and vigorously.'					

4.4.4 *Comparison*

Circumstances of Comparison construe similarity or difference; they can be queried by the interrogative expression 무엇처럼 *mueot cheoreom* 'like what' or 누구처럼 *nugu cheoreom* 'like whom'. They are realised by a nominal group marked by clitics 보다 *boda* 'than' or 처럼 *cheoreom* 'like' as in (105).

very docilely tamed'), with 아주 온순하게 *aju onsunhage* 'very docilely' realising a Circumstance:Manner qualifying the Process. Like other Manner Circumstances these can be be queried with 어떻게 *eotteoke* 'how' or 'in what way'.

4.4 The System of CIRCUMSTANTIATION

(105)

그 아이는 어른처럼 설명했다.							
geu	ai	=neun	eoreun	=*cheoreom*	seolmyeongha-et-da		
the	child		adult	like	explained		
P1:Sayer			Comparison		Process:verbal		
ng			ng		vg		
Deictic	Thing	TFM	Thing	EFM	Event		
determiner	noun	clitic	noun	clitic	verb		
					Head	TM	EM
					stem	sfx	sfx
'The child explained like an adult.'							

4.4.5 Means

Circumstances of Means focus on the instrument used to do something; they are typically realised by a nominal group marked by (으)로 *(eu)ro* 'by, with' as in (106) and (107); or they can be realised by a co-verbal phrase such as 을/를 가지고 *eul/reul gajigo* 'with' or by 을/를 통해서 *eul/reul tonghaeseo* 'through' as in (108). They can be queried by the interrogative expressions 무엇으로 *mueos euro*, 무엇을 가지고 *mueos eul gajigo*, etc., 'with what' in Korean.

(106)

스위치로 공기의 힘을 ...						
seuwichi	=*ro*	gonggi	=ui		him	=eul
switch	with	air			power	
Means		P2:Undergoer				
ng		ng				
Thing	EFM	Orient			Thing	EFM
noun	clitic	[ng]			noun	clitic
		Thing	Linking			
		noun	clitic			
'(You) ... the air power with the switch.'						

... 조절할 수 있다.			
jojeolha-l	*su*		*it-da*
control	can		
Process:material			
vg			
Event	Modal		
verb	word complex		
Head	Link	β	α
stem	sfx	bound noun	auxiliary verb
			Head / EM
			stem / sfx
... can control ...			

(107)

추젓은 가을 새우로 만든 새우젓 ...						
chujeos	*=eun*	*gaeul*	*saeu*	*=ro*	*mandeu-n*	*saeujeos*
chujeot		autumn	shrimp	with	make	shrimp pickle
P1:Token		P0:Value				
ng		ng				
Thing	TFM	Qualifier				Thing
noun	clitic	[[clause]]				noun
		Means			Process	
		ng			vg	
		Class	Thing	EFM	Event	
		noun	noun	clitic	verb	
					Head / RTM	
					stem / sfx	
'Chujeot ... pickle made with autumn shrimps.'						

4.4 The System of CIRCUMSTANTIATION

... 입니다.	
i-mnida	
is	
Process:relational	
vg	
Event	
verb	
Head	EM
stem	sfx
... is ...	

(108)

우리는 실습을 통해서 ...				
uri	*=neun*	*silseub*	*=eul*	*tonghaeseo*
we		practice		through
P1		Means		
ng		cvp		
Thing	TFM	Incumbent		**Role**
noun	clitic	[ng]		bound verb
		Thing	**EFM**	
		noun	clitic	
'We ... through practice.'				

... 이론을 배울 수 있었다.					
iron	*=eul*	*baeu-l*	*su*	*iss-eot-da*	
theory		learn	possibility	existed	
P2		Process			
ng		vg			
Thing	EFM	Event		Modal	
noun	clitic	verb		word complex	
		Head	Link	β	α
		stem	sfx	bound noun	aux verb
					Head	TM	EM
					stem	sfx	sfx
... could learn the theory ...					

4.4.6 Cause

Circumstances of Cause construe the reason why the process is actualised; they can be queried with the interrogative expression 왜 *wae* 'why'. They are realised by a nominal group that includes a bound noun 때문 *ttaemun* 'cause, reason' that culminates with the EFM 에 *e* as in (109), a nominal group marked by (으)로 *(eu)ro* 'due to' as in (110), or an embedded clause involving the Install or Installing functions as in (112) and (113) respectively.

(109)

나는 너 때문에 미치겠다.							
na	*neun*	=*neo*	***ttaemun***	=*e*	*michi-get-da*		
I		you	because of		become crazy		
P1:Senser		Cause			Process:mental		
ng		ng			vg		
Thing	TFM	Thing	**Perspective**[11]	**EFM**	Event		
pronoun	clitic	pronoun	bound noun	clitic	verb		
					Head	Modal	EM
					stem	sfx	sfx
'I'm going crazy because of you.'							

(110)

우천으로 소풍이 취소되었다.							
ucheon	=*euro*	*sopung*	=*i*	*chwisodoe-eot-da*			
rain	because of	excursion		was cancelled			
Cause		P1:Undergoer		Process:material			
ng		ng		vg			
Thing	**EFM**	Thing	**EFM**	Event			
noun	clitic	noun	clitic	verb			
				Head	TM	EM	
				stem	sfx	sfx	
'Because of the rain, the excursion was called off.'							

---

[11] We are extending our characterisation of the nominal group Perspective function here to include causality alongside location.

4.4 The System of CIRCUMSTANTIATION

Clause (110) has the same marker as the Manner of 'means' in (106) and (107). But only in Circumstances of Cause can this be replaced by the nominal group 때문에 *ttaemun e* 'because of', as in (111).

(111)

우천 때문에 소풍이 취소되었다.								
ucheon	***ttaemun***	=*e*	sopung	=*i*	chwisodoe-eot-da			
rain	because of		excursion		was cancelled			
Cause			P1:Undergoer		Process:material			
ng			ng		vg			
Thing	**Perspective**	**EFM**	Thing	EFM	Event			
noun	bound noun	clitic	noun	clitic	verb			
					Head	TM	EM	
					stem	sfx	sfx	
'Because of the rain, the excursion was called off.'								

The next two examples illustrate Circumstances of Cause realised through an embedded clause. Example (112) shows a Circumstance of Cause realised through the Install function involving the suffix 기 -*gi*; and (113) illustrates a Cause realised through an Installing function involving the bound noun 것 *geot*.

(112)

비가 오기 때문에 ...				
bi	*ga*	*o-gi*	*ttaemun*	=*e*
rain		come	because of	
Cause				
ng				
Thing			Perspective	EFM
[[clause]]			bound noun	clitic
P1	Process			
ng	vg			
Thing	EFM	Event		
noun	clitic	verb		
		Head	**Install**	
		stem	sfx	
'Because it was raining ...				

The Grammar of Experiential Meaning: TRANSITIVITY

... 소풍이 취소되었다.		
sopung	=*i*	*chwisodoe-eot-da*
excursion		was cancelled
P1:Undergoer		Process:material
ng		vg
Thing	EFM	Event
noun	clitic	verb
		Head / TM / EM
		stem / sfx / sfx
'... the excursion was called off.'		

(113)

어제 결석한 것 때문에 ...					
eoje	*gyeolseokha-n*	**geot**		*ttaemun*	=*e*
yesterday	skip class			because of	
Cause					
ng					
Thing				Perspective	EFM
[[clause]]				bound noun	clitic
Location:time	Process		**Installing**		
ng	vg		bound noun		
Thing	Event				
noun	verb				
	Head	Link			
	stem	sfx			
'Because (I) skipped class yesterday ...'					

4.4 The System of CIRCUMSTANTIATION

... 진단서를 내야 한다.							
jindanseo	=*reul*	*nae-ya*		*ha-n-da*			
medical certificate		submit		must			
P2:Undergoer		Process:material					
Ng		vg					
Thing	EFM	Event		Modal			
noun	clitic	verb		aux verb			
		Head	Link	Head		TM	EM
		stem	sfx	stem		sfx	sfx
'... (I) have to submit a medical certificate.'							

4.4.7 Purpose

Circumstances of Purpose can be realised by a co-verbal phrase, culminating with the bound verb 위해 *wihae* 'for' as in (114). They can be queried by the interrogative expression 누구를 (or 무엇을) 위해 *nugu reul* (or *mueos eul*) *wihae* 'for whom (or what)'.

(114)

그 신부는 가난한 사람들을 위해 ...						
geu	*sinbu*	=*neun*	*gananha-n*	*saram-deur*	=*eul*	*wihae*
that	priest		poor	people		for
P1:Actor			Purpose			
ng			cvp			
Deictic	Thing	TFM	Incumbent			Role
determiner	noun	clitic	[ng]			bound verb
			Epithet	Thing	EFM	
			adjective	noun	clitic	
			Head	Link		
			stem	sfx		
'That priest ... for the poor.'						

... 평생을 살았다.		
pyeongsaeng	*=eul*	*sar-at-da*
entire-life		lived
P2:E-Range		Process:material
ng		vg
Thing	EFM	Event
noun	clitic	verb
		Head / TM / EM
		stem / sfx / sfx
... lived his entire life ...		

A Circumstance of Purpose can also be realised through an embedded clause in a co-verbal phrase, involving the Install function realised by the suffix 기 *-gi* – as shown in (115).

(115)

내년에 한국에 가기 위해 ...					
naenyeon	*=e*	*hangug*	*=e*	*ga-**gi***	*wihae*
next year	in	Korea	to	go	for
Purpose					
cvp					
Incumbent					Role
[ng]					bound verb
Thing					
[[clause]]					
Location:time		Location:space		Process	
ng		ng		vg	
Thing	EFM	Thing	EFM	Event	
noun	clitic	noun	clitic	verb	
				Head / **Install**	
				stem / sfx	
'In order to go to Korea next year ...					

4.4 The System of CIRCUMSTANTIATION

... 저금을 하고 있다.				
jeogeum	=*eul*	*ha-go*		*it-da*
saving money		do		be doing
P2:P-Range		Process:material		
ng		vg		
Thing	EFM	Event		Dimension
noun	clitic	verb		aux verb
		Head	Link	Head	EM
		stem	sfx	stem	sfx
... (I) am saving money.'				

4.4.8 Concession

Circumstances of Concession provide the reason for something that is expected but does not happen.

Example (116) involves an expectation that the noise should have kept someone awake, but in fact it did not. This is realised by a co-verbal phrase with the bound verb 불구하고 *bulguhago* 'despite'; this bound noun can be elided, as in (117), giving the impression that Concession is realised by a nominal group.

Circumstances of Concession can be queried by the interrogative expression, 무엇에도 불구하고 *mueos e do bulguhago* 'in spite of what'.

(116)

소음에도 불구하고 그는 ...						
soeum	=*e*	=*do*	*bulguhago*	*geu*		=*neun*
noise	despite			he		
Concession				P1:Undergoer		
cvp				ng		
Incumbent			Role	Thing		TFM
[ng]			bound verb	pronoun		clitic
Thing	EFM	IFM				
noun	clitic	clitic				
'Despite the noise, he ...						

... 깊은 잠에 빠졌다.					
gip-eun	*jam*	=*e*	*ppajy-eot-da*		
deep	sleep	in	fell		
Location:space			Process:material		
ng			vg		
Epithet	Thing	EFM	Event		
adjective	noun	clitic	verb		
Head	Link		Head	TM	EM
stem	sfx		stem	sfx	sfx
... fell into a deep sleep.'					

(117)

소음에도 그는 ...				
soeum	=*e*	=*do*	*geu*	=*neun*
noise	despite		he	
Concession			P1:Undergoer	
ng			ng	
Thing	EFM	IFM	Thing	TFM
noun	clitic	clitic	pronoun	clitic
'Despite the noise, he ...				

... 깊은 잠에 빠졌다.					
gip-eun	*jam*	=*e*	*ppajy-eot-da*		
deep	sleep	in	fell		
Location:space			Process:material		
ng			vg		
Epithet	Thing	EFM	Event		
adjective	noun	clitic	verb		
Head	Link		Head	TM	EM
stem	sfx		stem	sfx	sfx
... fell into a deep sleep.'					

4.4 The System of CIRCUMSTANTIATION

Example (118) illustrates a Circumstance of Concession realised through an embedded clause. An Install function involving the suffix (으)ㅁ -(eu)m is the only option for realising the embedding here.

(118)

경고를 했음에도 불구하고 ...						
gyeonggo	=*reul*	*ha-ess-eum*		=*e*	=*do*	*bulguhago*
warning		did				despite
Concession						
cvp						
Incumbent						Role
[ng]						bound verb
Thing				EFM	IFM	
[[clause]]				clitic	clitic	
P2		Process				
ng		vg				
Thing	EFM	Event				
noun	clitic	verb				
		Head	TM	**Install**		
		stem	sfx	sfx		
'In spite of warning ...						

... 시위대는 저지선을 넘었다.						
siwidae	=*neun*	*jeojiseon*		=*eul*	*neom-eot-da*	
demonstrators		police line			crossed	
P1		P2			Process	
ng		ng			vg	
Thing	TFM	Thing		EFM	Event	
noun	clitic	noun		clitic	verb	
					Head	TM	EM
					stem	sfx	sfx
... the demonstrators crossed the police line.'						

4.4.9 Accompaniment

Circumstances of Accompaniment involve joint participation and construe the meaning of 'comitative' or 'reciprocal'.

As shown in (119), the Circumstance of Accompaniment is realised by a nominal group culminating with the clitic 와/과 *wa/gwa* 'with'; this nominal group can be optionally followed by an expression such as 같이/함께 *gachi/hamkke* 'together'. Korean School Grammar identifies the expressions *gachi* and *hamkke* as adverbs.

Circumstances of Accompaniment can be queried through the interrogative expression 누구와 (함께/같이) *nugu wa (hamkke/gachi)* '(together) with whom' or 무엇과 (함께/같이) *mueot kwa (hamkke/gachi)* '(together) with what'.

(119)

부부는 부모님과 휴가를 지냈다.								
bubu	=*neun*	*bumo-nim*	=*gwa*	*hyuga*	=*reul*	*jinae-t-da*		
couple		parents	with	holiday		spent		
P1:Actor		Accompaniment		P2:E-Range		Process:material		
ng		ng		ng		vg		
Thing	TFM	Thing	**EFM**	Thing	EFM	Event		
noun	clitic	noun	clitic	noun	clitic	verb		
		Head	Honour			Head	TM	EM
		root	sfx			stem	sfx	sfx
'The couple (spent) holiday with the parents.'								

4.4.10 Role

Circumstances of Role specify the part played by a Participant in a clause. The Circumstance of Role is realised as a nominal group with the clitic (으)로(서) *(eu)ro(seo)* 'as' as in (120). They can be queried through the interrogative expression 무엇으로(서) *mueos euro(seo)* 'as what'.

(120)

그는 현재 소설가로서 . . .				
geu	=*neun*	*hyeonjae*	*soseolga*	=*roseo*
he		at present	novelist	as
P1:Phenomenon		Location:time	Role	
ng		ng	ng	
Thing	TFM	Thing	Thing	**EFM**
pronoun	Clitic	noun	noun	clitic
'He . . . as a novelist at present.'				

4.4 The System of CIRCUMSTANTIATION

... 더 잘 알려져 있다.							
deo	*jal*	*ally-eo*		*jy-eo*		*it-da*	
more	well	known		is		be doing	
Manner		Process:mental					
advg		vg					
Head		Event		Valence		Dimension	
word complex		verb		aux verb		aux verb	
β	α	Head	Link	Head	Link	Head	EM
adverb	adverb	stem	sfx	stem	sfx	stem	sfx
... is better known ...							

4.4.11 Product

Product Circumstances construe the end state of a Participant that is transformed by the Process. They are realised as a nominal group culminating with the clitic (으)로 *(eu)ro* 'into', as in (121); they can be queried through the interrogative expression 무엇으로 *mueos euro* 'into what'.

(121)

2011 년에 이 작품이 ...							
2011	*nyeon*	*=e*		*i*		*jakpum*	*=i*
2011	year	in		this		work	
Location:time				P1:Undergoer			
ng				ng			
Quantity		EFM		Deictic		Thing	EFM
word complex		clitic		determiner		noun	clitic
α	β						
numeral	bound noun						
'This work ... in 2011.'							

... 영화로 만들어졌다.			
yeonghwa	*=ro*	*mandeur-eo*	*jy-eot-da*
film	into	made	was
Product		Process:material	
ng		vg	
Thing	**EFM**	Event	Valence
noun	clitic	verb	aux verb
		Head / Link	Head / TM / EM
		stem / sfx	stem / sfx / sfx
... was made into a drama film ...			

4.4.12 Angle

Circumstances of Angle are concerned with the perspective from which something is said or thought. They can be queried by an interrogative expression such as 누구에 의하면 *nugu e uihamyeon* 'according to whom' or 무엇에 따르면 *mueos e ttareumyeon* 'according to what'. The perspective involved can be that of a human being, an organisation, a newspaper, a report, research or a survey, or someone's memory, idea or estimation. Angle is realised by a co-verbal phrase that ends with bound verbs such as 의하면 *uihamyeon* 'leaning' or 따르면 *ttareumyeon* 'following' as in (122).

(122)

한 연구에 의하면 ...			
han	*yeongu*	*=e*	*uihamyeon*
one	study		leaning
Angle			
cvp			
Incumbent			**Role**
[ng]			bound verb
Deictic	Thing	**EFM**	
Determiner	noun	clitic	
'According to a study ...			

4.4 The System of CIRCUMSTANTIATION

... 인구 증가율은 ...		
ingu	*jeunggayur*	=*eun*
population	increasing rate	
P1:Carrier		
ng		
Class	Thing	TFM
noun	noun	clitic
... the increase in population ...		

... 약 10%이다.				
yak	10	*peosenteu*	*i-da*	
about	10	per cent	is	
P0:Attribute			Process:relational	
ng			vg	
Quantity			Event	
word complex			copula	
β	α		Head	EM
bound noun	word complex		stem	sfx
	α	β		
	number	bound noun		
'... is about 10 percent.'				

Circumstances of Angle can also be realised by a nominal group (marked with 에게 *ege* 'to') when the perspective is that of a specific person as in (123). In this case the Angle can be queried by the interrogative expression 누구에게 *nugu ege* 'to whom'.

(123)

그에게 나는 ...			
geu	=*ege*	*na*	=*neun*
he	to	I	
Angle		P1:Carrier	
ng		ng	
Thing	EFM	Thing	TFM
pronoun	clitic	pronoun	clitic
'To him, I ...			

... 전혀 다른 세계의 사람이었다.							
jeonhyeo	*dareun*	*segye*	*=ui*	*saram*	*i-eot-da*		
totally	different	world		person	was		
P0:Attribute					Process:relational		
ng					vg		
Orient				Thing	Event		
[ng]				noun	copula		
Epithet		Thing	Link		Head	TM	EM
word complex		noun	clitic		stem	sfx	sfx
β	α						
adverb	adjective						
... was a person from a totally different world.'							

4.4.13 Matter

Circumstances of Matter construe what is being talked or thought about. They can be queried by the interrogative expression such as 무엇에 대하여 *mueos e daehayeo* 'about what'. This function is realised by a co-verbal phrase that ends with the bound verb 대해 *daehae* 'concerning, about',[12] as in (124).

(124)

그 사고에 대해 사장은 ...					
geu	*sago*	*=e*	***daehae***	*sajang*	*=eun*
the	accident	concerning		boss	
Matter				P1:Senser	
cvp				ng	
Incumbent			**Role**	Thing	TFM
[ng]			bound verb	noun	clitic
Deictic	Thing	**EFM**			
determiner	noun	clitic			
'Concerning the accident, the boss ...					

[12] Note that there are two 'free' variation forms of the bound verb 대해 *daehae* 'concerning, about': (i) 대하여 *daehayeo* and (ii) 대해서 *daehaeseo*.

4.5 Concluding Remarks on TRANSITIVITY

... 책임을 느꼈다.		
chaegim	*=eul*	*neukky-eot-da*
responsibility		felt
P2:Phenomenon		Process:mental
ng		vg
Thing	EFM	Event
noun	clitic	verb
		Head / TM / EM
		stem / sfx / sfx
'... felt responsibility.'		

Table 4.7 summarises the realisation of Circumstances and the way they can be queried.

Table 4.7 *Realisation of Circumstances*

Circumstance	realisation				interrogative expression
	nominal group		adverbial group	co-verbal phrase	
		typical EFM employed			
Location:time	yes	에 *e* 'in/on/at'			언제 *eonje* 'when'
Location: space	yes	에 *e* 'in/on/at'; (으)로 *(eu)ro*, 'to'			어디 *eodi* 'where'
Extent:time	yes	동안 *dongan* 'for'; 부터 *buteo* 'from' + 까지 *kkaji* 'to'	잠깐 *jamkkan* 'a moment'		얼마(나) *eolma(na)* 'how long, to what extent'
Extent:space	yes	을/를 *eul/reul*	멀리 *meolli* 'far'		얼마(나) *eolma(na)* 'how far ..., to what extent'
Extent: frequency	yes	동안 *dongan* 'for'	언제나 *eonjena* 'always' 자주 *jaju* 'frequently'		몇번 *myeot beon* 'how many times', 몇시간 *myeot sigan* 'how many hours' 몇년 *myeot nyeon* 'how many years'.

Table 4.7 *(cont.)*

Circumstance	realisation				interrogative expression
	nominal group		adverbial group	co-verbal phrase	
	yes	typical EFM employed			
Manner			오손도손 *osondoson* 'harmoniously', 재미있게 *jaemiitge* 'fun', 함께 *hamkke* 'jointly'		어떻게 *eotteoke* 'how, in what way'
Comparison	yes	보다 *boda* 'than'; 처럼 *cheoreom* 'like'			무엇/누구보다 *mueot/nugu boda* 'than what/whom'; 무엇/누구처럼 *mueot/nugu cheoreom* 'like what/whom'
Means	yes	(으)로 *(eu)ro* 'by, with'		... 을/를 가지고 *eul/reul gajigo* ... 을/를 통해서 *eul/reul tonghaeseo* 'with, through'	무엇으로 *mueos euro* 'with what'; 무엇을 가지고 *mueos eul gajigo* 'with what'
Cause	yes	때문에 *ttaemun e* 'cause, reason' + 'in/on/at'; (으)로 *(eu)ro* 'due to'		... (으)로 인해 *(eu)ro inhae* 'because of'	왜 *wae* 'why'; 누구/무엇 때문에 *nugu/mueot ttaemun e* 'because of whom/what'; 누구/무엇으로 인해 *nugu/mueos euro inhae* 'caused by whom/what'
Purpose				... 을/를 위해 *eul/reul wihae* 'for the sake of'	누구를/무엇을 위해 *nugu reul/mueos eul wihae* 'for whom/what'
Concession	yes	에도 *e do* 'in/on/at' + 'even'		... 에도 불구하고 *edo bulguhago* 'in spite of'	무엇에도 불구하고 *mueos e do bulguhago* 'in spite of what'
Accompaniment	yes	와/과 *wa/gwa* 'with'			누구와/무엇과 (함께/같이) *nugu wa/mueot kwa (hamkke/gachi)* '(together) with whom/what'

4.5 Concluding Remarks on TRANSITIVITY

Table 4.7 (cont.)

Circumstance		realisation			interrogative expression
		nominal group			
		typical EFM employed	adverbial group	co-verbal phrase	
Role	yes	(으)로(서) (eu)ro(seo) 'as'			무엇으로(서) mueos euro(seo) 'as what'
Product	yes	(으)로 (eu)ro 'into'			무엇으로 mueos euro 'into what'
Angle	yes	에게 ege 'to'		... 에 의하면 e uihamyeon ... 에 따르면 e ttareumyeon 'according to'	누구/무엇에 의하면/따르면 nugu/mueos e uihamyeon/ttareumyeon 'according to whom/what'; 누구에게 nugu ege 'to whom'
Matter				... 에 대하여 e daehayeo 'about'	누구/무엇에 대하여 nugu/mueos e daehayeo 'about whom/what'

4.5 Concluding Remarks on TRANSITIVITY

In this chapter we have considered the experiential grammar of a Korean clause. We began with a brief survey of the key TRANSITIVITY functions and their realisation at different ranks – across clause, group/phrase and word structure. We then developed the system of EXPERIENTIAL CLAUSE TYPES in Korean and discussed in detail material, mental, relational and verbal clauses. Our analysis includes some innovative proposals for acts, facts and ideas in mental clauses and a generalisation about locative and possessive sub-types of relational clauses. We then moved on to the DIATHESIS system, which describes the alternative ways Participants are related to the Process. These have been more commonly discussed in terms of the contrast between 'active' and 'passive' voices and between 'causatives' and 'non-causatives'; but in this grammar the alternatives are treated as agnate expressions related to one another as paradigmatic options.

We then moved on to Circumstances. Circumstances are elements that essentially expand the experiential centre of the clause (i.e., the Participant(s) and Process configuration), construing a range of more peripheral meanings. We introduced thirteen types of circumstance in Korean, including consideration of time, space, manner and cause. Whereas Participants are specific to clause types, Circumstances tend to combine with a range of clause types.

276 The Grammar of Experiential Meaning: TRANSITIVITY

We conclude this chapter by providing an overview of experiential systems in Korean (Figure 4.9). Note that many of the sub-systems of CIRCUMSTANTIATION have been omitted to simplify the presentation. For restrictions on the co-selection of chocies from the systems EXPERIENTIAL CLAUSE TYPE and DIATHESIS, see Table 4.6.

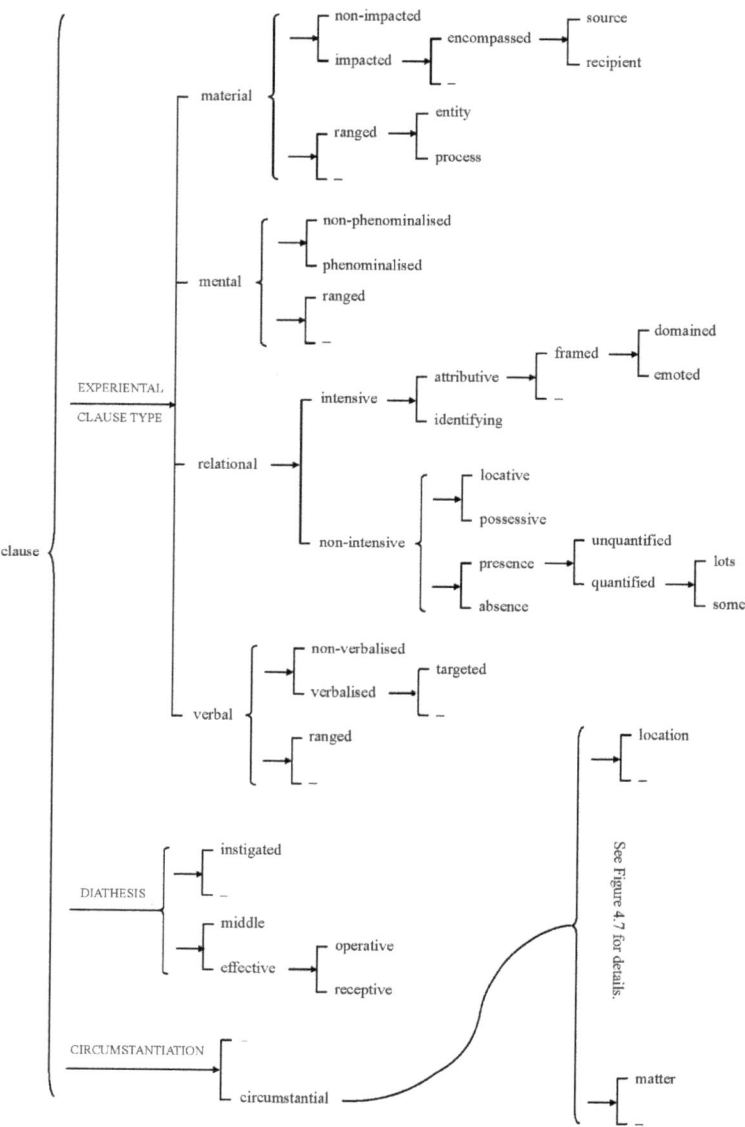

Figure 4.9 The system of TRANSITIVITY in Korean

5 The Grammar of Textual Meaning in Korean: THEME

5.1 Introduction to Textual Clause Structure

In Chapter 3 we explored interpersonal meaning, looking at how meaning is enacted in conversation as interlocutors take up different roles. In Chapter 4 we explored experiential meaning, focusing on how our experience of the world is construed. We now turn to textual meaning, considering how these experiential and interpersonal meanings are organised as a message that fits coherently into the flow of information as a text unfolds. Since we are working on grammar we will focus on the system of THEME, setting aside consideration of systems realised through prosodic phonology. For a full account of textual meaning in Korean we would of course have to address both grammatical and phonological resources.

Textual meaning has often been characterised metaphorically in terms of information flow. Pike, for example, refers to meanings 'flowing together like ripples on the tide, merging into one another in the form of a hierarchy of little waves ... on still bigger waves' (Pike 1982: 12–13). Halliday (in Thibault 1987: 612) refers to the 'periodic movement which is so characteristic of discourse at all levels' – movement he terms a 'hierarchy of periodicity'. This metaphor of waves upon waves has been applied to a range of modalities of communication alongside language, including image, music and paralanguage (Kress and van Leeuwen 1990, Ngo et al. 2021, O'Toole 1994, Painter et al. 2014, van Leeuwen 1999). As we have all experienced, no matter how long or short a piece of music is, it typically comes with a beat – the rhythm of the piece. Korean, like all languages, organises information flow along comparable lines.

As a speaker or writer, we chunk our ideas into pulses of information and guide the audience by highlighting the angle we are taking on what we are talking about. If we did not do this, it would be very hard to get the audience to predictively engage in an exchange of meaning, whether spoken or written. This is why we move around chunks of information (which can be a group of words, a clause or even a whole paragraph) from one place to another when we are editing, translating or authoring.

In this chapter, we are focusing on textual resources that enable Korean speakers to signal the beginning of waves and adjust their wavelength at clause rank. Importantly, we will look at how specific linguistic resources deployed at the clause level are related to their neighbouring discourse. As far as possible we will work with examples from phases of discourse in our data. This allows us to consider how information is organised beyond the clause (in paragraph-size units for example) and show how the choice of clause level topical Theme is very sensitive to the composition of longer wavelengths of information flow. Just as Theme orients the reader to the field at the clause level, Hyper-Theme and Macro-Theme play a similar role for longer stretches of discourse. As Martin notes, a Macro-Theme[1] is 'a sentence or a group of sentences (possibly a paragraph) which predicts a set of Hyper-Themes'; and a Hyper-Theme is 'an introductory sentence or group of sentences which is established to predict a particular pattern of interaction among strings, chains and Theme selection in the following sentences' (Martin 1992: 437). In writing, Macro-Themes are often realised graphologically as titles or subtitles in a text, scaffolding the phasing and staging of a text as it unfolds.

Consider text (1), which functions as the Macro-Theme of a children's fork story entitled *The Umbrella Seller and the Fan Seller* (The Educational Foundation for Koreans Abroad 2006):

(1) 옛날 어느 마을에 두 아들을 둔 어머니가 살았어요. 그런데 어머니는 늘 두 아들 때문에 마음이 편할 날이 없었지요. 왜냐하면 큰 아들은 우산 장수였고 작은 아들은 부채 장수였기 때문이에요.

Once upon a time in a village lived a mother who had two sons. However, the mother never had a day when her mind was peaceful because of the two sons. For the older son was an umbrella seller and the younger son was a fan seller.

This text is presented again, clause by clause, including transitivity analysis.

---

[1] Macro-Theme is commonly referred to as an introductory paragraph and Hyper-Theme as a topic sentence.

5.1 Introduction to Textual Clause Structure

(1')

Clause 1			
옛날 어느 마을에		두 아들을 둔 어머니가	살았어요.
yennal	eoneu maeur =e	du adeur =eul du-n eomeoni =ga	sar-ass-eo yo
once upon a time	in a certain village	mother who had two sons	lived
Cir:Loc:time	Cir:Loc:space	P1:Actor	Process
'Once upon a time in a village, a mother who had two sons lived.'			

Clause 2				
그런데	어머니는	늘 두 아들 때문에	마음이 편할 날이	없었지요.
geureonde	eomeoni =neun	neul du adeul ttaemun =e	maeum =i pyeonha-l nar =i	eops-eot-ji yo
However,	mother	always because of two sons	day when her mind was peaceful	did not have
	P1:Possessor	Cir:Cause	P1:Possession	Process
'However, the mother never had a worry-free day because of her two sons.'				

Clause 3			
왜냐하면	큰 아들은	우산 장수	였고
waenyahamyeon	keu-n adeur =eun	usan jangsu	y-eot-go
for	older son	umbrella seller	was and
	P1:Carrier	P0:Attribute	Process
'For the older son was an umbrella seller and			

Clause 4		
작은 아들은	부채 장수였기 때문이에요.	
jag-eun adeur =eun	buchae jangsu	y-eot-gi ttaemun-i-e yo
younger son	fan seller	was
P1:Carrier	P0:Attribute	Process
the younger son was a fan seller.'		

The first sentence is a typical way of beginning folk stories – namely, setting what happens in time and place and introducing the main characters. The mother is picked up at the beginning of the second clause. And the additional characters, her two sons, are picked up at the beginning of the third and fourth clauses. We will refer to the function of this clause initial position as Theme. Theme is the element of clause structure that establishes the angle that a message adopts on the field of a text (i.e., its 'subject matter') as it unfolds; the rest of the message is referred to as Rheme.

In Korean, the Theme can involve EFM, TFM and/or IFM clitics – depending on the role a Participant or Circumstance plays in co-text and context. For example, if a speaker selects an angle on the field that is anticipated, they choose a Theme with a TFM (i.e., 은/는 *eun/neun*). If they want to highlight the experiential role of a Theme that it is not readily anticipated in a given context, they choose an EFM (i.e., 이/가 *i/ga*). If they want to highlight an interpersonal dimension of a Theme, they may mark it with an IFM (e.g., 만 *man* 'only', 도 *do* 'also'). In spoken discourse, where explicit function marking is often dropped, the Theme can be recognised through early position in the clause alone.

It is important to point out that the concept of Theme is not the same as the concept of topic; the latter is a narrower concept, whose primary role is to signal what a message is about. This is the function of just one particular kind of Theme (what we call an angling topical Theme in Korean; see Section 5.2.1). SFL takes a broader view and recognises different kinds of Theme. A Theme that signals the angle a message adopts in relation to its field is called a topical Theme. In addition, we recognise textual Themes (that relate messages to their adjacent co-text) and interpersonal Themes (which highlight aspects of the interpersonal meaning of interacts).

In the remainder of this chapter we will explore different kinds of Theme and the distinct contributions they make in discourse. In our discussion we follow Fries (1981/1983), who argues that the clause Themes of a phase of discourse compose 'the method of development' of that phase. The term 'method of development' refers to a pattern of semantic relations among choices for Theme (Eggins 2004: Chapter 9, Martin 1992: Chapter 6, Martin and Rose 2007: Chapter 6). Linguists of the Prague School have explored closely related patterns in their studies of thematic progression (Fries 1981). To begin, we introduce each of the three main categories of Theme (i.e., topical, interpersonal and textual) and discuss different Theme choices within each category. We formalise our description step by step as a set of choices as we go. After reviewing all the possible Theme choices in Korean, we present an overall system network for THEME and propose a methodology for identifying Themes in discourse with reference to a few exemplary texts.

5.2 Topical Theme

As outlined in Chapter 1, in SFL social context is interpreted as patterns of meanings – with ideational meaning construing field, interpersonal meaning enacting tenor and textual meaning composing mode. In this model, field is understood as a set of activities orientated to some global institutional purpose, the taxonomies of items participating in these activities and their respective properties (Doran and Martin 2021, Martin 1992). From the perspective of field, for example, we might note that January is the time of year when professional tennis players compete in various tournaments in Australia. We experience them practising, playing matches, recovering from competition, being treated for injuries, being interviewed by the media, participating in award ceremonies, travelling to tournaments, endorsing products and so on. And depending on how much of a fan we are and how much tennis we have played in our lives, we know a lot about each of these activities – who is involved in them, how the players are ranked in relation to one another, what kinds of equipment and clothing are involved and who manufactures it, what kinds of courts and tennis balls are being used, how the weather affects the playing surface of the courts and so on (one of our authors could go on and on). All of this is field. Topical Theme is the clause function we use to let our readers and listeners know which aspect of this smorgasbord of knowledge we are on about.

Seen in these terms, a **topical Theme** flags the angle we are taking on the field. It orients the message to the field in one of two ways: either it establishes and then sustains an angle on the field by means of an entity (i.e., angling topical Theme) or it positions an angle on the field in time or space through a Circumstance (i.e., positioning topical Theme). Metaphorically speaking, we can think of topical Theme as a kind of movie camera, establishing and holding our attention during a filmic shot (angling Theme) or alternatively moving our gaze along from one shot to another (positioning Theme). We introduce the sub-systems of TOPICAL THEME one by one below.

5.2.1 The System of ANGLING THEME

There are two ANGLING THEME SYSTEMS – ESTABLISHING THEME and CONTINUING THEME. This reflects the fact that when we take up a particular angle on a field, we first establish the angle and then maintain it for as long as that angle is appropriate.

There are two distinctive ways of establishing an angle on a field in Korean. One of them is via the system of ESTABLISHING THEME. When the speaker establishes an angle on a field with a topic that the listener expects to hear about, the speaker places the topical Theme in an early clause position[2] and

---

[2] Initial position unless another type of Theme precedes.

marks it with the Textual Function Marker (TFM) 은/는 *eun/neun*. When, on the other hand, the speaker establishes an angle on a field through a topic that the listener is less likely to anticipate, they place it in an early clause position but do not use the TFM; rather the P1 Experiential Function Marker (EFM) 이/가 *i/ga* is used to focus readers' attention on the experiential role of the chosen Theme.

The former choice is referred to as anticipated Theme and realised by a clause initial nominal group marked by the TFM 은/는 *eun/neun*. The latter choice is referred to as non-anticipated Theme. It is usually realised by a clause initial nominal group marked by the P1 EFM 이/가 *i/ga*; the P2 EFM 을/를 *eul/reul* is occasionally used, as in examples (18) and (19) in Section 5.6. These choices are shown as the system of ESTABLISHING THEME in Figure 5.1, followed by realisation statements in Table 5.1.

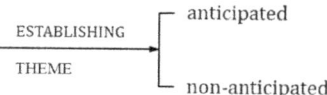

Figure 5.1 The system of ESTABLISHING THEME

Table 5.1 *Realisation statements for* ESTABLISHING THEME

anticipated	Theme: nominal group (TFM function marking)
non-anticipated	Theme: nominal group (EFM function marking)

We now consider two news stories, (2) and (3). The first was broadcast in a news programme (The Korean Broadcasting System 2014). As the purpose of news programmes is to deliver information that their audience is not necessarily aware of, the audience usually cannot be expected to precisely predict the news they will hear. Accordingly, it is not uncommon to observe a non-anticipated Theme in the leads for the top news stories of the day. This is illustrated in (2) – which was delivered at the beginning of news programmes on TV, before the newsreader went into detail for each news item.

(2)

Topical Theme		Rheme		
싸이의 강남 스타일 뮤직 비디오가		유튜브 사상 최초로 20 억 뷰를 돌파했습니다.		
Ssai =ui Gangnam Seutail myujik bidio	*=ga*	*Yutyubeu sasang choecho =ro*	*20 eok byu =reul*	*dolpaha-et-seumnida*
Psy's Gangnam Style music video	EFM: P1	for the first time in YouTube history	more than 2 billion viewings	recorded
P1:Actor		Cir:Location	P2:E-Range	Process
'Psy's Gangnam Style music video recorded more than 2 billion viewings in YouTube history for the first time.'				

5.2 Topical Theme

This story is about the high number of viewings of the 'Gangnam Style' music video, which became very popular after its release in 2012. Although the song itself is well-known in Korea and internationally, news about a pop music video is not a typical news item. This helps explain why Psy's Gangnam Style music video is a non-anticipated topical Theme marked by the EFM 가 *ga*.

On the other hand, when a news item that is regularly covered on TV news is mentioned (e.g., what the current president has done on the day), the audience more naturally expects the item. Accordingly, Themes of this kind tend to be marked by the TFM – as exemplified in (3).

(3)

Topical Theme			Rheme			
박근혜 대통령은			오늘 대국민 담화를 발표했습니다.			
Bakgeunhye daetongryeong	*=eun*	*oneul*	*daegungmin damhwa*	*=reul*	*balpyoha-et-seumnida*	
President Park Geunhye	TFM	today	national address	EFM	presented	
P1:Sayer		Cir:Loc:time	P2:Verbiage		Process	
'President Park Geunhye made a national speech today.'						

In spoken discourse, as noted above, a topical Theme may not involve explicit function marking. In such cases, taking context into account, it is not difficult to infer a suitable marker. Suppose example (4) is spoken by a wife when greeting her husband, who has come home in a wet coat. She is surprised because she was busy and didn't realise it was raining outside. In such a context, the topical Theme would most likely be a non-anticipated one if it were to be made explicit – marked by the EFM 가 *ga*.

(4)

Topical Theme	Rheme
비	와?
bi	*wa*
rain	come
P1:Actor	Process
'Is it raining?'	

TFM marking is commonly used for both P1 and P2 Participants in comparable contexts. In both (5) and (5'), for example, the experiential role of 한글 *Hangeul* 'Korean alphabet' is Undergoer, which is typically marked by the P2 EFM 을/를 *eul/reul* as in (5). However, it is replaced by the TFM in (5') –

where it is chosen as an anticipated topical Theme and placed at the initial position of the clause. As a result, examples (5) and (5') have different angling Themes even though they construe the same experiential meaning. Note that we use passive voice in the translation of (5') rather than what in English would be a very marked Theme (i.e., Hangeul, Great King Sejong created in 1443) because the Korean sentence is not highly 'marked'. This is an example of translation choices that prioritise textual meaning over experiential meaning (see more examples in Chapter 7, Section 7.3).

(5)

Topical Theme			Rheme		
세종대왕은			1443 년 한글을 창제하였다.		
Sejong Daewang	*=eun*	*1443 nyeon*	*Hangeur*	*=eul*	*changjeha-yeot-da*
Great King Sejong	TFM	in 1443 year	Hangeul	EFM	created
P1:Actor		Cir: Loc:time	P2:Undergoer		Process
'Great King Sejong created Hangeul in 1443.'					

(5')

Theme			Rheme		
한글은			1443 년 세종대왕이 창제하였다.		
Hangeur	*=eun*	*1443 nyeon*	*Sejong Daewang*	*=i*	*changjeha-yeot-da*
Hangeul	TFM	in 1443 year	Great King Sejong	EFM	created
P2:Undergoer		Cir:Loc:time	P1:Actor		Process
'Hangeul was created by Great King Sejong in 1443.'					

Note that not all anticipated Themes play an experiential role in clause structure. The anticipated Theme in (6), 한지는 *hanji neun* 'traditional Korean paper', does not function as a Participant or Circumstance in this material clause; it simply has a textual function.

5.2 Topical Theme

(6)

Topical Theme		Rheme			
한지는		바람이 잘 통한다			
hanji	*=neun*	*baram*	*=i*	*jal*	*tongha-n-da*
hanji	TFM	air	EFM	well	go through
		P1:Actor		Cir:Manner	Process
'As for Hanji (Korean paper), air passes through easily.'					

In some language descriptions, such Themes are referred to as absolute Themes (e.g., Halliday and McDonald 2004). However, we will not treat Themes that do not have an experiential function (as a Participant or Circumstance) separately from the other types of anticipated unmarked Themes that do have such a function. They both play the same role of flagging the clause's orientation to its field.

Once an orientation to the field is established through an anticipated or non-anticipated Theme, that orientation to the field can be sustained implicitly or explicitly affirmed. The system of CONTINUING THEME formalises options for these two kinds of Theme choice – as shown in Figure 5.2.

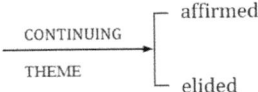

Figure 5.2 The system of CONTINUING THEME

Let's examine how the features [affirmed] and [elided] are used in a text. Example (7) is the first paragraph of a descriptive text entitled *The Dog* from a Primary School reading textbook for Year 3 children in Korea (Ministry of Education 2002a). The first paragraph and the title function as the Macro-Theme for the report.

The first clause starts with an anticipated Theme, 개는 *gae neun* 'dog', with TFM marking. A reader would naturally expect this owing to the title of the book, which is in effect its Macro-Theme. The topical Theme in the second clause, 사람들은 *saramdeur eun* 'people', is picked up from the Rheme of the first clause. The topical Themes of the first two clauses flag that this text is concerned with dogs and people. As 개는 *gae neun* 'dog' is not Theme in Clause (2), it is affirmed explicitly in Clause (3.1). It is then elided in subsequent clauses in the same clause complex where the chosen angle is maintained. This pattern of Theme choices (i.e., an anticipated and affirmed Theme followed by an elided Theme) is the typical way in which a text's method of development unfolds in Korean – that is, a topical Theme that is easily anticipated in a given context is chosen as the angle on the field, and this orientation is maintained for a phase of discourse (often a clause complex or two).

(7)

Cl. No.	Topical Theme			Rheme			
1	개는			사람과 가장 가까운 동물입니다.			
	gae		*=neun*	*saram =gwa gajang gakkau-n dongmur*			*i-mnida*
	dog		TFM	animal that is closest to people			is
	P1:Carrier			P0:Attribute			Process
	'The dog is an animal that is closest to people.'						
2	사람들은			먼 옛날부터 개를 길렀습니다.			
	saram-deur		*=eun*	*meon yetnal =buteo*		*gae =reul*	*gill-eot-seumnida*
	people		TFM	from long ago		dog	have kept
	P1:Actor			Cir:Extent		P2:Undergoer	Process
	'People have kept dogs from long ago.'						
3.1	원래, 개는			이리처럼 사나운 짐승이었는데,			
	wollae	*gae*	*=neun*	*iri =cheoreom sanau-n jimseung*			*i-eon-neunde*
	originally	dog	TFM	ferocious animal like wolf			was but
	Cir:Loc:time	P1:Carrier		P0:Attribute			Process
	'Originally, the dog was a ferocious animal like the wolf but						
3.2	(개는)			사람과 가까이 살면서			
	(*gae =neun*)			*saram =gwa gakkai*			*sal-myeonseo*
	(dog)			close to humans			lived while
	(P1:Actor)			Cir:Manner			Process
	while it lived close to humans						
3.3	(개는)			온순하게 길들여졌다고			
	(*gae =neun*)			*onsunhage*			*gildeury-eo jy-eot- da go*
	(dog)			docile			
	(P1:Undergoer)			Cir:Manner			Process
	the dog has been tamed to be docile						
3.4	(사람들은)						합니다.
	(*saramdeur =eun*)						*ha-mnida*
	(people)						say
	(P1:Sayer)						Process
	they say.'						

5.2 Topical Theme

Let's now consider (8), which includes two further clauses from the lead of the news story whose opening clause was analysed as (2). This text has the same pattern of thematic progression as text (7), except that the initial Theme (in Clause 7.1) is not easily anticipated by the listener – as noted for (2).

(8)

Cl. No.	Topical Theme		Rheme		
1	싸이의 강남 스타일 뮤직 비디오가		유튜브 사상 최초로 20 억 뷰를 돌파했습니다.		
	Ssai =ui Gangnam Seutail myujik bidio	*=ga*	*Yutyubeu sasang choecho =ro*	*20 eok byu =reul*	*dolpaha-et-seumnida*
	Psy's Gangnam Style music video	EFM	for the first time in YouTube history	2 billion viewings	recorded
	P1:Actor		Cir:Location	P2:E-Range	Process
	'Psy's Gangnam Style music video has recorded 2 billion viewings for the first time in YouTube history.'				
2	강남 스타일 뮤직 비디오는		오늘 낮 12 시 30 분 조회수 20 억 2 천 건을 기록했습니다.		
	Gangnam Seutail myujik bidio	*=neun*	*oneul nat 12 si 30 bun*	*johoesu 20 eok 2 cheon geon =eul*	*girokha-et-seumnida*
	Gangnam Style music video	TFM	today at 12.30 pm	2 billion 2 thousand viewings	recorded
	P1:Actor		Cir:Location	P2:E-Range	Process
	'The Gangnam Style music video had recorded 2 billion 2 thousand viewings as of 12.30 this afternoon.'				
3	(강남 스타일 뮤직 비디오는)		공개 1 년 10 개월 만에 대기록을 수립한 것입니다.		
	(Gangnam Seutail myujik bidio =neun)		*gonggae 1 nyeon 10 gaewol man =e*	*daegirog =eul*	*suripha-n geos i-mnida*
	(Gangnam Style music video)		within 1 year and 10 months since (its) release	great record	made
	(P1:Actor)		Cir:Extent	P2:E-Range	Process
	'The video produced a great record within 1 year and 10 months since its release.'				

Once the Psy's Gangnam Style music video has been established by the Theme in (8.1) as the angle on the field, it is marked by the TFM 는 *neun* in clause (8.2), where the audience expects to hear more about it – and gets elided in clause (8.3), where it sustains the angle on the field.

An elided Theme is often used in an answer to a question, as illustrated in (9). As 너 *neo* 'you' is explicitly established as an angling Theme by the question, the response does not need to repeat 나 *na* 'I'; the response simply gives the information asked for – that is, the name of the place where s/he lives.

(9)

Topical Theme		Rheme			
너	는	집	이	어디	니?
neo	*=neun*	*jib*	*=i*	*eodi*	*(i)-ni*
you	TFM	house	EFM	where	is
P1:Carrier-Domain		P1:Carrier		P0:Attribute	Process
'You, where's (your) house?'					
(나	는	집	이)	목동	(이야)
(na	**=neun**	*jib*	*=i*)	*mokdong*	*(i-ya)*
(I	**TFM**	house	EFM)	Mokdong	(is)
(P1:Carrier-Domain		P1:Carrier		P0:Attribute	(Process)
'(Me, (my) house is (in)) Mokdong.'					

In spoken discourse when two interlocutors are asking about one another, a topical Theme is regularly elided – as shown in (10). Both 너 *neo* 'you' and 나 *na* 'I' are implied.

(10)

Cl. No.	Topical Theme	Rheme
1	(너)	피곤해?
	(neo)	*pigonha-e*
	(you)	tired
	(P1:Carrier)	Attribute/Process
	'Are you tired?'	
2	(나)	피곤한 것 같네
	(na)	*pigonha-n geot gan-ne*
	(I)	tired it seems
	(P1:Carrier)	Attribute/Process
	'I think I am.'	

In summary we can say that anticipated and non-anticipated topical Themes in Korean use entities to establish an angle on the field and are chosen taking into account readers' expectations and relevant aspects of field. Once a specific angle on a field is established, it tends to be sustained implicitly in subsequent clauses – especially within the same clause complex, but also across clause complexes. Non-anticipated topical Themes are often used when news items are first introduced in news story texts.

5.2 Topical Theme   289

One significant linguistic pattern related to this discussion is that anticipated Themes marked by the TFM 은/는 *eun/neun* never appear in embedded clauses or hypotactically dependent ones – this is because embedded and dependent clauses do not participate directly in the composition of information flow for a text overall. From the perspective of textual meaning they are 'demoted' messages. This confirms the fact that the function of the particle 은/는 *eun/ neun* is textual rather than experiential.

5.2.2   The System of POSITIONING THEME

So far we have discussed how an angle is established through an anticipated or non-anticipated Theme and how it is maintained through affirmed or elided Themes. We now move on to consider positioning topical Themes, which establish an angle on the field through a particular Circumstance of time or place. A positioning Theme is typically realised by an adverbial group, co-verbal phrase or nominal group that functions as a Circumstance and comes before an angling Theme at the beginning of a clause. When analysing Themes in a Korean text, it is often helpful to make an elided angling Theme explicit to see whether the Circumstance naturally precedes (as positioning Theme) or follows – as the text unfolds. This is a matter of interpretation for an analyst, who has to find the best fit for the text at this moment in its development.

A positioning Theme can be realised with or without a TFM 은/는 *eun/neun*. A positioning Theme without a TFM involves transitional positioning and indicates that an angling Theme is going to be discussed in a particular setting in time or space; a positioning Theme with a TFM highlights contrastive positioning and indicates that the angling Theme is going to be discussed in a contrasting setting in time or space.

Consider example (11), which is the beginning of a famous Korean short story entitled 소나기 *sonagi* 'Shower' by Hwang Sun-won (Hwang 1952). After introducing the main characters, the boy and the girl, it describes something that happened between them over a few days. Clause (11.4.1) has a transitional positioning Theme 며칠째 *myeochiljjae* 'for a few days' (before the affirmed angling Theme 소녀는 *sonyeo neun* 'girl'); the transitional positioning Theme centres on time. The following two clauses have two contrastive positioning Themes, 어제까지는 *eojekkaji neun* 'until yesterday' and 오늘은 *oneul eun* 'today', marking an explicit contrast between up until yesterday and today. In both clauses the angling Theme, 소녀는 *sonyeo neun* 'girl', is elided (this phase of discourse is about a girl, who is realised by an angling Theme throughout – explicitly in clause (11.4.1) and implicitly thereafter).

These positioning Themes contrast with the Circumstance 개울에다 *gaeur eda* 'into the stream' in clause (11.2.1), which does not function as a positioning Theme. It comes after the angling Theme 소녀는 *sonyeo neun* 'girl' and simply functions experientially as a Circumstance of Place; it does not have a textual function.

(11)

Cl. No.	Topical Theme			Rheme			
1.1	소년은			<<1.2>> 곧 [[윤 초시네 증손녀 딸이라]]는 걸 알 수 있었다.			
	sonyeon	=eun		got	[[Yun chosi-ne jeungsonnyeo ttar i-ra]]neun geo =l		al su iss-eot-da
	boy	TFM		immediately	[[she was the granddaughter of Old Yun]]		could tell
	P1:Senser			Cir:Manner	P2:Phenomenon		Process
	'The boy <<1.2>> immediately could tell that she was the granddaughter of Old Yun.'						
1.2				개울가에서 소녀를 보자 >>			
				gaeulga =eseo	sonyeo =reul		bo-ja
	<<(boy)			by stream>>	girl		when (he) saw
	(P1:Senser)			Cir:Loc:space	P2:Phenomenon		Process
	<<when he saw the girl by the stream>>						
2.1	소녀는			개울에다 손을 잠그고			
	sonyeo	=neun		gaeur	=eda	son =eul	jamgeu-go
	girl	TFM		into stream		hand	immersing
	P1:Actor			Cir:Loc:space		P2:Undergoer	Process
	'The girl was immersing her hand in the stream and						
2.2				물장난을 하고 있는 것이다.			
				muljangnan =eul		ha-go	in-neun ges i-da
	(girl)			water play		was doing	
	(P1:Actor)			P2:P-Range		Process	
	(the girl) was playing with water.'						
3	서울서는			이런 개울물을 보지 못하기나 한 듯이.			
	Seoul =seo	=neun		ireon gaeulmur =eul		bo-ji mota-gi =na ha-n deusi	
	in Seoul	TFM	(she)	such stream		had never seen (as if)	
	Cir:Loc:space		(Senser)	P2: Phenomenon		Process	
	'It was as if in Seoul she had never seen such a stream.'						
4.1	벌써 며칠째 소녀는,			학교에서 돌아오는 길에 물장난이었다.			
	beolsseo myeochil jjae	sonyeo	=neun	hakgyo =eseo dorao-neun gir =e		muljangnan	i-eot-da
	already for several days now	girl	TFM	on way home from school		water playing	was
	Cir:Ext	P1:Actor		Cir:Loc:space		P0: 'Existent'[3]	Process
	'Already for several days the girl had been playing in the water on her way home from school.'						

---

[3] We do not recognise existential clauses in our grammar, and our analysis of this clause is therefore provisional. What we are labelling as an 'Existent' here realises a discourse semantic occurrence figure ('playing in water') and is predicated grammatically by the copula 이었다 *i-eot-da* 'was' – which amounts to construing the existence of the 'water play'.

5.2 Topical Theme

5.1	그런데 어제까지는			개울 기슭에서 하더니,	
	geureonde eoje =kkaji	*=neun*		*gaeul giseulg =eseo*	*ha-deoni*
	that said up until yesterday	TFM	(girl)	on bank and	had done (her water-stirring play)
	Cir:Loc:time		(Actor)	Cir:Loc:space	Process
	'That said up to yesterday she was doing it by the bank but,				
5.2	오늘은			징검다리 한가운데 앉아서	
	oneul	*=eun*		*jinggeomdari hangaunde*	*anj-aseo*
	today	TFM	(girl)	on one of stepping stone midstream	squatting
	Cir:Loc:time		(Actor)	Cir:Loc:space	Process
	today squatting on one of the stepping stones in midstream.'				
5.3				하고 있다.	
				ha-go it-da	
	(girl)			is doing (it)	
	(P1:Actor)			Process	
	she is doing it.'				
6.1	소년은			개울둑에 앉아 버렸다.	
	sonyeon	*=eun*		*gaeuldug =e*	*anj-a beory-eot-da*
	boy	TFM		on bank.	decided to sit down
	P1:Actor			Cir:Loc:space	Process
	'The boy decided to sit down on the bank.'				
7.1				소녀가 비키기를 기다리자는 것이다.	
				sonyeo =ga biki-gi =reul gidari-ja-neun geos	*i-da*
	(that)			to wait for her to give way.	is
	(P1:Token)			P2:Value	Process
	'That is to wait for her to give way.'				

In addition, in the locative type of relational clause, P3 EFM can be used as a positioning Theme. In (12) 오른쪽에 *oreunjjog e* 'on the right side' functions as Location and is the positioning Theme in the relational clause.

(12)

Topical Theme				Rheme
오른쪽에 벽난로가 있었다.				
oreunjjog	=*e*	*byeongnallo*	=*ga*	*iss-eot-da*
right side	EFM	fireplace		there was
P3:Location		P1:Located		Process:locative
'On the right side there was a fireplace.'				

Positioning Theme choices in Korean are presented in Figure 5.3.

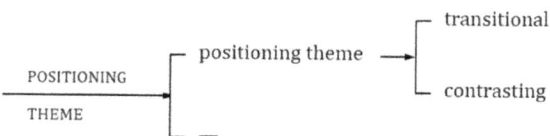

Figure 5.3 The system of POSITIONING THEME

5.3 Interpersonal Theme

Interpersonal Themes come before topical Themes in Korean. They are more common in conversation than in monologic registers. They highlight a speaker's attitude toward a proposition or proposal and/or make explicit reference to the addressee. Examples of interpersonal Themes are given in Table 5.2 – for Vocative elements (e.g., 선생님 *Seonsaeng-nim* 'Teacher') and Modal Adjunct or Comment functions (e.g., 아마도 *amado* 'perhaps' and 다행히도 *dahaenghido* 'fortunately'). When not thematic, these functions are positioned after P1.

Table 5.2 *Interpersonal Themes*

Modal Adjunct (e.g., 아마도 *amado* 'perhaps')
Comment (e.g., 불행히도 *bulhaenghido* 'unfortunately', 애석하게도 *aeseokhagedo* 'to my regret')
Vocative (e.g., 판사님 *Pansa-nim* 'Your Honour', 손님 *Son-nim* 'Mr or Ms guest')

5.3 Interpersonal Theme

Some examples are presented in (13). These are taken from a short story entitled 'On the Overhead Bridge' included in Cho (1978). In the story the protagonist Sinae tells a story about her younger brother, Tongsayng. He was a student activist during the politically unstable period of the 1970s and 1980s in Korea. He is now sick and does not have a proper job. All the doctors who had examined him recommended that he should be admitted into a hospital for treatment. The topical Theme, 의사 한 사람이 *uisa han saram i* 'one of the doctors' is preceded by a Comment, 다행히 *dahaenghi* 'fortunately' in (13). This indicates that Sinae is relieved that her brother has found a doctor who went to university with him, which in turn implies that they can trust the doctor.

(13)

Cl. No.	Theme		Rheme	
	Interpersonal	Topical		
1		[[동생을 본]] 의사들이	[[입원할 것]]을 권했다	
		[[dongsaeng =eul bo-n]] uisa-deur =i	*[[ibwonha-l ges]] =eul*	*gwonha-et-da*
		doctors who examined brother	[[(that he should) be hospitalised]]	recommended
		P1:Sayer	P2:Verbiage	Process
	'The doctors who examined my brother recommended that he should be hospitalised.'			
2	다행히	의사 한 사람이	동생의 대학 동기였다	
	dahaenghi	*uisa han saram =i*	*dongsaeng =ui daehak donggi*	*y-eot-da*
	fortunately	one of doctors	university mate of brother	was
	Cir:Manner	P1:Carrier	P0:Attribute	Process
	'Fortunately, one of the doctors was a university friend of my brother.'			

Example (14) has a Vocative, 의원님 *Uiwon-nim*, 'Mr Assemblyman', as interpersonal Theme. This Vocative includes –님 *-nim*, a suffix that shows respect toward the addressee (see Chapter 3, Section 3.7 for discussion).

(14)

Theme		Rheme
Interpersonal	Topical	
의원님,		안녕하십니까?
Uiwon-nim		*annyeongha-simnikka*
Mr Assemblyman	(you)	are well
Vocative		Process/Attribute
'Mr Assemblyman, how are you?'		

Interpersonal Themes are an optional resource, as outlined in Figure 5.4. More than one interpersonal Theme is possible.

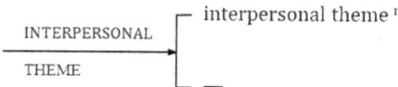

Figure 5.4 The system of INTERPERSONAL THEME

5.4 Textual Theme

Textual Themes come before topical Themes in Korean. If an interpersonal Theme is present, it usually precedes the textual Theme – but may follow.

Textual Themes orient the reader to the relationship of a clause with preceding discourse. They are realised as a Conjunctive Adjunct (examples are given in Table 5.3).

Conjunctive Adjuncts typically involve conjugations of the verb 그리하- *geuriha-* 'do so' or the verbalised adjective 그러하- *geureoha-* 'be so' in Korean. Examples include 그리고 *geurigo* 'that being the case, and', 그러나 *geureona* 'that being the case, but', 그런데 *geureonde* 'that being said', 그러니까 *geureonikka* 'because of that being the case', 그래서 *geuraeseo* 'that being the case, so' and so on. Korean school grammars treat these conjugations of 그리하- *geuriha-* and 그러하- *geureoha-* as conjunctive adverbs; no separate word class of 'conjunctives' is recognised.

Conjunctive Adjuncts are also realised through a handful of other expressions. Examples include 또 *tto* 'and' (literally 'again'), 또는 *ttoneun* 'and' or 'or', 또한 *ttohan* 'as well', 혹은 *hogeun* 'or', 따라서 *ttaraseo* 'therefore' (literally 'following') and so on.

Following Martin and Rose (2007: 133–41), in Table 5.3 we categorise Conjunctive Adjuncts into four types, depending on the connections they construe. In Martin and Rose's terminology they construe 'internal' relations, which organise a text rhetorically.

Table 5.3 *Conjunctive Adjuncts*

addition	그리고 *geurigo* 'and', 게다가 *gedaga* 'besides', 또 *tto* 'also', 아니면 *animyeon* 'alternatively, if not' add the one for 'or'
comparison	그러나 *geureona* 'but', 그런데 *geureonde* 'but'
time	그리고 나서 *geurigo naseo* 'and then', 먼저 *meonjeo* 'first of all'
consequence	그래서 *geuraeseo* 'so', 그러니까 *geureonikka* 'so that', 따라서 *ttaraseo* 'therefore', 그럼에도 *geureomedo* 'and yet'

5.4 Textual Theme

In (15), taken from a Primary School Reading Year 3 (Ministry of Education 2002f), there are two Conjunctive Adjuncts that serve as textual Themes – 또 *tto* 'also' in clause (15.1.1) and 그래서 *geuraeseo* 'therefore' in clause (15.2). Conjunctive Adjuncts are usually spoken on a separate tone group from the rest of the clause.

(15)

Cl. No.	Topical Theme		Rheme			
	Textual	Topical				
1.1	또,	숯은	[[쎅는 것을 막는]] 성질이 있어			
	tto	*such =eun*	*[[sseong-neun geos =eul mang-neun]] seongjir =i*	*iss-eo*		
	also	charcoal	function of preventing decay	has so		
		P1:Possessor	P1:Possession	Process		
	'In addition, charcoal prevents organic matters from rotting so[4]					
1.2			음식과 함께 놓아 두기만 해도			
			eumsik =gwa hamkke	*no-a du-gi =man ha-e-do*		
		(charcoal)	with foods	is only placed		
		(P2:Undergoer)	Cir:Acc	Process		
	when it is simply placed with food					
1.3			음식을 쉽게 썩지 않게 해준다.			
			eumsig =eul	*swipge*	*sseok-ji an-ke ha-e ju-n-da*	
		(charcoal)	food	easily	prevents from going bad	
		(P1:Actor)	P2: Undergoer	Cir: Man	Process	
	it prevents it from going bad.'					
2	그래서	옛 사람들은	광에 늘 숯을 넣어 두었다.			
	geuraeseo	*yet saram-deur =eun*	*gwang =e*	*neul*	*such =eul*	*neo-eo du-eot-da*
	therefore	olden-day people	in food storage room	always	charcoal	kept
		P1:Actor	Cir:Loc: space	Cir:Loc: time	P2: Undergoer	Process
	'Therefore people in the past always kept charcoal in food storage rooms.'					

---

[4] In Korean, linguistic devices that link clauses come at the very end of the verbal group. For details see Chapter 6.

These connectors relate one clause complex to another, within or between turns in discourse. Relations between clauses inside a clause complex are managed through clause final linkers (as discussed in Chapter 6). Thus textual Themes only handle relations between clause simplexes and clause complexes (i.e., complete sentences) in Korean (Figure 5.5).

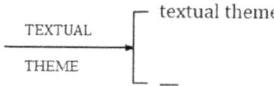

Figure 5.5 The system of TEXTUAL THEME

5.5 Theme Systems

A system network for THEME of Korean that encompasses all the options discussed above is presented in Figure 5.6. It consists of three main systems (i.e., TOPICAL THEME, INTERPERSONAL THEME and TEXTUAL THEME). The system of TOPICAL THEME specifies that speakers of Korean always choose an angling Theme and may as well choose a positioning Theme. The system of ANGLING THEME consists of two sub-systems that establish and maintain an angle on the field – ESTABLISHING THEME and CONTINUING THEME. The ESTABLISHING THEME system allows for anticipated Themes and non-anticipated Themes, both of which may be explicitly affirmed or be elided through the CONTINUING THEME system.

The POSITIONING THEME system orients the text to its field through a Circumstance of time or space. A transitional positioning Theme flags that the angling Theme is going to be discussed in a particular setting in time or space while a contrastive positioning Theme signals that the angling Theme is going to be discussed in a contrasting setting in time or space.

The optional INTERPERSONAL THEME and TEXTUAL THEME systems allow Korean speakers to give thematic prominence to an attitude and/or thematic prominence to rhetorical connections as the text unfolds.

5.6 Topical Theme Identification and Progression

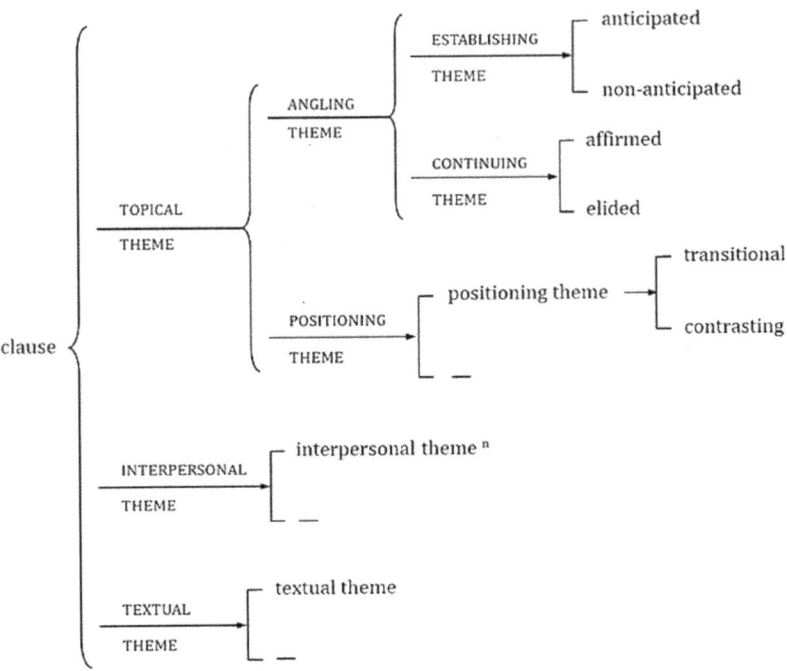

Figure 5.6 The system network of THEME in Korean

5.6 Topical Theme Identification and Thematic Progression

In this section, we will set out in practical terms a strategy for studying Theme and discussing the way different choices of Theme contribute to a text's method of development or thematic progression – that is, how Themes contribute to the cohesion and coherence of a text in relation to one other. In general terms, there are three typical types of thematic progression (Eggins 2004: 324–6) – namely, (i) Theme reiteration, which means a Theme is repeated in two or more consecutive clauses; (ii) the zig-zag pattern, which means a Theme picks up an element in the Rheme of a preceding clause and (iii) the multiple-Rheme pattern, which means two or more consecutive clauses pick up an element from the same Rheme in a preceding clause. They are illustrated in Figure 5.7.

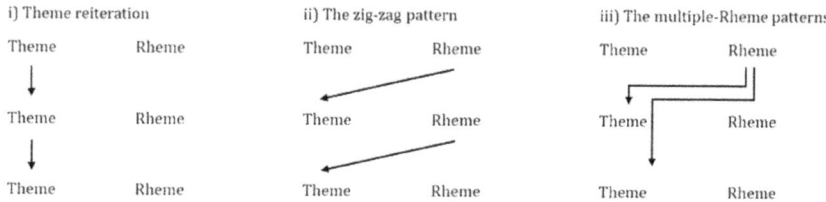

Figure 5.7 Three types of thematic progression

We need to emphasise that Theme analysis must be undertaken with due consideration for thematic progression in a text – taking both co-text (cohesion) and context (register and genre) into account. We suggest the following rules of thumb for Theme identification in Korean.

1. If a nominal group is marked by a TFM at the beginning of the clause, it is an anticipated topical Theme.
2. If a nominal group is marked by an P1 EFM (i.e., 이/가 *i/ga*) at the beginning of the clause, it is a non-anticipated topical Theme. However, it is not a Theme when it involves the experiential function of Carrier or Possession in a relational clause and a Carrier-Domain or Possessor is explicit in the previous clause. In such cases, the Carrier-Domain is the elided angling topical Theme.
3. If a Circumstance precedes an explicit topical Theme, it functions as a positioning Theme. If an angling Theme has been elided, careful consideration is required to determine whether or not a Circumstance has a textual function (as explained for example (11)). Caution is needed when a Theme in the locative type of relational clause is analysed. A nominal group with P3 EFM is not a Circumstance but rather a Location Participant (see Section 4.2.3.6 in Chapter 4). It functions as a positioning Theme.
4. When a Modal Adjunct, a Comment or a Vocative comes at the beginning of the clause before a Participant or Circumstance, it is an interpersonal Theme.
5. When a Conjunctive Adjunct comes at the beginning of the clause before a Participant or Circumstance, it is a textual Theme.

We consider some examples below. We return first to (16), which we introduced earlier on to introduce the angling Themes – in order to understand how to they contribute to thematic progression in the text. Example (16) has a Theme reiteration pattern. The nominal group 싸이의 강남 스타일 뮤직 비디오가 *Ssai ui Gangnam Seutail myujik bidio ga* 'Psy's Gangnam Style music video' is positioned at the beginning of clause (16.1), which functions as the Hyper-Theme of the text. We are at the beginning of the news story and the TV watchers cannot be expected to anticipate what the story is going to be about – other than the usual

5.6 Topical Theme Identification and Progression

topics that are covered in everyday news (as noted for (3)). The nominal group marked by the TFM 은/는 *eun/neun*, i.e., 강남 스타일 뮤직 비디오는 *Gangnam Seutail myujik bidio neun* 'Psy's Gangnam Style music video' in clause (16.2), is an anticipated affirmed topical Theme, since it has been introduced in the first clause. The anticipated topical Theme is elided in clause (16.3).

(16)

Cl. No.	Topical Theme		Rheme		
1	싸이의 강남 스타일 뮤직 비디오가		유튜브 사상 최초로 20 억 뷰를 돌파했습니다.		
	Ssai =ui Gangnam Seutail myujik bidio	*=ga*	*Yutyubeu sasang choecho =ro*	*20 eok byu =reul*	*dolpaha-et-seumnida*
	Psy's Gangnam Style music video	P1 EFM	for the first time in YouTube history	more than 2 billion viewing	recorded
	P1:Actor		Cir:Location	E-Range	Process
	'Psy's Gangnam Style music video recorded more than 2 billion viewings in YouTube history for the first time.'				
2	강남 스타일 뮤직 비디오는		오늘 낮 12 시 30 분 조회수 20 억 2 천 건을 기록했습니다.		
	Gangnam Seutail myujik bidio	*=neun*	*oneul nat 12 si 30 bun*	*johoesu 20 eok 2 cheon geon =eul*	*girokha-et-seumnida*
	Psy's Gangnam Style music video	TFM	today at 12.30 pm	2 billion 2 thousand viewing	recorded
	P1:Actor		Cir:Loc:time	E-Range	Process
	'The music video recorded 2 billion and 2 thousand viewings as of 12.30 pm today.'				
3			공개 1 년 10 개월 만에 대기록을 수립한 것입니다.		
			gonggae 1 nyeon 10 gaewol man =e	*daegirog =eul*	*suripha-n geos-i-mnida*
	(Psy's Gangnam Style music video)		within 1 year and 10 months,	great record	made
	(P1:Actor)		Cir:Ext	P-Range	Process
	'It made a great record within 1 year and 10 months since its release.'				

Interpreting these Theme choices from a discourse perspective, the non-anticipated established Theme, 싸이의 강남 스타일 뮤직 비디오가 *Ssai ui Gangnam Seutail myujik bidio ga* 'Psy's Gangnam Style music video', tells the listeners that this news story is about the Korean pop singer's music video called Gangnam Style. Once the newsworthy Theme has been established as the Theme of the news, it gets affirmed as the anticipated Theme in clause (16.2) (where the audience expects to hear more about it), and sustains this angle on the field in clause 16.3. The nominal group 공개 1 년 10개월 만에 *gonggae 1 nyeon 10 gaewol man e* 'within 1 year and 10 months' in clause (16.3) has no thematic prominence but simply functions as a Circumstance in the clause.

In (17) a biography text entitled 강감찬 Gang Gam-chan (17) (Ministry of Education 2002b), 소년 시절 *sonyeon sijeol* 'boyhood period' is the positioning

Theme in clause (17.1.1). It signals that the story will unfold in a chronical sequence; and Gang is selected as anticipated Theme – thereby composing the angle on the story. He then gets elided in the following relational attributive clauses (17.1.2 and 17.1.3). In clause (17.1.2), Gang Gam-chan is the elided Carrier-Domain and 성격이 *seonggyeog i* 'character' is the Domain of the relational clause. Accordingly the nominal group marked by the P1 EFM in clause (17.1.2) is part of the Rheme. This use of elided Themes to sustain an orientation to the field is commonplace in languages around the world (cf. Moyano 2016 on Spanish and the chapters in Caffarel et al. 2004). Like (16), (17) has a Theme reiteration pattern.

(17)

Cl. No.	Topical Theme			Rheme			
	Positioning	Angling					
1.1	소년 시절,	강감찬	은	행동이		바르고	
	sonyeon sijeol,	*Gang Gam-chan*	=*eun*	*haengdong*	=*i*	*bareu-go*	
	boyhood period,	Gang Gam-chan	TFM	behaviour	P1 EFM	is correct and	
	Cir:Loc:time	P1:Carrier-Domain		P1:Carrier		Attribute/Process	
	'During the boyhood, Gang Gam-chan behaved truthfully and						
1.2				성격이		대범하여	
				seonggyeog	=*i*	*daebeomha-yeo*	
		(Gang Gam-chan eun)		personality	P1 EFM	is brave so	
		P1:Carrier-Domain		P1:Carrier		Attribute/Process	
	had brave personality so						
1.3				칭찬을		많이	받았습니다.
				chingchan	=*eul*	*mani*	*bad-at-seumnida*
		(Gang Gam-chan)		praise	P2 EFM	a lot	received
		P1:Actor		P2:Goal		Cir: Manner	Process
	he received lots of praise.'						

As mentioned earlier, a nominal group marked by the P2 EFM can serve as the non-anticipated Theme. Example (18) is a short excerpt from a primary school textbook entitled 'Cave Pickled Shrimp' (Ministry of Education 2002g). In clauses (18.1) and (18.2), the clause-initial nominal group marked by a TFM is 새우젓은 *saeujeos eun* 'pickled shrimp'. It is an anticipated Theme (the title has already flagged what this text is about). In the following clauses (18.3.1 and 18.3.2), a nominal group marked by a P2 EFM comes at the beginning of each clause. We need to consider the text's method of

5.6 Topical Theme Identification and Progression

development to decide whether the nominal group is the Theme or whether the Theme is an elided Participant (i.e., a general human entity). The angling Theme in the first two clauses, pickled shrimp, clearly signals that this text is about pickled shrimp; and the second clause introduces the new information that shrimp are referred to differently depending on when they are caught. In this text, a reasonable analysis of the Theme in clauses 18.3.1 and 18.3.2 is to identify the nominal groups marked by the P2 EFM as non-anticipated Themes, rather than to analyse the elided participant as Theme.

(18)

Cl. No.	Topical Theme		Rheme		
1	새우젓은		[[작은 새우를 소금에 절여 3~4 개월동안 저장하여 삭힌]] 음식입니다.		
	saeujeos	=eun	[[jag-eun saeu =reul sogeum =e jeory-eo 3~4 gaewol =dongan jeojangha-yeo saki-n]] eumsig-i-mnida		
	pickled shrimps	TFM	are food [[that are salted, preserved and fermented for three to four months]]		
	P1:Carrier		Process		
	'Pickled shrimps are food that are salted, preserved and fermented for three to four months.'				
2	새우젓은		[[새우를 잡은]] 시기에 따라 이름이 다릅니다.		
	saeujeos	=eun	[[saeu =reul jab-eun]] sigi =e ttara ireum =i dareu-mnida		
	pickled shrimps	TFM	have different names depending on season [[they are caught]]		
	P1:Carrier-Domain		Cir:Ang		P1:Carrier	Process
	'Pickled shrimps have different names depending on the season they are caught.'				
3.1	[[5 월과 6 월에 잡은 새우로 만든]] 것을		각각 '오젓', '육젓'이라고 하고,		
	[[5 wol =gwa 6 wor =e jab-eun saeu =ro mandeu-n]] geos	=eul	gakgak 'ojeot', 'yukjeos' i-ra-go	ha-go,	
	ones [[made with shrimps caught in May and June]]	P2 EFM	'May pickle' and 'June pickle' each	(we) call and	
	P2:Value		P0:Token	Process	
	'The ones made with shrimps caught in May and June are called 'May pickle' and 'June pickle' respectively and				
3.2	[[가을에 잡은 새우로 만든]] 것을		'추젓'이라고 합니다.		
	[[gaeur =e jab eun saeu =ro mandeu-n]] geos	=eul	'chujeos' i-ra-go	ha-mnida	
	ones [[made with shrimps caught in autumn]]	P2 EFM	'autumn pickle'	(we) call	
	P2:Value		P0:Token	Process	
	the ones made with the shrimps caught in autumn are called 'autumn pickle'.'				

This kind of non-anticipated Theme marked by a P2 EFM *eul/reul* is regularly used in imperative clauses in texts such as (19). This is a recipe text written by a Year 4 primary school student in a Prezi slide show after a cooking class at school (Lee J. H. 2015).

(19)

Cl. No.	Topical Theme			Rheme		
1	과일, 채소		를	깨끗하게		씻는다
	gwail, chaeso		=*reul*	*kkaekkeuthage*		*ssin-neun-da*
	fruit, vegetable		P2 EFM	cleanly		wash
	P2:Undergoer			Cir:Man		Process
	'Wash the fruit and vegetables cleanly.'					
2	과일, 채소		를	적당한 크기로		자른다
	gwail, chaeso		=*reul*	*jeokdangha-n keugi* =*ro*		*jareu-n-da*
	fruits, vegetable		P2 EFM	in proper size		cut
	P2:Undergoer			Cir:Pro		Process
	'Cut the fruit and vegetables in a proper size.'					
3	주스 만드는 기계		에	과일, 채소를		넣는다
	juseu mandeu-neun gigye		=*e*	*gwail, chaeso* =*reul*		*neon-neun-da*
	juice machine		Cir EFM	fruit, vegetables		put
	Cir:Loc:space			P2:Undergoer		Process
	'Put the fruit and vegetables in a juicer.'					
4	주스		를	컵에		따른다
	juseu		=*reul*	*keob* =*e*		*ttareu-n-da*
	juice		P2 EFM	in cup		pour
	P2:Undergoer			Cir:Loc:space		Process
	'Pour the juice into a cup.'					
5	주스		를	마신다		
	juseu		=*reul*	*masi-n-da*		
	juice		P2 EFM	drink		
	P2:Undergoer			Process		
	'Drink the juice.'					

This text's method of development unfolds through non-anticipated Themes because the listener expects new information to be provided one clause after another in procedural discourse of this kind. Except for clause (19.3), all the other clauses have a non-anticipated Theme marked by a P2 EFM.

Example (20) is from a text about the history of Gyeongbokgung Palace (Gyeongbokgung Palace Management Office 2014). The angling

5.6 Topical Theme Identification and Progression

Theme, 경복궁은 *Gyeongbokgung eun* 'Gyeongbokgung Palace', is set up in the Hyper-Theme (clause 1) and elided in all the following clauses. A Circumstance:Location is used as a positioning Theme in each clause as the history of the palace is developed chronologically.

(20)

Cl. No.	Topical Theme		Rheme	
1	경복궁은		조선 왕조 제일의 법궁입니다.	
	Gyeongbokgung	=*eun*	*Joseon wangjo jeir* =*ui beobgung*	*i-mnida*
	Gyeongbokgung		Joseon Dynasty's principal palace	is
	P1:Carrier		P0:Attritute	Process
	'Gyeongbokgung Palace is the principal palace of the Joseon Dynasty.'			
2	1395 년		태조 이성계가	창건하였고
	1395 nyeon		*Taejo Iseonggye* =*ga*	*changgeonha-yeot-go*
	In 1395		King Taejo	built
	Cir:Loc:time		P1:Actor	Process
	'In 1395, Gyeongbokgung Palace was built by King Taejo and			
3	1592 년		임진왜란으로	불타 없어졌다가
	1592 nyeon		*Imjinwaeran* =*euro*	*bulta eops-eo jy-eot-daga*
	In 1592		because of the Japanese invasion	burnt down and disappeared
	Cir:Loc:time		Cir:Cause	Process
	in 1592, it was burnt down because of the Japanese invasion			
4	고종 때인 1867 년		다시	세워졌습니다.
	Gojong ttae-i-n 1876 nyeon		*dasi*	*sew-eo jy-eot-seumnida*
	In 1876 of King Gojong period		again	was built
	Cir:Loc:time			Process
	in 1867 during King Gojong period it was built again.'			

Note that a receptive clause (see Chapter 4, Section 4.3), including a verbal group Valence function realising [diminish], has been used in clauses (20.3) and (20.4) in order to maintain the text's angle on its field. This function is realised by the auxiliary verb 지 *jy-* in both of the clauses – as analysed in (21) (see Chapter 2, Section 2.4.2 for a discussion of VALENCY).

(21)

세워졌습니다				
sew-eo		*jy-eot-seumnida*		
was built				
Process				
verbal group				
Event		Valence:diminish		
verb		auxiliary verb		
Head	Link	Head	Tense Mark	Exchange Mark
stem	suffix	stem	suffix	suffix
'was built'				

If as an alternative we make the Actor of each clause Theme, we would end up composing a substantially different thematic progression. As shown in (22), instead of having 경복궁 *Gyeongbokgung* 'Gyeongbokgung Palace' functioning as our angle on the field and building up information about the palace, we would have a text oriented to who did what to the palace.

(22)

Cl. No.	Topical Theme			Rheme	
1	1395 년	태조 이성계가		경복궁을	창건하였고
	1395 nyeon	*Taejo Iseonggye =ga*		*Gyeongbokgung =eul*	*changgeonha-yeot-go*
	In 1395	King Taejo		Gyeongbok Palace	built
	Cir:Loc:time	P1:Actor		P2:Undergoer	Process
	'In 1395, King Taejo built Gyeongbokgung Palace and				
2	1592 년	일본침략자가			불태워 없애버렸으나
	1592 nyeon	*Ilbon chimnyakja =ga*			*bultaew-o eopsae beory-eoss-euna*
	In 1592	Japanese invaders			burnt down
	Cir:Loc:time	P1:Actor			Process
	in 1592, Japanese invaders burnt it down but				
3	1867 년	고종이	다시		세웠습니다.
	1876 nyeon	*Gojong =i*	*dasi*		*sew-eot-seumnida*
	In 1876	King Gojong	again		built
	Cir:Loc:time	P1:Actor			Process
	in 1867 Gojong rebuilt it.'				

Finally, consider example (23). This spoken discourse is from the first episode of 'Coffee Friends', a cooking variety television show broadcast in January 2019. This example is from a telephone conversation between Yeongsuk and Sejong; Sejong is younger than Yeongsuk and therefore calls him 형님 *Hyeong-nim* 'Big Brother'. After greeting each other, Yeonsuk is asking Sejong what he is doing eliding a topical Theme 너 *neo* 'you' in clause (23.1). Sejong picks it up in his reply with 저 *jeo* 'I', in clause (23.2).

(23)

Cl. No.		Textual Theme	Interpersonal Theme	Topical Theme	Rheme		
1	Yeongsuk			(너)	뭐		하니?
				(neo)	mwo		ha-ni
				(you)	what		do
				P1:Actor	P2:P-Range		Process
	'What are you doing?'						
2	Sejong	네	형님	저	운동		가려구요
		ne	Hyeong-nim	jeo	undong		ga-ryeogu yo
		well	Big Brother	I	exercise		intend to go
				P1:Actor	P2:E-Range		Process
	'Ah, Big Brother, I'm planning to go exercise.'						

As mentioned in Section 5.3, in spoken discourse interpersonal Themes are more frequently used than in written discourse; and when the interlocutors are referring to one other, they often elide the topical Theme.

In this section, we have suggested a set of principles for Theme identification in Korean and demonstrated with a number of examples how these principles need to apply in relation to the development of method. In adopting these principles it is essential to interpret the grammar of textual meaning in relation to how it contributes to the waves of meaning being composed as the text unfolds.

5.7 Conclusion

In Chapter 5, we have explored the grammar of textual meaning in clauses – discussing various Theme choices at clause rank and how they contribute to the thematic progression of text (using a number of example texts). We have also proposed a THEME system network and outlined a method for identifying Themes in Korean. We have not undertaken a comprehensive analysis of rhythm and intonation in Korean, which are additional resources for composing textual meaning in Korean. The relation of anticipated vs non-anticipated Themes to intonational prominence in different MOOD types (i.e., declarative, interrogative and imperative) is an important subject for future research.

6 The Grammar of Logical Meaning in Korean:
CLAUSE COMPLEXING

In Chapter 5, we discussed the system of THEME in Korean – the grammatical resources for organising interpersonal and experiential meaning as a message. We now consider the systems for clause complexing – the grammatical resources construing logical relations between clauses.

6.1 Introduction to Clause Complexing

Logical meaning is concerned with connecting clauses to one another. More specifically, the resources of the logical component of the ideational metafunction provide a grammatical device for relating experiential occurrences and states, one clause after another, as a text unfolds. As opposed to the structures we analysed for TRANSITIVITY, the structure at stake here is a serial one – involving the repetition of a single variable (albeit with distinctive subtypes of 'repetition'). So we might find one clause quoting another clause, which is in turn sequenced before another clause (as in *He said, "Look before you leap."*) and so on.

By way of introduction, we begin with a text extracted from a Primary School Reading Year 3 (Ministry of Education 2002c). It discusses *hanji*, a type of paper used for books, fans, kites, and other products depending on light, tough, well-ventilated paper.

> 한지는 종이이다. 한지는 가볍고 질기며 공기도 잘 통한다. 옛날 사람들은 한지로 책도 만들고, 부채와 연 등을 만들기도 하였다. 오늘날에도 한지를 많이 만들고 있다. 한지의 좋은 점을 알고 찾는 사람들이 늘고 있기 때문이다. 요즈음에는 한지에 물을 들여 여러 색깔의 한지를 만들기도 한다.

As we can see from the Korean script, the text is organised graphologically into six sentences (each ending with a full stop). As noted in Chapter 1, from a grammatical point of view these sentences are clause complexes, each consisting of one or more clauses. We re-present the text below, one clause at a time (1). In doing so we follow the SFL convention of using '|||' to separate clause complexes (which may consist of one or more clauses), and '||' to separate clauses within a clause complex (the text also includes one embedded clause, which we have enclosed in double square brackets – [[clause]]).

(1)   한지는 종이이다. |||
        hanji neun jongi i-da
        'Hanji is (a type of) paper.'

        한지는 가볍고 질기며 ||
        hanji neun gabyeop-go jilgi-myeo
        'Hanji is light and tough and

        공기도 잘 통한다. |||
        gonggi do jal tongha-n-da
        (it) ventilates well.'

        옛날 사람들은 한지로 책도 만들고 ||
        yennal saram-deur eun hanji ro chaek do mandeul-go
        'Ancient people made books with hanji and

        부채와 연 등을 만들기도 하였다. |||
        buchae wa yeon deung eul mandeul-gi do ha-yeot-da.
        also made fans, kites and so on.'

        오늘날에도 한지를 많이 만들고 있다. |||
        oneulnar e do hanji reul mani manduel-go it-da.
        'Even today (people) manufacture a large quantity of hanji.'

        [[한지의 좋은 점을 알고 찾는]] 사람들이 늘고 있기 때문이다. |||
        [[hanji ui joheun jeom eul al-go chan-neun]] saram-deur i neul-go it-gi ttaemun i-da.
        'This is because there are more people [[who understand the merits of hanji and want it]].'

        요즈음에는 한지에 물을 들여 ||
        yojeueum e neun hanji e mur eul deury-eo
        'These days (manufacturers) dye hanji and

        여러 색깔의 한지를 만들기도 한다. |||
        yeoreo saekkar ui hanji reul mandeul-gi do ha-n-da.
        make hanji available in various colours.'

Clause complexing is concerned with how clauses are combined. As we have just illustrated, in text analysis we may find a simple clause standing on its own as well as combinations of two or more interdependent clauses. Combinations of clauses are linked through a variety of logico-semantic relations such as cause and effect or quoted and quoting. In Korean these relations are signalled through a suffix (at word rank) or a clitic (at group or phrase rank); we refer to their functions as Link (at word rank) or Linking (at group or phrase rank). In addition we will introduce a clause rank function, Linker, realised through a particle. In this chapter, we will focus on the various types of clause combination and the Link, Linking or Linker functions that are used in different types of clause combination.

6.1 Introduction to Clause Complexing

Let's now consider two examples from the *hanji* text. Example (2) is a single clause (a clause simplex) and Example (3) involves two clauses (a clause complex). The clause in (2) is an attributive relational clause, and has two Participants (한지 *hanji* the Carrier and 종이 *jongi* 'paper' the Attribute) and one Process realised through the copula 이다 *i-da* 'be'. The clause complex in (3) on the other hand has two Processes (one in a relational clause realised by the verbalised adjective 'be light' and another in a mental clause realised by the verb 'like'). The two clauses are connected through the relation 'reason', which is realised through the Link 어서 *-eoseo* (a linking suffix culminating the verbalised adjective 가벼워서 *gabyeow-* is light-**because**). Note that in Korean a dependent clause of this kind always precedes the clause it is dependent on.

(2)   a clause simplex

한지는 종이이다.				
hanji	*=neun*	*jongi*	*i-da*	
hanji		paper	is	
P1:Carrier		P0:Attribute	Process	
ng		ng	vg	
Thing	TFM	Thing	Event	
noun	clitic	noun	copula	
			Head	EM
			stem	sfx
'Hanji is paper.'				

(3)   a clause complex

한지는 가벼워서 사람들이 좋아한다.								
hanji	*=neun*	*gabyeow-eoseo*		*saram-deur*	*=i*	*johaha-n-da*		
hanji		is light-**because**		people		like		
P1:Carrier		Attribute/ Process		P1:Senser		Process		
ng		vg		ng		vg		
Thing	TFM	Event		Thing	EFM	Event		
noun	clitic	verbalised adjective		noun	clitic	verb		
		Head	Link			Head	TM	EM
		stem	**sfx**			stem	sfx	sfx
'Because hanji is light people like (it).'								

Clause complexing has two dimensions. One has to do with the logico-semantic relations in play between clauses; this dimension is referred to as LOGICO-SEMANTIC RELATION. The other dimension concerns whether one clause has the same status as the other one or is dependent on it; this dimension is called TAXIS. These two sub-systems are configured with a curly bracket in Figure 6.1 – showing that a clause complex chooses from both the LOGICO-SEMANTIC RELATION and TAXIS systems. There are two types of logico-semantic relation – [projection] and [expansion]; and there are two types of taxis – [hypotaxis] and [parataxis].

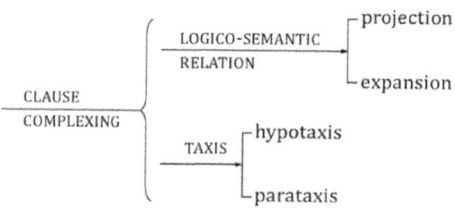

Figure 6.1 Clause complex systems (primary delicacy)

Before exploring LOGICO-SEMANTIC RELATION and TAXIS options, it is necessary to briefly discuss two foundational points – (i) the distinction between a verbal group complex and a clause complex, and (ii) the concept of a combination of clauses (i.e., a 'clause nexus').

6.2　Verbal Group Complex vs Clause Complex

Before we move into a detailed discussion of logical meaning, we need to clarify the distinction between a verbal group complex (i.e., a combination of verbal groups) and a clause complex (i.e., a combination of clauses). This is an important distinction to make when analysing Korean texts.

A verbal group complex may appear similar to a clause complex when the two clauses share a Participant that has been elided, leaving only the verbal groups realising the Processes. To differentiate a verbal group complex from a clause complex we propose the following two criteria. The first criterion has to do with whether both verbal groups share the same experiential clause functions – that is, the Participants and Circumstances (but not verbal group functions such as Modal, Dimension, etc.). The second criterion is the tendency for verbal group complexes to prevent a clause constituent from interrupting them (i.e., to come in between the verbal groups).

Based on the criteria, (4) is a verbal group complex. Both verbal groups have the same Participants – P1 (사용자 *sayongja* 'user') and P2 (한셀 2010

6.2 Verbal Group Complex vs Clause Complex

Hansel 2010 referring to computer software). In addition, it is awkward to position a Circumstance function between the two verbal groups. This strongly suggests that the two verbal groups do not realise two separate Processes. In (5) and (6) the interruption of the two groups by a circumstantial element results in awkwardness.

(4)   verbal group complex

사용자는 한셀 2010 을 선택하여 실행한다.								
sayongja	=neun	Hansel2010	=eul	seontaekha-yeo	silhaengha-n-da			
user		Hancell2010		select and	execute			
P1		P2		Process				
ng		ng		vg complex				
Thing	TFM	Thing	EFM	β	α			
noun	clitic	noun	clitic	vg	vg			
				Event	Event			
				verb	verb			
				Head	Link	Head	TM	EM
				stem	sfx	stem	sfx	sfx
'The user selects and executes Hancell2010.'								

(5)

?? 사용자는 한셀 2010 을 선택하여	한 시간동안	실행한다.
sayongja =neun Hansel2010 =eul seontaekha-yeo	**han sigan =dongan**	*silhaengha-n-da*
	for one hour	
	Cir:Location:time	
'The user selects and for one hour executes Hancell2010.'		

(6)

?? 사용자는 한셀 2010 을 선택하여	천천히	실행한다.
sayongja =neun Hansel2010 =eul seontaekha-yeo	**cheoncheonhi**	*silhaengha-n-da*
	slowly	
	Cir:Manner	
'The user selects and slowly executes Hancell2010.'		

On the other hand, (7) is a clause complex in terms of our criteria. There are two Participants (P1 사람들이 *saram-deur i* 'people' and P2 한지의 장점을 *hanji ui jangjeom eul* 'merits of hanji') in (7); but the two verbal groups are related to only one of them – the P1. The P2, 'merits of hanji', is only related to the first verbal group 알고 *al-go* 'know and'; a different P2, 한지를 *hanji reul* 'hanji', is implied in the second clause. Like the P1 사람들이 *saram-deur i* 'people', the P2 has been elided in the second clause. Note that realising a Circumstance function between the two verbal groups as in (8) and (9) does not result in awkwardness.

(7) clause complex

사람들이 한지의 장점을 알고 ...						
saram-deur	=*i*	*hanji*	=*ui*	*jangjeom*	=*eul*	*al-go*
people		hanji		merits		know and
P1		P2				**Process**
ng		ng				vg
Thing	EFM	Orient		Thing	EFM	Event
noun	clitic	[ng]		noun	clitic	verb
		Thing	Linking			Head	Link
		noun	clitic			stem	sfx
'People know the merits of hanji and ...						

... 찾는다.		
chan-neun-da		
seek		
Process		
vg		
Event		
verb		
Head	TM	EM
stem	sfx	sfx
... seek out (hanji).'		

(8)

사람들이 한지의 장점을 알고	이른 새벽부터	찾는다.
saram-deur =i hanji =ui jangjeom =eul al-go	***ireu-n saebyeok =buteo***	chan-neun-da
	Cir:Location:time	
'People know the merits of hanji and seek out (hanji) from early in the morning.'		

(9)

사람들이 한지의 장점을 알고	필사적으로	찾는다.
saram-deur =i hanji =ui jangjeom =eul al-go	***pilsajeogeuro***	chan-neun-da
	Cir:Manner	
'People know the merits of hanji and seek out (hanji) desperately.'		

From this point on we exclude verbal group complexes from the discussion.

6.3 Clause Nexus and Relevant Notation

A pair of interdependent clauses may stand in either an equal relation to one another or a dependent relation. For an equal relation, we have an initiating clause followed by a continuing clause; the structure is paratactic (comparable to coordination in traditional grammar). With a dependent relation, the first clause (i.e., the dependent clause) comes before the second clause (i.e., the dominant clause); the structure is hypotactic (one type of what traditional grammars refer to as subordination).

The sequencing for a dependent relation in Korean is the same as in Japanese (Teruya 2007), but different from English (since in English the dependent clause can come either before or after the dominant clause). Sequences of equal and dependent relations in Korean are tabulated in Table 6.1. Following the notation deployed in Halliday and Matthiessen (2014), we represent an equal relation as 1 2 (1 stands for an initiating clause, 2 for a continuing one), and we represent a dependent relation as β α (β for a dependent clause, α for a dominant one).

Table 6.1 *Primary and secondary clauses in a clause nexus*

	First clause	Second clause
Equal relation	1 (initiating)	2 (continuing)
Dependent relation	β (dependent)	α (dominant)

In (10), we have a clause complex, where the P1 of the initiating clause (한지는 *hanji neun* 'hanji') is shared by the continuing clause. The initiating clause is relational and the P1 is Carrier. The continuing clause is also relational and the second P1 there (공기도 *gonggi do* 'air') is also Carrier. The shared P1, which has the role of Carrier in the initiating clause, plays the role of Carrier-Domain in the continuing clause. The dependency relation between the two clauses is an equal one, as the second clause could have been chosen as the initiating clause. The structure is paratactic and we label the relation between the two clauses as 1 and 2.

(10)   paratactic

1	한지는 가볍고 질기며						
	hanji	*=neun*	*gabyeop-go*		*jilgi-myeo*		
	hanji		light and		tough and		
	P1:Carrier		Attribute/Process:relational				
	ng		vg complex				
	Thing	TFM	1		2		
	noun	clitic	vg		vg		
			Event		Event		
			verb		verb		
			Head	Link	Head	Link	
			stem	sfx	stem	sfx	
	'Hanji is light and tough and						

+2	(한지는) 공기도 잘 통한다.						
	(hanji =neun)		*gonggi*	*=do*	*jal*	*tongha-n-da*	
	(hanji)		air	too	well	go through	
	(P1:Carrier-Domain)		P1:Carrier		Attribute/Process:relational		
	(ng)		ng		vg		
	(Thing	TFM)	Thing	IFM	Property	Event	
	(noun	clitic)	noun	clitic	advg	verb	
					Head	Head	TM	EM
					adv	stem	sfx	sfx
	(hanji) ventilates well.'						

6.3 Clause Nexus and Relevant Notation

By contrast, the clause complex in (11), where the elided P1 (사람들이 *saram-deur i* 'people') is shared, has a dependent clause followed by a dominant one. The structure is hypotactic and we label the relation between the clauses as β and α. Unlike the clause complex in (10), the sequence of the two clauses in (11) cannot be changed. We further develop our criteria for distinguishing types of dependency relations in Section 6.4.1.

(11)   hypotactic

β	요즈음에는 ...							
	yojeueum	=*e*	=*neun*					
	these days							
	Cir:Location							
	ng							
	Thing	EFM	TFM					
	noun	clitic	clitic					
	'These days ...							

	... (사람들이) 한지에 물을 들여 ...							
	(*saram-deur*	=*i*)	*hanji*	=*e*	*mur*	=*eul*	*deury-eo*	
	(people)		hanji		water		dye-by	
	(P1)		P3		P2		Process	
	(ng)		ng		ng		vg	
	(Thing	EFM)	Thing	EFM	Thing	EFM	Event	
	(noun	clitic)	noun	clitic	noun	clitic	verb	
							Head	Link
							stem	sfx
	... (people) by dyeing hanji ...							

α	... (사람들이) 여러 색깔의 한지를 ...						
	(*saram-deur*	=*i*)	*yeoreo*	*saekkal*	=*ui*	*hanji*	=*reul*
	(people)		many	colour		hanji	
	(P1)		P2				
	(ng)		ng				
	(Thing	EFM)	Orient			Thing	EFM
	(noun	clitic)	[ng]			noun	clitic
			Quantity	Thing	Linking		
			adjective	noun	clitic		
	... (people) hanji in various colours ...						

... (사람들이) 만들기도 한다.							
(saram-deur	=i)	mandeul-gi	=do	ha-n-da			
(people)		make		as well			
(P1)		Process					
(ng)		vg					
(Thing	EFM)	Event		Mo... <<IFM>> ...dal			
(noun	clitic)	verb		clitic	aux verb		
		Head	Link		Head	TM	EM
		stem	sfx		stem	sfx	sfx
... (people) would make (hanji in various colours).'							

In addition to dependency relations, a clause complex involves various logico-semantic relations. These logico-semantic relations between clauses can be grouped into two general types: projection and expansion. Projection relations involve locutions (indicated by '') projected by a verbal clause, or ideas (indicated by ') projected by a mental clause. With expansion, one clause is elaborated, that is, its meaning is specified (indicated by =), or it is extended, that is, meaning is added (indicated by +), or it is enhanced, that is, one meaning is qualified by another (indicated by x). Here again we follow the notation deployed in Halliday and Matthiessen 2014 (as tabulated in Table 6.2).

Table 6.2 *Logico-semantic relations between clauses in a clause nexus*

general types	specific types	notation
projection	locution	''
	idea	'
expansion	elaborated	=
	extended	+
	enhanced	x

Example (12), which we divide into (12.1), (12.2) and (12.3) for reference purposes, provides a transitivity analysis of a long clause complex with diverse relations among the clauses inside. This example is taken from a primary school text entitled 'Seokjumyeong' (Ministry of Education 2002e). To

6.3 Clause Nexus and Relevant Notation

understand how this kind of long clause complex is structured, we need to establish two things. One is the concept of 'nesting', by which we mean the presence of layers of internal bracketing. The other is the distinction between the dependent clause and a circumstantial element.

(12.1...)

석주명은 나비를 찾기 위하여 ...							
Seokjumyeong	*=eun*	*nabi*		*=reul*	*chat-gi*		*wihayeo*
Seokjumyeong		butterflies			search		for
P1:Actor		Circumstance:Purpose						
ng		co-verbal phrase						
Thing	TFM	Incumbent					Role
noun	clitic	[[clause]]					co-verb
		P2			Process		
		ng			vg		
		Thing	EFM		Event		
		noun	clitic		verb		
					Head	Install	
					stem	sfx	
'Seok Jumyeong, in search of butterflies ...							

(12.2)

... 풀숲도 헤쳐보고 ...					
pulsup	*=do*	*hechy-eo*		*bo-go*	
bush	even	whack			
P2:Undergoer		Process			
ng		vg			
Thing	IFM	Event		Dimension	
noun	clitic	verb		aux verb	
		Head	Link	Head	Link
		stem	sfx	stem	sfx
... pushing open bushes and ...					

(12.3)

... 나뭇가지도 흔들어 보며 ...			
namutgaji	=do	heundeur-eo	bo-myeo
tree branch	also	shake	
P2:Undergoer		Process	
ng		vg	
Thing	IFM	Event	Dimension
noun	clitic	verb	aux verb
		Head / Link	Head / Link
		stem / sfx	stem / sfx
... shaking tree branches ...			

(...12.1)

... 온 산을 헤매고 다녔다.				
on	san	=eul	hemae-go	dany-eot-da
entire	mountain		wandering	went around
P2:E-Range			Process	
ng			vg	
Epithet	Thing	EFM	Event	Dimension
adjective	noun	clitic	verb	aux verb
			Head / Link	Head / TM / EM
			stem / sfx	stem / sfx / sfx
... was wandering around the entire mountain.'				

Note that the clause complex in (12) consists of three clauses; we number them as (12.1), (12.2) and (12.3) respectively. Note also that (12.1) is discontinuous, interrupted by (12.2) and (12.3). This clause complex involves nesting – that is, it has two layers. The outer layer is a hypotactic complex, relating the dominant clause (12.1) to its dependent clauses (12.2) and (12.3); the inner layer is a paratactic complex, relating the initiating clause (12.2) and its continuing clause (12.3). The clauses in the outer layer in (12) are presented in (13).

6.3 Clause Nexus and Relevant Notation

(13) α... <<xβ>> ... α

Clause	Logical structure	
(12.1...)	α ...	석주명은 ... *Seokjumyeong =eun*[1]
		'Seokjumyeong, ...
(12.2)–(12.3)	<<xβ>>	<<풀숲도 헤쳐보고>> <<*pulsup =do hechy-eo bo-go*>>
		... pushing open bushes and ...
(...12.1)	... α	... 온산을 헤매고 다녔다. *on san =eul hemae-go dany-eot-da*
		... was wondering around the entire mountain.'

In this notation '^' represents the sequence (for example, β ^ α means β precedes α); the symbol 'x' signifies the enhancing logical relation (see Table 6.2); and the dependent β clause, which interrupts its α, is marked with double angled brackets, <<clause>>, in analysis. The nested paratactic clauses are presented in (14).

(14) 1 ^ +2

Clause	Logical structure	
(12.2)	1	풀숲도 헤쳐보고 *pulsup =do hechy-eo bo-go*
		'pushing open bushes and
(12.3)	+2	나뭇가지도 흔들어 보며 *namutgaji =do heundeur-eo bo-myeo*
		shaking tree branches'

---

[1] The reason that the Participant 석주명 *Seokjumyeong* is treated as part of the α clause, not the β clause of the outer layer, is threefold. First, it is typical in Korean for the dependent clause in a clause complex to be enclosed within the dominant clause; second, if a Participant is shared by both clauses, the Participant of the main clause is signalled explicitly while that of the dependent clause is left implicit (note that a textual function marker, TFM, is never used in dependent clauses, but only in dominant clauses); and third, the Participant is spoken on a separate tone group from the β clause.

The whole clause complex is reassembled as (15). In the linear notation next to the example number, the parentheses group clauses that taken together are related to other clauses.

(15)   α ... <<xβ (1 ^ +2)>> ... α

Clause	Logical structure		
(12.1...)	α ...		석주명은 나비를 찾기 위하여 ... Seokjumyeong =eun [[nabi =reul chat-gi]] wihayeo
			'Seokjumyeong, in search of butterflies ...
(12.2)	<<xβ>>	1	<<풀숲도 헤쳐보고 pulsup =do hechy-eo bo-go
			<<pushing open bushes and
(12.3)		+2	나무가지도 흔들어보며>> namugaji =do heundeur-eo bo-myeo
			shaking tree branches>>
(...12.1)	... α		... 온산을 헤매고 다녔다. onsan =eul hemae-go dany-eot-da
			... was wondering around the entire mountain.'

Note that in (12.1...) the α clause includes an embedded clause, which realises the Incumbent role in a co-verbal phrase (as analysed in (12.1...)). Its distinctive Install function (see Section 4.2.2.3 in Chapter 4), realised by the suffix 기 -gi, clearly marks it as an embedded, not a dependent clause.

We now explore clause complexing in Korean in more detail.

6.4   CLAUSE COMPLEXING

Figure 6.2 represents the system of CLAUSE COMPLEXING in Korean we propose.

As we introduced above, clause complexing has two dimensions: the dependency relation between clauses and the logico-semantic relation between clauses. In Figure 6.2, the two dimensions are presented as the TAXIS and the LOGICO-SEMANTIC RELATION systems. The TAXIS system distinguishes parataxis (equal status) from hypotaxis (unequal status). The LOGICO-SEMANTIC

6.4 CLAUSE COMPLEXING

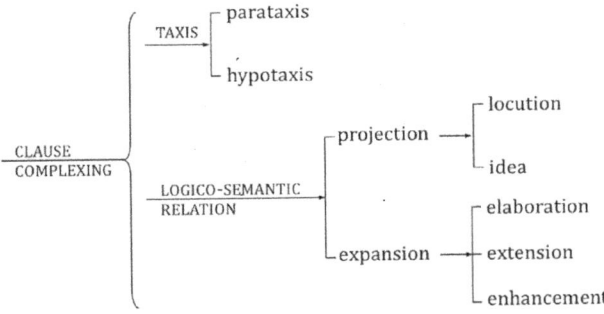

Figure 6.2 The system of CLAUSE COMPLEXING in Korean

RELATION system handles sub-types of interdependency between clauses – that is, PROJECTION (one clause represents the linguistic content of the other as an idea or locution) or EXPANSION (one clause expands the other by elaborating, extending or enhancing it).

6.4.1 Paratactic vs Hypotactic Relations

With respect to TAXIS in Korean, we propose two criteria to determine whether a clause nexus involves a paratactic or hypotactic relation. The criteria are:

i. Symmetry:
   With parataxis either clause can play the role of initial or continuing clause and still involve the same logico-semantic relationship (Halliday and Matthiessen 2014: 451–3); but this is not possible for hypotaxis.

ii. Negotiability:
   With parataxis, both clauses, 1 and 2, are negotiable (they can be argued about); MOOD is made explicit in the continuing clause (2) but not marked in the initial clause (1). In Korean the speech function of the initial clause is determined by the mood of the continuing clause. With hypotaxis only the α clause is negotiable and it is always marked for MOOD; MOOD is not marked on the β clause, which has no directly negotiable speech function.

Example (16) is a paratactic clause complex, where two clauses are joined by the Link 고 -go 'and'. As illustrated in (17) the two clauses involve the same logico-semantic relationship if their order is reversed; the two events are simply listed (there is no temporal connection).

(16)

1	현우가 기타를 치고						
	Hyeonu	=*ga*	*gita*	=*reul*	*chi-**go**		
	Hyunwoo		guitar		play **and**		
	P1		P2		Process		
	ng		ng		vg		
	Thing	EFM	Thing	EFM	Event		
	noun	clitic	noun	clitic	verb		
					Head	**Link**	
					stem	**sfx**	
	'Hyunwoo plays the guitar and						
+2	지혜가 노래를 부른다 .						
	Jihae	=*ga*	*norae*	=*reul*	*bureu-n-da*		
	Jihae		song		sing		
	P1		P2		Process		
	ng		ng		vg		
	Thing	EFM	Thing	EFM	Event		
	noun	clitic	noun	clitic	verb		
					Head	TM	EM
					stem	sfx	sfx
	Jihae sings a song.'						

6.4 CLAUSE COMPLEXING

(17)

1	지혜가 노래를 부르고						
	Jihae	*=ga*	*norae*	*=reul*	*bureu-go*		
	Jihae		song		sing **and**		
	P1		P2		Process		
	ng		ng		vg		
	Thing	EFM	Thing	EFM	Event		
	noun	clitic	noun	clitic	verb		
					Head	**Link**	
					stem	**sfx**	
	'Jihae sings a song and						

+2	현우가 기타를 친다.						
	Hyeonu	*=ga*	*gita*	*=reul*	*chi-n-da*		
	Hyunwoo		guitar		play		
	P1		P2		Process		
	ng		ng		vg		
	Thing	EFM	Thing	EFM	Event		
	noun	clitic	noun	clitic	verb		
					Head	TM	EM
					stem	sfx	sfx
	Hyunwoo plays the guitar.'						

If we compare (16) with (18) we see that the initiating clause in (16) is understood as a statement; but in (18) the first clause is understood as a question (although the initiating clauses in the examples lack explicit morphology indicating the MOOD they are enacting).

(18)

1	현우가 기타를 치고				
	Hyeonu	=*ga*	*gita*	=*reul*	*chi-**go***
	Hyunwoo		guitar		play **and**
	P1		P2		Process
	ng		ng		vg
	Thing	EFM	Thing	EFM	Event
	noun	clitic	noun	clitic	verb
					Head / **Link**
					stem / **sfx**
	'Does Hyunwoo play the guitar and				

+2	지혜가 노래를 부르니?				
	Jihae	=*ga*	*norae*	=*reul*	*bureu-ni*
	Jihae		song		sing
	P1		P2		Process
	ng		ng		vg
	Thing	EFM	Thing	EFM	Event
	noun	clitic	noun	clitic	verb
					Head / EM:**inter**
					stem / sfx
	does Jihae sing a song?'				

Further, if we compare (19) with (16) and (18), we see that the initiating clause in (19) is now understood as a command (although once again it is not marked grammatically for MOOD).

(19)

1	현우는 기타를 치고				
	Hyeonu	=*neun*	*gita*	=*reul*	*chi-go*
	Hyunwoo		guitar		play **and**
	P1		P2		Process
	ng		ng		vg
	Thing	TFM	Thing	EFM	Event
	noun	clitic	noun	clitic	verb
					Head / **Link**
					stem / **sfx**
	'Hyunwoo (you) play the guitar and				

+2	지혜는 노래를 불러라.				
	Jihae	=*neun*	*norae*	=*reul*	*bull-eora*
	Jihae		song		sing
	P1		P2		Process
	ng		ng		vg
	Thing	TFM	Thing	EFM	Event
	noun	clitic	noun	clitic	verb
					Head / EM:**imp**
					stem / sfx
	Jihae (you) sing a song.'				

Evidence that the initiating clause in (19) is understood as a command can be found by negating the verbal group 치고 *chi-go* 'play and'. As we saw in Chapter 3 (Section 3.5), the auxiliary verb used for negative indicatives (i.e., declaratives and interrogatives) is 않 *an-* 'am/are/is not' or 'do/does not'; but the auxiliary verb used for negative imperatives is 말 *mal-* 'don't do ...'. This is illustrated in (20) and (21) (for more detail about the difference between 않 *an-* and 말 *mal-*, see (45) and (48) in Section 3.5 of Chapter 3).

(20)

1	현우는 기타를 치지 않았고								
	Hyeonu	*=neun*	*gita*	*=reul*	*chi-ji*		**an**-*at-go*		
	Hyunwoo		guitar		play		**did not** and		
	P1		P2		Process				
	ng		ng		vg				
	Thing	TFM	Thing	EFM	Event		Negation		
	noun	clitic	noun	clitic	verb		aux verb		
					Head	Link	Head	TM	Link
					stem	sfx	stem	sfx	sfx
	'Hyunwoo did not play the guitar and								

+2	지혜도 노래를 부르지 않았다.								
	Jihae	*=do*	*norae*	*=reul*	*bureu-ji*		*an-at-da*		
	Jihae		song		sing		did not		
	P1		P2		Process				
	ng		ng		vg				
	Thing	IFM	Thing	EFM	Event		Negation		
	noun	clitic	noun	clitic	verb		aux verb		
					Head	Link	Head	TM	EM:**decl**
					stem	sfx	stem	sfx	sfx
	Jihae did not sing a song either.'								

(21)

1	현우는 기타를 치지 말고								
	Hyeonu	*=neun*	*gita*	*=reul*	*chi-ji*		**mal**-*go*		
	Hyunwoo		guitar		play		**don't** and		
	P1		P2		Process				
	ng		ng		vg				
	Thing	TFM	Thing	EFM	Event		Negation		
	noun	clitic	noun	clitic	verb		aux verb		
					Head	Link	Head	Link	
					stem	sfx	stem	sfx	
	'Hyunwoo (you) don't play the guitar and								

6.4 CLAUSE COMPLEXING

+2	지혜도 노래를 부르지 마라.							
	Jihae	*=do*	*norae*	*=reul*	*bureu-ji*		*ma-ra*	
	Jihae	even	song		sing		don't	
	P1		P2		Process			
	ng		ng		vg			
	Thing	IFM	Thing	EFM	Event		Negation	
	noun	clitic	noun	clitic	verb		aux verb	
					Head	Link	Head	EM: **imp**
					stem	sfx	stem	sfx
	'Jihae (you) don't sing a song either.'²							

By contrast, in a hypotactic clause complex, the clauses are non-symmetrical. If the order in the clause complex in (22) is changed while retaining the same Link as well as TENSE and MOOD, the meaning differs from the original. The reversed sequence with the contrasting meaning is illustrated in (23).

(22)

α...	현우가 . . .	
	Hyeonu	*=ga*
	Hyunwoo	
	P1	
	ng	
	Thing	EFM
	noun	clitic
	'(Did) Hyunwoo . . .	

---

² This is imperative mood in Korean, not declarative.

<<xβ>>	... 기타를 치려고 ...		
	gita	=*reul*	*chi-ryeogo*
	guitar		play-in order to
	P2		Process
	ng		vg
	Thing	EFM	Event
	noun	clitic	verb
			Head / Link
			stem / sfx
	... in order to play guitar ...		

...α	... 집에 왔니?				
	jib	=*e*	*w-an-ni*		
	home		came		
	Circumstance:Location		Process		
	ng		vg		
	Thing	EFM	Event		
	noun	clitic	verb		
			Head	TM	EM
			stem	sfx	sfx
	... come home?'				

(23)

α...	현우가 ...	
	Hyeonu	=*ga*
	Hyunwoo	
	P1	
	ng	
	Thing	EFM
	noun	clitic
	'(Did) Hyunwoo ...	

6.4 CLAUSE COMPLEXING

<<xβ>>	... 집에 오려고 ...		
	jib	=e	o-ryeogo
	home		come-in order to
	Circumstance:Location		Process
	ng		vg
	Thing	EFM	Event
	noun	clitic	verb
			Head / Link
			stem / sfx
	... in order to come home ...		
...α	... 기타를 쳤니?		
	gita	=reul	chi-eon-ni
	guitar		played
	P2:Entity-Range		Process
	ng		vg
	Thing	EFM	Event
	noun	clitic	verb
			Head / TM / EM
			stem / sfx / sfx
	... play guitar?'		

In a hypotactic clause, such as the β clause in (22) and (23), the β clause simply provides contingent information that is not negotiable. In addition there is no possibility of deploying the auxiliary verb 말 *mal-* 'don't do ...', which realises the Negation function in an imperative clause; only 않 *an-* 'am/are/is not or do/does not' is possible (as we saw in (20) *an-* realises Negation in indicative clauses). Thus, the ungrammaticality of (24), with 말 *mal-*.

(24)

<<xβ>>	잊어버리지 않으려면 ...		
	ij-eo	*beori-ji*	***an**-euryeomyeon*
			***mal-lyeomyeon**
	forget	'completely'	in order not to
	Process		
	vg		
	Event	Dimension	**Negation**
	verb	aux verb	**aux verb**
	Head / Link	Head / Link	Head / Link
	stem / sfx	stem / sfx	stem / sfx
	'If (you) want **not** to forget ...		
...α	... 적어라.		
	jeog-eora		
	write		
	Process		
	vg		
	Event		
	verb		
	Head / EM		
	stem / sfx		
	... write (it) down'		

6.4.2 PROJECTION *and* EXPANSION

In our grammar PROJECTION contrasts with EXPANSION. EXPANSION is a direct representation of events and states (e.g., 'People like hanji because it is light'); this contrasts with PROJECTION, which involves a representation of a linguistic representation – that is, a locution or idea (e.g., 'People say hanji is light'). In other words, while EXPANSION is concerned with a 'complex phenomenon', PROJECTION involves different orders of experience – a relation between a projecting phenomenon (a verbal or mental process) and an idea or a statement concerning a phenomenon (a 'metaphenomenon'). As noted above, locutions (i.e., direct and indirect speech) are indicated as ", and ideas (i.e., direct and indirect thought) are indicated as '.

6.4.3 Projection

Below we explore projected locutions and projected ideas. We begin with paratactic projection and then move on to hypotactic projection.

6.4.3.1 Paratactic Projection

There are two types of paratactic projection, involving either locutions or ideas. We consider paratactically projected locutions first.

A paratactic clause complex involving a locution quotes speech directly. The quoted locution involves all the choices available for a ranking clause – for example, MOOD, STANCE, ADDRESSEE DEFERENCE and so on. In a projecting clause complex, the projecting and the projected clauses have an equal status. In general, the projecting clause encloses the projected clause in Korean, although the projecting clause does in some cases follow its projected clause.

The projected clause is marked by the clause rank particles 라고 *rago* or 하고 *hago*. We refer to the function of this particle as Linker. We treat the Linker as part of the projecting clause, not of the projected clause, on intonational and graphological grounds. In spoken Korean, if the projecting clause complex is spoken on two tone groups, then the second intonational phrase begins with 라고 *rago* or 하고 *hago*. In addition, if there is a break in the rhythm, it falls naturally before *rago* or *hago*, not after. Korean graphology also supports this analysis. At the conclusion of a paratactic locution and before 라고 *rago* or 하고 *hago* we regularly find a closing double quotation mark and often a space – a graphological indication that the Linker is not part of the projected clause.

In (25), the projecting clause is divided into two parts by the projected clause – the first part consists of the P1: Sayer, 그는 *geu neun* 'he', and the second part consists of the Linker, 라고 *rago* and the Process, 말했다 *malha-et-da* 'said'. These two parts surround the projected clause, 소년들의 건강상태가 양호합니다 *sonyeon-deur ui geongang sangtae ga yanghoha-mnida* 'the boys' health condition is good'. Examples of this kind are likely to be spoken on three tone groups – one for the Sayer, one for the projected locution and one for the rest of the projecting clause. Korean graphology once again reflects this analysis. We find an opening double quotation mark and a space between the Sayer and the paratactic locution, in addition to a closing quotation mark and often a space at the end of the projected clause (as partly reflected in the Hangeul).[3]

---

[3] In 표준국어대사전 *pyojungugeodaesajeon* 'Standard Korean Language Dictionary', published by the National Institute of Korean Language (1999), it is noted that no space is used after a closing quotation mark (i.e. after a projected clause). A quick Google search however reveals that Koreans commonly provide a space after a closing quotation mark. In our view, the practice of the general public better reflects our interpretation grammar and phonology of Korean – in which 하고 *hago* and 라고 *rago* are clause rank particles (i.e., words).

(25)   1... <<"2>> ...1

1...	그는 ...							
	geu	=neun						
	He							
	P1:Sayer							
	ng							
	Thing	TFM						
	noun	clitic						
	'He...							
"2	... "소년들의 건강상태가 양호합니다" ...							
	sonyeondeur	=ui		geongang	sangtae	=ga	yanghoha-mnida	
	boys			health	condition		is good	
	<<P1						Attribute/Process>>	
	ng						vg	
	Deictic			Classifying	Thing	EFM	Event	
	[ng]			noun	noun	clitic	verbalised adj	
	Thing	Linking					Head	EM
	noun	clitic					stem	sfx
	... "the boys' health condition is good" ...							
...1	... 라고 말했다							
	rago	malha-et-da						
		said						
	Linker	Process						
	ptcl	vg						
		Event						
		verb						
		Head	TM	EM				
		stem	sfx	sfx				
	... said.'							

As mentioned above, it is also possible, although less frequent, to have a construction where the whole projecting clause, 그는 말했다 *geu neun malha-et-da* 'he said' is preceded by the projected clause. In this construction, separate tone groups are used for (i) the projected clause and (ii) the projecting clause

6.4 CLAUSE COMPLEXING 333

(including the 라고 *rago* or 하고 *hago* particle). In such a structure, the Sayer cannot be elided. Example (26) illustrates this pattern.

(26)   "1^2

"1	"소년들의 건강상태가 양호합니다"							
	sonyeondeur	=*ui*	*geongang*	*sangtae*	=*ga*	*yanghoha-mnida*		
	boys		health	condition		is good		
	<<P1					Attribute/Process>>		
	ng					vg		
	Deictic		Classifying	Thing	EFM	Event		
	[ng]		noun	noun	clitic	verbalised adj		
	Thing	Link				Head	EM	
	noun	clitic				stem	sfx	
	' "The boys' health condition is good"							
2	라고 그는 말했다.							
	rago	*geu*	=*neun*	*malha-et-da*				
		he		said				
	Linker	P1:Sayer		Process				
	ptcl	ng		vg				
		Thing	TFM	Event				
		noun	clitic	verb				
				Head	TM	EM		
				stem	sfx	sfx		
	he said.'							

Paratactic idea complexes quote thought directly in a clause complex involving clauses with equal status and are projected by mental clauses with cognitive Processes – for example, 생각하다 *saenggakha-da* 'think', 의심하다 *uisimha-da* 'doubt' and so on. The projected ideas in these complexes can realise choices for MOOD, STANCE and ADDRESSEE DEFERENCE.

As with paratactically projected locutions, the projecting clause typically encloses the projected clause (i.e., 1...<<'2>>...1); this is illustrated in (27). Note that the projected idea is notated with a single quotation mark in the

Hangeul (i.e., the single inverted comma illustrated). The Linker in a paratactic idea clause complex is realised through 라고 *rago* and 하고 *hago* – the same connectors used when quoting a locution.

(27)   1... <<'2>> ...1

1	지혜는 ...				
	Jihae	=*neun*			
	Jihae				
	P1:Senser				
	ng				
	Thing	TFM			
	noun	clitic			
	'Jihae...				
'2	... '전화를 해야지' ...				
	jeonhwa	=*reul*	*ha-eya-ji*		
	telephone		do		
	<<P2		Process>>		
	ng		vg		
	Thing	EFM	Event		
	noun	clitic	verb		
			Head	Modality Mark	Stance Mark
			stem	sfx	sfx
	... "(I) have to make a phone call"...				

6.4 CLAUSE COMPLEXING

(1)

1	... 하고 생각했다.			
	hago	*saenggakha-et-da*		
		thought		
	Linker	Process		
	ptcl	vg		
		Event		
		verb		
		Head	TM	EM
		stem	sfx	sfx
	'... thought.'			

Less commonly the projecting clause can follow its projected clause (i.e., '1 ^ 2) as in (28).

(28)   '1 ^ 2

'1	'전화를 해야지'			
	jeonhwa	=*reul*	*ha-eya-ji*	
	telephone		do	
	<<P2		Process>>	
	ng		vg	
	Thing	EFM	Event	
	noun	clitic	verb	
			Head	Modality Mark	Stance Mark
			stem	sfx	sfx
	' "(I) have to make a phone call"			

2	하고 지혜는 생각했다.			
	hago	*Jihae*	*=neun*	*saenggakha-et-da*
		Jihae		thought
	Linker	P1:Senser		Process
	ptcl	ng		vg
		Thing	TFM	Event
		noun	clitic	verb
				Head	TM	EM
				stem	sfx	sfx
Jihae thought.'				

Regarding the issue of whether the Linker (realised through the clause rank particle 하고 *hago* or 라고 *rago*) is part of the projecting or the projected clause, the arguments presented above all hold. The Linker is part of the projecting clause on intonational and graphological grounds.

An interrupted paratactic idea clause complex such as (27) is likely to be spoken on three tone groups – one for the Senser, one for the projected idea and one for the rest of the projecting clause including the Linker. Korean graphology once again reflects this analysis. There will be an opening quotation mark and a space between the Senser and the paratactic idea, in addition to a closing quotation mark and in general a space at the end of the projected clause.

The two clauses in examples such as (27) would be spoken on separate tone groups; the second intonation unit will begin with 하고 *hago* or 라고 *rago*. In addition, at the conclusion of a paratactic idea and before 하고 *hago* or 라고 *rago* there is a closing single quotation mark and potentially a space – a graphological indication that the Linker is not part of the projected clause.

In closing, we note that school grammars of Korean treat 라고 *rago* as a particle; but they treat 하고 *hago*, the literal meaning of which is 'say and', as a 'verb'. However, 하고 *hago* is a frozen expression and following many Korean linguists (e.g., Kwon 2012: 220) we take it as a particle like 라고 *rago*. We also note that there are subtle differences between 하고 *hago* and 라고 *rago*. For instance, when paratactic locution or idea clause complexes project minor clauses, only 하고 *hago* (not 라고 *rago*) can be deployed to realise the Linker – as shown in (29) and (30).

(29) 라고 *rago* is not possible

그는 "야" 하고 탄성을 질렀다.								
geu	=neun	ya	**hago**	tanseong	=eul	jill-eot-da		
he		wow		exclamation		shouted		
1 ...		"2	... 1					
clause ...		interjection	... clause					
P1:Sayer			Linker	P2		Process		
ng			ptcl	ng		vg		
Thing	TFM			Thing	EFM	Event		
noun	clitic			noun	clitic	verb		
						Head	TM	EM
						stem	sfx	sfx
'He exclaimed, "Wow!" '								

(30) 라고 *rago* is not possible

'옳지' 하고 엄마는 생각했다.							
olchi	**hago**	eomma	=neun	saenggakha-et-da			
right		mum		thought			
'1	2						
interjection	clause						
	Linker	P1:Senser		Process			
	ptcl	ng		vg			
		Thing	TFM	Event			
		noun	clitic	verb			
				Head	TM	EM	
				stem	sfx	sfx	
'Mum thought, "Right." '							

6.4.3.2 *Hypotactic Projection*

There are two types of hypotactic projection, involving either locutions or ideas. We consider hypotactically projected locutions first.

A hypotactic clause complex involving a locution reports speech indirectly. The projecting and projected clauses have unequal status. There are two possible sequences – α... <<"β>> ...α or "β^α.

In contrast with paratactically projected locutions, two major grammatical differences stand out. One is the projection signals. Above, we treated the paratactic Linkers, 라고 *rago* or 하고 *hago*, particles operating at clause rank, as Linker; and we argued on intonational and graphological grounds that Linker is part of the projecting clause, not the projected one (examples (25)–(30)).

By contrast, the hypotactic projection signals (다고 *-da-go*, 냐고 *-nya-go*, 라고 *-ra-go* and 자고 *-ja-go*) are verbal suffixes involving the functions Projected Mood Mark and Link; they are affixed to verbs or verbalised adjectives. These hypotactic projection signals[4] are operating at word rank and the morpheme *-go* is a connecting suffix, not a particle like *rago* or *hago*. For instance, 양호하다고 *yanghoha-**da-go*** 'that (it) is good' and 양호하냐고 *yanghoha-**nya-go*** 'whether (it) is good', appearing respectively in (31) and (32), are words (verbalised adjectives) – without 다고 *-da-go* and 냐고 *-nya-go* the projected clauses are 'incomplete'. In addition, while the Linker (in parataxis) generally begins a new tone group, the morpheme 고 *-go* after a Projected Mood Mark (in hypotaxis) typically ends a tone group. Turning to graphology, hypotactic projection does not involve a space between a Projected Mood Mark and 고 *-go*, nor a quotation mark; but as noted above we generally need a space before the paratactic Linkers 라고 *rago* and 하고 *hago*. We thus treat the structure Projected Mood Mark and Link as part of the projected clause.

The other grammatical difference between hypotactically and paratactically projected locutions is that unlike in paratactic locutions, ADDRESSEE DEFERENCE is not available in hypotactic ones. Examples (31) and (32) exemplify hypotactic locutions in two different projected moods; in these locutions ADDRESSEE DEFERENCE is not possible.

(31)   α...<<"β>>...α

α...	그는 ...	
	geu	*=neun*
	He	
	P1:Sayer	
	ng	
	Thing	TFM
	noun	clitic
	'He ...	

---

[4] Note that 다고 *-da-go* consists of the projected declarative suffix and the connecting suffix, 냐고 *-nya-go* consists of the projected interrogative suffix and the connecting suffix, 라고 *-ra-go* consists of the projected jussive suffix and connecting suffix and 자고 *-ja-go* consists of the projected cohortative suffix and the connecting suffix.

6.4 CLAUSE COMPLEXING

"β

... 소년들의 건강상태가 ...					
sonyeon-deur	*=ui*		*geongang*	*sangtae*	*=ga*
boys			health	condition	
P1						
ng						
Deictic			Classifying	Thing	EFM
[ng]			noun	noun	clitic
Thing	Linking					
noun	clitic					
... that the boys' health condition ...						

... 양호하다고 ...			
*yanghoha-**da**-go*			
is good			
Attribute/Process			
vg			
Event			
verbalised adjective			
Head	**Projected Mood Mark (declarative)**		Link
stem	sfx		sfx
... was good ...			

...α

공손히 말했다			
gongsonhi	*malha-et-da*		
courteously	said		
Cir:manner	Process		
advg	vg		
Property	Event		
adverb	verb		
	Head	TM	EM
	stem	sfx	sfx
... said courteously.'			

(32) α...<<"β>>...α

α...	그는 ...				
	geu	=*neun*			
	He				
	P1:Sayer				
	ng				
	Thing	TFM			
	noun	clitic			
	'He ...				

"β	... 소년들의 건강상태가 ...				
	sonyeon-deur	=*ui*	*geongang*	*sangtae*	=*ga*
	boys		health	condition	
	P1:Sayer				
	ng				
	Deictic		Classifying	Thing	EFM
	[ng]		noun	noun	clitic
	Thing	Linking			
	noun	clitic			
	... if the boys' health condition ...				

6.4 CLAUSE COMPLEXING

	... 양호하냐고 ...		
	*yanghoha-**nya**-go*		
	is good		
	Attribute/Process		
	vg		
	Event		
	verbalised adjective		
	Head	**Projected Mood Mark (interrogative)**	Link
	stem	sfx	sfx
	... was good ...		
...α	공손히 물었다		
	gongsonhi	*mur-eot-da*	
	courteously	asked	
	Cir:manner	Process	
	advg	vg	
	Property	Event	
	adverb	verb	
		Head	TM	EM
		stem	sfx	sfx
	... asked courteously.'		

We now move on to projected ideas. Hypotactic idea complexes report thought indirectly in a clause complex in which two clauses have unequal status (with the sequence α... <<'β>> ...α or less commonly 'β ^ α) – as shown in (33) and (34) respectively.

342   The Grammar of Logical Meaning: CLAUSE COMPLEXING

(33)   α... <<'β>> ...α

α...	나는 ...						
	na	=*neun*					
	I						
	P1:Senser						
	ng						
	Thing	TFM					
	noun	clitic					
	'I ...						

'β	... 온유의 말이 맞다고 ...							
	Onyu	=*ui*	*mal*	=*i*	*mat-**da**-go*			
	Onyu		word		right			
	P1				Attribute/Process			
	ng				vg			
	Deictic		Thing	EFM	Event			
	[ng]		noun	clitic	verbalised adj			
	Thing	Linking			Head	PMM	Link	
	noun	clitic			stem	sfx	sfx	
	... that Onyu is right ...							

...α	... 생각한다.		
	saenggakha-n-da.		
	think		
	Process		
	vg		
	Event		
	verb		
	Head	TM	EM
	stem	sfx	sfx
	... think.'		

6.4 CLAUSE COMPLEXING

(34)

'β	무언가 이상하다고			
	mueonga	*isangha-**da-go***		
	something	strange		
	P0	Attribute/Process		
	ng	vg		
	Thing	Event		
	pronoun	verbalised adjective		
		Head	Projected Mood Mark	Link
		stem	sfx	sfx
	'That something was strange'			

α	이강은 느꼈다.			
	Igang	*=eun*	*neukky-eot-da*	
	Igang		felt	
	P1:Senser		Process	
	ng		vg	
	Thing	TFM	Event	
	noun	clitic	verb	
			Head	TM	EM
			stem	sfx	sfx
	Igang felt.'			

Hypotactic ideas are similar to hypotactic locutions. As with hypotactic locutions, ADDRESSEE DEFERENCE is not available in the β clause in hypotactic idea complexes. In addition, the Projected Mood Mark and Link structure is part of the β clause. As we observed above for hypotactic locutions, hypotactic ideas are not spoken on a separate tone group; and in terms of graphology, no space is provided between the projected idea and 다고 -*da-go* (the Projected Mood Mark and Link), nor are any quotation marks used (to separate the projecting clause from the projected clause).

The clause type of the α clause in hypotactic idea complexes is mental, and generally limited to cognitive clauses. There are four subtypes of mental clause: perceptive, emotive, desiderative and cognitive, as discussed in Chapter 4 (see Section 4.2.2.3 and Table 4.5). All four types allow for embedded ideas. So (34) would be interpreted as a cognitive clause – it does not reference sensing (via touching, smelling, etc.), but rather apprehension.

The mood of a hypotactically projected idea is declarative. This is true for a wide range of mental verbs, for example, 생각하다 *saenggakha-da* 'think', 의심하다 *uisimha-da* 'doubt', and so on. As in (33) and (34), the projected declarative suffix plus the connecting suffix is 다고 *-da-go*. Examples with other Projected Mood Mark functions do not occur.

Before closing this section, we address two further issues that present themselves while we are considering types of projection. One has to do with a structure involving unspecified Sayers; the issue is whether we treat this structure as a clause complex or a clause simplex. The other has to do with cases situated in a region between a hypotactic idea clause complex and a clause simplex with an embedded idea.

Example (35) illustrates the first challenge. It differs from examples such as (31) and (32) in that it only has a Process in its projecting clause (합니다 *ha-mnida* 'say'). It is often not easy to recover a Sayer from the co-text or context of examples like these; and the tense for the Process in what we might take as the projecting clause tends to be present. Constructions like (35) are commonly found in Korean genres such as political speeches, where the identity of the source of the locution is not specified; the source can only be inferred in general terms. In a sense they present information as received wisdom.

(35)　　Clause simplex with unspecified Sayer/s

세월은 유수와 같다고 합니다.							
sewol	*=eun*	*yusu*	*=wa*	*gat-dago*		*ha-mnida*	
time		flowing water		resemble		(they) say	
P1:Token		Px[5]:Value		Attribute/Process			
ng		ng		vg			
Thing	TFM	Thing	EFM	Event		Dimension	
noun	clitic	noun	clitic	verbalised adjective		aux verb	
				Head	Link	Head	EM
				stem	sfx	stem	sfx
'It's said that time resembles flowing water.'							

---

[5] School grammars in Korea identify 와 *wa* or 과 *gwa* as variants (와 *wa* after a vowel, and 과 *gwa* after a consonant) of the comitative case marker, and 같다 *gat-da* as an adjective, meaning 'being the same kind'.

In our grammar, 와 *wa* or 과 *gwa* are two variants of a clitic that operates at group rank, realising either the Linking function between two nominal groups in a nominal group complex or an EFM function. In the latter case, the nominal group that culminates with the EFM function can realise a Participant or a Circumstance of Accompaniment. In Chapter 2 Section 2.7 we

6.4 CLAUSE COMPLEXING

In our grammar, we treat this structure as a clause simplex, not as a clause complex. Accordingly we recognise a single Process – realised by a verbal group, which is in turn realised by an Event and a Dimension. Note that the Link that connects the Event and the Dimension is limited to 다고 -*dago*. This contrasts with hypotactic locutions in a clause complex such as (31) where the β clause can involve all four projected moods – via 다고 -*da-go* (projected declarative), 냐고 -*nya-go* (projected interrogative), 라고 -*ra-go* (projected jussive) and 자고 -*ja-go* (projected cohortative). In (35), if we replace 다고 -*dago* with any of the other Projected Mood Mark functions (plus the Link), the clause will not involve a 'locution with unspecified Sayers' any more. The same is true if we change the tense of the verbalised adjective, 같다 *gat-da* 'resemble' (which is present tense in (35)) to past. While we accept 다고 -*dago* in (35) has evolved from the 'projected declarative suffix plus connecting suffix', we contend that it now has a different function.

In Chapter 2, we proposed four subtypes of the Dimension function (see Section 2.4.3 and Table 2.18): aspectual, phrasal, 'projectional' and others. The Dimension realised in (35) can be aligned with the 'projectional' subtype (alongside desideratives, realised by the auxiliary adjective 고 싶다 -*go sip-da* 'wanting to do ...' and by the auxiliary verb 기로 하다 -*giro ha-da* 'decide to do ...').

So far, we have considered hypotactically as well as paratactically projected locutions and ideas. In Chapter 4, we also considered embedded ideas, together with embedded acts and facts – all as realisations of the Phenomenon function in a mental clause. What makes the embedded clauses different from the comparable ranking clauses is that (i) an embedded clause can be marked by an EFM (like nominal groups), which is impossible with the projected locution and idea clauses; and (ii) an embedded clause does not use a link that distinguishes moods, whereas a projected locution and a projected idea clause do (via 다고 -*da-go*, 냐고 -*nya-go*, 라고 -*ra-go*, or 자고 -*ja-go* – projected declarative, interrogative, imperative jussive, or imperative cohortative respectively).

However, there are cases situated in an ambiguous region between a hypotactic idea clause complex and a clause simplex with an embedded idea. In Korean, culminating interrogative suffixes such as 느냐 -*neunya* and (으)냐 -*(eu)nya*, which realise the Exchange Mark function ([interrogative;

---

considered examples of 와 *wa* or 과 *gwa* realising the Linking function, and in Chapter 4 Section 4.4.9 we saw 와 *wa* or 과 *gwa* realising a Circumstance of Accompaniment; we are concerned here only with 와 *wa* or 과 *gwa* realising a Participant function.

The Process realised by the verbalised adjective 같다 *gat-da* is relational. 같다 *gat-da* contrasts with 이다 *i-da*, the positive copula; semantically, the former has to do with resemblance and the latter with identification. Grammatically, in both clauses, the Token is a P1; but the Value is P0 in the case of 이다 *i-da*. In the case of 같다 *gat-da*, the Value is something we label Px (where the relevant clitic is 와 *wa* or 과 *gwa*). Interestingly, we observe that the clitic 와 *wa* or 과 *gwa* can be elided when realising the Value in a relational clause. But the clitic 와 *wa* or 과 *gwa* can never be elided when realising a linking function, nor when realising a Circumstance of Accompaniment.

dominant]), occur at the very end of a clause. However, they can be followed by an EFM as in Example (36).

(36)

우리는 재료를 어떻게 확보하느냐를						
uri	=neun	jaeryo	=reul	eotteoke	hwakboha-neunya	=reul
we		materials		how	secure	
P1:Senser		P2:Phenomenon				
ng		[[clause]]⁶				
Thing	TFM	P2		Cir: Manner	Process	EFM
noun	clitic	ng		advg	vg	clitic
		Thing	EFM	Property	Event	
		noun	clitic	adverb	verb	
					Head	EM
					stem	sfx
'We (must decide) how (we) secure the materials						

결정해야 한다.				
gyeoljeongha-eya	ha-n-da			
decide	must			
Process				
vg				
Event	Modal			
verb	aux verb			
Head	Link	Head	TM	EM
stem	sfx	stem	sfx	sfx
must decide.'				

Examples of this type can be interpreted logically (as a clause complex) or experientially (as a clause simplex). Logically, they have an 'interrupted' structure (as we have seen with projecting clauses enclosing their projected clause); and the clause type of the projecting clause is [mental:cognitive].

---

[6] To simplify the analysis of embedded locutions and ideas in this chapter, we embed them directly in the Phenomenon.

6.4 CLAUSE COMPLEXING

Experientially, they can be viewed as clause simplexes with another clause embedded in them. The embedded clause can be treated as a Phenomenon (a Participant normally realised by a nominal group) because of the P2 EFM (를 *reul*). We have favoured an embedding analysis in (36), in part because the clause does not employ the Link suffix 고 *-go*.

In addition, like other clauses with two Participants, there is a possible thematic equative counterpart ('what we have to decide is how we secure the materials') – as shown in (37). Thematic equatives involve clause constituents, not interdependent clauses; this favours an embedding analysis.

(37)

우리가 결정해야 하는 것은					
uri	*=ga*	*gyeoljeongha-eya*	*ha-neun*	*geos*	*=eun*
we		decide	have to	thing	
P1					
[[clause]]					
P1:Senser	Process			**Installing**	TFM
ng	vg			**bound noun**	clitic
Thing	EFM	Event	Modal		
noun	clitic	verb	aux verb		
		Head	Link	Head	**Link**
		stem	sfx	stem	**sfx**
'What we have to decide					

재료를 어떻게 확보하느냐이다					
jaeryo	*=reul*	*eotteoke*	*hwakboha-neunya*	*i-da*	
materials		how	secure	is	
P0				Process	
[[clause]]				vg	
P2		Cir:Manner	Process	Event	
ng		advg	vg	copula	
Thing	EFM	Property	Event	Head	EM
noun	clitic	adverb	verb	stem	sfx
			Head	EM	
			stem	sfx	
is how we secure the materials.'					

In this grammar, comparable borderline constructions are treated as clause simplexes, which means we privilege the P2 (을 *eul* or 를 *reul*) and the possibility of a thematic equative in support of an experiential rather than a logical interpretation.

6.4.4 Expansion

Expansion (cf. Halliday and Matthiessen 2014: 444) builds on a clause (i) by *elaborating* it (e.g., restating it in other words, specifying it in greater detail, exemplifying it or commenting on it), (ii) by *extending* it through addition or replacement (e.g., by adding some new element, giving an exception to it or offering an alternative) or (iii) by *enhancing* it (e.g., by qualifying it with some circumstantial feature of time, place, cause or condition).

Expansion involves specific verbal suffixes that connect the initiating clause to the continuing one (in parataxis) and that connect the dependent clause to the dominant one (in hypotaxis). We will identify the function realised by this suffix as Link.

Below we consider hypotactic elaboration, paratactic and hypotactic extension and hypotactic enhancement; these are the most commonly found expanding clause complex relations in Korean. In Korean elaborating and enhancing clause complexes are realised hypotactically rather than paratactically, while extending clause complexes are realised paratactically as well as hypotactically.

6.4.4.1 Hypotactic Elaboration

We begin by pointing out that paratactic elaboration is rare in Korean. It is more natural in Korean to juxtapose two independent clauses as in (38), rather than deploy a clause complex.

(38)

늦었어.				벌써 자정이 넘었어.			
neuj-eoss-eo				*beolsseo*	*jajeong*	=*i*	*neom-eoss-eo*
late				already	midnight		passed
Attribute/Process				Modal Adjunct	P1		Process
vg				adverb	ng		vg
Event					Thing	EFM	Event
verbalised adjective					noun	clitic	verb
Head	TM	SM					Head	TM	SM
stem	sfx	sfx					stem	sfx	sfx
'It's late.'				'It's already past midnight (lit. Midnight passed).'			

6.4 CLAUSE COMPLEXING

A hypotactic elaborating clause complex uses the connector (으)ㄴ데 –(eu)nde or (느)ㄴ데 –(neu)nde, which signals that significant information is forthcoming; it typically combines clauses through a relation of comment (as in (39)) or specification (as in (40)).

(39)   =β ^ α

=β	다윈에 갔다왔는데				
	Dawin	=e	gatdaw-an-neunde		
	Darwin	to	went and came back		
	Circumstance:Location		Process		
	ng		vg		
	Thing	EFM	Event		
	noun	clitic	verb		
			Head	TM	Link
			stem	sfx	sfx
	'I went to Darwin				
α	참 좋더라.			
	cham	jo-teora		
	very	good		
	Attribute/Process			
	vg			
	Degree	Event		
	adverb	verbalised adjective		
		Head	SM:witnessed	
		stem	sfx	
	(it, i.e., the city) was very good.'			

(40)   =β ^ α

=β	누나가 방에 들어왔는데				
	nuna	*=ga*	*bang*	*=e*	*deureow-an-neunde*
	older sister		room	to	entered
	P1		Circumstance: Location		Process
	ng		ng		vg
	Thing	EFM	Thing	EFM	Event
	noun	clitic	noun	clitic	verb
					Head / TM / Link
					stem / sfx / sfx
	'(My) older sister entered the room				

α	아기를 안고 있었다.			
	agi	*=reul*	*an-go*	*iss-eot-da*
	baby		embrace	be (past) doing
	P2		Process	
	ng		vg	
	Thing	EFM	Event	Dimension
	noun	clitic	verb	aux verb
			Head / Link	Head / TM / EM
			stem / sfx	stem / sfx / sfx
	(she) was holding a baby in (her) arms.'			

We take the connector 는데 *-neunde* as a verbal suffix signalling hypotaxis, not embedding (an embedding analysis would treat 는데 as the suffix *-(n)eun* followed by the bound noun *de*). This is based on our observation that no clitic realising an EFM can occur after 는데 *-neunde*. In addition, 는데 *-neunde* can occur with a Tense Mark (e.g., *-an* 'past tense') as in (39) and (40); but the Relative Tense Mark suffixes, (으)ㄴ*-(eu)n*, 는 *neun*, or (으)ㄹ*(eu)l*, that we find in embedded clauses are not possible in =β clauses.

6.4 CLAUSE COMPLEXING

Note also that English hypotactic elaborating clauses, which focus on a Participant (i.e., non-restrictive relative clauses) and which are often included in a dominant clause, elaborate the dominant clause as in (41). However, as we saw in (39) and (40), in Korean it is the dominant clause that 'elaborates' the dependent one.

(41) Melbourne,   which I seldom visit,   is my friend's favourite city.
       α...   <<=β >>   ...α

In fact, grammatically speaking, the so-called 'non-restrictive relative clause' is not possible in Korean. In a clause such as (42), the clause 내가 좋아하는 *nae ga joaha-neun* '(who) I like' functions as a Qualifying function in a nominal group, not an =β clause. This embedded clause is not spoken on a separate tone group in Korean and there is no punctuation separating it from the rest of the clause. Critically the clause ends with the Relative Tense Mark (RTM) 는 -*neun* associated with embeddings – as opposed to 는데 -*neunde* as in (39) and (40).

(42)

내가 좋아하는 온유가 왔다.							
nae	=ga	joaha-neun	Onyu	=ga	w-at-da		
I		like	Onyu		came		
P1					Process		
ng					vg		
Qualifying			Thing	EFM	Event		
[[clause]]			noun	clitic	verb		
P1		Process			Head	TM	EM
ng		vg			stem	sfx	sfx
Thing	EFM	Event					
noun	clitic	verb					
		Head	RTM				
		stem	sfx				
'Onyu who I like has come.'							

6.4.4.2 *Paratactic and Hypotactic Extension*

Paratactic extending clause complexes are divided into three subcategories – *additive* (where information is added), *adversative* (where information is contrasted) and *replacive* (where information is substituted).

A typical example for paratactic extension clause complex is shown in (43). The clause complex in the example is paratactic as it respects both criteria for parataxis – the two clauses in the clause complex can realise either the initiating or the continuing clause and both clauses are negotiable.

(43)　　1 +2

1	말하기는 음성 언어 활동이고					
	malhagi	*=neun*	*eumseong*	*eoneo*	*hwaldong*	*i-go*
	speaking		spoken	language	activity	is
	P1		P0			Attribute/Process
	ng		ng			vg
	Thing	TFM	Classifying	Classifying	Thing	Event
	noun	clitic	noun	noun	noun	copula
						Head / Link
						stem / sfx
	'Speaking is a spoken language activity **and**					

+2	읽기는 문자 언어 활동이다.					
	ilki	*=neun*	*munja*	*eoneo*	*hwaldong*	*i-da*
	reading		written	language	activity	is
	P1		P0			Attribute/Process
	ng		ng			vg
	Thing	TFM	Classifying	Classifying	Thing	Event
	noun	clitic	noun	noun	noun	copula
						Head / EM
						stem / sfx
	reading is a written language activity.'					

Hypotactic extension, like paratactic extension, makes use of three relations: additive, adversative and replacive. The clauses have unequal status.

The clause complex in (44) involves an additive relation, realised through a hypotactic extension Link (아 or 어)서-(*a* or *eo*)*seo*.

6.4 CLAUSE COMPLEXING

(44) α... <<+β>> ^ ...α

α...	나는 ...		
	na	=*neun*	
	I		
	P1		
	ng		
	Thing	TFM	
	noun	clitic	
	'I ...		

<<+β>>	... 시장에 가서 ...			
	sijang	=*e*	*ga-seo*	
	market	to	go	
	Circumstance:Location		Process	
	ng		vg	
	Thing	EFM	Event	
	noun	clitic	verb	
			Head	Link
			stem	sfx
	... went to the market and (lit. going to the market ...)			

...α	... 포도를 샀다.				
	podo	=*reul*	*sa-t-da*		
	grapes		bought		
	P2		Process		
	ng		vg		
	Thing	EFM	Event		
	noun	clitic	verb		
			Head	TM	EM
			stem	sfx	sfx
	... bought grapes.'				

The clause complex in (45) realises the replacive relation, as encoded through the negative copula 아니- *ani-* 'be not' and a hypotactic extension Link 라 *-ra* (example taken from a primary school textbook, Ministry of Education 2002d). Clause complexes with the replacive relation often display different polarity values, with one being 'positive' and the other 'negative'. In example (45), the dependent clause has the negative value (without a Tense Mark) and the dominant clause has the positive one (with a Tense Mark).

(45)   α ... <<+β>> ^ ...α

α...	주인공은 ...		
	juingong	=*eun*	
	main character		
	P1		
	ng		
	Thing	TFM	
	noun	clitic	
	'The main character...		
+β	... 사람이 아니라 ...		
	saram	=*i*	*ani-ra*
	human		not be
	P1		Attribute/Process
	ng		vg
	Thing	EFM	Event
	noun	clitic	negative copula
			Head	Link
			stem	sfx
	... (the main character) being not a human ...		

6.4 CLAUSE COMPLEXING

...α	... 강아지였다.			
	gangaji	*y-eot-da*		
	puppy	was		
	P0	Attribute/Process		
	ng	vg		
	Thing	Event		
	noun	copula		
		Head	TM	EM
		stem	sfx	sfx
	'... was a puppy.'			

6.4.4.3 Hypotactic Enhancement

Examples (46)–(49) illustrate hypotactic enhancing relations signalled by a Link suffix. In (46) the Link is realised by (아 or 어)서-(*a* or *eo*)*seo* 'after ...', which is attached to the last element of the verbal group in a β clause – here the auxiliary verb 나 *na-*, which indicates the 'completion' of an action encoded by the main verb (in our terms it realises the Dimension verbal group function; see Chapter 2, Section 2.4.3).

(46)   xβ ^ α

xβ	온유가 밥을 하고 나서					
	Onyu	=*ga*	*bab*	=*eul*	*ha-go*	*na-seo*
	Onyu		rice-cooking		do	'complete'-after
	P1		P2		Process	
	ng		ng		vg	
	Thing	EFM	Thing	EFM	Event	Dimension
	noun	clitic	noun	clitic	verb	aux verb
					Head | Link	Head | **Link**
					stem | sfx	stem | **sfx**
	'After Onyu cooked rice'					

α	미나가 국을 끓였다.			
	Mina	=*ga*	*gug*	=*eul*	*kkeury-eot-da*
	Mina		soup		boiled
	P1		P2		Process
	ng		ng		vg
	Thing	EFM	Thing	EFM	Event
	noun	clitic	noun	clitic	verb
					Head	TM	EM
					stem	sfx	sfx
	Mina boiled soup.'				

Note that in (47) the P1 is shared across clauses and so the unmarked position for P1 is at the beginning of the clause complex. An example such as (47) is spoken on three tone groups, with optional punctuation (i.e., commas) before and after the xβ clause. In this respect it contrasts with (46), where the clauses have different P1s (*Onyu* and *Mina*) and the complex is spoken on two tone groups.

(47)   α... << xβ>> ...α

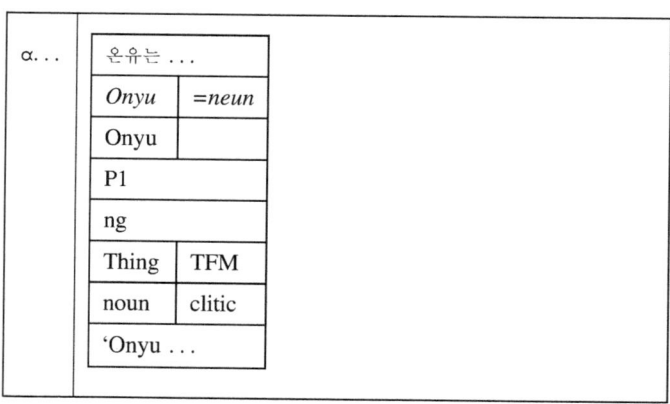

α...	온유는 ...	
	Onyu	=*neun*
	Onyu	
	P1	
	ng	
	Thing	TFM
	noun	clitic
	'Onyu ...	

6.4 CLAUSE COMPLEXING

xβ	... 밥을 하고 나서 ...						
	bab	*=eul*	*ha-go*		*na-seo*		
	rice-cooking		do		'complete'-after		
	P2		Process				
	ng		vg				
	Thing	EFM	Event		Dimension		
	noun	clitic	verb		aux verb		
			Head	Link	Head		**Link**
			stem	sfx	stem		**sfx**
	... after (she) cooked rice ...						

...α	... 국을 끓였다.				
	gug	*=eul*	*kkeury-eot-da*		
	soup		boiled		
	P2		Process		
	ng		vg		
	Thing	EFM	Event		
	noun	clitic	verb		
			Head	TM	EM
			stem	sfx	sfx
	... (she) boiled soup.'				

In (48), the Link is realised by the suffix (으)면 -(*eu*)*myeon* 'if ...', which is attached to the last element of the verbal group (namely the verb 필요하 *piryoha-* 'need'). Note that the person who needs the syrup is not made explicit in this xβ clause; but the suffix 시 -*si* indicates that they are someone respected by the speaker.

(48) xβ ^ α

xβ	혹시 시럽 필요하시면					
	hoksi	*sireop*	*piryoha-si-myeon*			
	by any chance	syrup	need if			
	Modal Adjunct	P0	Attribute/Process			
	adverb	ng	vg			
		Thing	Event			
		noun	verbalised adjective			
			Head	Participant Deference Mark		Link
			stem	sfx		sfx
	'If (you, respected one) need syrup by any chance					

α	말씀해 주세요.				
	malsseumha-e	*ju-s-e*		*yo*	
	speak	give			
	Process			Politeness Marker	
	vg			ptcl	
	Event	Dimension			
	verb	aux verb			
	Head	Link	Head	PDM	SM
	stem	sfx	stem	sfx	sfx
	please let me know (lit. speak to me).'				

In (49), the Link is realised by the suffix (으)니까 -*(eu)nikka* 'since, because ...', which is attached to the last element of the verbal group (namely the verbalised adjective 유명하- *yumyeongha-* 'be famous' in the β clause); it indicates the 'reason' for the action encoded by the main verb.

6.4 CLAUSE COMPLEXING

(49)

xβ	흑돼지가 유명하니까				
	heukdwaeji	=ga	*yumyeongha-nikka*		
	black pig		are famous because		
	P1		Attribute/Process		
	ng		vg		
	Thing	EFM	Event		
	noun	clitic	verbalised adjective		
			Head	Link	
			stem	sfx	
	'Since black pigs are famous				

α	흑돼지로 돼지고기 스튜를 만듭시다.					
	heukdwaeji	=ro	*dwaejigogi*	*seutyu*	=reul	*mandeupsida*
	black pig	with	pork	stew		make let's
	Cir:Means		P2			Process
	ng		ng			vg
	Thing	EFM	Classifying	Thing	EFM	Event
	noun	clitic	noun	noun	clitic	verb
						Head	EM
						stem	sfx
	let's make pork stew with black pork.'					

Note that no paratactic enhancing clause complexes have been found in the data surveyed for this study; Korean relies on hypotaxis when organising enhancing clause complexes. In fact, hypotactic enhancing clauses and paratactic extending ones are the two main types of clauses discussed in Korean grammar books (Choe 1937/1971, Heo 1983, Im and Chang 1995, Kwon 1985, Lee 1999, Nam and Ko 1985/1993).

Hypotactic enhancing clause complexes can be divided into two broad subcategories – 'temporal' and 'causal-conditional'. Temporal relations can be further classified into 'same time' and 'different time'; and causal-conditional relations can be divided into 'reason', 'purpose', 'result', 'condition' and 'concession'. Numerous verbal suffixes are deployed to realise Link function in Korean.[7] Table 6.3 lists some of the more common of these suffixes.

As a final note, in contrast with (46), example (50) illustrates how a temporal relation can be realised by an embedded clause functioning as a Circumstance (as introduced in Chapter 4, Section 4.4). The temporal connection in this case involves a bound noun following a verb or verbalised adjective that culminates with a 'specific' verbal suffix (realising one of the three possible realisations of Relative Tense Mark). In (50) the bound noun employed is 뒤 *dwi* 'after' (literally 'the back side') and the verb preceding it culminates with the verbal suffix ㄴ *-n* (relative past). Following our analysis of this structure in Chapter 4, we treat 뒤 *dwi* as realising an Installing function culminating the verbal group realising the Process of the embedded clause.

(50)

온유가 밥을 한 뒤에						
Onyu	=*ga*	*bab*	=*eul*	*ha-n*		*dwi*	=*e*
Onyu		rice-cooking		do		after	
Circumstance:Location							
[[clause]][8]							
P1		P2		Process			EFM
ng		ng		vg			clitic
Thing	EFM	Thing	EFM	Event		Installing	
noun	clitic	noun	clitic	verb		bound noun	
				Head	Link		
				stem	sfx		
'After Onyu cooked rice,							

---

[7] Note that Korean grammarians refer to the verbal suffixes that we treat as realising the Link function as 접속어미 *jeopsogeomi* 'conjunctive verbal suffixes'. Depending on how one categorises these verbal suffixes in Korean, there are between 30 and 100 of them (Kwon 2012: 167).
[8] To simplify the analysis of the embedded clause in this example, we embed it directly in the Circumstance.

6.4 CLAUSE COMPLEXING

미나가 국을 끓였다.						
Mina	=ga	gug	=eul	kkeury-eot-da		
Mina		soup		boiled		
P1		P2		Process		
ng		ng		vg		
Thing	EFM	Thing	EFM	Event		
noun	clitic	noun	clitic	verb		
				Head	TM	EM
				stem	sfx	sfx
'Mina boiled soup.'						

The suffix ㄴ -*n* in (50) links the clause to the bound noun 뒤 *dwi* 'after'. This bound noun carries some residual lexical meaning (enough to distinguish types of Circumstance) – mainly having to do with space, time and manner. The bound noun in this construction can be followed by the clitic 에 *e* 'at, on, in', a Circumstance EFM function.

The grammatical resources used by the different types of taxis and logico-semantic relations that have been identified in this chapter are summarised in Table 6.3. This table is not exhaustive; additional detail depends on further research.

The grammatical resources in Table 6.3 make explicit what has to be understood as far as logico-semantic relations between clauses are concerned. But from a discourse semantic perspective we may need to infer more to understand a text. In example (51) 고 -*go* 'and' makes explicit that the two clauses are related via paratactic addition; but from the perspective of discourse semantics we may need to read more into the picture for a full interpretation. Accordingly the discourse semantic system of CONJUNCTION proposed in Martin (1992) and Martin and Rose (2007) allows for implicit connections. So in (51), although the grammar tells us simply that there is an additive relation between the two clauses, we can in addition infer that the two events took place at the same time. The grammar does not make this explicit; but there is an implicit conjunctive relation there that we can reasonably abduce. The example shows that for a full analysis of the relationships between clauses in a text we need to take both explicit grammatical and implicit discourse semantic relations into account.

Table 6.3 *Basic types of inter-clausal connectors in Korean*

			parataxis	hypotaxis
PROJECTION				
locution			하고 *hago* 라고 *rago*	다, 냐, 라 or 자-고 *-da, nya, ra* or *ja-go*
idea			하고 *hago* 라고 *rago*	다고 *-da-go*
EXPANSION				
elaboration				(으)ㄴ데 *-(eu)nde* 는데 *-neunde*
extension		additive	고 *-go* (으)며 *-(eu)myeo*	아 or 어(서) *-a* or *eo(seo)* (으)며(ㄴ서) *-(eu)myeo(nseo)*
		adversative	지만 *-jiman* (으)나 *-(eu)na*	
		replacive	거나 *-geona*	라 *-ra*
enhancement	temporal	same time		(으)면서 *-(eu)myeonseo* (으)며 *-(eu)myeo*
		different time		고(나서) *-go(naseo)* 아 or 어(서) *-a* or *eo(seo)* 자(마자) *-ja(maja)*
	causal-conditional	reason		아 or 어(서) *-(a* or *eo)seo* (으)니(까) *-(eu)ni(kka)*
		purpose		(으)러 *-(eu)reo* (으)려고 *-(eu)ryeogo*
		result		(으)니(까) *-(eu)ni(kka)* 게 *-ge* 도록 *-dorok*
		condition		(으)면 *-(eu)myeon* (아 or 어)야 *-(a* or *eo)ya*
		concessive		(아 or 어)도 *-(a* or *eo)do* 더라도 *-deorado* (으)ㄴ데(도) *-(eu)nde(do)* (으)면서도 *-(eu)myeonseodo*

(51)

xβ	서로 부등켜안고					
	seoro	*budungkyeoan-**go***				
	each other	embrace				
	Cir:manner	Process				
	advg	vg				
	Property	Event				
	adverb	verb				
		Head	TM	**Link**		
		stem	sfx	**sfx**		
	'(They) embraced each other and					

α	기쁨의 눈물을 흘렸다.						
	gippeum	*=ui*	*nunmul*	*=eul*	*heuly-eot-da*		
	joy		tears		shed		
	P2:P-Range				Process		
	ng				vg		
	Orient		Thing	EFM	Event		
	[ng]		noun	clitic	verb		
	Thing	Linking			Head	TM	EM
	noun	clitic			stem	sfx	sfx
	(at the same time) (they) shed tears of joy.'						

6.5 Discussion of a Long Clause Complex

By way of closing, we analyse one longer more complex example involving nesting of relations. Example (52) is adapted from a news story. It is composed of five clauses, which are combined through both expansion and projection.

(52)

그는 "우리 배의 항로가 . . .						
geu	*=neun*	*uri*	*bae*	*=ui*	*hangno*	*=ga*
he		our	boat		route	
1		"2 β				
P1		<<P1				
ng		ng				
Thing	TFM	Orient			Thing	EFM
pronoun	clitic	[ng]			noun	clitic
		Deictic	Thing	Linking		
		possessive determiner	noun	clitic		
'He (said,) "if our vessel's route . . .						

. . . 1km 만 벗어났더라도 . . .			
1km		*=man*	*beoseona-t-deorado*
1km		only	missed if
"2 β			
P2:E-Range			Process
ng			vg
Thing		IFM	Event
word complex		clitic	verb
α	β		Head	TM	Link
cardinal number	bound noun		stem	sfx	sfx
. . . missed by only 1km . . .			

6.5 Discussion of a Long Clause Complex

... 소년들이 탄 배를 ...				
sonyeon-deur	=i	ta-n	bae	=reul
boys		board	boat	
"2 α				
P2				
ng				
Qualifying			Thing	EFM
[[clause]]			noun	clitic
P1		Process		
ng		vg		
Thing	EFM	Event		
noun	clitic	verb		
		Head	RTM	
		stem	sfx	
... the boat the boys boarded ...				

... 찾지 못했을 것" 이라고 하며[9] ...								
chat-ji	mota-ess-eulgeosi-ra-go						ha-myeo	
find	would not have been able						said-and	
"2 α							... 1	
Process>>							Process	
vg							vg	
Event	Negation						Event	
verb	auxiliary verb						verb	
Head	Link	Head	TM	Modal Mark	PMM: decl	Link	Head	Link
stem	sfx	stem	sfx	sfx	sfx	sfx	stem	sfx
... (we) wouldn't have been able to find..." (he) said, and ...								

[9] In the original example in the source text, 못했을 것" 이라고 하며 *mota-ess-eulgeosi-ra-go ha-myeo* appears as 못했을 것" 이라며 *mota-ess-eulgeosi-ra-myeo*. The configuration 이라며 *i-ra-myeo* is in fact 'shortened' from 이라(고 하)며 *i-ra(-go ha-)myeo* (see Kim et al. 2005b: 440 and 444 for details). The elisions involved are the Link 고 -*go* and the verbal Process 하 *ha-* 'say'; what is left, 며 -*myeo* 'and', is in fact the paratactic Link suffix. We provide the full form in the example to clarify that we are dealing with a clause that is connected paratactically to the following clause.

... 이들을 찾은 것은 ...					
i-deur	*=eul*	*chaj-eun*		*geos*	*=eun*
them		finding			
+2 "β					
<<P1					
ng					
Thing					TFM
[[clause]]					clitic
P2		Process			
ng		vg			
Thing	EFM	Event		Installing	
noun	clitic	verb		bound noun	
		Head	Link		
		stem	sfx		
... that (they) had found them ...					

... 기적이라고 했다.				
gijeog	*i-ra-go*			*ha-et-da*
miracle	is			said
+2 "β				+2 α
P0	Attribute/Process>>			Process
ng	vg			vg
Thing	Event			Event
noun	verb			verb
	Head	PMM	Link	
	stem	sfx	sfx	
... was a miracle (he) said.'				

Given the length of the clause complex, the English translation provided above may not be immediately clear. We'll take a moment here to clarify our translation. Essentially, this clause complex has two projecting clauses, which are linked paratactically:

6.5 Discussion of a Long Clause Complex

1   He said, "If our vessel missed the route by only 1km, we wouldn't have been able to find the boat the boys boarded"
+2 and he said it was a miracle to find them

The first clause complex above is paratactic (it involves directly quoted speech); the second clause complex is hypotactic (it involves indirectly reported speech).

The paratactically projected locution in the first clause complex involves two clauses that are linked hypotatically (an enhancing relation):

xβ If our vessel missed the route by only 1km
α   we wouldn't have been able to find the boat the boys boarded

The hypotactically projected locution in the second clause complex consists of one clause.

The Korean clause complex in (52) can be developed step by step – as illustrated in (53.1) to (53.3). In the outer layer are two projecting clauses (each enclosing a projected locution); they are linked paratactically through the Link 며 -*myeo* 'and'. These relations are displayed in (53.1). The two projecting clauses are paratactically connected. As such each can play the role of either an initiating or continuing clause and still involve the same logico-semantic relation; and the initiating clause has the potential for variation in SPEECH FUNCTION (it is a statement but could be changed to a question). We use Roman numerals to number the clauses in (53.1) to (53.3).

(53.1)   1+2

Clause	Logical structure	
I...	1	그는 *geu =neun* He
II		" ... "
...I		이라고 하며 *i-ra-go ha-**myeo*** said and
IV	+2	이들을 찾은 것은 기적이라고 *ideur =eul chaj-eun ges =eun gijeog-i-ra-go* it was a miracle [[to find them]]
V		했다. *ha-et-da.* said

In the inner layer of the initiating clause complex (I and II, analysed as 1 in (53.1) and then developed as I..., II, III and ...I – analysed as 1... "2 and ...1 in (53.2)), we have a paratactically projected locution (the locution is enclosed in double quotation marks). Its structure however is somewhat different from the projecting structure we considered in (25) and (26). The quoted locution is 'incomplete' – in the sense that it does not culminate with an Exchange Mark, as we would expect in paratactic projections. Instead, we have a Projected Mood Mark 라 -*ra* (projected declarative) – a defining characteristic of the hypotactic projection (as we have seen (31) and (32)). A detailed analysis has been given in (52).

(53.2)   1 (1... << "2 >> ...1) +2 (<<"β>> α)

Clause	Logical structure		
I...	1	1...	그는 *geu =neun* He
II		"2	"우리 배의 항로가 1km 만 벗어났더라도 *uri bae =ui hangno =ga 1km =man beoseona-t-deorado* If our vessel missed the route by only 1km
III			소년들이 탄 배를 찾지 못했을 것" *sonyeon-deur =i ta-n bae =reul chat-ji mot ha-ess-eul ges* (we) wouldn't have been able to find the boat [[the boys boarded]]
...I		...1	이라고 하며 *i-ra-go ha-myeo* said, and
IV	+2	"β	이들을 찾은 것은 기적이라고 *ideur =eul chaj-eun ges =eun gijeog-i-**ra-go*** it was a miracle [[to find them]]
V		α	했다. *ha-et-da.* said

This 'hybrid' type of projection is a genre-specific way of quoting others' speech in news stories, reflecting a strategic practice found in newspapers – the double quotation marks function as what we might characterise as 'scare

6.6 Conclusion

quotes', indicating that what is said is not the opinion of the reporter but rather that of the interviewee.

In the inner layer of the continuing clause complex (IV and V, analysed as +2 in (53.1) and developed as "β and α in (53.2)), we have a hypotactic locution (IV), which culminates with 라고 – the PMM 라 -ra (projected declarative mood), followed by the Link 고 -go. See (52) for a detailed analysis.

Finally, as illustrated in (53.3), the clauses (II and III) projected by 그는 ... 이라고 하며 *geu neun ... i-ra-go ha-myeo* 'he said ... and' are connected through conditional hypotactic enhancement – 더라도 *-deorado* 'if' (in II).

(53.3)   1 (1... << "2 (xβ ^ α) >> ...1) +2 ("β α)

Clause	Logical structure			
I...	1	1...		그는 ***geu =neun*** He
II		"2	xβ	"우리 배의 항로가 1km 만 벗어났더라도 *uri bae =ui hangno =ga 1km =man beoseona-t-**deorado*** If our vessel missed the route by only 1km
III			α	소년들이 탄 배를 찾지 못했을 것" *sonyeon-deur =i ta-n bae =reul chat-ji mot ha-ess-eul ges* (we) wouldn't haven't been able to find the boat [[the boys boarded]]
...I		...1		이라고 하며 ***i-ra-go ha-myeo*** said and
IV	+2	"β		이들을 찾은 것은 기적이라고 *ideur =eul chaj-eun ges =eun gijeot-i-ra-go* it was a miracle [[to find them]]
V			α	했다. *ha-et-da.* said

It might be useful at this point to repeat the English translation: 'He said, "If our vessel missed the route by only 1km, we wouldn't have been able to find the boat the boys boarded" and he said it was a miracle to find them.'

6.6 Conclusion

This chapter has introduced an outline of clause complexing in Korean – the grammatical resources for logical meaning. We have proposed a system that involves two sub-systems – TAXIS and LOGICO-SEMANTIC RELATION. For TAXIS, we proposed symmetry and negotiability as the criteria to determine whether a clause nexus involves a paratactic or hypotactic relation; and for LOGICO-SEMANTIC RELATION we presented projection and expansion as subtypes of interdependency between clauses. We noted that in projection, both locutions and ideas can be projected paratactically and hypotactically. In expansion, on the other hand, while extension is expressed both paratactically and hypotactically, elaboration and enhancement relations are realised hypotactically.

7 Two Applications

7.1 Introduction to Using Our Korean Grammar

This book is not a pedagogic grammar, designed for students learning Korean. Nor is it a translator's handbook. But it is an appliable linguistics grammar – one that has grown out of a dialectic of theory, description and practice in applied contexts.

This culminating chapter illustrates the relevance of our functional grammar of Korean to two particular contexts of application – teaching Korean as a foreign language and translation and interpreting (T&I). As noted in Chapter 1, these contexts of application were what motivated us to prepare this grammar of Korean as a meaning-making resource.

Both of the applied contexts we focus on here are multilingual ones, involving Korean and English.[1] As work on functional language typology has shown, SFL is particularly well suited to application in multilingual contexts because of the range of perspectives it offers for comparing languages. As reviewed in Martin and Quiroz (2020, 2021), based on work by Matthiessen (2004, 2014, 2018), comparing and contrasting languages in SFL takes advantage of four descriptive motifs and generalisations:

1. Languages tend to differ more with respect to more delicate distinctions in system networks than more general ones (so SFL's formalisation of paradigmatic relations is critical).
2. Languages tend to differ more with respect to syntagmatic relations than paradigmatic ones (so SFL's complementarity of system and structure is insightful).
3. Languages tend to differ more at lower ranks than higher ones (so SFL's rank-based model of constituency is advantageous).

---

[1] In other parts of the world, languages other than English would of course be used to support learning Korean or for translation and interpreting. Fortunately, SFL descriptions of the main languages likely to be involved (e.g., Chinese, Japanese, French and Spanish) are well-developed ones.

4. Languages tend to differ more at lower strata than at higher ones (so SFL's stratified content plane – as lexicogrammar realising discourse semantics – is beneficial).

A schematic outline of these complementary perspectives is provided in Figure 7.1 (a diagram intended for Matthiessen 2018 and later published in Martin et al., 2022: 78).

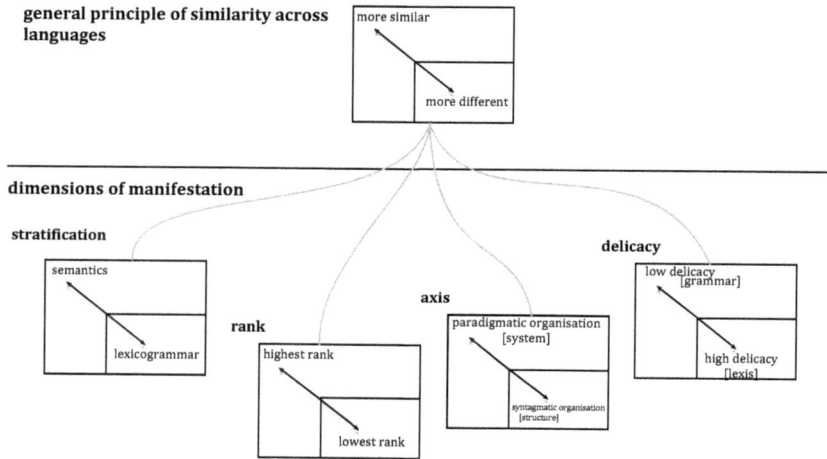

Figure 7.1 Complementary perspectives on comparing and contrasting languages

These parameters allow translators, interpreters and language teachers and learners to shift 'back and forth' between languages and 'up and down' functional descriptions of languages. This greatly facilitates explanations of practical T&I and language teaching/learning issues.

7.2 Teaching Korean as a Foreign Language

Innovative programming for language teaching and learning is one well-developed application of SFL. In this section we will illustrate how our grammar can be used for Korean language teaching and learning. Our discussion focuses on the needs of adult learners and their interest in meaning-oriented explanations of Korean structure.

Below we show how SFL genre pedagogy, specifically Reading to Learn (Rose and Martin 2012), can take advantage of our functional grammar of Korean. We chose this pedagogy because it has been designed to draw on rich functional grammars such as the one we have presented for Korean – both in terms of selecting texts that foreground specific aspects of grammar that need attention and

7.2 Teaching Korean as a Foreign Language

in terms of providing opportunities for students and teachers to build up explicit knowledge about language as part of their teaching and learning.

We concentrate on a short descriptive text that foregrounds Korean attributive and locative relational clauses. We decided to focus on this area of our grammar because of the important differences between Korean and many other languages as far as the grammar of description is concerned. The Korean text we focus on has been adapted from a Korean translation (Lee, J. H. 2018) of the P. D. James novel *An Unsuitable Job for a Woman* (1977). James is well known for the cultivated literary style of her crime fiction and for her passages of description in particular. We knew that selecting a passage of this kind would highlight some of the major relational clause grammar challenges faced by many learners of Korean and would also provide a useful point of transition for the translation and interpreting section that follows on in this chapter. That said, it was necessary to simplify the text in some respects, to avoid constructions that would over-complicate our presentation of Reading to Learn pedagogy and over-burden students in the earlier stages of a university Korean language programme. The original text and its translation are provided in the Appendix to this chapter. The simplified text, its Romanisation and its back translation into English is provided in example (1).

(1) 오른쪽에 벽난로가 있었는데, 구식 철제 레인지였다. 화덕은 좀 더러웠다. 난로 안에 하얀 재가 많이 있었다. 난로 앞에는 작은 통나무가 많았다. 불쏘시개는 없었다. 난로 옆에 낡은 의자가 있었다. 전에는 아름다운 의자였다고 코델리아는 말했다.

oreunjjog e byeongnallo ga iss-eon-neunde, gusik cheolje reinji y-eot-da. hwadeog eun jom deoreow-ot-da. nallo an e haya-n jae ga mani iss-eot-da. nallo ap e neun jag-eun tongnamu ga man-at-da. bulssosigae neun eops-eot-da. nallo yeop e nalg-eun uija ga iss-eot-da. jeon e neun areumdau-n uija y-eot-dago Kodellia neun malha-et-da.

'On the right side there was a fireplace, (it) was an old-fashioned iron range. The ovens were a bit unclean. In the stove there were a lot of white ash. In front of the stove there were lots of small logs. There was no kindling wood. Next to the stove there was an old chair. Cordelia said that previously (it) had been a beautiful chair.'

7.2.1 Traditional Approaches to Teaching Korean as a Foreign Language

In a traditional pedagogy of the kind students of Korean commonly experience in universities around the world, our focus text would be used for reading practice. The text would typically be presented in Hangeul, followed by a list of 'unfamiliar' Korean words, together with their English translations. This would be followed by grammar notes that 'unpack' the meaning of unfamiliar expressions – with or without referring explicitly to their 'grammar'. This would be followed by an English translation. An example of how our text might appear in a textbook or materials prepared for students is presented in (2).

374 Two Applications

(2)   A sample handout for a reading class

오른쪽에 벽난로가 있었는데, 구식 철제 레인지였다. 화덕은 좀 더러웠다. 난로 안에 하얀 재가 많이 있었다. 난로 앞에는 작은 통나무가 많았다. 불쏘시개는 없었다. 난로 옆에 낡은 의자가 있었다. 전에는 아름다운 의자였다고 코델리아는 말했다.

Illustration 7.1 An old-fashioned iron range

New words

- 벽난로   fireplace
- 철제   (made with) iron
- 더럽다   dirty, messy
- 통나무   log
- 낡다   old (inanimate)
- 아름답다 beautiful
- 구식   old-style
- 화덕   oven
- 재   ash
- 불쏘시개 kindling wood
- 전에   before

Grammar notes

· 의자였다고: This construction involves reported speech, reporting what other people have SAID. It is one of the four options, and the other three are reporting what other people have ASKED, COMMANDED and SUGGESTED.

English equivalent

On the right side there was a fireplace, (it) was an old-fashioned iron range. The ovens were a bit unclean. In the stove there were a lot of white ash. In front of the stove there were lots of small logs. There was no kindling wood. Next to the stove there was an old chair. Cordelia said that previously it had been a beautiful chair.

7.2 Teaching Korean as a Foreign Language

In Australian contexts, a text of this kind might appear in the second half of a beginner's level or the first half of the lower intermediate level tertiary course in Korean. It could be studied as an example of the description of things found in a domestic setting – for a 50-minute class including follow-up writing exercises.

In this pedagogy in order to help students understand the text (word by word and sentence by sentence) the teacher would first give a brief description of the scene that the text depicts – supported where possible through visual aids (such as photos and video clips), together with background information (such as where the text comes from). The teacher's initial descriptions and explanations will most likely be a 'mixture' of Korean and English at this level of study; the teacher knows which Korean expressions his/her students can, or cannot, understand and the teacher's descriptions and explanations might involve story-telling combined with questions and answers to get the students engaged. For instance, the teacher can start off by showing a photo of an old-fashioned fireplace range (such as the one in (2)) and asking what students can see in the photo – introducing the word for fireplace in Korean and commenting briefly on the goal of the lesson. In example (3) we provide some instances of how this might proceed. (The '...' notation indicates a pause in the teacher's moves).

(3) Teacher: 여기 이 사진에 뭐가 있어요?
yeogi   i   sajin   e   mwo ga isseo   yo?
here   this   photo   in   what   is there
'Here... in this photo... what's there?'

Students: A fireplace!

Teacher: 네, 벽난로예요.   벽...   난...   로...
ne   byeongnallo ye   yo. byeong   nal   lo
yes   fireplace   it is   fireplace...
'Yes, it's a fireplace. Fire... place... (syllable by syllable, for pronunciation)'

오래된 영국식 벽난로예요.
oraedoen   yeongguksik   byeongnallo ye   yo.
old   UK-style   fireplace   it is
'It's an old, UK-style fireplace.'

오늘 공부할 내용은 이 벽난로가 있는 방인데,
oneul   gongbuhal   naeyong   eun   i   byeongnallo ga   inneun   bang inde,
today   study   content   this fireplace   there is   room is
'What we are studying today is the room where this fireplace is –

이 방에 벽난로하고 또 뭐가 있는지 알아볼 거예요.
i   bang e   byeongnallo hago tto   mwo   ga   inneunji   arabolgeoye yo.
this   room in   fireplace   and   also what   there is   investigate
we will investigate, in addition to a fireplace, what else there is in this room.'

At this point, the teacher would distribute handouts (e.g., like those in (2)) to the class, say where the text comes from, and explain briefly in English who Mark and Cordelia are in the story. The teacher might wish to go through the 'new words', focusing on the pronunciation and etymology – words such as 구식 *gusik* 'old-style' and 철제 *cheolje* 'iron-made' are Sino-Korean words and the meanings of individual syllables can be explained and related to words learned previously (e.g., 한식 *hansik* 'Korean-style'). Then the class could be instructed to go through the text themselves in pairs or small groups. The teacher would move around the class and provide individualised explanations if necessary.

This work in pairs or groups might be followed by a series of questions that are intended to help the students understand further details. Some instances are given in (4).

(4) 화덕이 어땠어요? 깨끗했어요?
    hwadeog   i   eottaesseo   yo?   kkaekkeutaesseo   yo?
    oven   how was   neat
    'How were the ovens? Were they tidy?'

    벽난로는 사용되고 있었어요? 어떻게 알아요?
    byeongnallo   neun   sayongdoe-go   iss-eoss-eo   yo?   eotteoke   ar-a   yo?
    fireplace   was used   was...ing   how   know
    'Was the fireplace being used? How do we know?'

    의자는 어디에 있었어요?
    uija   neun   eodi   e   isseosseo   yo?
    chair   where   at   was
    'Where was the chair?'

    코델리아는 의자가 깨끗하다고 말했어요?
    Kodellia   neun   uija   ga   kkaekkeutaetdago   malhaesseo   yo?
    Cordelia   chair   neat   said
    'Did Cordelia say that the chair was neat?'

Students might also be asked to draw a picture based on the information they obtain from the text. They could, for example, be asked to draw a similar picture but with the locations of the fittings and furniture varied, and then attempt to write in Korean a paragraph describing what they have drawn as a follow-up writing exercise.

As all Korean teachers know, some students will be better able to answer questions and complete tasks of this kind than others – which are in effect testing students' understanding of the text. This reflects the fact that in a pedagogy of this kind some students will inevitably do much better than others and that over time some students will become far better speakers and readers than others. An alternative pedagogy, designed to ensure success for all students, is outlined below.

7.2.2 An Alternative 'Reading to Learn' (R2L) Perspective

The pedagogy we suggest below has been carefully designed to address the gap between successful and less successful language learners. In general terms the pedagogy is built up around the cycle of activity outlined in Figure 7.2. Central to each cycle is a task that students must perform. To ensure that students will be successful in completing the task, the teacher carefully prepares students with what they need to know and focuses their attention by zeroing in on what is required. Completion of the task is then positively evaluated, even if students miss the mark because they have not been properly prepared and focused. Finally the teacher elaborates on the task in a way that benefits all students, potentially drawing more or less explicitly on our grammar in ways we illustrate below.

At the scale of classroom teacher/learner interactions, the task of learners is generally to respond to teachers' focused questions. Successful student responses are then used to elaborate with further information toward the lesson's curriculum goals. This analysis reinterprets the widely discussed 'initiation–response–feedback' pattern of classroom discourse (Sinclair and Coulthard 1975) in terms of pedagogic activity – that is, teaching/learning cycles. R2L redesigns this ubiquitous pattern, scaffolding learning to ensure that every student is continually successful and thus well positioned to develop control of spoken and written Korean.

Figure 7.2 R2L's teaching/learning cycle

As concisely synthesised in Rose (2020a,b, 2022), Reading to Learn (hereafter R2L) programmes draw on both a culture's reservoir of knowledge genres (i.e., what students need to read and write) and a teacher's repertoire of designed curriculum genres (i.e., how to teach so all students can learn). An outline of relevant curriculum genres is presented as Figure 7.3. The model involves three layered cycles of activity; we'll focus on just the middle layer here (Detailed Reading, Joint Rewriting and Individual Rewriting) – its Detailed Reading phase in particular. This layer is designed to scaffold students as they gain control of challenging texts. So our discussion below is oriented to a class of students all of whom would struggle to read our Korean description without scaffolding by the teacher.

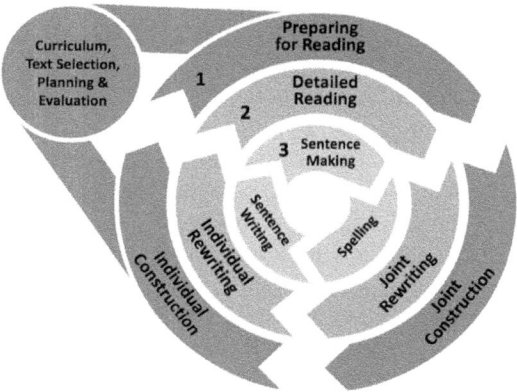

Figure 7.3 Rose's model of R2L curriculum genres (Rose 2020a: 252)

Detailed Reading deploys the Prepare ^ Focus ^ Task ^ Evaluate ^ Elaborate teaching/learning cycle outlined in Figure 7.2 to support all learners in a class to read a text with detailed comprehension. The central task in Detailed Reading cycles is to identify wordings in the text, whose meanings may then be elaborated. Students use highlighters to mark wordings on their own copy of the focus text. In the cycles we model here, the focus of elaborations is locative and attributive clauses, and highlighting is used to mark nominal groups and verbal groups. Elaborations are also used to introduce metalinguistic terms, adapted from our grammar, which are useful for discussing the grammatical structure of descriptions.

The pedagogic principle in play here is that linguistic functions are learnt by experiencing instances in meaningful texts (as in first language learning in the

7.2 Teaching Korean as a Foreign Language

home), but that learning is enhanced and accelerated by teacher guidance. We suggest that this is more effective for most learners than the traditional method of memorising linguistic patterns in paradigms with decontextualised examples, before applying this abstract knowledge to actual language tasks. Instead, Detailed Reading guides learners to recognise the functions under focus in actual texts and builds on this recognition to generalise these functions using relevant metalanguage. The grammar we presented in Chapters 1 to 6 of this book would emerge selectively in student consciousness from instances organised along just these lines.

The suggestions we are making below for Detailed Reading would follow on from the implementation of the Preparing for Reading curriculum genre (see Figure 7.3). Preparing for Reading involves two steps with descriptive texts. First the field is prepared, making clear any background knowledge students need to comprehend and engage with the text. In this case, the description is dealing with an old-fashioned cast iron open fire cooking range stove for which a photo would need to be provided (since such a stove would be unfamiliar to most students). The teacher could explain why the stove is being presented in detail in this text and how the description fits into the crime novel as a whole. This would be followed up by a summary of the features covered in the description text. This preview gives students a semantic 'roadmap' that supports them to follow as the teacher reads the text to the class.

For the Detailed Reading activity we have in mind, A4 copies of the description are prepared, copied and distributed to each student so that they can easily read the description and highlight it as the lesson unfolds. The teacher can point out to the class that their focus will be on how Korean grammar is used to describe a scene in which significant action has taken place, or is ongoing, or is about to happen.

We will now suggest some cycles of Detailed Reading focusing on Korean locative and attributive clauses. Before each cycle we present a grammatical analysis of the part of the text being focused on. The first sentence of the description, which appeared in (1), has two clauses – the first is a locative relational clause and the second is an attributive one. We provide an ideational analysis at clause and group rank in (5) (and for other examples); our teaching/learning cycle however will concentrate on transitivity (relational clauses in particular).

(5)

오른쪽에 벽난로가 있었는데,				
oreunjjog	*=e*	*byeongnallo*	*=ga*	*iss-eon-neunde*
right side	LOC	fireplace		was present
=β				
clause (locative)				
P3:Location		P1:Located		Process
ng		ng		vg
Thing	EFM	Thing	EFM	Event
noun	clitic	noun	clitic	verb
				Head / TM / Link
				stem / sfx / sfx
'On the right side there was a fireplace,				

구식 철제 레인지였다.			
gusik	*cheolje*	*reinji*	*y-eot-da*
old-fashioned	iron	range	was
α			
clause (attributive)			
P0:Attribute			Process
ng			vg
Classifying	Classifying	Thing	Event
noun	noun	noun	copula
			Head / TM / EM
			stem / sfx / sfx
(it) was an old-fashioned iron range.'			

In our first cycle the teacher draws students' attention to the two parts of the sentence – 오른쪽에 벽난로가 있었는데 *oreunjjog e byeongnallo ga iss-eon-neunde* 'on the right side there was a fireplace' and 구식 철제 레인지였다 *gusik cheolje reinji y-eot-da* '(it) was an old-fashioned iron range'. In presenting Korean expressions in the elicitation tables (6), we continue our practice of giving Hangeul, romanisation and where necessary a gloss, for example, 한글 *Hangeul* 'Korean alphabet'; the Romanisation and glosses are provided for the convenience of English-speaking readers (they are not part of the teaching/learning interactions we are modelling here).

(6)

Teacher	The first sentence has two parts. It tells us that there was a fireplace in the room, on the right side, and that it was an old-fashioned iron range.	Prepare sentence
	The two parts are divided by a comma. Can you see the first part?	Focus on wording
Student	오른쪽에 벽난로가 있었는데 *oreunjjog e byeongnallo ga iss-eon-neunde* 'on the right side there was a fireplace'	Identify wording
Teacher	Right.	Affirm
	This part depends on the second part, doesn't it? The verb 있었는데 *iss-eon-neunde* 'there was' tells us there is more to come.	Elaborate grammar
	Which part of the verb connects the two clauses? It's at the end of the verb.	Focus on wording
Student	는데 *-neunde*	Identify wording
Teacher	Very good. Highlight 는데 *-neunde*.	Affirm
	That ending tells us we need to keep going.	Elaborate wording
	What is the second part of the sentence, after the ending?	Focus on wording
Student	구식 철제 레인지였다 *gusik cheolje reinji yeot-da* '(it) was an old-fashioned iron range'	Identify wording
Teacher	Exactly.	Affirm
	This second part refers to a range, like the one we have in the picture up here and tells us it was an old-fashioned iron range.	Elaborate grammar

S/he then deals with each of the two clauses (7). The first clause is a locative one; it introduces an entity (벽난로 *byeongnallo* 'fireplace') in relation to its location (오른쪽 *oreunjjog* 'right side').

(7)

오른쪽에 벽난로가 있었는데,						
oreunjjog	=*e*	*byeongnallo*	=*ga*	*iss-eon-neunde*		
right side	LOC	fireplace		was present		
clause (locative)						
P3:Location		P1:Located		Process		
ng		ng		vg		
Thing	EFM	Thing	EFM	Event		
noun	clitic	noun	clitic	verb		
				Head	TM	Link
				stem	sfx	sfx
'On the right side there was a fireplace.'						

The teacher begins by getting the students to identify the wording realising the Location and Located functions in this locative clause (8).

(8)

Teacher	Now the first clause tells us that there was a fireplace on the right side of the room we are describing.	Prepare clause
	It begins with the location. Can you see the words that tell us where the fireplace was?	Focus on wording
Student	오른쪽에 *oreunjjog e* 'on the right side'	Identify wording
Teacher	Very good. Highlight 오른쪽에 *oreunjjog e*.	Affirm
	The little word 에 *e* marks the location, doesn't it?	Elaborate grammar
	Can you see the following words that tell us what we are locating?	Focus on wording
Student	벽난로가 *byeongnallo ga* 'a fireplace'	Identify wording
Teacher	Right. Highlight 벽난로가 *byeongnallo ga*.	Affirm
	The 가 *ga* tells us that the fireplace is what is located.	Elaborate grammar

S/he then focuses on the locative verb (9).

7.2 Teaching Korean as a Foreign Language

(9)

Teacher	At the end of the clause we have the verb 있었는데 *iss-eon-neunde* 'there was'.	Prepare clause
	Can you see the part of the verb that tells us something is located somewhere? Just before the 는데 *-neunde*.	Focus on wording
Student	있었 *iss-eon*	Identify wording
Teacher	Very good. That's exactly right. Highlight 있었 *iss-eon*.	Affirm
	This verb tells us that we are locating an entity; in this clause we position the fireplace on the right side of the room.	Elaborate grammar

The second clause is an attributive one; it tells us that the fireplace was an old-fashioned iron range (구식 철제 레인지 *gusik cheolje reinji*). Here the Carrier is the fireplace that was introduced by the previous 는데 *-neunde* clause and thus is understood and not mentioned (10).

(10)

구식 철제 레인지였다.					
gusik	*cheolje*	*reinji*	*y-eot-da*		
old-fashioned	iron	range	was		
α					
clause (attributive)					
P0:Attribute			Process		
ng			vg		
Classifying	Classifying	Thing	Event		
noun	noun	noun	copula		
			Head	TM	EM
			stem	sfx	sfx
'(it) was an old-fashioned iron range.'					

The teacher begins by getting the students to identify the wording, beginning by filling in the elliptical Carrier function (11).

(11)

Teacher	The second clause describes the fireplace. But it doesn't actually mention the fireplace, does it? Because the fireplace was just mentioned in the first clause.	Prepare clause
	What was the word that referred to the fireplace?	Focus on wording
Student	벽난로 *byeongnallo*	Identify wording
Teacher	Yes. Excellent.	Affirm
	In Korean, you don't have to mention what you're talking about when you believe your hearer knows what it is. But what happens if you do? Well, your sentence will not be ungrammatical, but it won't sound like natural Korean.	Elaborate grammar

S/he then turns to the P0:Attribute function (12).

(12)

Teacher	How is the fireplace described?	Prepare clause
	Can you see the words that jointly describe the fireplace? There are three all together.	Focus on wording
Student	구식 철제 레인지 *gusik cheolje reinji*	Identify wording
Teacher	Yes. Highlight 구식 철제 레인지 *gusik cheolje reinji*.	Affirm
	It's a special type of fireplace, isn't it? It is described as a range (레인지 *reinji*), made out of iron (철제 *cheolje*) and which is old-fashioned (구식 *gusik*).	Elaborate grammar

7.2 Teaching Korean as a Foreign Language

S/he now turns to the Process function (13).

(13)

Teacher	At the end of the clause, we have a special verb, also called a copula, which says 'something is'.	Prepare clause
	Can you see it?	Focus on wording
Student	였다 *y-eot-da*.	Identify wording
Teacher	Perfect. Exactly right. Highlight 였다 *y-eot-da*.	Affirm
	We have seen 였다 *y-eot-da* many times before. It means 'something was', and here the something is 구식 철제 레인지 *gusik cheolje reinji*. This is one of the two ways that Korean clauses that describe things work. We put a noun and then add a copula.	Elaborate grammar

The next sentence has one clause and is the other type of attributive clause, involving the conflated Attribute/Process function (14).

(14)

화덕은 좀 더러웠다.			
hwadeog	=*eun*	*jom*	*deoreow-ot-da*
oven		a bit	unclean
P1:Carrier		Mod Adj	Attribute/Process
ng		adv	vg
Thing	TFM		Event
noun	clitic		verbalised adjective
			Head / TM / EM
			stem / sfx / sfx
'The ovens were a bit unclean.'			

The teacher would begin again by getting the students to identify the wording realising the Carrier and Attribute functions (15).

(15)

Teacher	This clause describes the ovens, which as we see in the photo are attached to both sides of the range.	Prepare clause
	The clause begins by referring to the ovens. Can you see the words that refer to the ovens? The last one of the words is 은 *eun*.	Focus on wording
Student	화덕은 *hwadeog eun* 'the stove'	Identify wording
Teacher	Yes. Highlight 화덕은 *hwadeog eun*.	Affirm
	The word 은 *eun* makes the ovens prominent, because we are shifting our focus from the range to the ovens.	Elaborate grammar
	At the end of the clause, the verb gives us some more information.	Prepare clause
	Can you see the verbalised adjective there? It ends with 웠다 *w-ot-da*.	Focus on wording
Student	더러웠다 *deoreow-ot-da* 'was unclean'	Identify wording
Teacher	Perfect. Exactly right. Highlight 더러웠다 *deoreow-ot-da*.	Affirm
	In Korean we turn adjectives into verbs at the end of clauses, don't we? So here the adjective 더럽다 *deoreop-da* is conjugated as a verb by adding 웠다 *w-ot-da* to the stem.	Elaborate grammar
	What's another adjective we could have used as a verb here whose stem ends in ㅂ *p*?	Focus on wording
Student	무거웠다 *mugeow-ot-da* 'heavy', maybe?	Propose wording
Teacher	Good.	Affirm
	Another one, whose stem does not end in ㅂ *p*?	Focus on wording
Student	깨끗했다 *kkaekkeuta-et-da* 'clean'	Propose wording
Teacher	Very good.	Affirm
	This is the other way Korean clauses that describe things work. They start with the thing you are describing, like our ovens here, and they end with the description – an adjective turned into a verb.	Elaborate grammar

7.2 Teaching Korean as a Foreign Language

The next sentence in (16) is a locative clause, which can be handled very similarly to the locative clause (7). The structural differences are that (16) is not a dependent clause (but (7) is) and that (16) includes the Manner Circumstance (많이 *mani* 'a lot'). Because we are dealing now with a second example of this locative clause type, a teacher might use elaboration moves to introduce elements of our functional description of this clause type – naming the Location and Located functions, for example.

(16)

난로 안에 하얀 재가 많이 있었다.							
nallo	an	=e	haya-n	jae	=ga	mani	iss-eot-da
stove	inside	LOC	white	ash		a lot	was present
α							
clause (locative)							
P3:Location			P1:Located			Cir: Manner	Process
ng			ng			advg	vg
Thing	Perspective	EFM	Epithet	Thing	EFM	Grader	Event
noun	bound noun	clitic	adjective	noun	clitic	adverb	verb
			Head	Link			Head	TM	EM
			stem	sfx			stem	sfx	sfx
'In the stove there was a lot of white ash.'							

This is followed by another locative clause; but this time the Process indicates that lots of logs are being located (17).

(17)

난로 앞에는 작은 통나무가 많았다.							
nallo	ap	=e	=neun	jag-eun	tongnamu	=ga	man-at-da
stove	front	LOC		small	log		were lots
P3:Location				P1:Located			Process
ng				ng			vg
Thing	Perspective	EFM	TFM	Epithet	Thing	EFM	Event
noun	bound noun	clitic	clitic	adjective	noun	clitic	verb
				Head	Link			Head	TM	EM
				stem	sfx			stem	sfx	sfx
'In front of the stove there were lots of small logs.'							

The teacher could begin again by getting the students to identify the wording realising the Location and Located functions (18).

(18)

Teacher	The next sentence tells us that there were a number of small logs in front of the stove.	Prepare clause
	It begins with the location. Can you see the words that tell us where the logs were?	Focus on wording
Student	난로 앞에는 *nallo ap e neun* 'in front of the stove'	Identify wording
Teacher	That's right. Highlight 난로 앞에는 *nallo ap e neun*.	Affirm
	The little word 에 *e* marks the location, here; and the word 는 *neun* makes the location prominent, because we are shifting our focus from the sides to in front of the stove.	Elaborate grammar
	Can you see the following words that tell us what we are locating?	Focus on wording
Student	작은 통나무가 *jag-eun tongnamu ga* 'small logs'	Identify wording
Teacher	Good. Highlight 작은 통나무가 *jag-eun tongnamu ga*.	Affirm
	The 가 *ga* tells us that the small logs are what we are locating.	Elaborate grammar

The teacher can now focus on the different types of locating verb in Korean – beginning by drawing attention to the difference between *it-da* 'be present' and *man-ta* 'be lots' (19).

7.2 Teaching Korean as a Foreign Language

(19)

Teacher	Now look at the last word, the verb.	Focus on wording
Student	많았다 man-at-da 'there were many'.	Identify wording
Teacher	Well done. Highlight 많았다 man-at-da.	Affirm
	Earlier in the text we had 있다 it-da 'there is/are' as our locating verb; but now we have 많다 man-ta. Can anyone see the difference?	Elaborate grammar
	How does 있다 it-da contrast with 많다 man-ta?	Focus on wording
Student	Does it have to do with how many things we are locating?	Propose
Teacher	Very clever!	Affirm
	In Korean we can use the locating verb to signal whether we are locating one thing or many. We can use 많다 man-ta for many things, and if there are just a few, we can use 적다 jeok-da 'there are few'.	Elaborate grammar

The next sentence is yet another locative clause; but this time the Process indicates that there was no kindling (20).

(20)

불쏘시개는 없었다.				
bulssosigae	neun	eops-eot-da		
kindling		was absent		
P1:Located		Process		
ng		vg		
Thing	TFM	Event		
noun	clitic	verb		
		Head	TM	EM
		stem	sfx	sfx
'There was no kindling.'				

This gives the teacher an opportunity to focus students' attention on another locative verb, 없다 eop-da 'there isn't/aren't', which is used to signal the absence of things (21).

(21)

Teacher	Now, the next sentence tells us that there wasn't in fact any kindling by the fireplace; there were just small logs. Maybe all the kindling had been used up.	Prepare clause
	Can you see the words that refer to the kindling? The first two words.	Focus on wording
Student	불쏘시개는 *bulssosigae neun* 'kindling'	Identify wording
Teacher	That's right. Highlight 불쏘시개는 *bulssosigae neun*.	Affirm
	And the rest of the sentence is the verb.	Focus on wording
Student	없었다 *eops-eot-da* 'there wasn't/weren't'	Identify wording
Teacher	Excellent.	Affirm
	This is a negative verb, isn't it? It tells us there wasn't any kindling. So when we are locating things in Korean, we often use 있다 *it-da*. But if we want to be explicit about how many we can use 많다 *man-ta* for many things and 적다 *jeok-da* for a few. And if we expect there to be something but there isn't any, we use 없다 *eop-da*.	Elaborate grammar

The next clause, (22), introduces the chair next to the stove. It is a locative clause like (7) and (17) and so can be treated in the same way. As for (17), repeated consideration of the same clause type creates opportunities for teachers to extend the technicality of the discussion, drawing on our grammar – noting for example how this clause type treats the Location as positioning Theme and Located as angling Theme (see Chapter 5).

(22)

난로 옆에 낡은 의자가 있었다.								
nallo	*yeop*	*=e*	*nalgeu-n*	*uija*	*=ga*	*iss-eot-da*		
stove	next	LOC	old	chair		was present		
P3:Location			P1:Located			Process		
ng			ng			vg		
Thing	Perspective	EFM	Epithet	Thing	EFM	Event		
noun	bound noun	clitic	adjective	noun	clitic	verb		
			Head	Link		Head	TM	EM
			stem	sfx		stem	sfx	sfx
'Next to the stove there was an old chair.'								

7.2 Teaching Korean as a Foreign Language

The final sentence in this text (23) once again has two clauses, in this case an attributive clause projected by a verbal one. Its attributive clause has a (Carrier) Attribute Process structure, like that in (16) – once again with an elliptical Carrier. The teacher could use this clause to reinforce the difference between a P0:Attribute realised by a nominal group and a conflated Attribute/Process structure like that in (14).

(23)

전에는 아름다운 의자였다고								
jeon	=e	=neun	areumda-un		uija	y-eot-da-go		
before	LOC		beautiful		chair	was		

"β								
clause (attributive)								
Cir:Location:time			P0:Attribute			Process		
ng			ng			vg		
Thing	EFM	TFM	Epithet		Thing	Event		
noun	clitic	clitic	adjective		noun	copula		
			Head	Link		Head	TM	PMM	Link
			stem	sfx		stem	sfx	sfx	sfx
'(that it) had been a beautiful chair previously …								

코델리아는 말했다.					
Kodellia	=neun	malha-et-da			
Cordelia		said			
Theme		Rheme			
α					
clause (verbal)					
P1:Sayer		Process			
ng		vg			
Thing	TFM	Event			
noun	clitic	verb			
		Head	TM	EM	
		stem	sfx	sfx	
Cordelia said.'					

As a next step the teacher could move on to a Joint Rewriting step in the pedagogy. This would involve a student scribe listing the highlighted Korean words and phrases in Hangeul on a white board or smart board at the front of the class – scribing suggestions offered by peers (with prompts from the teacher as required). This creates opportunities for the teacher to make further comments on the grammar and help students with their Hangeul spelling if required. The next step would be to jointly construct a new version of the description drawing on the list of highlighted wordings – with students making suggestions as another student scribes the new text on the white board or smart board. This could be followed by individual writing – possibly, if students are ready, a description of a room with another kind of fireplace or perhaps a modern stove. The ultimate aim of the pedagogy is of course to enable all the students in the class to be able to read and write a short descriptive text in Korean, involving a range of locative and attributive relational clauses.

Readers will have noticed that in the teaching/learning cycles illustrated above, the terminology developed in our grammar of Korean was only gradually and selectively introduced. Ideally the teacher would have benefited by drawing on our grammar to develop the tasks; but in our examples s/he tended to rely on just a few traditional terms to explain Korean locative and attributive clauses. We exemplified our pedagogy in this way because we want to leave open the important issue of how much technicality teachers need to know and share with their students. This depends of course on the opportunities a teacher has had to study our grammar and how s/he feels about the importance of explicitly sharing knowledge about language with students. The main point we want to make is that this knowledge should not be provided in a lecture about Korean relational clauses. Rather it should be introduced gradually, in teaching/learning cycles like those illustrated above – making use of Preparation and Elaboration moves around tasks that students are successfully prepared to accomplish and for which they constantly receive positive affirmation. The basic philosophy of Reading to Learn is that whenever students' struggle with a task, it is up to their teachers to adjust their teaching/learning cycles so that no student is left behind.

Having made this point, it is important to draw attention to the inner circle activities outlined in Figure 7.3. It is here that the pedagogy creates opportunities for an explicit focus on structures that need special attention – beyond what is possible in teaching/learning cycles like those illustrated above. At teachers' discretion, a more explicit uptake of the technicality of our grammar could be enacted there. Jones and Lock (2011) provide a number of useful suggestions for teaching grammar in context along these lines.

As Korean readers will appreciate, when we simplified the Korean translation of the P. D. James text we avoided one type of structure used by the translator when translating English existential clauses – which we felt was too

7.2 Teaching Korean as a Foreign Language

challenging for the task to hand. It does however create a relevant bridge to our section on translation and interpreting below. This structure is illustrated in both clauses of (24). Taken at face value this structure involves a receptive material clause whose Process is realised through a diminished verbal group (쌓였고 *ssa-y-eot-go* 'was piled up' and 놓였다 *no-y-eot-da* 'was placed'). Accordingly the Undergoer is marked as P1 (재가 *jae ga* 'ash' and 의자가 *uija ga* 'a chair'). And each clause has a Circumstance of Location as Theme.

(24)

난로 안에 재가 쌓였고 ...									
nallo	*an*		=*e*		*jae*	=*ga*	*ssa-y-eot-go*		
stove	inside				ash		was piled up		
1									
clause (material)									
Theme									
Cir:Location					P1:Undergoer		Process		
ng					ng		vg		
Thing	Perspective		EFM		Thing	EFM	Event		
noun	bound noun		clitic		noun	clitic	verb		
							Head	VM	TM	Link
							stem	sfx	sfx	sfx
'Inside the stove a mound of ash was piled up and ...'									

난로 한쪽 옆에 의자가 놓였다.									
nallo	*hanjjok*	*yeop*	=*e*		*uija*	=*ga*	*no-y-eot-da*		
stove	one side	next			chair		was placed		
+2									
clause (material)									
Theme									
Cir:Location					P1:Undergoer		Process		
ng					ng		vg		
Thing	Perspective		EFM		Thing	EFM	Event		
noun	word complex		clitic		noun	clitic	verb		
	β	α					Head	VM	TM	Link
	noun	noun					stem	sfx	sfx	sfx
'... on one side of the stove was placed a chair.'									

The discourse semantic function of receptive material clauses of this kind is very similar to that of the locative clauses we focused on above – so much so that it is tempting to see these clauses as a kind of blend of material and locative (notated 'material/locative'). A blended analysis is suggested as (25) (we've adjusted the translations toward the locative clause reading).

(25)

난로 안에 재가 쌓였고 ...								
nallo	*an*	*=e*	*jae*	*=ga*	*ssa-y-eot-go*			
stove	inside		ash		was piled up			
1								
clause (material/locative)								
Theme								
Cir/P3:Location			P1:Undergoer/Located		Process			
ng			ng		vg			
Thing	Perspective	EFM	Thing	EFM	Event			
noun	noun	clitic	noun	clitic	verb			
						Head	VM	TM	Link
						stem	sfx	sfx	sfx
'There was a mound of ash in the stove and ...'								

난로 한쪽 옆에 의자가 놓였다.								
nallo	*hanjjok*	*yeop*	*=e*	*uija*	*=ga*	*no-y-eot-da*		
stove	one side	next		chair		was placed		
+2								
clause (material/locative)								
Theme								
Cir/P3:Location				P1:Undergoer/Located		Process		
ng				ng		vg		
Thing	Perspective		EFM	Thing	EFM	Event		
noun	word complex		clitic	noun	clitic	verb		
	β	α						
	noun	noun				Head	VM	TM	Link
						stem	sfx	sfx	sfx
'... on one side of the stove was a chair.'								

7.2 Teaching Korean as a Foreign Language

Another good example of a blended material/locative structure of this kind can be found in the original Korean translation of the P. D. James text (26).

(26)

난로 한쪽 옆에는 통나무도 마련되어 있었다.										
nallo	hanjjok	yeop	=e	=neun	tongnamu	=do	maryeondoe-eo	iss-eot-da		
stove	one side	next			log	too	prepared	were		
clause (material/locative)										
Theme					Rheme					
Cir/P3:Location					P1:Undergoer/Located		Process			
ng					ng		vg			
Thing	Perspective		EFM	TFM	Thing	IFM	Event	Dimension		
noun	word complex		clitic	clitic	noun	clitic	verb	aux verb		
	α	β						Head	Link	Head	TM	EM
	noun	noun						stem	sfx	stem	sfx	sfx
'On one side of the stove, there were logs prepared too.'										

The 'passive' verb 마련되 *maryeondoe-* 'be prepared' and the suffix 어 *-eo* along with the verbal group Dimension function (realised by 있 *iss-*) is an important part of this structure – clearly pushing toward a relational clause reading (with the meaning 'a continuing situation which is the result of some action').

Similar examples abound immediately before and after the excerpt we studied. We list just three of them (27), (28) and (29).

(27)

문 앞에 장화가 놓여 있었다.									
mun	ap	=e	janghwa	=ga	no-y-eo		iss-eot-da		
door	front	at	boots		placed		were		
Cir/P3:Location			P1:Undergoer/Located		Process				
ng			ng		vg				
					Event		Dimension		
					verb		aux verb		
					Head	VM	Link	Head	TM	EM
					stem	sfx	sfx	stem	sfx	sfx
'In front of the door were placed boots.'									

(28)

가운데에 쇠고리가 박혀 있었는데 ...									
gaunde	*=e*	*soegori*	*=ga*	*bak-y-eo*					*iss-eon-neunde*
middle	in	iron hook		pegged					was
Cir/P3: Location		P1:Undergoer/ Located		Process						
ng		ng		vg						
				Event				Dimension	
				verb				aux verb	
				Head	VM	Link	Head	TM	Link
				stem	sfx	sfx	stem	sfx	sfx
'In the middle was pegged a butcher hook ...'									

(29)

난로에 재가 쌓여 있었다.									
nalo	*e*	*jae*	*ga*	*ssa-y-eo*					*iss-eot-da*
stove	in	ash		mounded					was
Cir/P3: Location		P1: Undergoer/ Located		Process						
ng		ng		vg						
				Event				Dimension	
				verb				aux verb	
				Head	VM	Link	Head	TM	EM
				stem	sfx	sfx	stem	sfx	sfx
'In the stove were mounded ashes.'									

We would predict that this clause type would certainly be favoured by translators for English existential clauses such as the following:

> *On the table (there) sat a vase of flowers.*
> *In the corner (there) stood a coat rack.*
> *On the wall (there) hung a portrait of the owner.*

Such clauses do not have natural middle material equivalents in Korean, so a receptive material clause with a diminished verbal group (beefed up by an aspectual Dimension) is an attractive alternative. Contrastive analysis of this

7.3 Translation and Interpreting Korean

kind, focusing as it does on complementary systems and structures across languages, brings us to the next section of our applications chapter – which deals with translation and interpreting Korean.

7.3 Translation and Interpreting Korean

The most influential early application of SFL to translating and interpreting is Catford (1965) – although the earliest discussion is Halliday (1962). Since then it has provided a critical lens through which a number of questions about translation have been explored (e.g., Steiner and Yallop 2001). Ongoing developments are canvassed in Kim et al. (2021) and Wang and Ma (2020, 2021, 2022). The discussion of translation and interpreting in this section focuses on how our functional description of Korean grammar can be used for both practical and research purposes in translation and interpreting studies.

There is general agreement about the theoretical notion that translating is a process of making choices (e.g., Catford 1965, Munday 2016, Steiner and Yallop 2001, Vinay and Darbelnet 1958) and that it involves prioritising a particular aspect of meaning in a given context whenever translating the multi-dimensional meaning of the source text 'literally' into a target text is not possible (e.g., Kim 2009). But appreciating and justifying specific choices made at the lexicogrammar level in a given translation remains a challenge. This makes it difficult to discuss translation choices constructively. One scholar or practitioner may think a particular translation choice is well-motivated; but another may think there has been an unnecessary shift or even an unacceptable choice that distorts the meaning of the source text.

Our grammar has been written as a resource that can be drawn on when such disagreements arise – because it provides an explicit description of the meaning potential of Korean grammar. With this description, we can consider translation choices constructively by discussing the impact they make on specific aspects of meaning rather than entering into a frustrating debate involving unreconcilable opinions about what is right or wrong. In other words, our grammar is designed to enable translators to understand the choices that are available and make informed choices in a given context. In this section we will illustrate how our grammar can be used to understand choices made in one interpreted text and one translated text – texts that reinstantiate Korean into English.

7.3.1 Interpretation Example

We begin with an interpretation that was broadcast around the world in February 2020 when Director Bong Joon-ho won the Best Director Oscar for his dark social satire 'Parasite'. He made a short speech right after his win was announced during the Oscar Award Presentations night; and his remarks were interpreted consecutively.[2] We will analyse two excerpts (30) and (31), in which we can observe numerous shifts. Matthiessen (2001) suggests five types of shift – shifts between metafunctions, shifts within a metafunction, shifts in rank, shifts in delicacy and shifts in structure (cf. Figure 7.1). Here we will focus on shifts in metafunction.

In the excerpts (Seong 2020), Bong's Korean speech is presented first, followed by a literal translation and the interpretation (without any grammatical analysis). Following this presentation we zero in on shifts made in the interpretation. The literal translations provided here are close to a word-for-word translation, involving structure that English speakers can make sense of.

The most conspicuous shifts made in the interpretation in (30) have to do with logical meaning (shifts in clause complexing). Bong's speech reflects the nature of spoken Korean, where there is a tendency to combine a series of clauses into a single clause complex. His clause complex was broken up in the interpretation – as two complexes and one simplex (we base this analysis on the absence of linking conjunctions and the interpreter's intonation).

(30)

> Bong: 제가 학교에서 마틴 영화를 보면서 공부했던 그런 사람인데 같이 후보에 오른 것만도 영광인데 상을 받을 줄 정말 몰랐었구요 예...
>
> Literal translation: I am the kind of person who studied in school watching Martin's films and being nominated together itself is a huge honour and really (I) didn't know (I) would receive the award yeah...
>
> Interpreter: When I was in school, I studied Martin Scorsese's films. Just to be nominated was a huge honour. I never thought I would win.

In (31) we provide a clause complex analysis of the Korean source text. Bong's speech involves a clause complex (31.I) consisting of three clauses (numbered 31.i, 31.ii, 31.iii). Bong links his clauses together with the connector ㄴ데 -nde – a signal that significant information is forthcoming (see Chapter 6, Section 6.4.4.1). As shown in (31), his first clause is dependent on his second, and these two together are dependent on his third – a =β (=β α) α structure.

---

[2] In consecutive interpreting, the interpreter starts interprets as the speaker pauses. This contrasts with simultaneous interpretation, where the interpreter interprets in real-time.

7.3 Translation and Interpreting Korean

(31) Logical relations in the first part of Bong's speech

Clause complex	Clause	Logical structure		Korean and literal translation
I	i	=β	=β	제가 [[학교에서 마틴 영화를 보면서 공부했던]] 그런 사람인데 *je ga [[xβ hakgyo =eseo Matin yeonghwa =reul bo-myeonseo α gongbuha-et-deon]] geureon saram i- nde* I am the kind of person [[who studied while watching Martin's films in school]]
	ii		α	같이 후보에 오른 것만도 영광인데 *[[gachi hubo =e oreu-n geot =man =do]] yeonggwang i-nde* [[being nominated together itself]] is an honour
	iii		α	상을 받을 줄 정말 몰랐었구요 *[[sang =eul bad-eul jul]] jeongmal moll-ass-eot-gu yo* (I) wasn't really aware [[that (I) would receive the award]]

In (32) we provide a clause complex analysis of the Korean interpretation. The interpretation unfolds as three clause complexes (32.I, 32.II, 32.III). The first clause complex (32.I) comprises two clauses in an enhancing relationship (32.i and 32.ii). The second (32.II) comprises one clause (32.iii). The third (32.III) comprises two clauses (32.iv and 32.v) in a projecting relationship. Bong's first clause (31.i) is reworked as an enhancing clause complex in the interpretation (32.I), with information he had embedded in a nominal group Qualifier (i.e., 학교에서 마틴 영화를 보면서 공부했던 *hakgyo eseo Matin yeonghwa reul bo-myeonseo gongbuha-et-deon*, 'who studied while watching Martin's films in school') now distributed across two ranking clauses (32.i and 32.ii). For Bong's second and third clauses the opposite move is made. His dependent clause (31.ii) is turned into a clause simplex (32.iii) and his dominant clause (31.iii) is turned into a projecting clause complex (32.iv and 32.v).

(32) Logical relations in the interpretation of the first part of Bong's speech

Clause simplex/ complex	Clause	Logical structure	Interpretation
I	i	xβ	When I was in school,
	ii	α	I studied Martin Scorsese's films.
II	iii		Just to be nominated was a huge honour.
III	iv	α	I never thought
	v	'β	I would win.

In addition, the interpreter treated the embedded clause in clause (31.iii) of the source text (i.e., 상을 받을 줄 *sang eul bad-eul jul* 'would receive (the) award') as a dependent ranking projected clause 'I would win' (32.v).

We can also observe shifts in experiential, interpersonal and textual meaning. In (31.iii) there is an embedded clause 상을 받을 줄 *sang eul bad-eul jul* '[[that (I) would receive the award]]'. In the interpretation is an experiential shift in DIATHESIS (32.v) – from effective (with an Actor (Bong) and Undergoer (the award)) in the source text to middle (just an Actor, Bong) in the interpretation – eliding what Bong won (which is of course obvious given the context of the presentation ceremony). This shift is analysed in (33) and (34). The interpreter used *I* in her projecting clause complex (32.III), which was not explicit in the source text (31.iii). This choice reflects the fact that English needs a Subject to show declarative mood (Halliday and Matthiessen 2014: Chapter 4), while Korean does not (see Chapter 3 of this volume). This interpersonal shift in turn causes a shift in textual meaning – from an elided topical Theme in Korean to an explicit topical Theme in English.

(33)   Transitivity analysis of clause (31.iii) of the source text (with an embedded idea)

상을 받을 줄 정말 몰랐어구요.						
[[sang	=eul	bad-eul	jul]]	jeongmal	moll-ass-eot-gu	yo
award		receive		really	didn't know	
P2:Phenomenon					Process	
[[clause]]³					vg	
P2:Undergoer		Process				
ng		vg				
Thing	EFM	Event	Installing			
noun	clitic	verb	bound noun			
… (I) really didn't know (I) would receive the award.'						

(34)   Multifunctional analyses of clauses (32.iv) and (32.v) of the target text (with a projected idea)

I	never	thought	I	would	win
α			'β		
Senser		Process	Actor	Process	
Subject	Mood Adjunct	Finite/Predicator	Subject	Finite	Predicator
Theme	Rheme		Theme	Rheme	

Logical metafunction shifts are also present in the interpretation of Bong's next utterance (following (31)). His wording, a literal translation and its interpretation are presented in (35).

---

[3] As in Chapter 6, we have simplified the analysis by embedding the idea directly in the Phenomenon.

402 Two Applications

(35)
> Bong: 그, 저의 영화를 미국의 관객들이나 사람들이 모를 때 항상 제 영화를 리스트에 뽑고 좋아했던 우리 퀜틴 형님이 계신데, 정말 사랑합니다.
>
> Literal translation: Well, our Big Brother Quentin who put my films on his list and liked (them) when audiences or people in the US did not know them is here, (I) really love you.
>
> Interpreter: When people in the US were not familiar with my films, Quentin always put my films on his list. He's here. Thank you so much.
>
> Bong: Quentin, I love you!

There are two ranking clauses in the source text in (35). Their relationship is analysed in (36).

(36) Logical relations in the second part of Bong's speech

Clause complex	Clause	Logical structure	Korean and literal translation
I	i	=β	그, [[embedded clause complex]] 우리 퀜틴 형님이 계신데, [[embedded clause complex]] *uri Kwentin Hyeong-nim =i gyesi-nde* Well, [[embedded clause complex]] our Big Brother Quentin is here,
	ii	α	정말 사랑합니다. *jeongmal sarangha-mnida* (I) really love you.

As noted, the first clause (36.i) includes a long embedded clause complex – 저의 영화를 미국의 관객들이나 사람들이 모를 때 항상 제 영화를 리스트에 뽑고 좋아했던, *jeo ui yeonghwa reul migug ui gwangaek-deur ina saram-deur i moreu-l ttae hangsang je yeonghwa reul riseuteu e ppop-go joaha-et-deon* 'who put my films on his list and liked (them) when audiences or people in the US did not know them'. A clause complex analysis of the embedded clause is provided in (37).

7.3 Translation and Interpreting Korean

(37)

Clause	Logical structure	Korean and literal translation
i	xβ	저의 영화를 미국의 관객들이나 사람들이 모를 때 *jeo =ui yeonghwa =reul migug =ui gwangaek-deur =ina saram-deur =i moreu-l ttae* when audiences or people in the US did not know my films
ii	α	α	항상 제 영화를 리스트에 뽑고 *hangsang je yeonghwa =reul riseuteu =e ppop-go* put my films on his list and
iii		+β	좋아했던 *joaha-et-deon* liked

The interpretation of (36) is presented as (38). As we can see the elaborating clause complex in the source text (36.i and ii) was interpreted as an enhancing clause complex (38.i and ii) and two simplexes in the target text (38.iii and iv). Information that was embedded in the source text (37) is rendered as two ranking clauses in the target text (clause complex I). The rest of the information in (36) (i.e., the information that was not embedded) is interpreted as a clause simplex (II). And clause (36.ii) from the source text is presented on its own as a clause simplex (III). The last clause in the embedded clause (37.iii), 좋아했던 *joaha-et-deon* 'liked', was not interpreted.

(38)

Clause simplex/ complex	Clause	Logical structure	Interpretation
I	i	xβ	When people in the US were not familiar with my films,
	ii	α	Quentin always put my films on his list.
II	iii		He's here.
III	iv		Thank you so much.

The interpreter also makes some interesting shifts in interpersonal meaning. Bong's second excerpt is not straightforward to interpret in English because the two languages have different VOCATION system options and these options are used differently in apparently comparable contexts. For one thing, Bong referred to Quentin Tarantino as 우리 퀜틴형님 *uri Kwentin Hyeong-nim* 'our Big Brother Quentin'. Bong's choice is influenced by Korean culture, wherein people often use kinship terms to address one another and talk about each other as they get close to one another; in addition Bong uses 우리 *uri* 'our' to mark a close relationship. This vocative was presented as *Quentin* in the interpretation. The interpreter appears to have tried to convey a degree of interpersonal solidarity by calling Quentin by his first name, as someone's first name is an important resource used to indicate solidarity in many English-speaking cultures. In addition Bong used the verb 계시- *gyesi-* 'be (respectful)', a choice that draws on the PARTICIPANT DEFERENCE system to show respect to Tarantino; this enactment of respect is lost in the interpretation.

There is also a shift from an experiential mental clause in the source text to a minor clause in the interpretation (a leave-taking formula). Bong said 정말 사랑합니다 *jeongmal sarangha-mnida* '(I) really love (you)', which enacts a high degree of affection for Tarantino. But this was interpreted as 'Thank you so much'. As soon as the interpreter finished her turn, Bong, perhaps noticing this shift, added in English, 'Quentin, I love you!'

In this section, we have discussed various shifts made in the interpretation, drawing on the grammatical descriptions provided in our book – without attempting to evaluate the quality of the interpretation. Such value-neutral analysis is a useful starting point for exploration of a number of interesting research questions. For instance, one could explore how interpreters perceived their role and the nature of expectations by others – including the commissioner who initiates and pays for the interpreting service, and the Source Text audience and the Target Text audience.[4] Such studies would need to collect additional data (e.g., through interviews, surveys or focus groups) such as that employed in the study discussed in the next section.

7.3.2 Translation Examples

We now focus on translation choices that have an impact on textual meaning – drawing on a study by Kim (2011), which shows how translation choices that give textual prominence to different meanings have elicited different reactions from target readers.

A survey was conducted with 42 native speakers of English with the two versions of translation presented in (39). The source text for the translations is the beginning part of a Korean short story titled *On the Overhead Bridge* by Cho Se-hui (Buzo 1980). Translation 1 (T1) is an English native speaker's translation published in the *Korea Journal* in 1980. Translation 1 was revised

---

[4] This particular interpreter has been highly praised by many, including Director Bong who has described her as 'the best interpreter' on YouTube and mass media (e.g., www.youtube.com/watch?v=xvvK_JOJbrQ).

7.3 Translation and Interpreting Korean

by one of our authors (Kim) as Translation 2 (T2), maintaining the ideational and interpersonal meanings constant while varying the content of two of the three Theme choices. The survey questionnaire is presented below.

(39) The following texts are two versions of translation of the beginning of a Korean short story. Please read them and answer the questions below:

Translation 1
Sinae was walking in the centre of Seoul, distracted. All she could see in front of her were people, buildings and cars. On the pavement the smell of oil, the smell of people and the smell of scorched rubber hung in the air. Just to stand still and look about her would take an effort. People packed the pavement, cars packed the street. There was no place to stop, no place to stop even for a few seconds to try to control her depression.

Translation 2
Sinae was walking in the centre of Seoul, distracted. All she could see in front of her were people, buildings and cars. On the pavement the smell of oil, the smell of people and the smell of scorched rubber hung in the air. Just to stand still and look about her would take an effort. The pavement was overflowing with people, the road was overflowing with cars. There was no place for her, no place for her to stop even for a few seconds to try to control her depression.

1. Which version do you prefer?
2. Please specify reasons for your preference.

7.3.2.1 Survey Results

As Table 7.1 shows, only 19 per cent of those surveyed did not have a preference for one translation or the other. Even though the two texts were very short and almost identical except for a few Theme choices 81 per cent had a preference. The preferences were distributed unevenly. There was a strong preference for the second version, 55 per cent versus 26 per cent.

Table 7.1 *Results of the Survey*

Preference	No. of people	Percentage
Translation 1	11	26
Translation 2	23	55
No preference	8	19
Total	42	100

What is even more interesting than the quantitative data is the findings from a qualitative analysis of the various reasons mentioned for the survey participants' preferences; these are shown in Tables 7.2 and 7.3.

Table 7.2 *Reasons for Preferring Translation 1*

Reasons	No. of respondents
Concise and short expression	7
Better way to describe traffic and busy pavements	7
Text flows well	3
Sense of alienation	2
Impression of immediacy	2

Table 7.3 *Reasons for Preferring Translation 2*

Reasons	No. of respondents
Text flows well	10
Nice link with the main character and the circumstance	9
Very emotive	6
More graphic and evocative	4
Greater sense of exclusion	3
More engaging	2
Makes the scene seem busier	1

Table 7.2 shows that 26 per cent of those surveyed preferred T1 because (a) they liked its concise and short expressions – such as *packed* (7) and (b) they could better appreciate the 'harsh' and 'suffocating' circumstances of the traffic and busy pavements (7). On the other hand, 55 per cent of those surveyed preferred T2 because it 'seems to flow and reads more cohesively' (10). Also a number of survey participants pointed out that the choice of 'for her' in the last sentence of the second version helped them better understand both the situation and the character's feelings (9).

There was an interesting response from one participant who did not have a strong preference but liked different aspects of each translation. Because he liked both the choice of 'packed' in T1 and the choice of 'for her' in T2, he could not choose between them. He wrote:

I have a slight preference for the sentence that uses *packed* in T1 rather than *overflowing* in T2 as *the pavement was overflowing with people* [...] T2 sounds a little over-descriptive somehow, making the repetition here cumbersome. *People packed the pavement* [...] is more compact and 'tight', I think, and so the repetition works better. I have a slight preference, however, for the final sentence in T2, as I think the phrase *there was no place for HER* [...] is more powerful than *there was no place to stop* [...] – the sentence in T2 creates the impression of a street scene in which Sinae, with her private needs, did not have a place.

Two main points emerge from the responses from the survey. The first is the issue of word choice: *packed* versus *overflowing*. As mentioned above, most of the respondents liked *packed*; but more than half of them regarded it as less important than the overall flow of the text. The second is the issue of style versus flow – that is, whether a reader would prefer a text on the basis of stylistic effects alone or on the basis of a coherent textual flow. One respondent who liked the second version stated her criteria very clearly:

As this is a piece of descriptive prose, I'm considering more the effectiveness of communication rather than the correctness of grammar. As Sinae is feeling depressed, the author's job is to convey the individual's mental experience. The author uses Sinae's perceptions of her surroundings to convey her feelings of depression.

This statement provides a succinct summary of translation issues involved in this particular study – namely, the translator's need to take into account the purpose and effect of the source text in creating his/her translation.

7.3.2.2 Analysis We will now focus on the Theme choices in the source text and the translations. In the source text (provided in (40)), an analysis of the clausal Themes shows an interesting thematic progression in the beginning of the short story. The author starts the story from Sinae's perspective by choosing *Sinae* as an angling Theme in clause (40.1). As explained in Chapter 5 (see Section 5.2.1), the angling Theme establishes a particular gaze on a field and sustains it while that gaze is appropriate. An angling Theme is marked by the TFM 은/는 *eun/neun* when it is expected within the context and is called an anticipated Theme in our grammar. When not predictable, it is marked by the P1 EFM 이/가 *i/ga* or the P2 EFM 을/를 *eul/reul*, which results in a non-anticipated Theme. Interestingly, the angling Theme chosen in the very first clause is an anticipated angling Theme marked by 는 *neun* – as if the reader already knows whose story it is from the outset. This is not unusual in narrative genres (e.g., a short story or novel), designed to draw the reader into the tale. This Theme is elided in clause (40.2), which is a very common way of realising an anticipated Theme if the same Theme is selected in immediately following clauses.

Clauses (40.4), (40.6) and (40.7) include positioning Themes; 거리에서는 *geori eseo neun* 'on the street' in clause (40.4), 인도에 *indo e* 'on the pavement' in clause (40.6) and 차도에 *chado e* 'on the road' in clause (40.7); each is followed by a non-anticipated Theme. Such Themes establish an angle on the field through a particular Circumstance of Location in time or space (see

Chapter 5, Section 5.2.2) and shift the angle from Sinae in clauses (40.1) and (40.2) to the places in clauses (40.4), (40.6) and (40.7). The last two clauses are possessive relational clauses with the Possessor Sinae elided (40.8) and (40.9). As detailed in Chapter 5, Section 5.6, when the Possessor is elided but recoverable from the co-text, it plays the role of anticipated topical Theme. Therefore Sinae is the topical Theme in the relational clauses (40.8) and (40.9). These Theme choices create a camera-like panning effect, starting with Sinae, moving on to her environs and returning to Sinae again; this helps the reader relate the busy street to Sinae's depressed feelings.

(40)   Korean source text with a close to literal translation

Cl. No.	Theme(s)			Rheme		
1		신애는		시내 중심가를 걸으며		
		Sinae =neun		sinae jungsimga =reul		geor-eumyeo
		Sinae		the centre of the city		was walking
		P1:Actor		P2:Entity-Range		Process
	Sinae was walking in the centre of the city (while)					
2		(Sinae)		정신을 차릴 수 없었다.		
		(Sinae)		jeongsin =eul		chari-l su eops-eot-da
		(Sinae)		(her) mind		couldn't focus
		P1:Actor		P2:Entity-Range		Process
	(she) couldn't focus her mind (i.e., couldn't concentrate).					
3		[[그녀가 볼 수 있는]] 것은		사람, 건물, 자동차 뿐이었다.		
		[[geunyeo =ga bo-l su in-neun]] geos =eun		saram, geonmul, jadongcha ppun		i-eot-da
		What she could see		people, buildings and cars only		were
		P1:Value		P0:Token		Process
	What she could see was only people, buildings and cars.					
4	거리에서는	기름 타는 냄새, 사람 냄새, 고무 타는 냄새가		났다.		
	geori eseo =neun	gireum ta-neun naemsae, gomu ta-neun naemsae =ga		na-t-da		
	On the street	smell of burning oil, smell of people, smell of burning rubber		emerged		
	Cir:Loc: space	P1:Actor		Process		
	On the street smell of burning oil, smell of people, smell of burning rubber emerged.					

7.3 Translation and Interpreting Korean

5			잠시 서서 주위를 둘러 보기도 어려울 정도였다.	
			[[jamsi seo-seo juwi =reul dul-leo bo-gi =do eoryeo-ul]] jeongdo	y-eot-da
			the degree that even stopping briefly to look around was difficult	was
			P0:'Existent'⁵	Process
	(It) was to a degree that even stopping briefly to look around was difficult.			
6	인도에	사람들이	넘치고,	
	indo =e	saram-deur =i		neomchi-go
	On the pavement	people		were overflowing (and)
	Cir:Loc: space	P1:Actor		Process
	On the pavement people were overflowing (and)			
7	차도에	자동차들이	넘쳤다.	
	chado =e	jadongcha-deur =i		neomchy-eot-da
	On the road	cars		were overflowing
	Cir:Loc: space	P1:Actor		Process
	on the road, cars were overflowing.			
8		(Sinae)	[[몸둘]] 곳이 없었다.	
		(Sinae)	[[momdu-l]] gos =i	eops-eot-da.
		(Sinae)	a place [[to lay (her) body]]	did not have
		P1:Possessor	P1:Possession	Process
	(Sinae) did not have a place to lay her body (e.g., no place to stand still).			
9		(Sinae)	[[단 몇 초 동안이라도 걸음을 멈추고 우울을 달랠]] 곳이 없었다.	
		(Sinae)	[[dan myeot cho dongan i-rado georeum =eul meomchu-go uur =eul dallae-l]] gos =i	eops-eot-da
		(Sinae)	a place [[to stop just for a few seconds to soothe (her) depressed feelings]].	did not have
		P1:Possessor	P1:Possession	Process
	(Sinae) did not have a place to stop for a few seconds to soothe her depression.			

The Thematic progression of (41) is different from that of the source text. Following clauses (41.1) and (41.2) the text's method of development shifts from Sinae to her environs in clauses (41.4), (41.6) and (41.7). These Theme

---

⁵ This clause type is discussed in footnote 5 in Chapter 5.

choices fail to create the camera-like panning effect from place to place that is evident in the source text; this arguably weakens the thematic link between Sinae's environs and her emotions.

(41)   English translation 1

Cl. No.	Theme(s)	Rheme
1	Sinae	was walking in the centre of Seoul,
2	(she)	distracted.
3	All she could see in front of her	were people, buildings and cars.
4	On the pavement the smell of oil, the smell of people and the smell of scorched rubber	hung in the air.
5	Just to stand still and look about her	would take an effort.
6	People	packed the pavement,
7	cars	packed the street.
8	There	was no place [[to stop]], no place [[to stop even for a few seconds to try to control her depression]].

Similarly, (42) does not include a positioning Theme in clauses (42.6) or (42.7); there places are made Theme – *the pavement* in clause (42.6) and *the road* in clause (42.7). These places could have been selected as positioning Themes as in the source text – by writing *on the pavement (people were packed)* and *on the road (cars were packed)*. However, this was avoided because one of the motivations for creating T2 was to maintain the same category of Theme (i.e. anticipated topical There) as T1 while changing some of their content.

The only other change made in T2 was the addition of *for her* in the last two clauses (42.7) and (42.8) – to show the connection between the physical environment and the protagonist (which involves implicit Themes in the source text). The connection derives from the implicit Theme *Sinae* and the varied qualifications of *place* in the last two clauses of the source text (40.8) and (40.9). In the source text (40), 곳이 *gos i* 'place' is repeated, but each time is qualified by a different embedded clause that refers to Sinae's inner state (몸둘 *momdu-l* 'to lay (her) body', alluding to her physical exhaustion and

우울을 달랠 *uur eul dallae-l* 'to soothe (her) depressed feelings', alluding to her emotional state).

(42)   English translation 2

1	Sinae	was walking in the centre of the city,
2	(she)	distracted.
3	All she could see in front of her	were people, buildings and cars.
4	On the pavement the smell of oil, the smell of people and the smell of scorched rubber	hung in the air.
5	Just to stand still and look about her	would take an effort.
6	The pavement	was overflowing with people
7	The road	was overflowing with cars.
8	There	was no place [[to stop for her]], no place [[for her to stop even for a few seconds to try to control her depression]].

In summary, the analysis of Theme choices in the source and target texts clearly revealed that Theme choices made at the clause level create significant patterns as the texts unfold. The Theme choices in the source text created a camera-like panning effect, starting with an anticipated angling Theme, Sinae, in clauses (40.1) and (40.2), moving on to her environs with positioning Themes in clauses (40.4), (40.6) and (40.7) and returning to Sinae again in clauses (40.8) and (40.9). This helps the reader relate the busy street to Sinae's depressed feelings. Target readers did respond differently to the two translations even though there were only small adjustments to textual meaning. The Theme choices in T2 were not identical to those of the source text but did reflect the thematic progression of the source text. The survey results showed that target readers are sensitive to clause orientation and its subsequent impact on information flow. It can also be inferred from the results that making lexical choices motivated by a sense of the thematic progression in the source text (e.g., *for her* in clause (42.8) in T2) can be a useful translation strategy for taking into account its purpose and effect.

What we have discussed above are just a few examples of many translation and interpreting questions that can be investigated using SFL. Critical here is the paradigmatic orientation of our grammar, which allows translators and interpreters to establish similarity between languages from the perspective of system – taking advantage of the point introduced in (7.1) about languages tending to be more comparable from the perspective of paradigmatic relations than the syntagmatic structures through which systems are realised. In practical terms this allows translators/interpreters to transcend structural differences between two languages, find common ground (e.g., MOOD systems in Korean and say English) and then move on to the structures that negotiate a comparable proposition or proposal in the target text. A model of this process is outlined in Figure 7.4 (from de Souza 2010; cf. de Souza 2013) – as it moves 'up' from the source text to the source text systems it is instantiating, then 'across' from source text systems to relevant target text systems, and then 'down' to the target text.

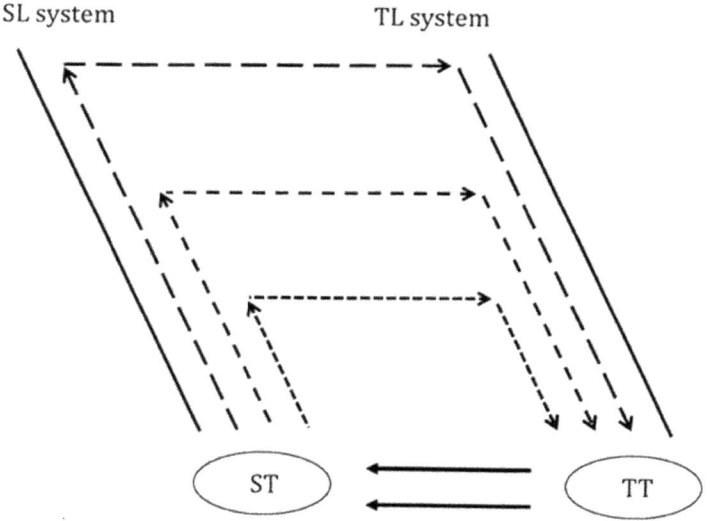

Figure 7.4 T&I as a process of reinstantiation

The T&I process is of course more complex than the figure might suggest owing to the multi-dimensionality of meaning involving ideational, interpersonal and textual resources. T&I is after all a process of ongoing decision-making because it involves prioritising certain dimensions of meaning over others in a given context. We expect that our grammar will provide a useful tool for practitioners to refer to in their work and for translation educators to help future practitioners develop the ability to make informed choices. In addition, we believe that it has established the ground on which researchers in the T&I field can explore challenging issues arising from text analysis more efficiently. This will in turn advance our understanding of translation.

7.4 Further Applications

In this chapter we have reviewed two applications of our grammar – for language teaching and for translation and interpreting. As surveyed in Caldwell et al. (2022) there are in fact many more possibilities, including applications in ecolinguistics, forensic linguistics, medical discourse, the language of administration and so on. Most of these applications draw on a model of context (as register and genre) such as that introduced in Martin (1992) and Martin and Rose (2008). Many also involve a focus on meaning beyond the clause, with reference to the framework introduced in Martin and Rose (2003/ 2007). These approaches to context and co-text were based on the rich functional grammar of English that inspired this volume (most recently consolidated as Halliday and Matthiessen 2014). We hope that our grammar enables and inspires description and practice of this kind for Korean, and we look forward to the contributions that this work will make to Korean society – fostering a better world than the one many of us are struggling to sustain right now.

Appendix

Hangeul translation

오른쪽에 벽난로가 있었는데 아궁이 양옆에 화덕이 달린 구식 철제 레인지였다. 마크가 종이와 나무로 불을 폈던 모양인지, 난로 안에 하얀 재가 소복하게 쌓였고 다가올 저녁을 대비한 불쏘시개와 작은 통나무도 마련되어 있었다. 난로 한쪽 옆에는 빛바랜 쿠션이 깔린 키 작은 널빤지 의자가 하나 놓였고 반대편에는 나무다리를 톱으로 잘라내고 그 자리에 바퀴를 달아놓은 의자가 하나 있었다. 아마도 아기를 돌볼 수 있게 일부러 낮게 만든 의자 같았다. 다리를 잘라내기 전에는 분명히 아름다운 의자였을 거라고 코델리아는 생각했다. (Lee, J. H. 2018)

Romanisation

oreunjjog e byeongnallo ga iss-eon-neunde agungi yangyeop e hwadeog i dal-li-n gusik cheolje reinji y-eot-da. Makeu ga jongi wa namu ro bur eul ttae-t-deon moyang i-nji, nallo an e hayan jae ga sobokage ssa-y-eot-go dagao-l jeonyeog eul daebiha-n bulssosigae wa jag-eun tongnamu do maryeondoe-eo iss-eot-da. nallo hanjjok yeop e neun bitbarae-n kusyeon i kkal-li-n ki jag-eun neolppanji uija ga hana no-y-eot-go bandaepyeon e neun namudari reul tob euro jal-la nae-go geu jari e bakwi reul dar-a no-eun uija ga hana iss-eot-da. amado agi reul dolbo-l su it-ge ilbureo natge mandeu-n uija gat-at-da. dari reul jal-la nae-gi jeon e neun bunmyeonghi areumda-un uija y-eoss-eulgeo-ra go Kodellia neun saenggaka-et-da. (Lee, J. H. 2018)

English source text

To the right was a fireplace, an old-fashioned iron range with ovens each side of the open fire. Mark had been burning wood and papers; there was a mound of white ash in the grate and a pile of kindling wood and small logs placed ready for the next evening. On one side of the fire was a low wooden slatted chair with a faded cushion and on the other a wheel-backed chair with the legs sawn off, perhaps to make it low enough for nursing a child. Cordelia thought that it must have been a beautiful chair before its mutilation. (James 1977)

References

Primary Sources

Buzo, A. (1980). On the Overhead Bridge (Translation of Cho, S. 1978). *Korea Journal, 20*(10), 30–5.

Cho, S. (1978). *Nanjangiga Ssoaolin Jageun Gong* (난장이가 쏘아올린 작은 공) *[A Dwarf Launches a Little Ball]*. Seoul: Munji Publishing.

Coffee Friends, Episode 1 (at 14.08) [TV series; tvN]. (Broadcast at 9.10 pm on 4 January 2019).

Gyeongbokgung Palace Management Office. (2014). *Gyeongbokgungui Yeoksa* (경복궁의 역사) *[The History of Gyeongbokgung]*. Seoul: Gyeongbokgung Palace Management Office. www.royalpalace.go.kr/content/data/data_01.asp.

Hwang, S. (1952/2002). *Sonagi* (소나기) *[Shower]*. Seoul: Darim.

James, P. D. (1977). *An Unsuitable Job for a Woman (Cordelia Gray Mystery Series)*. Faber & Faber. Kindle Edition.

The Korean Broadcasting System. (2014). *Gangnamseutail, Yutyubeu Cheot 20eok Byu Dolpa* ('강남스타일', 유튜브 첫 '20억 뷰'돌파) *[Gangnam Style Became the First to Record 2 Billion YouTube Viewings]*. http://news.kbs.co.kr/news/view.do?ncd=2869726.

Lee, Je-Hee. (2015). *Masinneun Sagwajuseu Mandeulgi* (맛있는 사과주스 만들기) *[How to Make Delicious Apple Juice]*. https://prezi.com/q-jdobxkxfsh/presentation/.

Lee, Ju-Hye. (2018). *Yeojaege Eoulliji Anneun Jigeop* (여자에게 어울리지 않는 직업) *[An Unsuitable Job for a Woman]* (Translation of James, P. D. 1977). Seoul: Ajak.

Ministry of Education. (2002a). Gae (개) [Dog]. In *Chodeunghakgyo Gugeoilki 3-1* (초등학교 국어읽기 3-1) *[Primary School Reading Year 3]*.

——— (2002b). Gang Gam-chan, Sonyeon Sijeol (강감찬, 소년시절) [Gang Gam-chan, Boyhood Period]. In *Chodeunghakgyo Gugeoilki 3-1* (초등학교 국어읽기 3-1) *[Primary School Reading Year 3]*.

——— (2002c). Hanji Gongjangeul Danyeowaseo (한지 공장을 다녀와서) [After Having Been to Hanji Factory]. In *Chodeunghakgyo Gugeoilki 3-2* (초등학교 국어읽기 3-2) *[Primary School Reading Year 3]*.

——— (2002d). Nuga Gajang Meonjeo Ujue Gasseulkkayo? (누가 가장 먼저 우주에 갔을까요?) [Who Went First to the Universe?]. In *Chodeunghakgyo Gugeoilki 1-2* (초등학교 국어읽기 1-2) *[Primary School Reading Year 1]*.

——— (2002e). Seokjumyeong (석주명) [Seokjumyeong]. In *Chodeunghakgyo Gugeoilki 3-2* (초등학교 국어읽기 3-2) *[Primary School Reading Year 3]*.

(2002f). Sut (숯) [Charcoal]. In *Chodeunghakgyo Gugeoilki 5-1* (초등학교 국어읽기 5-1) *[Primary School Reading Year 3]*.

(2002g). Toguljeot (토굴젓) [Cave Pickled Shrimp]. In *Chodeunghakgyo Gugeoilki 3-2* (초등학교 국어읽기 3-2) *[Primary School Reading Year 3]*.

Seong, J. (2020). *'Gisaengchung' Oseuka Gamdoksang Susang Sungan* ('기생충' 오스카 감독상 수상 순간) *['Parasite' Oscar Director Award Winning Moment]*. www.youtube.com/watch?v=0rb2MVZFNoY.

The Educational Foundation for Koreans Abroad. (2006). *Hangeulhakgyo Haksaengyong Donghwaro Baeuneun Hangugeo* (한글학교 학생용 동화로 배우는 한국어) *[Korean Learning through Children's Stories: For Korean School Students]*. Seoul: The Educational Foundation for Koreans Abroad.

Secondary Sources

Aikenvald, A. (2004). *Evidentiality*. Oxford: Oxford University Press.

Aikenvald, A., and Dixon, R. M. W. (2003). *Studies in Evidentiality*. Amsterdam: John Benjamins.

Caffarel, A., Martin, J. R., and Matthiessen, C. M. I. M. (Eds.). (2004). *Language Typology: A Functional Perspective*. Amsterdam: John Benjamins.

Caldwell, E. D., Knox, J., and Martin, J. R. (Eds.). (2022). *Appliable Linguistics and Social Semiotics: Developing Theory from Practice*. Bloomsbury Studies in Systemic Functional Linguistics. London: Bloomsbury.

Catford, J. C. (1965). *A Linguistic Theory of Translation*. London: Oxford University Press.

Chafe, W., and Nichols, J. (Eds.). (1986). *Evidentiality: The Linguistic Coding of Epistemology*. Norwood, NJ: Ablex.

Choe, H. (1937). *Urimalbon* (우리말본) *[Our Language Structure]*. Seoul: Jeongeumsa [reprinted in 1971].

Choi, G. (2013). *A Study on Logical Meaning Using SFL and the Implications of This for Translation Studies*. PhD Thesis, University of New South Wales.

Doran, Y. J., and Martin, J. R. (2021). Field Relations: Understanding Scientific Explanations. In K. Maton, J. R. Martin, and Y. J. Doran (Eds.), *Teaching Science: Knowledge, Language, Pedagogy* (pp. 105–33). London: Routledge.

Eggins, S. (2004). *An Introduction to Systemic Functional Grammar* [2nd Ed.]. London: Continuum.

Eggins, S., and Slade, D. (1997). *Analysing Casual Conversation*. London: Equinox.

Fries, P. H. (1981/1983). On the Status of Theme in English: Arguments from Discourse. *Forum Linguisticum*, 6(1), 1–38 [reprinted in J. S. Petöfi and E. Sözer (Eds.), *Micro and Macro Connexity of Texts*. Papers in Textlinguistics, 45. Hamburg: Helmut Buske Verlag, 1983, pp. 116–52].

Gleason, H. A. Jr. (1965). *Linguistics and English Grammar*. New York: Holt, Rinehart & Winston.

Halliday, M. A. K. (1962). Linguistics and Machine Translation. *Zeitschrift für Ponetik, Sprachwissenschaft und Kormunikationsforschung*, 15(1/2), 145–58 [reprinted in Angus McIntosh and M. A. K. Halliday, *Patterns of Language: Papers in General, Descriptive and Applied Linguistics*. Longmans Linguistic Library. London: Longman, 1966, pp. 134–50].

References

(1967). Notes on Transitivity and Theme in English: Part 1. *Journal of Linguistics*, *3* (1), 37–81.

(1985). *An Introduction to Functional Grammar* [1st Ed.]. London: Edward Arnold.

(1994). *An Introduction to Functional Grammar*. London: Arnold.

(2008). Working with Meaning: Towards an Appliable Linguistics. In J. J. Webster (Ed.), *Meaning in Context: Implementing Intelligent Applications of Language Studies* (pp. 7–23). London: Continuum.

Halliday, M. A. K., and Matthiessen, C. M. I. M. (1999). *Construing Experience through Meaning: A Language-based Approach to Cognition*. London and New York: Cassell.

(2014). *Halliday's Introduction to Functional Grammar*. London: Routledge.

Halliday, M. A. K., and McDonald, E. (2004). Metafunctional Profile of the Grammar of Chinese. In A. Caffarel, J. R. Martin, and C. M. I. M. Matthiessen (Eds.), *Language Typology: A Functional Perspective* (pp. 305–96). Current Issues in Linguistic Theory. Amsterdam: John Benjamins.

Han, J., and Shin, G. (2006). On the Choice of a Romanisation System. *International Review of Korean Studies*, *3*(1), 91–105.

Heo, W. (1983). *Gugeohak* (국어학) *[Korean Linguistics]*. Seoul: Saem Munhwasa.

(1995). *20 Segi Uri Marui Hyeongtaeron* (20세기 우리말의 형태론) *[20th Century Korean Morphology]*. Seoul: Saem Munhwasa.

Im, H., and Chang, S. (1995). *Gugeomunbeopnon* (국어문법론) *[A Theory of Korean Grammar]*. Seoul: Hankuk Bangsong Tongsin Daehakkyo Chulpanbu.

Jones, R. H., and Lock, G. (2011). *Functional Grammar in the ESL Classroom: Noticing, Exploring and Practising*. London: Palgrave Macmillan.

Kim, C., Pak, D., Lee, B., Lee, H., Jeong, H., Choe, J., and Heo, Y. (2005a). *Oegugineul wihan Hangugeo Munbeop* (외국인을 위한 한국어 문법) *[Korean Grammar for Foreign Learners]* (Vol. 1). Seoul: Communication Books.

(2005b). *Oegugineul wihan Hangugeo Munbeop* (외국인을 위한 한국어 문법) *[Korean Grammar for Foreign Learners]* (Vol. 2). Seoul: Communication Books.

Kim, M. (2007). *A Discourse Based Study on Theme in Korean and Textual Meaning in Translation*. PhD Thesis, Macquarie University.

(2009). Meaning-based Assessment of Translations: SFL and Its Application to Formative Assessment. In C. Angelelli and H. Jacobson (Eds.), *Testing and Assessment in Translation and Interpreting* (pp. 123–57). Amsterdam and Philadelphia: John Benjamins.

(2011). Hanyeong Danpyeon Soseol Beonyeoge Isseo 'Ikkeumbu(Theme)'ui Seontaeg (한영 단편 소설 번역에 있어 '이끔부(Theme)'의 선택이 독자에게 미치는 영향) [A Study on Target Reader Reactions to Different Theme Choices in Two Different Versions of English Translations of a Korean Short Story]. In E. Cho (Ed.), *Beonyeokhak, Mueosseul Yeonguhaneunga Eoneojeok, Munhwajeok, Sahwoejeok Jeopgeun* (번역학, 무엇을 연구하는가 언어적, 문화적, 사회적 접근) *[Translation Studies, What Does It Study, Linguistic, Cultural and Social Approaches]* (pp. 53–84). Seoul: Dongkuk University Press.

Kim, M., Munday, J., Wang, Z., and Wang, P. (Eds.). (2021). *Systemic Functional Linguistics and Translation Studies*. London and New York: Bloomsbury Academic.

Kress, G., and van Leeuwen, T. (1990). *Reading Images*. Geelong, Vic.: Deakin University Press [revised as *Reading Images: The Grammar of Visual Design*. London: Routledge, 1996] [Rev. 2nd Ed. 2006].

   (2021). *Reading Images: The Grammar of Visual Design*. London: Routledge.

Kwon, J. (1985). *Gugeoui Bokammun Guseong Yeongu* (국어의 복합문 구성 연구) *[A Study of Korean Combined Sentence Composition]*. Seoul: Jimmundang.

   (2012). *Hangugeo Munbeopnon* (한국어 문법론) *[A Theory of Korean Grammar]*. Seoul: Tae Hak Sa.

Lee, G. (1999). Daedeungmun Jongsongmun Busajeol Gumunui Byeonbyeol Teukseong (대등문·종속문·부사절 구문의 변별 특성) [The Criteria for Distinguishing Coordination, Subordination and 'Adverbial Phrase']. *Seoncheongeomun*, 27(1), 753–80.

Lee, H., and Lee, J. (2010). *Eomi, Josa Sajeon: Jeonmunga Yong* (어미, 조사 사전: 전문가용) *[A Dictionary of (Korean) Suffixes and 'Clitics': For Professionals (in Korean Language Studies)]*. Seoul: Hanguk Munhwasa.

Lee, I., and Chae, W. (1999/2013). *Gugeo Munbeopnon Gangui* (국어 문법론 강의) *[A Lecture on Korean Grammar]*. Seoul: Hak Yeon Sa.

Lee, K. (1993). *A Korean Grammar on Semantic-Pragmatic Principles*. Seoul: Hanguk Munhwasa.

Martin, J. R. (1992). *English Text: System and Structure*. Amsterdam: John Benjamins (reprinted Peking University Press, 2004).

   (2016). Meaning Matters: A Short History of Systemic Functional Linguistics. *Word*, 62(1), 35–58.

Martin, J. R., and Doran, Y. J. (Eds.). (2015a). *Grammatics*. Critical Concepts in Linguistics: Systemic Functional Linguistics, Vol. 1. London: Routledge.

   (Eds.). (2015b). *Grammatical Descriptions*. Critical Concepts in Linguistics: Systemic Functional Linguistics, Vol. 2. London: Routledge.

   (Eds.). (2015c). *Around Grammar: Phonology, Discourse Semantics and Multimodality*. Critical Concepts in Linguistics: Systemic Functional Linguistics, Vol. 3. London: Routledge.

   (Eds.). (2015d). *Context: Register and Genre*. Critical Concepts in Linguistics: Systemic Functional Linguistics, Vol. 4. London: Routledge.

   (Eds.). (2015e). *Language in Education*. Critical Concepts in Linguistics: Systemic Functional Linguistics, Vol. 5. London: Routledge.

Martin, J. R., and Matthiessen, C. M. I. M. (1991). Systemic Typology and Topology. In F. Christie (Ed.), *Literacy in Social Processes: Papers from the Inaugural Australian Systemic Linguistics Conference, Held at Deakin University, January 1990* (pp. 345–83). Darwin: Centre for Studies in Language in Education, Northern Territory University.

Martin, J. R., and Quiroz, B. (2020). Functional Language Typology: A Discourse Semantic Perspective. In J. R. Martin, Y. J. Doran, and G. Figueredo (Eds.), *Systemic Functional Language Description: Making Meaning Matter* (pp. 189–235). London: Routledge.

   (2021). Functional Language Typology: Systemic Functional Linguistic Perspectives. In M. Kim, J. Munday, P. Wang, and Z. Wang (Eds.), *Systemic Functional Linguistics in Translation Studies* (pp. 7–33). London: Bloomsbury.

References

Martin, J. R., and Rose, D. (2007). *Working with Discourse: Meaning beyond the Clause*. London: Continuum.

(2008). *Genre Relations: Mapping Culture*. London: Equinox.

Martin, J. R., and Shin, G. (2021). Korean Nominal Groups: System and Structure. *Word*, 67(3) (Special Issue on the Nominal Group edited by Y. Doran, J. R. Martin and D. Zhang), 387–429.

Martin, J. R., and White, P. R. R. (2005). *The Language of Evaluation: Appraisal in English*. London: Palgrave.

Martin, J. R., Wang, B. and Ma, Y. (2022). Contributions to Translation from the Sydney School of Systemic Functional Linguistics. In B. Wang & Y. Ma (Eds.), *Key Themes and New Directions in Systemic Functional Translation Studies* (pp. 75–86). Routledge Advances in Translation and Interpreting Studies. London: Routledge.

Martin, J. R., Wang, P., and Zhu, Y. (2013). *Systemic Functional Grammar: A Next Step into the Theory – Axial Relations*. Beijing: Higher Education Press.

Matthiessen, C. M. I. M. (2001). The Environments of Translation. In E. Steiner and C. Yallop (Eds.), *Exploring Translation and Multilingual Text Production: Beyond Content* (pp. 41–124). Berlin and New York: Mouton de Gruyter.

(2004). Descriptive Motifs and Generalisations. In A. Caffarel, J. R. Martin, and C. M. I. M. Matthiessen (Eds.), *Language Typology: A Functional Perspective* (pp. 537–673). Current Issues in Linguistics Theory. Amsterdam: John Benjamins.

(2014). Choice in Translation: Metafunctional Considerations. In K. Kunz, E. Teich, S. Hansen-Schirra, S. Neumann, and P. Daut (Eds.), *Caught in the Middle – Language Use and Translation (A Festschrift for Erich Steiner on the Occasion of His 60th Birthday)* (pp. 271–334). Saarbrücken: Saarland University Press.

(2018). The Notion of a Multilingual Meaning Potential: A Systemic Exploration. In A. S. Baklouti and L. Fontaine (Eds.), *Perspective from Systemic Functional Linguistics* (pp. 90–120). London and New York: Routledge.

Matthiessen, C. M. I. M., Lam, M., and Teruya, K. (2010). *Key Terms in Systemic Functional Linguistics*. London: Continuum.

Moyano, E. (2016). Theme in English and Spanish: Different Means of Realization for the Same Textual Function. In B. Clark and J. Arús (Eds.), *English Text Construction*, 9(1) (Special Issue on Communicative Dynamism), 190–220.

Munday, J. (2016). *Introducing Translation Studies: Theories and Application* [4th Ed.]. London: Routledge.

Mwinlaaru, I. N., and Xuan, W. W. (2016). A Survey of Studies in Systemic Functional Language Description and Typology. *Functional Linguistics*, 3, (8).

Nam, K., and Ko, Y. (1985/1993). *Pyojun Gugeo Munbeopnon* (표준 국어 문법론) *[A Theory of Standard Korean Grammar]*. Seoul: Tap Chulpansa [reprinted in 2003].

National Institute of Korean Language. (1999). *Pyojungugeodaesajeon* (표준국어대사전) *[Standard Korean Language Dictionary]*. Seoul: National Institute of Korean Language.

Ngo, T., Hood, S., Martin, J. R., Painter, C., Smith, B., and Zappavigna, M. (2022). *Modelling Paralanguage Using Systemic Functional Semiotics*. Bloomsbury Studies in Systemic Functional Linguistics. London: Bloomsbury.

O'Toole, M. (1994). *The Language of Displayed Art*. London: Leicester University Press (a Division of Pinter) [2nd Rev. Ed. Routledge 2011].

Painter, C., Martin, J. R., and Unsworth, L. (2013). *Reading Visual Narratives: Image Analysis of Children's Picture Books*. London: Equinox.

Park, K. (2013). *The Experiential Grammar of Korean: A Systemic Functional Perspective*. PhD Thesis, Macquarie University.

Perlmutter, D. (Ed.). (1983). *Studies in Relational Grammar 1*. Chicago: University of Chicago Press.

Perlmutter, D., and Rosen, C. (Eds.). (1984). *Studies in Relational Grammar 2*. Chicago: University of Chicago Press.

Pike, K. L. (1982). *Linguistic Concepts: An Introduction to Tagmemics*. Lincoln: University of Nebraska Press.

Postal, P. M., and Joseph, B. D. (Eds.). (1990). *Studies in Relational Grammar 3*. Chicago: University of Chicago Press.

Quiroz, B. (2013). *The Interpersonal and Experiential Grammar of Chilean Spanish: Towards a Principled Systemic-Functional Description Based on Axial Argumentation*. PhD Thesis, University of Sydney.

Rose, D. (2020a). Building a Pedagogic Metalanguage I: Curriculum Genres. In J. R. Martin, K. Maton, and Y. J. Doran (Eds.), *Accessing Academic Discourse: Systemic Functional Linguistics and Legitimation Code Theory* (pp. 236–67). London: Routledge.

  (2020b). Building a Pedagogic Metalanguage II: Knowledge Genres. In J. R. Martin, K. Maton, and Y. J. Doran (Eds.), *Accessing Academic Discourse: Systemic Functional Linguistics and Legitimation Code Theory* (pp. 268–302). London: Routledge.

  (2022). Designing Pedagogic Registers: Reading to Learn. In D. Caldwell, J. Knox, and J. R. Martin (Eds.), *Applicable Linguistics and Social Semiotics: Developing Theory from Practice* (pp. 103–25). Bloomsbury Studies in Systemic Functional Linguistics. London: Bloomsbury

Rose, D., and Martin, J. R. (2012). *Learning to Write, Reading to Learn: Genre, Knowledge and Pedagogy in the Sydney School*. London: Equinox [Swedish translation: K. Alden, *Skriva, Läsa – Lära: genre, kunskap och pedagogic*. Stockholm: Hallgren and Fallgren. 2013; Spanish translation: *Leer para aprender: Lectura y escritura en las áreas del currículo*. Madrid: Ediciones Pirámide (part of Anaya), 2018].

Shin, G. (2018). Interpersonal Grammar of Korean: A Systemic Functional Perspective. *Functions of Language*, 25(1), 20–53.

Shin, G., and Kim, M. (2008). A Systemic Functional Analysis of Topic NPs in Korean. In C. Wu, C. M. I. M. Matthiessen, and M. Herke (Eds.), *Proceedings of 35th International Systemic Functional Congress* (pp. 213–18). Sydney: Linguistics Department, Macquarie University.

Sinclair, J. M., and Coulthard, R. M. (1975). *Towards an Analysis of Discourse: The English Used by Teachers and Pupils*. London: Oxford University Press.

Sohn, H. (1999). *The Korean Language*. Cambridge: Cambridge University Press.

Song, J. (1977). The So-called Plural Copy in Korean as a Marker of Distribution and Focus. *Journal of Pragmatics*, 27(2), 203–24.

Song, S. (1988). *Explorations in Korean Syntax and Semantics*. Berkeley: University of California, Institute of East Asian Studies.

de Souza L. M. F. (2010). *Interlingual Re-instantiation: A Model for a New and More Comprehensive Systemic Functional Perspective on Translation*. PhD Thesis, Federal University of Santa Catarina.

— (2013). Interlingual Re-instantiation – A New Systemic Functional Perspective on Translation. *Text & Talk, 33*, 575–94.

Steiner, E., and Yallop, C. (Eds.). (2001). *Exploring Translation and Multilingual Text Production: Beyond Content*. Berlin and New York: Mouton de Gruyter.

Strauss, S. (2005). Cognitive Realization Markers in Korean: A Discourse-pragmatic Study of the Sentence-ending Particles *-kwun*, *-ney* and *-tela*. *Language Sciences, 27*, 437–80.

Teruya, K. (2004). Metafunctional Profile of the Grammar of Japanese. In A. Caffarel, J. R. Martin, and C. M. I. M. Matthiessen (Eds.), *Language Typology: A Functional Perspective* (pp. 185–254). Current Issues in Linguistic Theory. Amsterdam: John Benjamins.

— (2007). *The Functional Grammar of Japanese*. London: Continuum.

Thibault, P. (1987). An Interview with Michael Halliday. In R. Steele and T. Threadgold (Eds.), *Language Topics: Essays in Honour of Michael Halliday* (Vol. 2, pp. 601–28). Amsterdam: John Benjamins.

Thompson, G. (2014). *Introducing Functional Grammar* (3rd Ed.). London: Routledge.

van Leeuwen, T. (1999). *Speech, Music, Sound*. London: Macmillan.

van Valin, R. D., and Rapolla, R. D. (1997). *Syntax: Structure, Meaning and Function*. Cambridge: Cambridge University Press.

Vinay, J. P., and Darbelnet, J. (1958). *Stylistique Comparée du Francais et de l'Anglais: Méthode de Traduction*. Paris: Didier (Transl. and Ed. by J. C. Sager and M. J. Hamel as *Comparative Stylistics of French and English: A Methodology for Translation*. Amsterdam and Philadelphia: John Benjamins, 1985).

Wang, B., and Ma, Y. (2020). *Teahouse and Its Two English Translations*. London and New York: Routledge.

— (2021). *Systemic Functional Translation Studies: Theoretical Insights and New Directions*. Sheffield and Bristol: Equinox.

Wang, B., & Ma, Y. (Eds.). (2022). *Key Themes and New Directions in Systemic Functional Translation Studies*. London: Routledge.

Wang, P. (2020). Axial Argumentation and Cryptogrammar in Interpersonal Grammar: A Case Study of Classical Tibetan Mood. In J. R. Martin, Y. J. Doran, and G. Figueredo (Eds.), *Systemic Functional Language Description: Making Meaning Matter* (pp. 73–101). New York and London: Routledge.

Yeon, J. (2011). *Hangugeo Gumun Yuhyeongnon (한국어 구문 유형론) [A Typological Study on Korean Grammatical Constructions]*. Seoul: Thaehaksa.

Yu, H., Han, J., Kim, H., Lee, J.-T., Kim, S., Kang, H., Koo, B., Lee, B., Hwang, H., and Lee, J.-H. (2018). *Hangugeo Pyojun Munbeop (한국어 표준 문법) [Standard Korean Grammar]*. Seoul: Jipmoondang.

Index

Accompaniment 268
Actor 189
ADDRESSEE DEFERENCE 109, 111–12, **115–20**, 139, 338, 343
   dominant 112
   equal 118–19
   junior 118–19
   venerate 118
adverbial group 17, **93–9**, 107, 174, 183
   advg 183
affirm 131
Affirm 381
agnate expression 237
Angle 270–2
appliable linguistics 371
Attribute 213–15
   classifying 215
   describing 215
Attribute/Process 215
attributive clause 212
   Attribute 213–15
   Attribute/Process 215
   Carrier 213, 221
   Carrier-Domain 219
   Emoter 221–2
   P0:Attribute 213
   P1:Attribute 214
auxiliary verb 20

blend (material/relational) 394–7
bound noun 46, 150, 360–1
bound verb 18, 42, 99–100

Carrier 213, 221
Carrier-Domain 219, 221
   absolute Theme, Chinese 220
   Theme, Japanese 220
causal-conditional relation 359
   concession 360
   condition 360
   purpose 360
   reason 360
   result 360
causative 60
causativisation 60, 237
Cause 260–3
CIRCUMSTANTIATION 246
   types of Circumstance 246
Circumstance 9, 182
   Accompaniment 268
   Angle 270–2
   Cause 260–3
   Cir 183
   Comparison 256–7
   Concession 265–7
   Extent 252–5
   Location (Circumstance) 195, 227, 246–51
   Manner 255–6
   Matter 272–3
   Means 257–9
   Product 269–70
   Purpose 263–5
   Role 268–9
class 3, 6
CLASSIFICATION 27
Classifying 25–7
clause 4
clause complex 104, **308**, 313–16, 320
   long clause complex 316–20, 363–9
   vs clause simplex 309
   vs verbal group complex 310
CLAUSE COMPLEXING
   LOGICO-SEMANTIC RELATION 310
   TAXIS 310
clause nexus 310, 313
clause simplex 309
clitic 9, 20, 51, 108
co-verbal phrase 17–18, 42, **99–102**, 107, 320
   Incumbent 42, 99–100
   Role 42, 99
cognitive clause 343
cohortative 112, 122

Index

COMMENT 173–5
Comment 96, 111, 173, 292
comparison 29
Comparison 256–7
compound noun 25
Concession 265–7
concession 360
condition 360
conjugatable 28
CONJUNCTION 361
Conjunctive Adjunct 97, 294
consciousness 226
coordination 313
curriculum genre 377

declarative 11, 111
deferential 116
DEGREE 82
Degree 81–3
degree 163
DEIXIS 34
Deictic 32–5
dependency relation 320
descriptive motifs and generalisation 371
Detailed Reading 378–91
determiner 32
DIATHESIS 60, 236–45
  agnate expression 237
  effective 237
  information flow 238
  instigated 243
  receptive 238, 241–2
  Valence 60, 239, 241–3
  Voice Mark 238, 241, 243
different time 359
DIMENSION TYPE 70, 76
Dimension 65–70, 345
diminish 62–4
dominant 112, 116
double angled bracket 319
double quotation mark 331

Elaborate grammar 381
elemental 115, 123
embedded clause 89, 202, 204, 308, 343, 345, 360
  act 206
  fact 206
  idea 208–9
  Location 248
  Install 204–6
  Installing 204–5
  Location 248
embedding 41
Emoter 221–2

Entity-Range 196–7
  E-Range 196
EPITHESIS 31
Epithet 28–31
-er 108
equal 118–19
Event 58–9, 345
EVENT TYPE 59
Exchange Mark 110, 116, 183, 345
  EM 183
exchange marking 109
expansion 310, 316, 348
  elaboration 316
  enhancement 316
  extension 316
EXPANSION 330
  hypotactic elaboration 348–51
  hypotactic enhancement 348, 359, 355–60
  hypotactic extension 348, 352–5
  paratactic elaboration 348
  paratactic enhancement 359
  paratactic extension 348, 351–2, 359
experience 180
experiential meaning (metafunction) 3, 8, **180**
EXPERIENTIAL CLAUSE TYPE 187–8, 246
  material 187
  mental 187
  relational 187
  verbal 187
Experiential Function Marking 10, 50, 182
  EFM 10, 50, 182, 280
  EFM and IFM 184–5
  EFM and TFM 184–5
EXPLETION 175–7
Expletive 111, 176
extension 316
  additive 351
  additive 352
  adversative 351
  replacive 351, 354
Extent 252–5
  Extent:frequency 255
  Extent:space 254–5
  Extent:time 252–3

Focus on wording 381
formal 119, 139, 177
FORMAL MOOD 109, 111–15, 139
  cohortative 112
  elemental 115, 123
  imperative 111, 115, 141
  indicative 111, 115
  interrogative 111, 115
  jussive 112, 114, 122
  permission 159

FORMAL MOOD (cont.)
  polar 115, 123
  cohortative 112, 122
formal system 111
FORMALITY 139, 142, 177
  informal 136, 139, 177
function 3, 6
Function Marking 49–53
FUNCTION MARKING 52

gradable 29
Grader 93
group 4

hago and *rago* 336
Hangeul 6
heard 127–8, 129–31
HIGHLIGHT 79–80, 115, 165–8
Highlight 79, 165
Hyper-Theme 278, 303
hypotactic 313
  dependent clause 313
  dominant clause 313
hypotactic clause complex
  α clause 343
  β clause 343
hypotactic elaboration 348–51
  comment 349
hypotactic enhancement 348, 359, 355–60
  causal-conditional relation 359, 359
  temporal relation 359–60
hypotactic projection 337–8
  -da-go, *-nya-go*, *-ra-go*, *-ja-go* 338
  hypotactic idea 341–5
  hypotactic locution 338–41
  projected cohortative 345
  projected declarative 345
  projected interrogative 345
  projected jussive 345
  Projected Mood Mark and Link 338, 343

ideation 3
Identify wording 381
identifying clause 212
  Token 216
  Value 216
  Token^Value sequence 216–17
identifying verb 218
imperative 11, 111, 115, 141
inclination 73, 148, 160
Incumbent 42, 99–100, 111, 115
Individual Rewriting 378
informal 136, 139, 177
informal clause 120
INFORMAL MOOD 109, 121–4, 134, 139

elemental 115, 123
heard 127–8, 129–31
interrogative 111, 115
note 127–8, 131
permission 159
polar 115, 123
presume 127, 131
pronounce 132–3
propose 127
settled 124–7
settling 124–5, 127
substantiate 128
witnessed 127–9
informal system 111
inner circle activity 392
Inquirer 111, 115
Install 204–6, 320
Installing 204–5, 360
instantiating 412
instigated 243
internal bracketing 317
interpersonal meaning (metafunction) 3
Interpersonal Function Marking 50, 183
  IFM 50, 140, 151, 156, 183, 280
Interrogative 11, 111, 115

Joint Rewriting 378, 392
junior 118–19
jussive 112, 114, 122

kinship term 171
knowledge genre 377

language typology 372
lexical verb 20, 58
Link 308, 345, 348, 355, 357
Link *-go* 321
Linker 308, 331, 334, 336
Linking 103–4, 308
linking suffix 42
Located 223, 224
Location (Circumstance) 195, 227, 246–51
  Location:source 195
  Location:space 249–51
  Location:time 246–9
  consciousness 226
Location (Participant) 223–4
locative clause 212, 224, 228
  Located 223–4
  Location (Participant) 223–4
  locative;absence 223
  locative;lots 223
  locative;some 223
  locative;unquantified 223
logical meaning (metafunction) 3, 307

Index

LOGICO-SEMANTIC RELATION 310, 320
  expansion 310, 316, 348
  projection 310, 316
logico-semantic relation 308, 316, 320
lots 223

Macro-Theme 278
M-Range 198
Manner 255–6
material clause 187, 189
  Actor 189
  doing 189
  happening 189
  Range 195–6
  Recipient 191
  Source 193–5
  Undergoer 190
MATERIAL CLAUSE TYPE 188–98
Matter 272–3
Means 257–9
measure 46
mental clause 187, 198, 206, 316, 333, 343
  Senser 198–9
  Phenomenon 199, 202–11, 198
  Mental Range 198, 200–1
  cognitive 206
  desiderative 206
  emotive 206
  perceptive 206
MENTAL CLAUSE TYPE 198–212
  types of mental clause 206
Mental Range 198, 200–1
  M-Range 198
metafunction 3, 16
method of development 280, 407
middle 238
Modal 73, 148, 151, 158
Modal Adjunct 96, 148, 153, 159–60, 163–5, 292
Modal Mark 148, 152, 160
Modalisation 73, 75, 148, 157, 150–7
  probability 73
  usuality 73
modality
  Modal 73
  Modal Adjunct 96
  modalisation 73, 75
  modulation 73–6
  VERBAL GROUP MODALITY 73–9
MODALITY 115, 121, 148–65
  inclination 148, 160
  obligation 148, 158, 162
  probability 148
  usuality 148, 155, 159, 165

modulation 73–6, 148, 158–62
  inclination 73
  obligation 73
MOOD 7, 10, 13–14
morpheme 4
Negate 70–3, 75, 81, 143, 145
Negating 70–3, 75, 143, 145
negation 146
negative auxiliary 146
negotiability 321
Negotiator 10, 110, 138
nesting 317
neutral 62, 240
-ng 108
nominal group 5, 17, 19, 22–57, 183
  ng 183
nominal group complex 103
nominal group system 53
non-conjugatable 28
non-intensive relational clause 223
  absence 223
  lots 223
  presence 223
  some 223
  unquantified 223
non-restrictive relative clause 351
note 127–8, 131

obligation 73, 148, 158, 162
ORDINATION 28
Ordering 27–8
ORIENTATION 39, 56–7
Orient 35–40

P-Range 196–7
  Sino-Korean 197
paradigmatic relation 13
paratactic 313
  continuing clause 313
  initiating clause 313
paratactic elaboration 348
paratactic enhancement 359
paratactic extension 348, 351–2, 359
paratactic idea 333–6
paratactic locution 331, 331, 331–3
paratactic projection 331
  paratactic idea 333–6
  paratactic locution 331
  rago or *hago* 331
Participant 8–9
  Actor 189
  Attribute 213–15
  Carrier 213, 221
  Carrier-Domain 219, 221
  Emoter 221–2

Participant (cont.)
  Entity-Range 196–7
  Located 223–4
  Location (Participant) 223–4
  Mental Range 198, 200–1
  Phenomenon 198–9, 202–11, 347
  Possession 223, 229
  Possessor 223, 229
  Process-Range 196–7
  Receiver 235
  Recipient 191
  Sayer 232, 331
  Senser 198–9, 336
  Source 193–5
  Token 216
  Undergoer 190
  Value 216
  Verbiage 232–4
Participant 1 182
  P1 182
Participant 2 182
  P2 182
Participant 3 182
  P3 182
PARTICIPANT DEFERENCE 139–42, 404
  respect 118
Participant Deference Mark 83, 139
  PDM 83, 139
particle 22, 108, 183
  ptcl 183
passive voice 60
passivisation 59, 237
pedagogy 392
permission 159
personal name 171
PERSPECTIVISATION 49
Perspective 47–9
Phenomenon 198–9, 202–11, 347
  act 202, 206
  fact 202
  idea 202
phrase 4
plural 25
POLARITY 72, 143–8
  Negate 70–3, 75, 81
  Negating 70–3, 75
POLITENESS 109, 121, 135–9
  prosodic 138
Politeness Marker 111, 138, 183
  PM 138, 183
Possession 223, 229–31
possessive clause 212, 228
  possession 223, 229
  possessive;absence 223
  possessive;lots 223

possessive;some 223
possessive;unquantified 223
Possessor 223, 229
possessive determiner 33
Possessor 223, 229
Prepare clause 382
Prepare sentence 381
presume 127, 131
probability 73, 148
Process 8
Process-Range 196–7
  P-Range 196–7
  Sino-Korean 197
Product 269–70
projected idea 336, 341
Projected Mood Mark 345
Projected Mood Mark and Link 338, 343
projection 130, 310, 316
  idea 316, 331
  locution 234, 316, 330
PROJECTION 330
pronounce 132–3
Property 93–5
propose 127
Purpose 263–5

QUALIFICATION 45
Qualifying 41–5
QUANTIFICATION 47
Quantity 46–7

R2L teaching/learning cycle 377
rago or *hago* 331
Range 195–6
  Entity-Range 196–7
  Process-Range 196–7
rank 4, 16, 19
rank-shift 202
Reading to Learn (R2L) 372, 377–92
realisation 2–3
Receiver 235
Recipient 191
  giving clause 191
  consciousness 191
recursive system 30
reinstantiation 412
relational clause 212
  attributive 212, 213–15, 219–23
  identifying 212, 216–19
  intensive 212–23
  locative 212, 224–8
  non-intensive 212, 223–31
  possessive 212, 228–31
RELATIONAL CLAUSE TYPE 212–31
RELATIVE TENSE 85, 88–92

Index

Relative Tense Mark 204, 351, 360
  RTM 204, 351
respect 118
Revised Romanisation of Korean 7
  RRK 7
Rheme 12, 280
Role 42, 99, 268–9
romanisation 6

same time 359
Sayer 232, 331
  unspecified Sayer 344
scare quote 368
Senser 198–9, 336
settled 124–7
settling 124–5, 127
single quotation mark 333
some 223
Source 193–5
  non-conscious Source 193
  receiving clause 193
STANCE 109, 121, 124–35, 139
  affirm 131
Stance Mark 121, 124, 136, 138, 183
  SM 138, 183
stance marking 109
Standard 29, 94–5
strata 2–3
subordination 313
substantiate 128
suffix 20, 108, 183
  sfx 183
symmetry 321
system network 14
systemic functional linguistics 1
  SFL 2

TAXIS (feature) 310, 320
  hypotaxis 310, 359
  parataxis 310
TAXIS (criteria) 321–30
  negotiability 321
  symmetry 321
teaching Korean as a foreign language 372
temporal 359–60
tense
  ABSOLUTE TENSE 85–8
  RELATIVE TENSE 85, 88–92
TENSE MARKING 121
Tense Mark 85–92, 138, 183
  TM 138, 183
textual meaning (metafunction) 3, 282, 289, 299–300, 400
Textual Function Marking 50, 183, 283
  TFM 50, 183, 280, 289

thematic equative 347
thematic progression 297, 407 (see method of development)
THEME 7, 296
  ANGLING THEME 281
  CONTINUING THEME 285
  ESTABLISHING THEME 281
  INTERPERSONAL THEME 292
  POSITIONING THEME 296
  TEXTUAL THEME 296
Theme 12–13, 50, 278–80
  absolute Theme 280, 285
  absolute Theme in Chinese 220
  affirmed Theme 285
  angling Theme 298, 407
  anticipated Theme 282
  anticipated affirmed topical Theme 299
  camera-like panning effect 408
  contrastive positioning 289
  elided 285, 300, 407–8
  interpersonal Theme 292
  non-anticipated Theme 282, 300
  non-anticipated established Theme 299
  positioning Theme 289, 299, 303, 407
  Theme choices in translation 411
  Theme in spoken discourse 283, 288, 305
  topical Theme 281
  textual Them 294
  transitional positioning 289
  Theme, Japanese 220
Theme identification 298
THING TYPE 23
Thing 23–5
Token 216
traditional pedagogy 373–7
TRANSITIVITY 7, 14, 180, 276
translation and interpreting 397
  interpretation example 397–404
  process of making choices 397
  Theme choices in translation 411
  translation example 404–11
translation shift
  experiential shift 400
  interpersonal shift 400
  logical meaning shift 398

Undergoer 190
usuality 73, 148, 155, 159, 165

V-Range 235
VALENCY 59–65, 240
  augment 61, 240, 242–3
  causative 60
  diminish 238, 240–2
  neutral 62, 240

VALENCY (cont.)
  passive voice 60
  passivisation 59
Valence 60, 239, 241–3
Value 216
venerate 118
verbal clause 231, 316, 187
  Receiver 235
  Sayer 232
  Verbiage 232–4
  Verbal-Range 235
VERBAL CLAUSE TYPE 231–6
verbal group 5, 17, 19–20, 57–92, 183
  Process 182
  vg 183
verbal group complex 103, 105, 310–11
VERBAL GROUP MODALITY 73–9

VERBAL GROUP PARTICIPANT DEFERENCE 83–5
verbal group system 92
Verbal-Range 235
  V-Range 235
verbalised adjective 58
Verbiage 232–4
VOCATION 168–73
Vocative 111, 168, 292
voice 236
Voice Mark 61, 238, 241, 243
  middle 238
  operative 238, 241
  VM 238, 241, 61

witnessed 127–9
word 4, 20
word complex 26, 46

For EU product safety concerns, contact us at Calle de José Abascal, 56–1°,
28003 Madrid, Spain or eugpsr@cambridge.org.

www.ingramcontent.com/pod-product-compliance
Ingram Content Group UK Ltd.
Pitfield, Milton Keynes, MK11 3LW, UK
UKHW022121130426
469895UK00018B/346